Behave yourself. You are the mascot of this book.
Nobody will mind at all.

TENSHI JA NAI!!

Translation –Christine Schilling
Adaptation -- Mallory Reaves
Lettering – Jennifer Skarupa
Production Manager – James Dashiell
Editor – Brynne Chandler

A Go! Comi manga

Published by Go! Media Entertainment, LLC

Tenshi Ja Nai!! Volume 6
© TAKAKO SHIGEMATSU 2005
Originally published in Japan in 2005 by Akita Publishing Co., Ltd., Tokyo.
English translation rights arranged with Akita Publishing Co., Ltd.
through TOHAN CORPORATION, Tokyo.

Visit us online at www.gocomi.com
e-mail: info@gocomi.com

ISBN 978-1-933617-13-8

First printed in March 2007

1   2   3   4   5   6   7   8   9

Manufactured in the United States of America

TENSHI JA NAI!!

I'm No Angel!

Volume 6

Story and Art by
Takako Shigematsu

go!comi

Concerning Honorifics

At Go! Comi, we do our best to ensure that our translations read seamlessly in English while respecting the original Japanese language and culture. To this end, the original honorifics (the suffixes found at the end of characters' names) remain intact. in Japan, where politeness and formality are more integrated into every aspect of the language, honorifics give a better understanding of character relationships. They can be used to indicate both respect and affection. Whether a person addresses someone by first name or last name also indicates how close their relationship is.

Here are some of the honorifics you might encounter in reading this book:

-san: This is the most common and neutral of honorifics. The polite way to address someone you're not on close terms with is to use "-san." it's kind of like Mr. or Ms., except you can use "-san" with first names as easily as family names.

-chan: Used for friendly familiarity, mostly applied towards young girls. "-chan" also carries a connotation of cuteness with it, so it is frequently used with nick-names towards both boys and girls (such as "Na-chan" for "Natsu").

-kun: Like "-chan," it's an informal suffix for friends and classmates, only "-kun" is usually associated with boys. it can also be used in a professional environment by someone addressing a subordinate.

-sama: indicates a great deal of respect or admiration.

Sempai: in school, "sempai" is used to refer to an upperclassman or club leader. it can also be used in the workplace by a new employee to address a mentor or staff member with seniority.

Sensei: Teachers, doctors, writers or any master of a trade are referred to as "sensei." When addressing a manga creator, the polite thing to do is attach "-sensei" to the manga-ka's name (as in Shigematsu-sensei).

Onii: This is the more casual term for an older brother. Usually you'll see it with an honorific attached, such as "onii-chan."

Onee: The casual term for older sister, it's used like "onii" with honorifics.

[blank]: Not using an honorific when addressing someone indicates that the speaker has permission to speak intimately with the other person. This relationship is usually reserved for close friends and family.

CONTENTS

SCENE 26 9

SCENE 27 49

SCENE 28 87

SCENE 29 123

SCENE 30 161

Translator's Notes 198

VOL .6

Hikaru Takabayashi

The reluctant star of the series. Hikaru wants nothing more than to be left alone, but ever since she transferred to the prestigious Seika Academy, she's been stuck in the spotlight. Being roommates with a cross-dressing pop idol is bad enough, but now Izumi is blackmailing her into helping with his modeling job. Will Hikaru ever catch a break?

Izumi is one of the hottest new female pop idols in Japan. The only problem is...she's a guy! Only two people knew his secret—Yasukuni, his bodyguard and childhood friend, and Akizuki his manager. When Hikaru finds out, Izumi blackmails her into helping him maintain his secret. Izumi needs the modeling money to pay off his father's medical bills.

Izumi Kido

Yasukuni Inukai

Yasukuni is fiercely loyal to Izumi. A bastard child disowned by his father, Izumi is the only family he has. Now that Hikaru has won his trust, he's taken to looking out for her, as well. Much of his past remains a mystery, such as why he's missing his right eye. He does double duty as the school janitor so he can always be close to Izumi.

SUMIKKO

MOMOCHI

AKIZUKI

Hikaru's best friend in the world. Yasukuni takes care of her while Hikaru's at school.

Star reporter for the school paper, Momochi is always on the lookout for gossip!

President of the Akizuki Talent Agency and Izumi's manager.

Cast of Characters

Wall of Memories

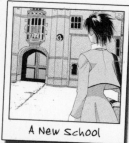

A New School

When her mom and step-dad move to France, Hikaru transfers to her mother's alma mater, the prestigious Seika Academy, an all-girls finishing school.

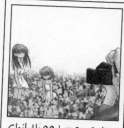

Childhood memories

When she was seven years old, Hikaru modeled in a series of ads. Her jealous classmates picked on her relentlessly so now Hikaru's greatest wish is to be left alone.

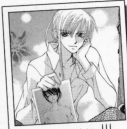

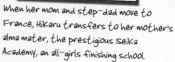

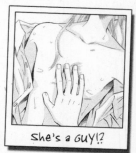

She's a GUY!?

Hikaru discovers that her roommate, Izumi, is actually a guy!

BLACKMAIL!!!

To keep Hikaru quiet and in order to enlist her help, Izumi and Yasukuni blackmail Hikaru with naked photos.

Hikaru turns out to be a blessing in disguise for Izumi. Having a female conspirator by his side helps him maintain his cover in the trickiest circumstances.

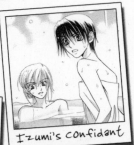

Izumi's Confidant

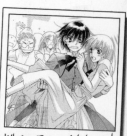

When Fans Attack!

It's not easy being a celebrity on campus. Half the students worship Izumi, the other half resent her. And Hikaru's stuck in the middle!

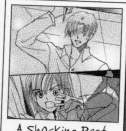

A Shocking Past

After being betrayed and left for broke, Izumi's father attempted to commit suicide but ended up in a coma. Now Izumi has to work as a model to pay off his dad's medical bills.

TENSHI JA NAI!!

I'm No Angel!

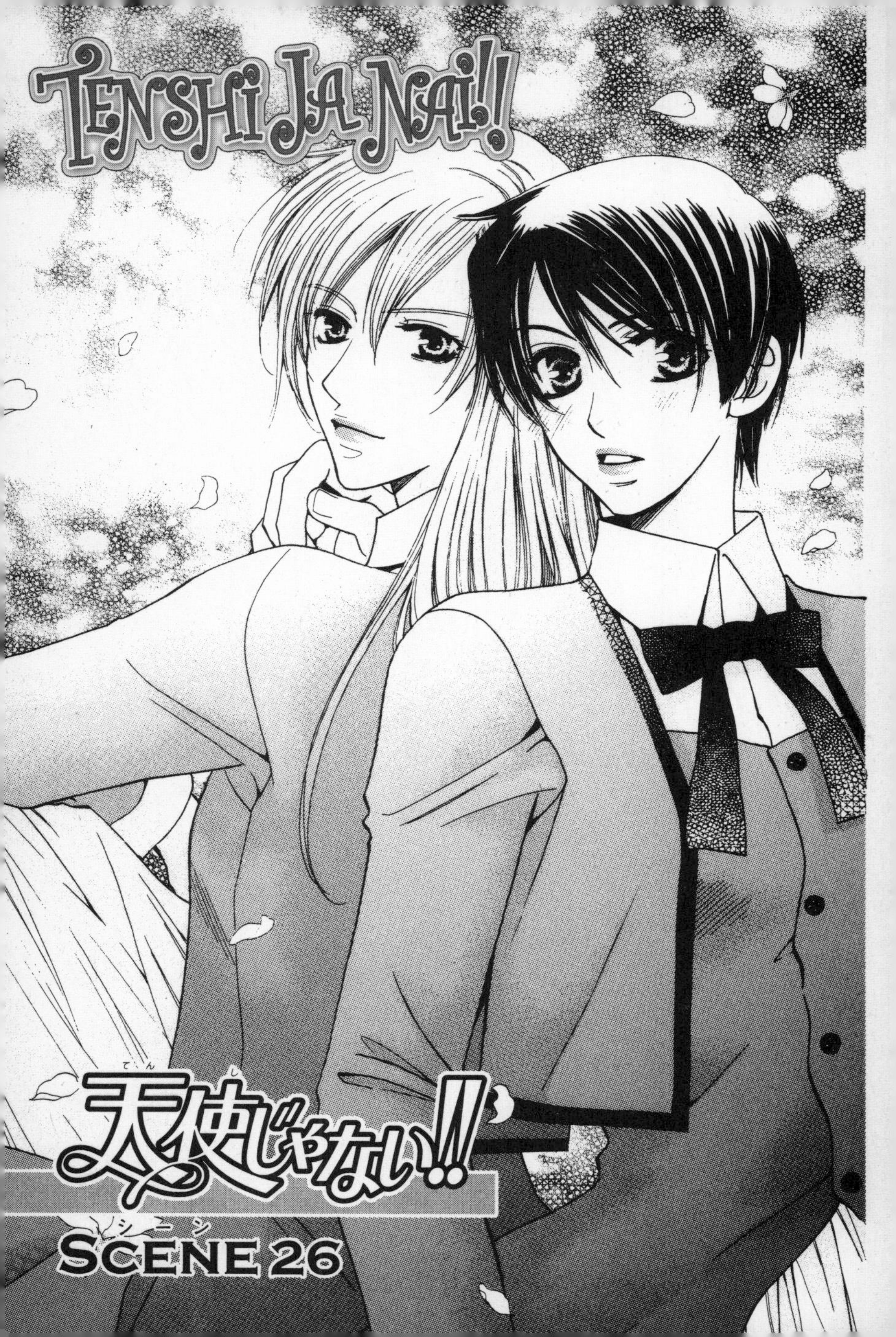

TENSHI JA NAI!!
天使じゃない!!
SCENE 26

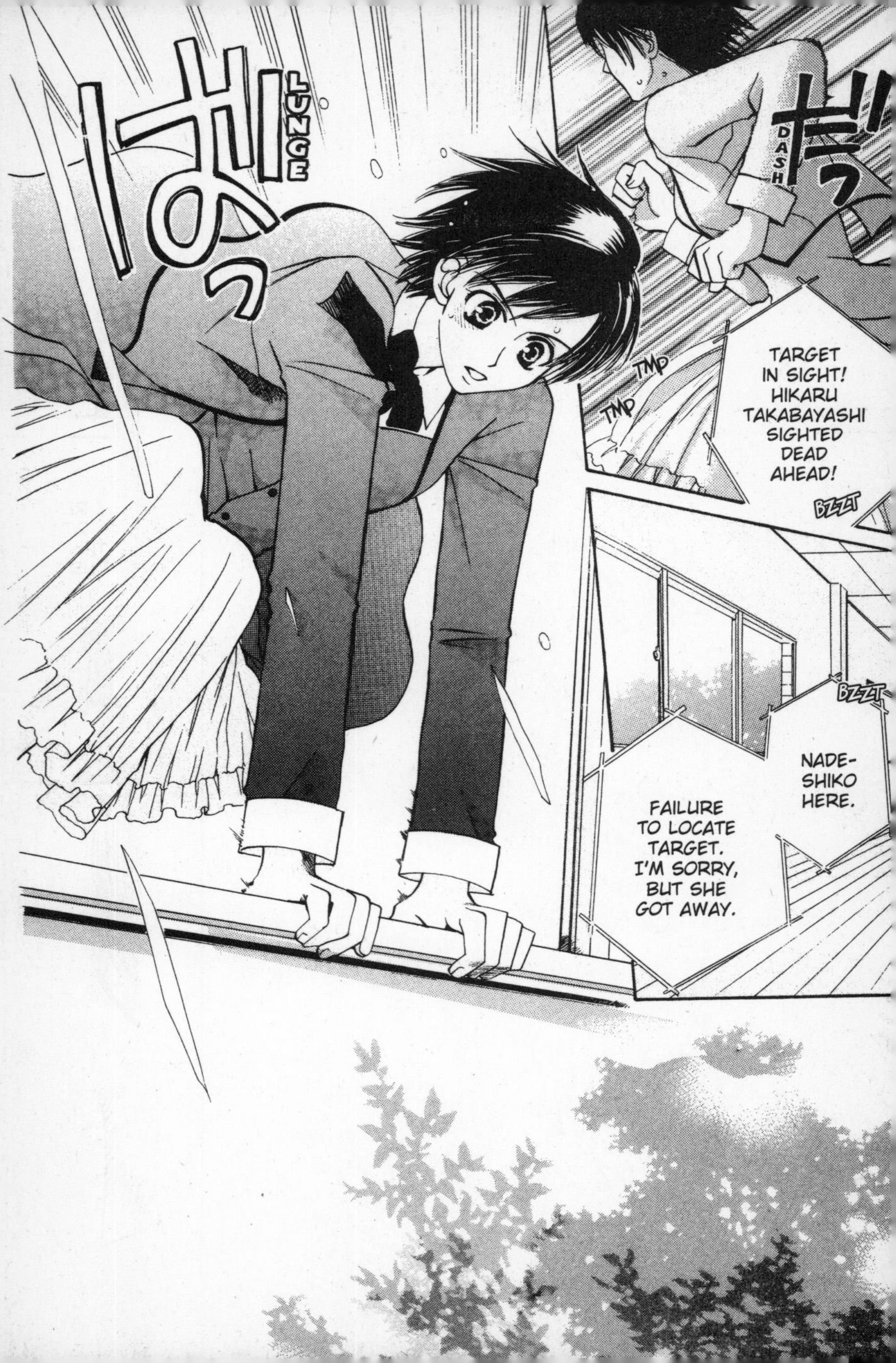
DASH
TMP
TMP
TARGET IN SIGHT! HIKARU TAKABAYASHI SIGHTED DEAD AHEAD!
BZZT
BZZT
NADE-SHIKO HERE.
FAILURE TO LOCATE TARGET. I'M SORRY, BUT SHE GOT AWAY.
LUNGE

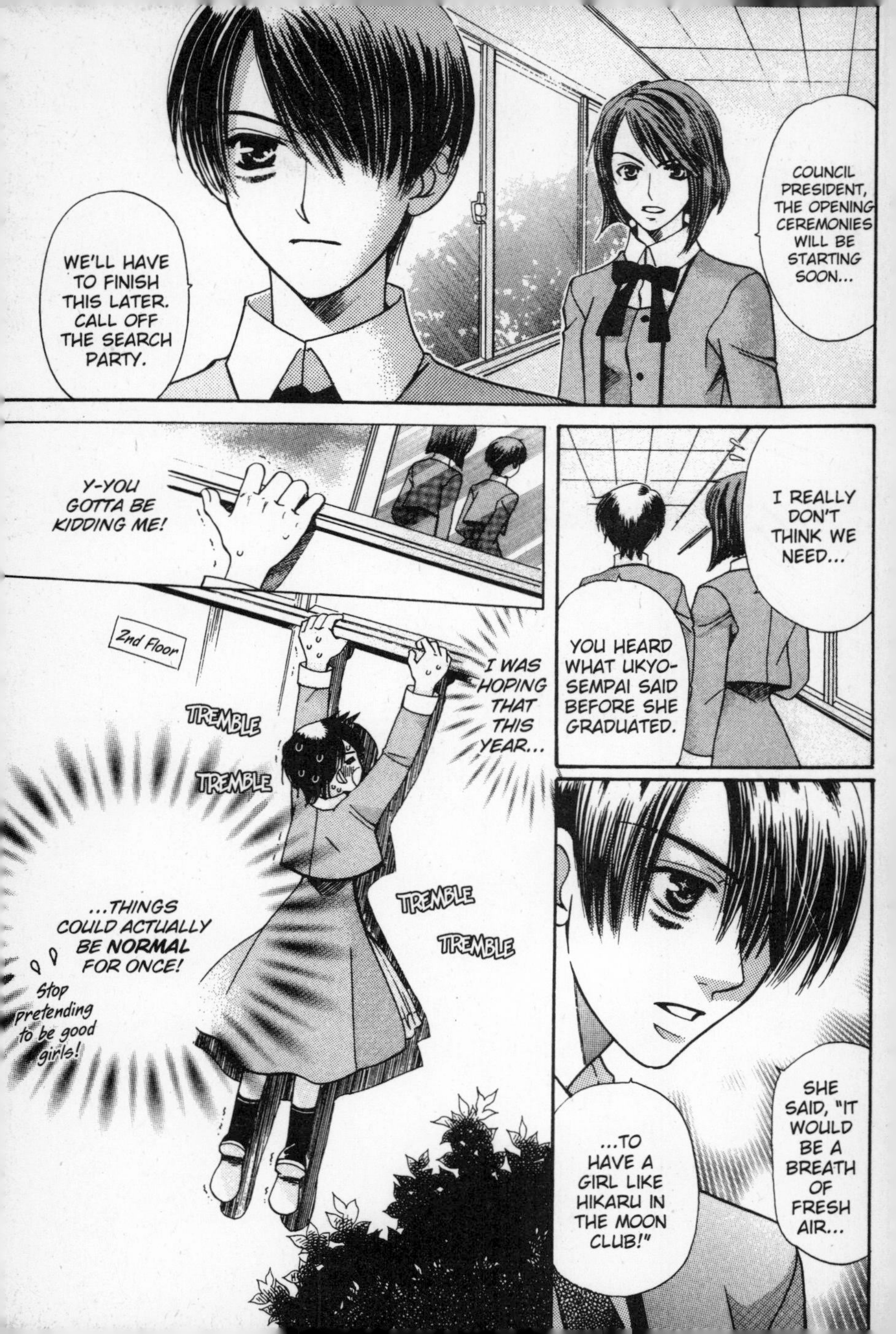
COUNCIL PRESIDENT, THE OPENING CEREMONIES WILL BE STARTING SOON...
WE'LL HAVE TO FINISH THIS LATER. CALL OFF THE SEARCH PARTY.
I REALLY DON'T THINK WE NEED...
YOU HEARD WHAT UKYO-SEMPAI SAID BEFORE SHE GRADUATED.
SHE SAID, "IT WOULD BE A BREATH OF FRESH AIR...
...TO HAVE A GIRL LIKE HIKARU IN THE MOON CLUB!"
Y-YOU GOTTA BE KIDDING ME!
2nd Floor
I WAS HOPING THAT THIS YEAR...
TREMBLE
TREMBLE
...THINGS COULD ACTUALLY BE NORMAL FOR ONCE!
Stop pretending to be good girls!
TREMBLE
TREMBLE

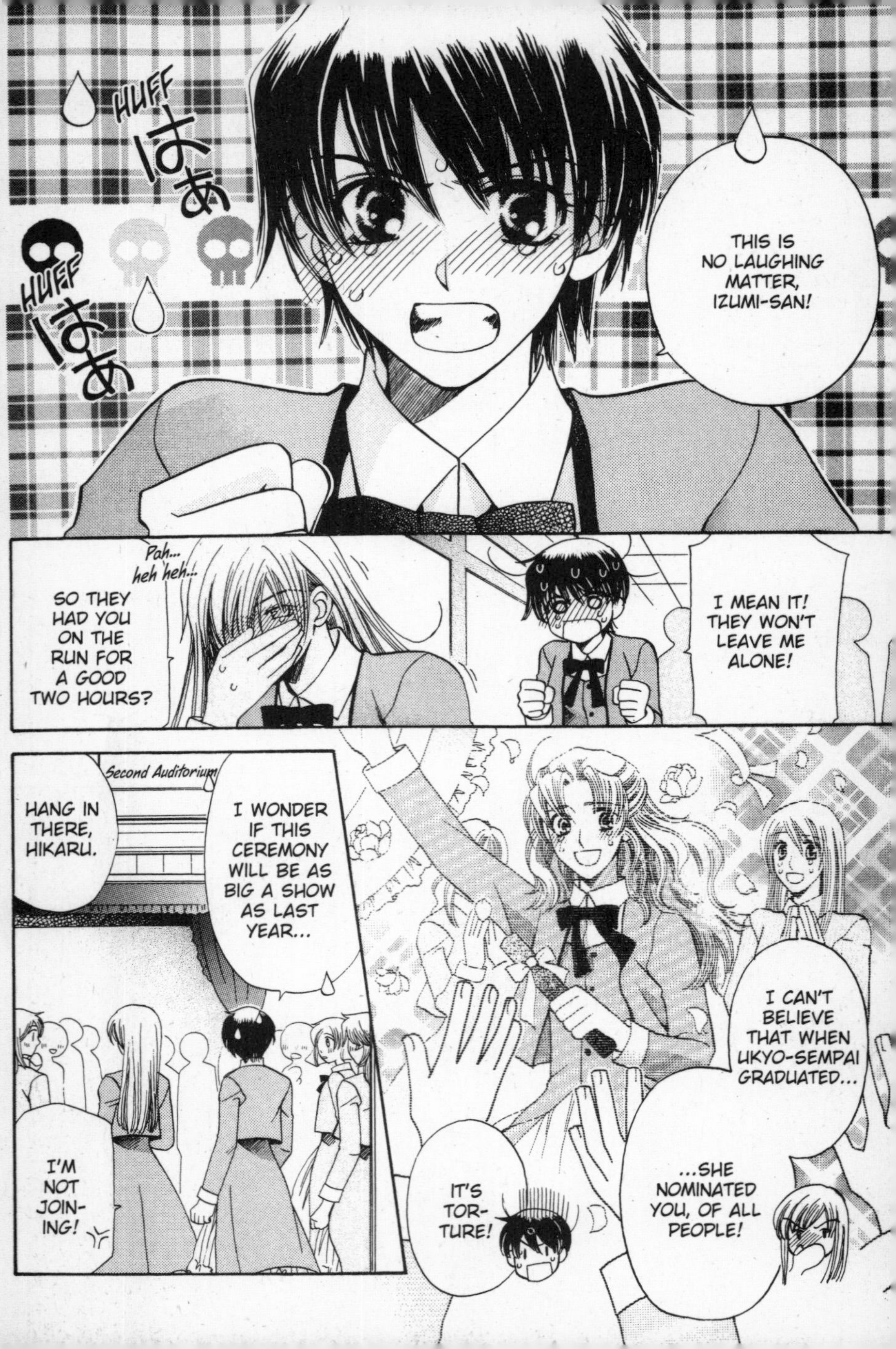
THIS IS NO LAUGHING MATTER, IZUMI-SAN!
HUFF はぁ
HUFF はぁ
I MEAN IT! THEY WON'T LEAVE ME ALONE!
Pah... heh heh...
SO THEY HAD YOU ON THE RUN FOR A GOOD TWO HOURS?
I CAN'T BELIEVE THAT WHEN UKYO-SEMPAI GRADUATED...
...SHE NOMINATED YOU, OF ALL PEOPLE!
IT'S TOR-TURE!
Second Auditorium
I WONDER IF THIS CEREMONY WILL BE AS BIG A SHOW AS LAST YEAR...
HANG IN THERE, HIKARU.
I'M NOT JOIN-ING!

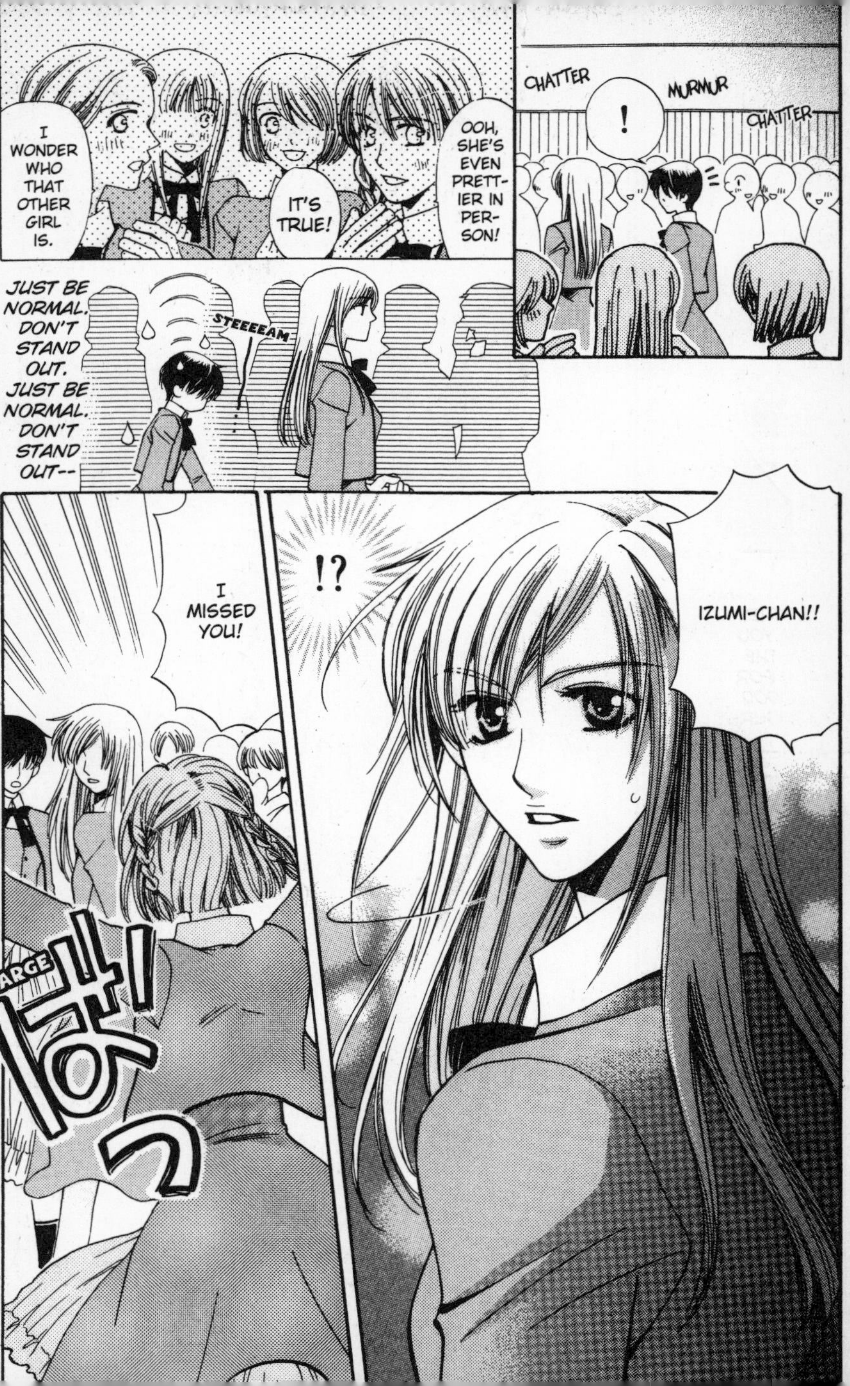
CHATTER
MURMUR
!
CHATTER
OOH, SHE'S EVEN PRETTIER IN PERSON!
IT'S TRUE!
I WONDER WHO THAT OTHER GIRL IS.
STEEEEAM
JUST BE NORMAL. DON'T STAND OUT. JUST BE NORMAL. DON'T STAND OUT--
IZUMI-CHAN!!
!?
I MISSED YOU!
CHARGE
ばっ

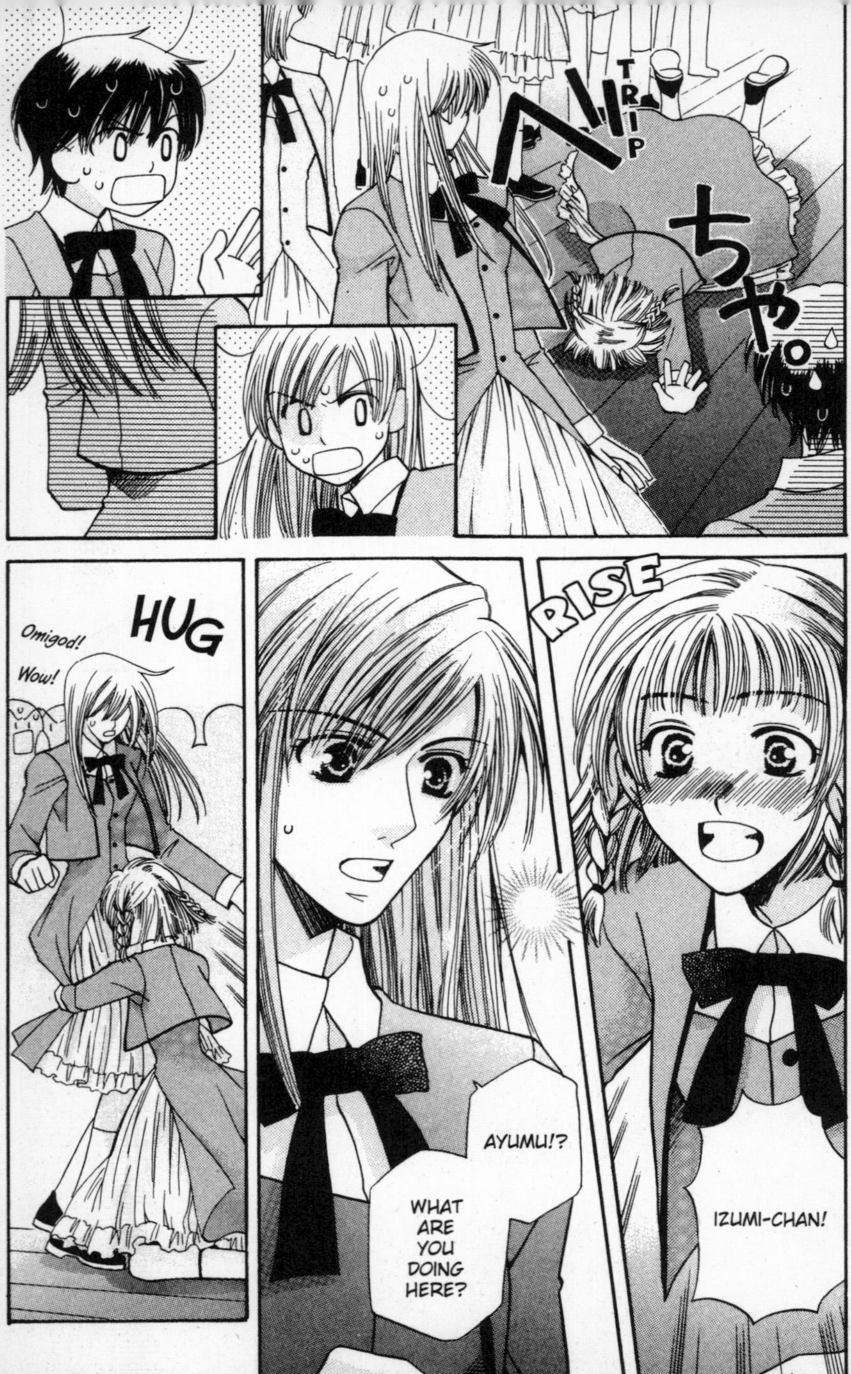
TRIP
ちゃ。
RISE
IZUMI-CHAN!
AYUMU!?
WHAT ARE YOU DOING HERE?
HUG
Omigod!
Wow!

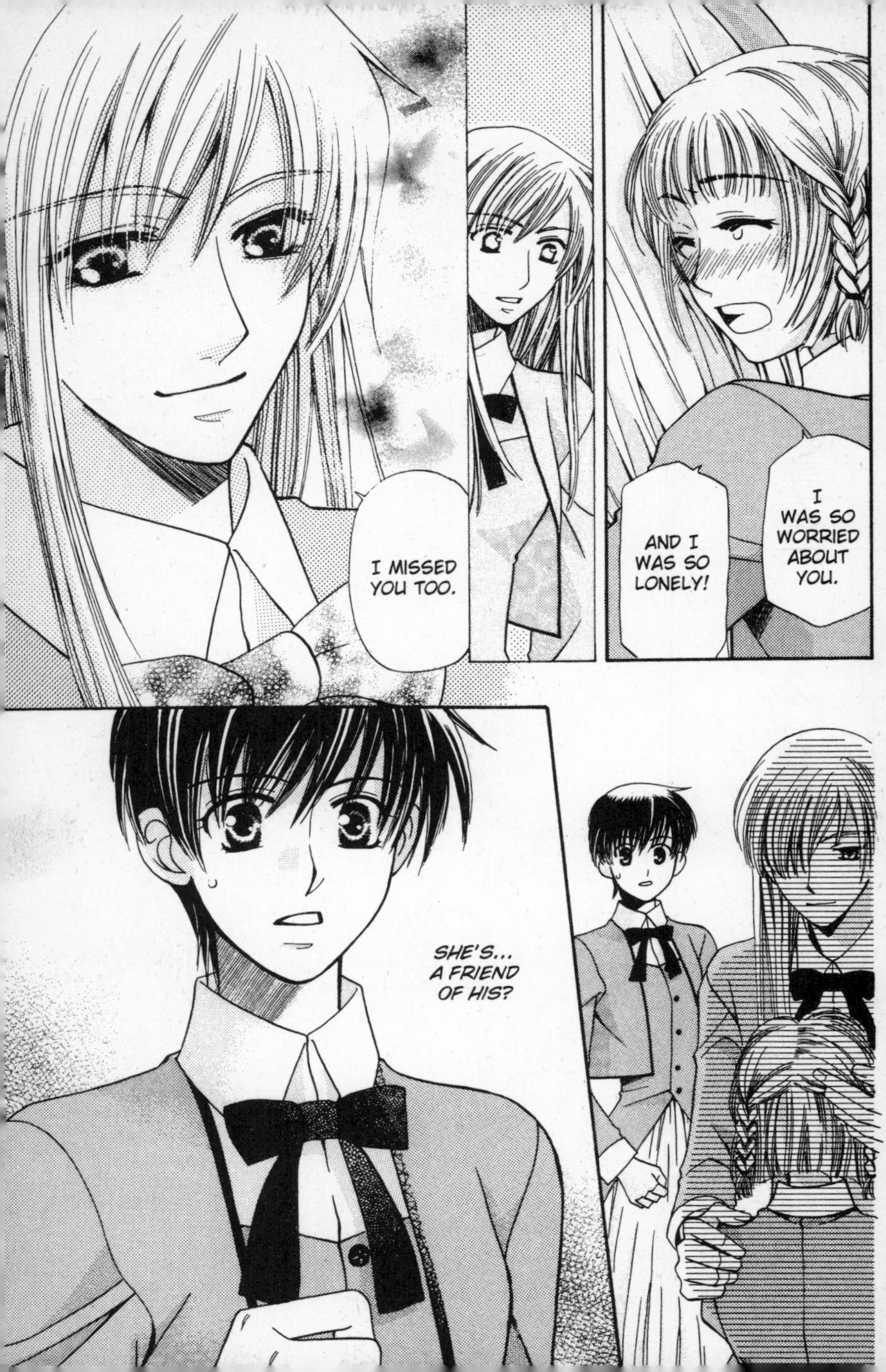
I WAS SO WORRIED ABOUT YOU.
AND I WAS SO LONELY!
I MISSED YOU TOO.
SHE'S... A FRIEND OF HIS?

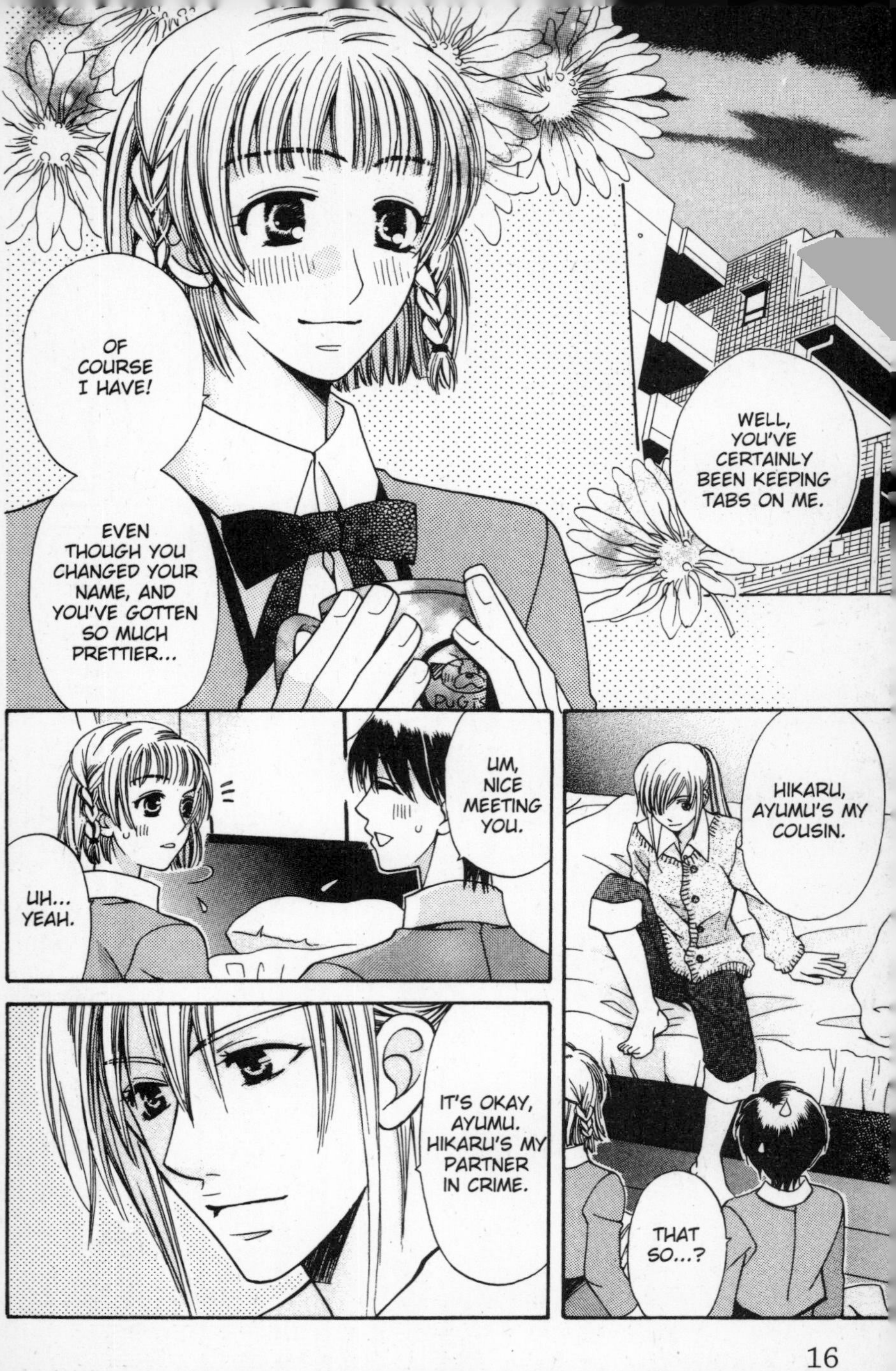
WELL, YOU'VE CERTAINLY BEEN KEEPING TABS ON ME.
OF COURSE I HAVE!
EVEN THOUGH YOU CHANGED YOUR NAME, AND YOU'VE GOTTEN SO MUCH PRETTIER...
HIKARU, AYUMU'S MY COUSIN.
THAT SO...?
UM, NICE MEETING YOU.
UH... YEAH.
IT'S OKAY, AYUMU. HIKARU'S MY PARTNER IN CRIME.

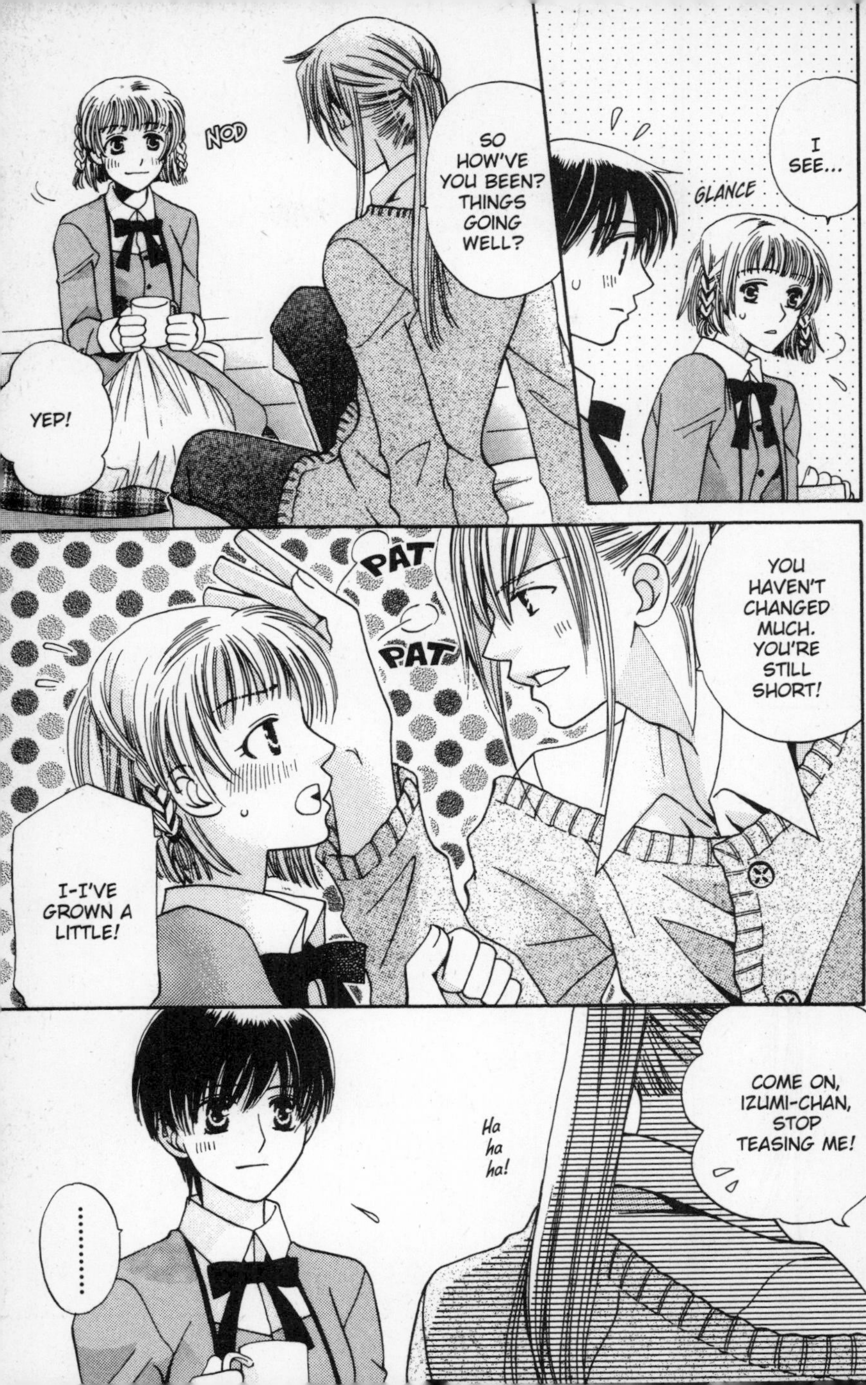
I SEE...
GLANCE
SO HOW'VE YOU BEEN? THINGS GOING WELL?
NOD
YEP!
YOU HAVEN'T CHANGED MUCH. YOU'RE STILL SHORT!
PAT
PAT
I-I'VE GROWN A LITTLE!
COME ON, IZUMI-CHAN, STOP TEASING ME!
Ha ha ha!
....

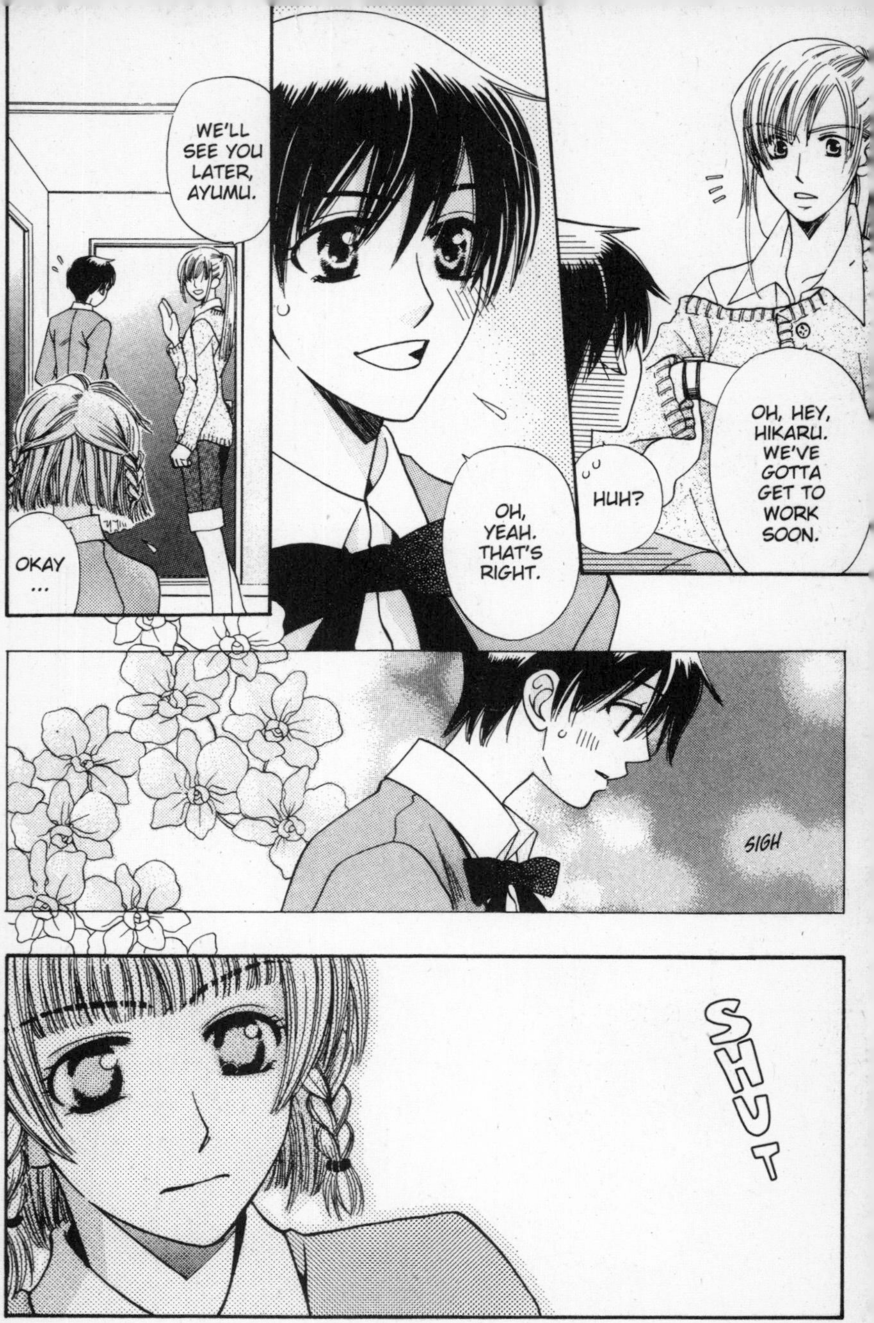
OH, HEY, HIKARU. WE'VE GOTTA GET TO WORK SOON.
HUH?
OH, YEAH. THAT'S RIGHT.
WE'LL SEE YOU LATER, AYUMU.
OKAY ...
SIGH
SHUT

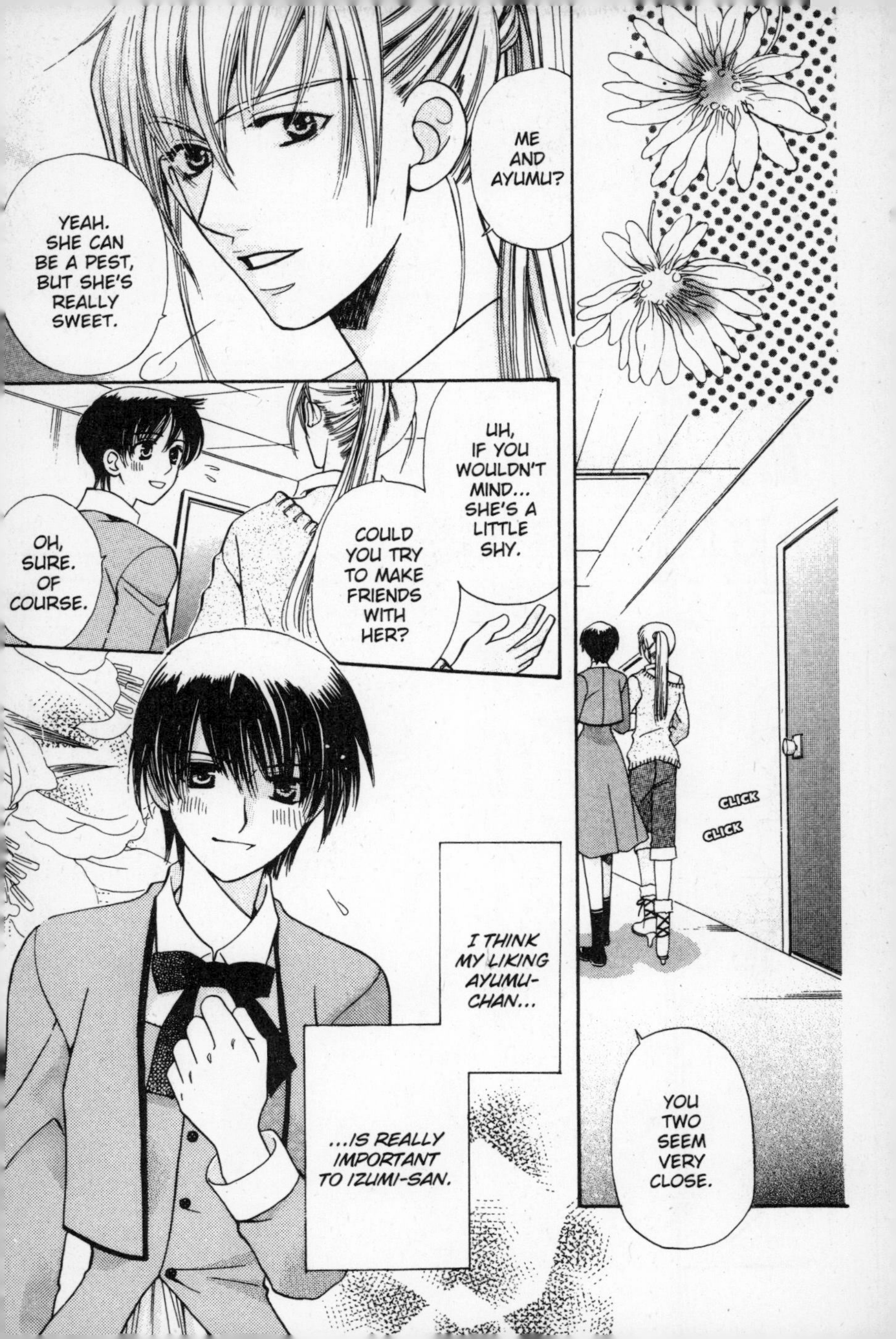
CLICK
CLICK
YOU TWO SEEM VERY CLOSE.
ME AND AYUMU?
YEAH. SHE CAN BE A PEST, BUT SHE'S REALLY SWEET.
UH, IF YOU WOULDN'T MIND... SHE'S A LITTLE SHY.
COULD YOU TRY TO MAKE FRIENDS WITH HER?
OH, SURE. OF COURSE.
I THINK MY LIKING AYUMU-CHAN...
...IS REALLY IMPORTANT TO IZUMI-SAN.

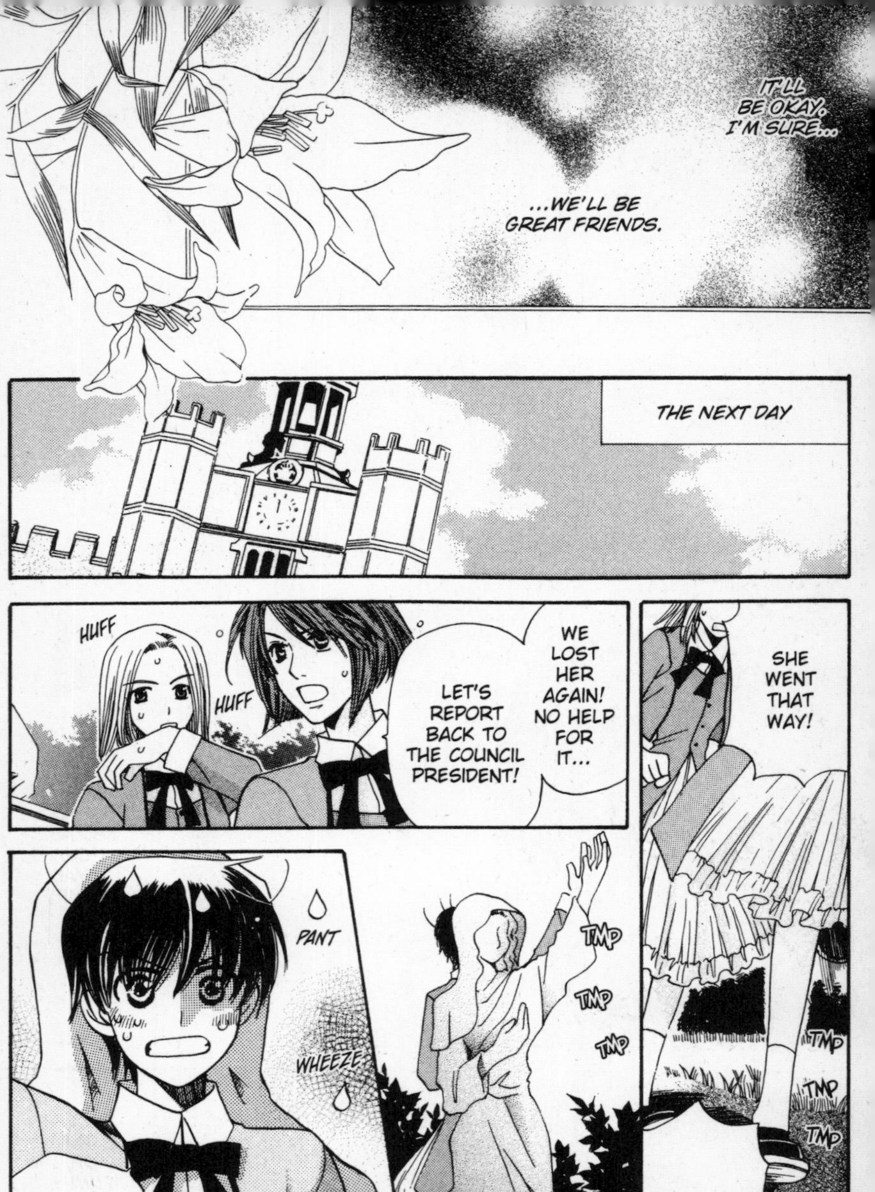
IT'LL BE OKAY. I'M SURE...
...WE'LL BE GREAT FRIENDS.
THE NEXT DAY
SHE WENT THAT WAY!
TMP
TMP
TMP
GOD, SHE'S FAST!
WE LOST HER AGAIN! NO HELP FOR IT...
LET'S REPORT BACK TO THE COUNCIL PRESIDENT!
HUFF
HUFF
TMP
TMP
TMP
PANT
WHEEZE
WHEN WILL THEY GIVE UP, ALREADY?

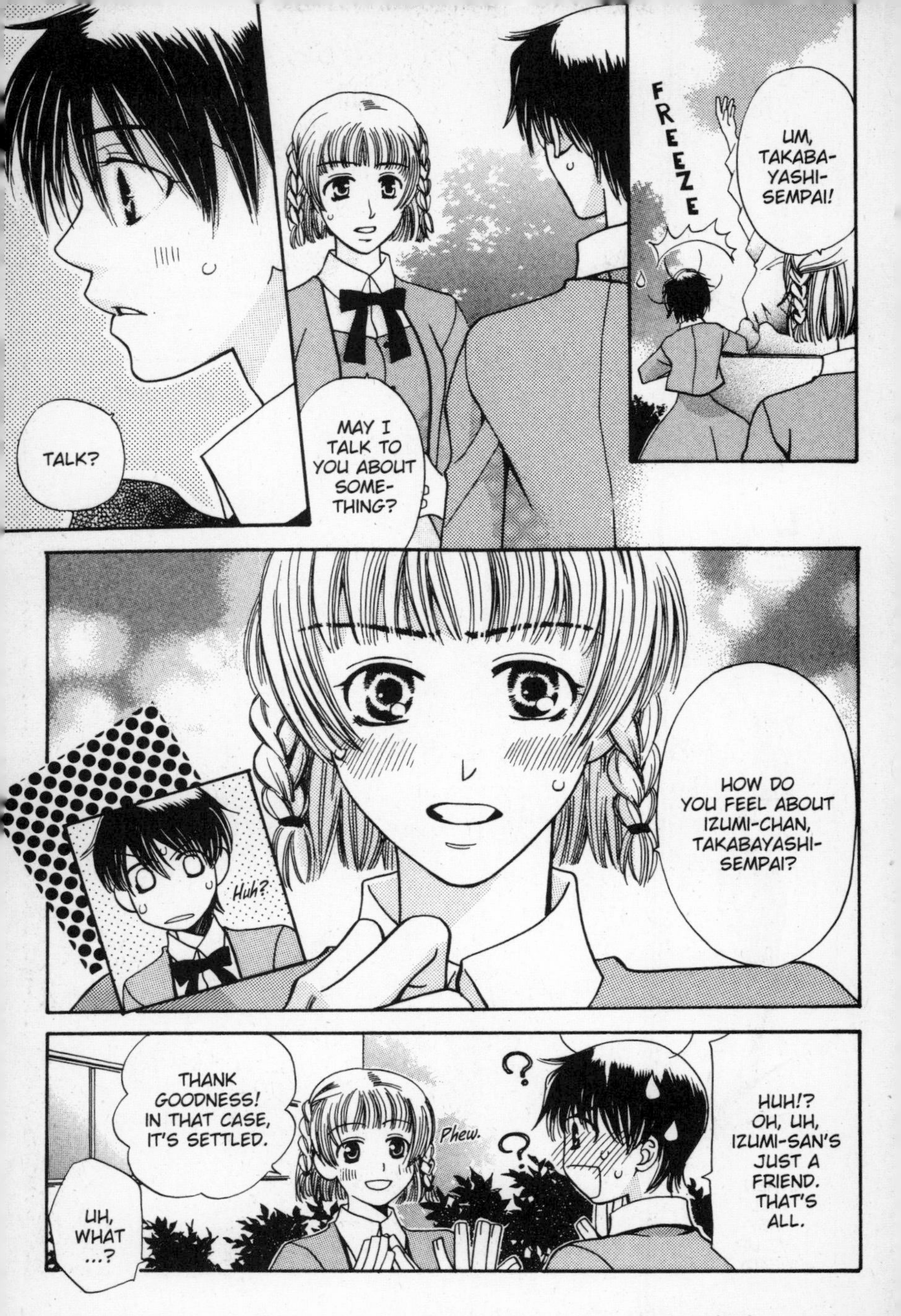
UM, TAKABAYASHI-SEMPAI!
FREEZE
MAY I TALK TO YOU ABOUT SOMETHING?
TALK?
HOW DO YOU FEEL ABOUT IZUMI-CHAN, TAKABAYASHI-SEMPAI?
Huh?
HUH!? OH, UH, IZUMI-SAN'S JUST A FRIEND. THAT'S ALL.
Phew.
THANK GOODNESS! IN THAT CASE, IT'S SETTLED.
UH, WHAT ...?

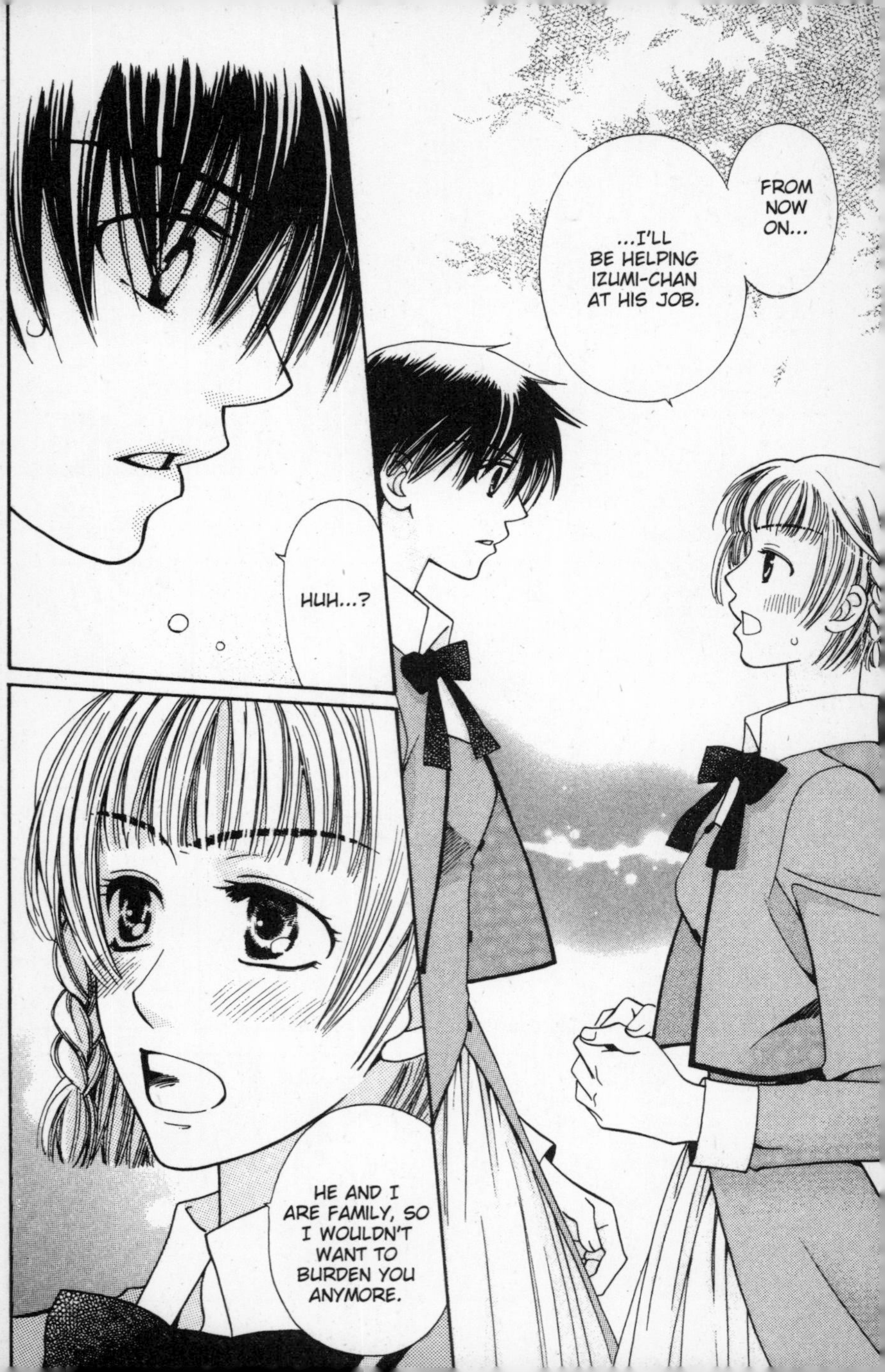
FROM NOW ON...
...I'LL BE HELPING IZUMI-CHAN AT HIS JOB.
HUH...?
HE AND I ARE FAMILY, SO I WOULDN'T WANT TO BURDEN YOU ANYMORE.

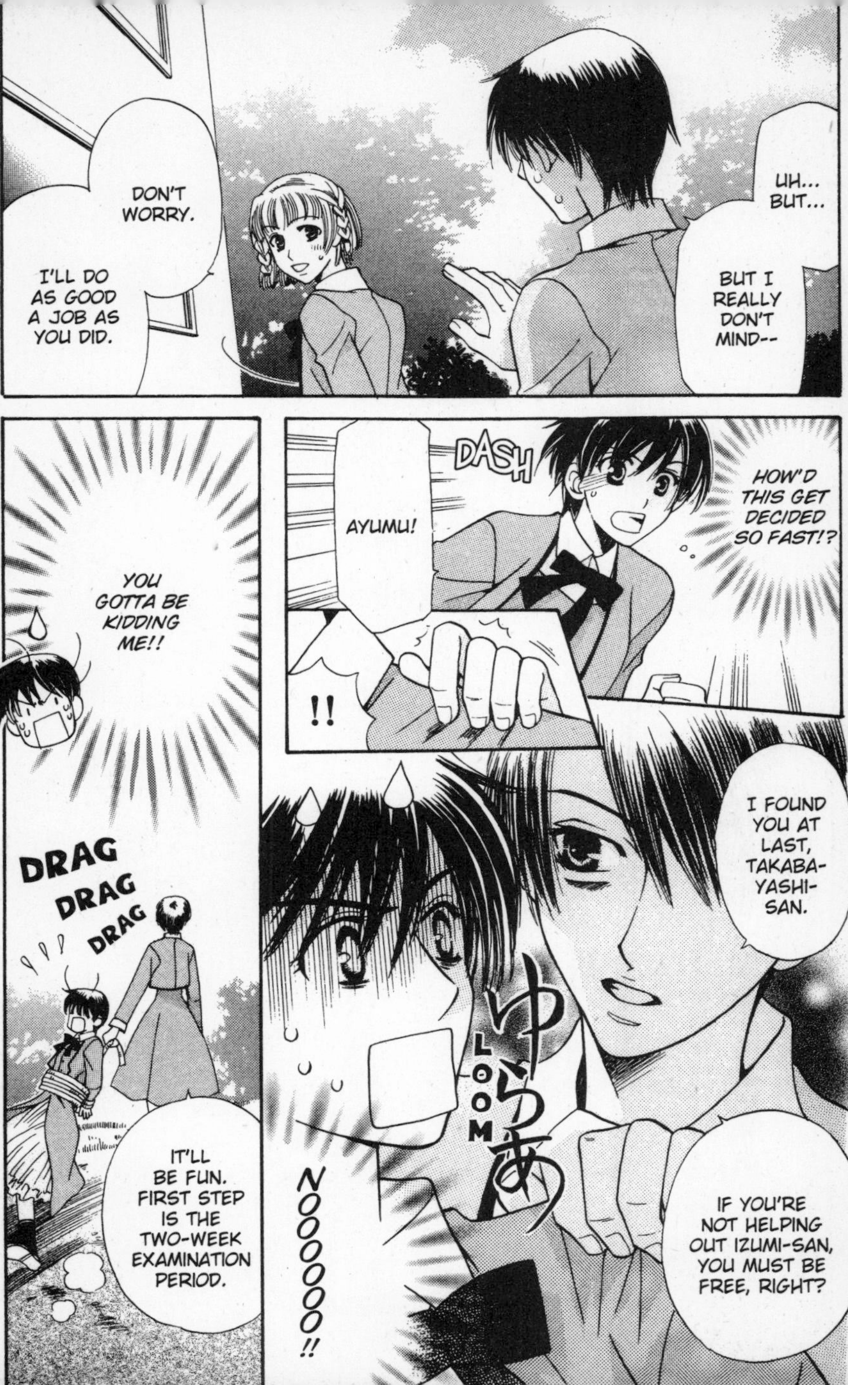

UH... BUT...
BUT I REALLY DON'T MIND--
DON'T WORRY.
I'LL DO AS GOOD A JOB AS YOU DID.
DASH
HOW'D THIS GET DECIDED SO FAST!?
AYUMU!
!!
I FOUND YOU AT LAST, TAKABA-YASHI-SAN.
ゆらあ
LOOM
IF YOU'RE NOT HELPING OUT IZUMI-SAN, YOU MUST BE FREE, RIGHT?
NOOOOOOO!!
YOU GOTTA BE KIDDING ME!!
DRAG DRAG DRAG
IT'LL BE FUN. FIRST STEP IS THE TWO-WEEK EXAMINATION PERIOD.

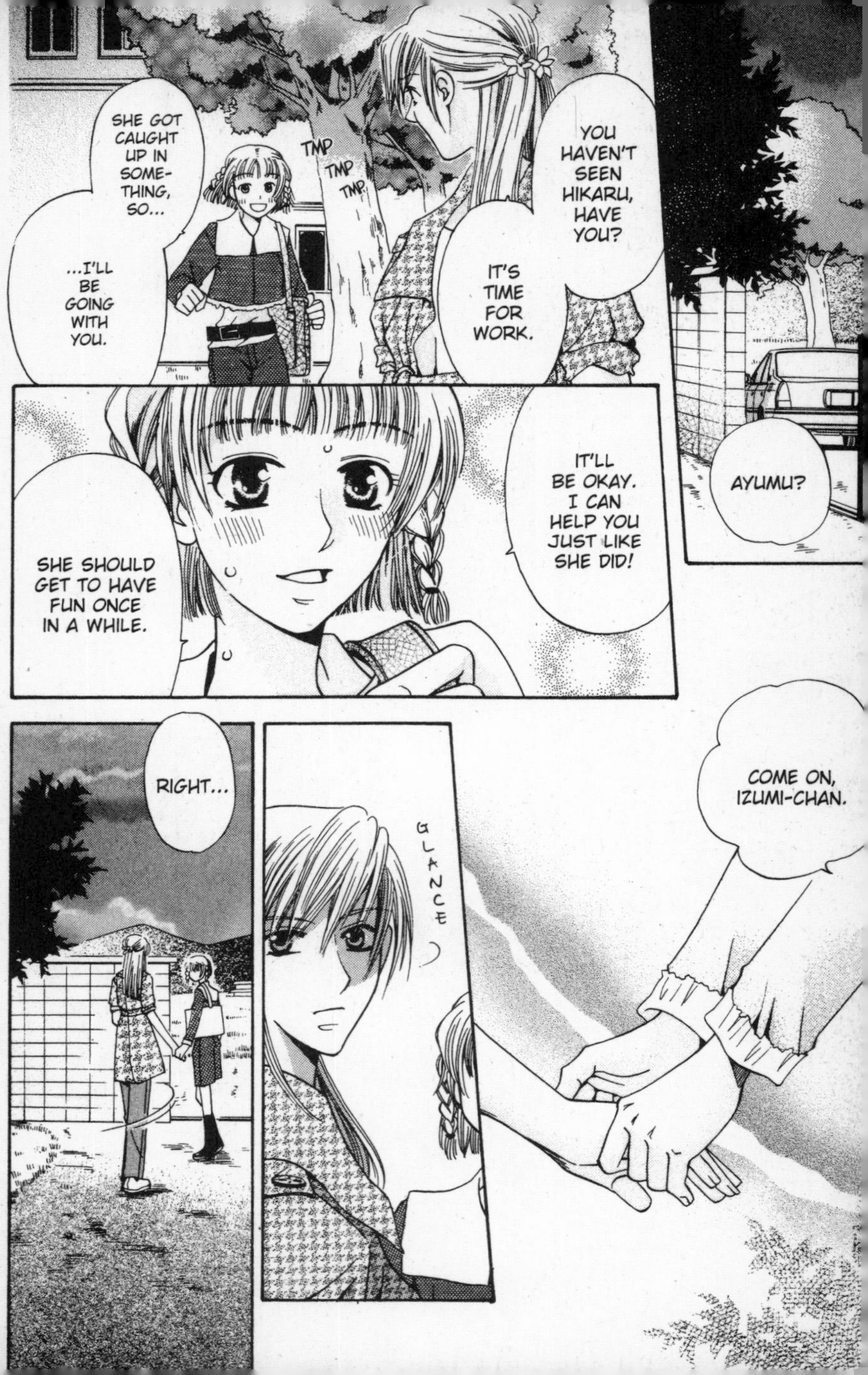
AYUMU?
YOU HAVEN'T SEEN HIKARU, HAVE YOU?
IT'S TIME FOR WORK.
TMP TMP TMP
SHE GOT CAUGHT UP IN SOME-THING, SO...
...I'LL BE GOING WITH YOU.
IT'LL BE OKAY. I CAN HELP YOU JUST LIKE SHE DID!
SHE SHOULD GET TO HAVE FUN ONCE IN A WHILE.
COME ON, IZUMI-CHAN.
GLANCE
RIGHT...

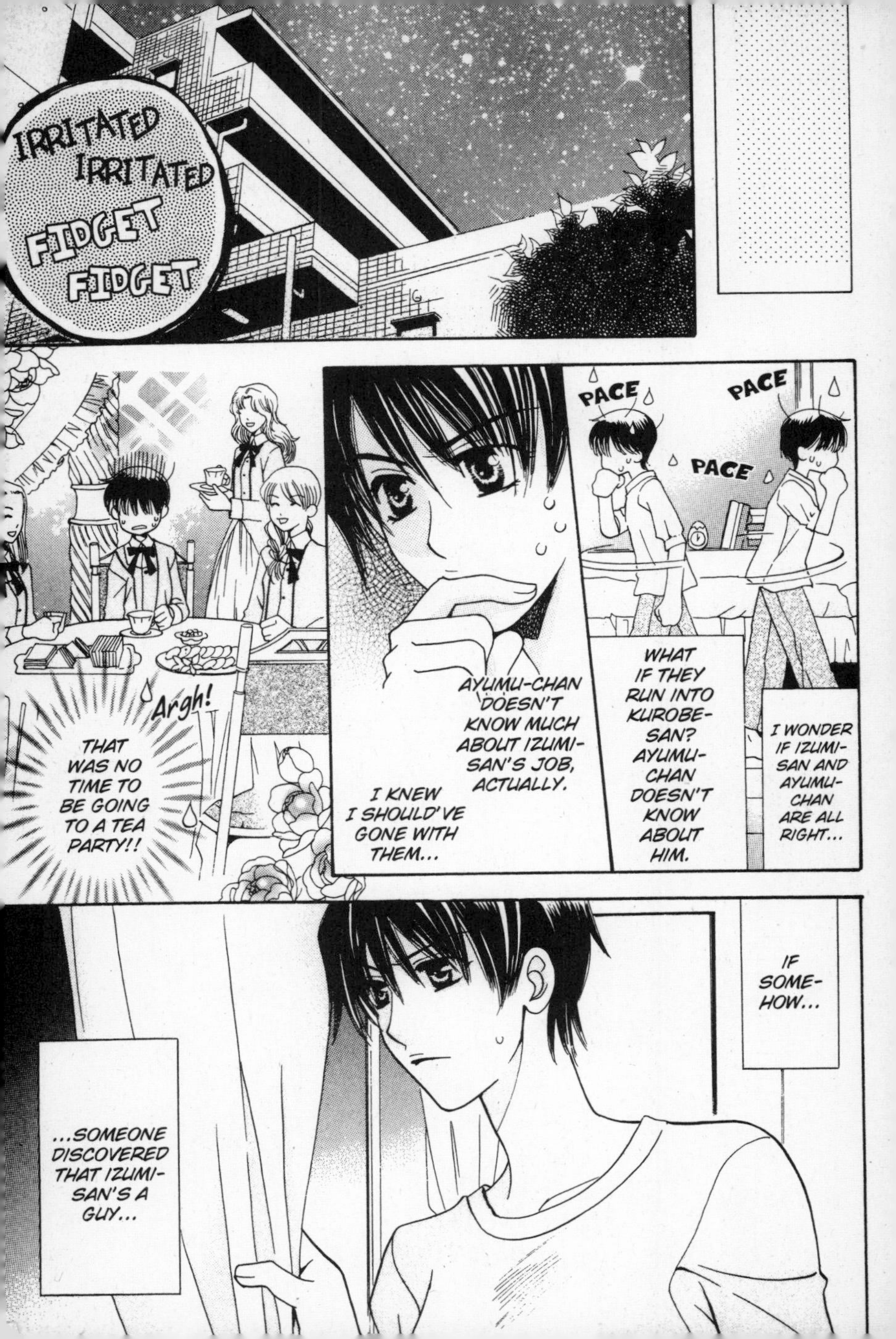
IRRITATED IRRITATED
FIDGET FIDGET
PACE
PACE
PACE
I WONDER IF IZUMI-SAN AND AYUMU-CHAN ARE ALL RIGHT...
WHAT IF THEY RUN INTO KUROBE-SAN? AYUMU-CHAN DOESN'T KNOW ABOUT HIM.
AYUMU-CHAN DOESN'T KNOW MUCH ABOUT IZUMI-SAN'S JOB, ACTUALLY.
I KNEW I SHOULD'VE GONE WITH THEM...
Argh!
THAT WAS NO TIME TO BE GOING TO A TEA PARTY!!
IF SOMEHOW...
...SOMEONE DISCOVERED THAT IZUMI-SAN'S A GUY...

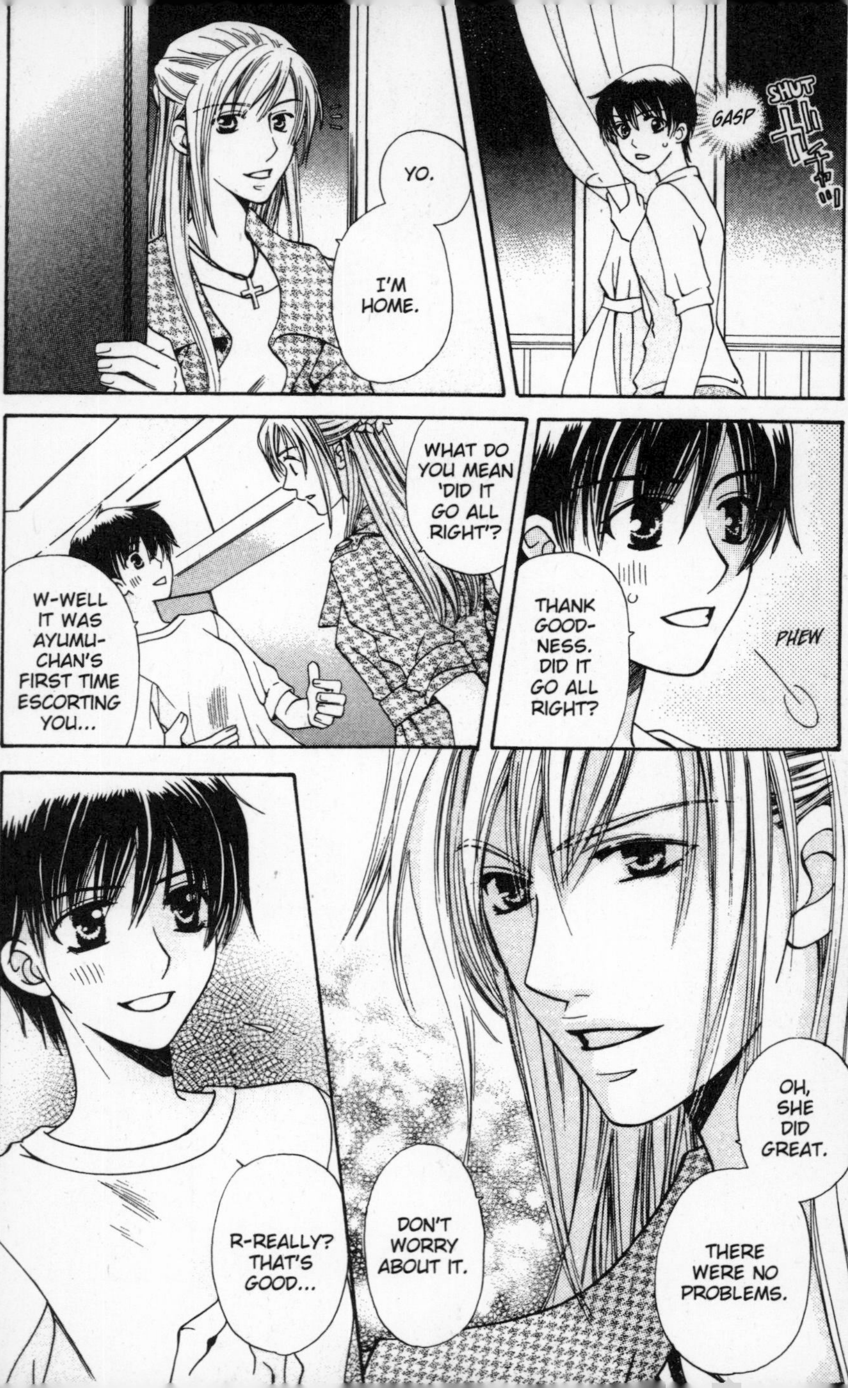
GASP
SHUT
YO.
I'M HOME.
THANK GOODNESS. DID IT GO ALL RIGHT?
PHEW
WHAT DO YOU MEAN 'DID IT GO ALL RIGHT'?
W-WELL IT WAS AYUMU-CHAN'S FIRST TIME ESCORTING YOU...
OH, SHE DID GREAT.
THERE WERE NO PROBLEMS.
DON'T WORRY ABOUT IT.
R-REALLY? THAT'S GOOD...

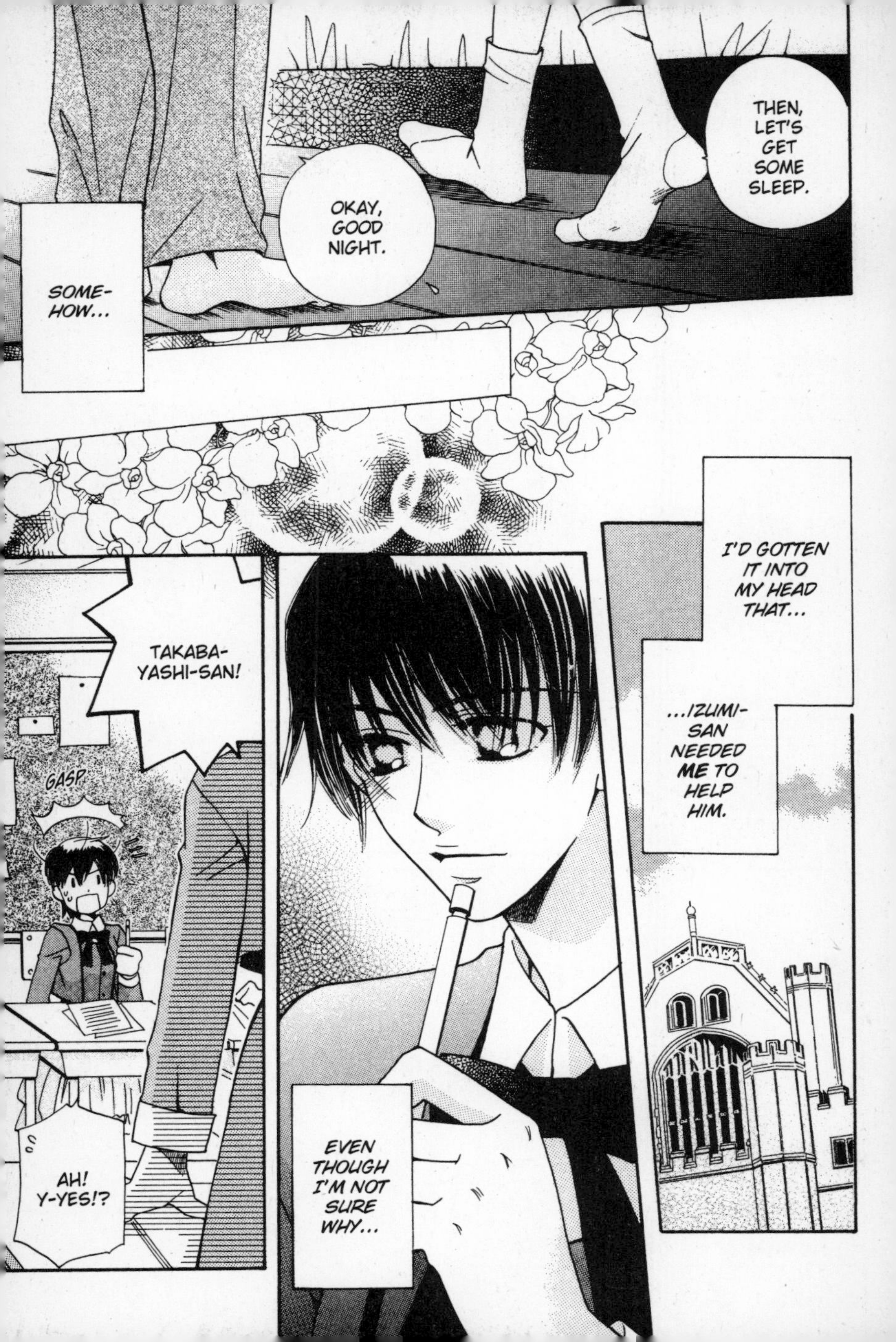
THEN, LET'S GET SOME SLEEP.
OKAY, GOOD NIGHT.
SOME-HOW...
I'D GOTTEN IT INTO MY HEAD THAT...
...IZUMI-SAN NEEDED ME TO HELP HIM.
EVEN THOUGH I'M NOT SURE WHY...
TAKABA-YASHI-SAN!
GASP
AH! Y-YES!?

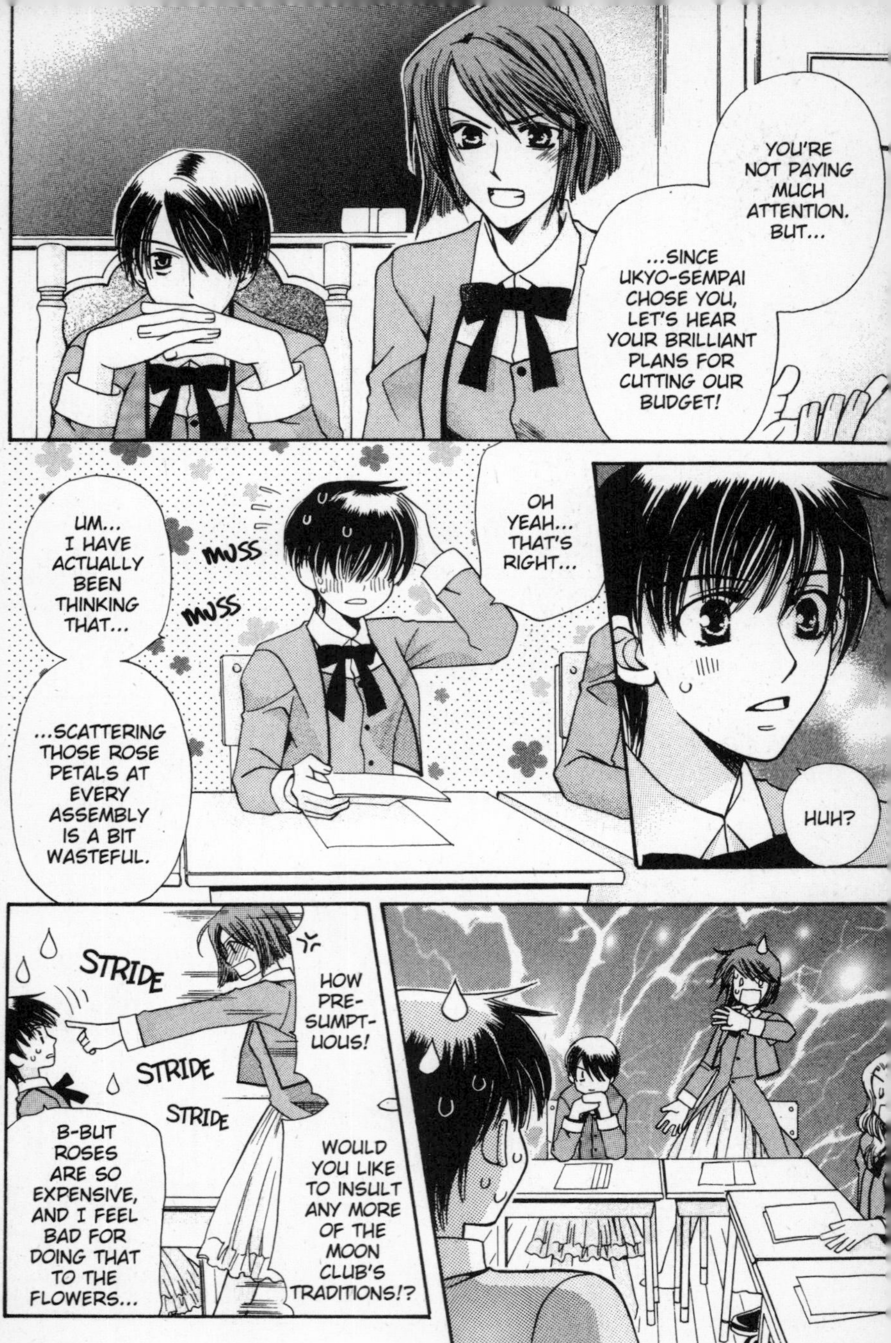
YOU'RE NOT PAYING MUCH ATTENTION. BUT...
...SINCE UKYO-SEMPAI CHOSE YOU, LET'S HEAR YOUR BRILLIANT PLANS FOR CUTTING OUR BUDGET!
HUH?
OH YEAH... THAT'S RIGHT...
MUSS
MUSS
UM... I HAVE ACTUALLY BEEN THINKING THAT...
...SCATTERING THOSE ROSE PETALS AT EVERY ASSEMBLY IS A BIT WASTEFUL.
HOW PRE-SUMPT-UOUS!
STRIDE
STRIDE
STRIDE
WOULD YOU LIKE TO INSULT ANY MORE OF THE MOON CLUB'S TRADITIONS!?
B-BUT ROSES ARE SO EXPENSIVE, AND I FEEL BAD FOR DOING THAT TO THE FLOWERS...

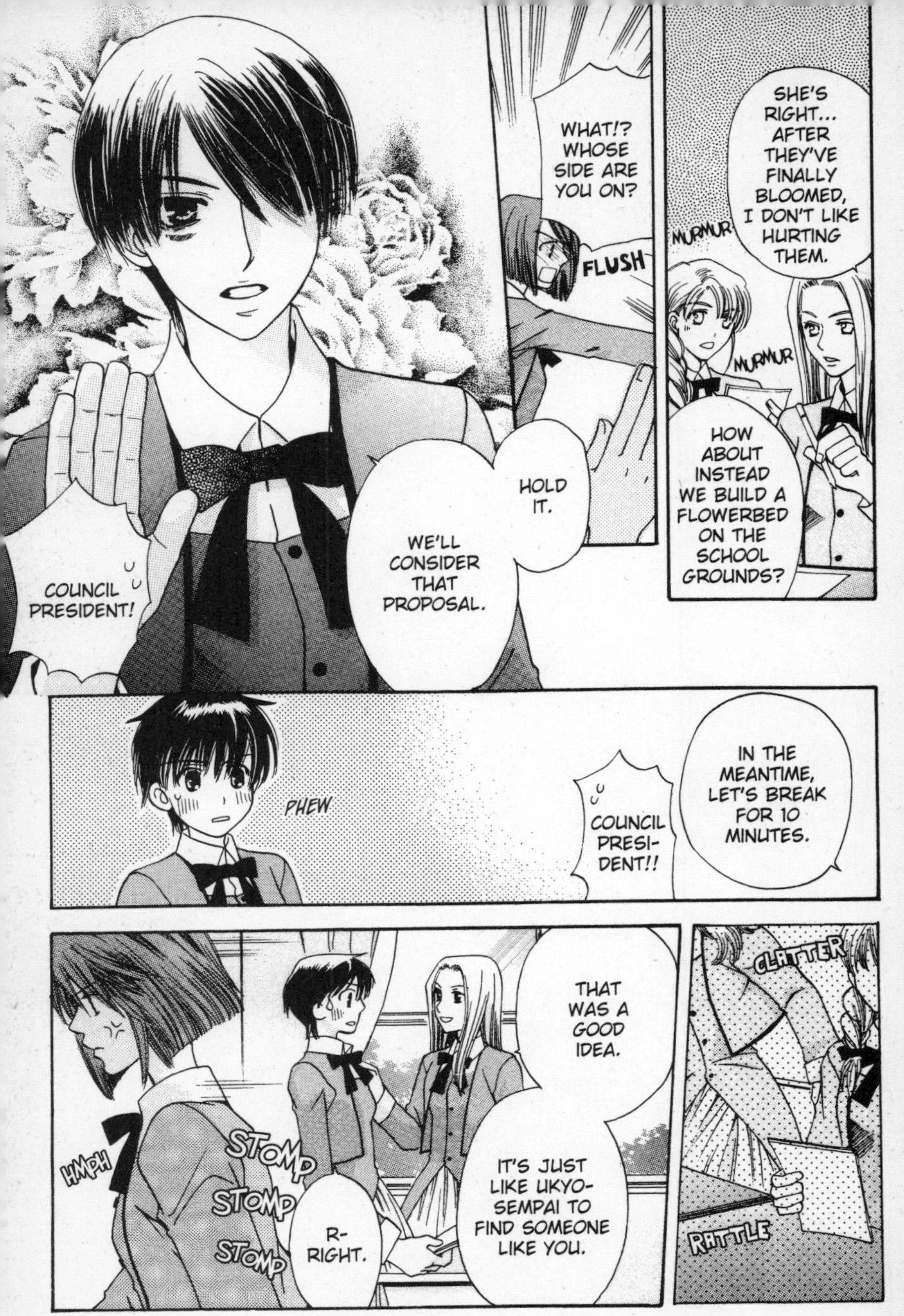
SHE'S RIGHT... AFTER THEY'VE FINALLY BLOOMED, I DON'T LIKE HURTING THEM.
MURMUR
MURMUR
HOW ABOUT INSTEAD WE BUILD A FLOWERBED ON THE SCHOOL GROUNDS?
WHAT!? WHOSE SIDE ARE YOU ON?
FLUSH
HOLD IT.
WE'LL CONSIDER THAT PROPOSAL.
COUNCIL PRESIDENT!
IN THE MEANTIME, LET'S BREAK FOR 10 MINUTES.
COUNCIL PRESI-DENT!!
PHEW
CLATTER
RATTLE
THAT WAS A GOOD IDEA.
IT'S JUST LIKE UKYO-SEMPAI TO FIND SOMEONE LIKE YOU.
R-RIGHT.
STOMP
STOMP
STOMP
HMPH

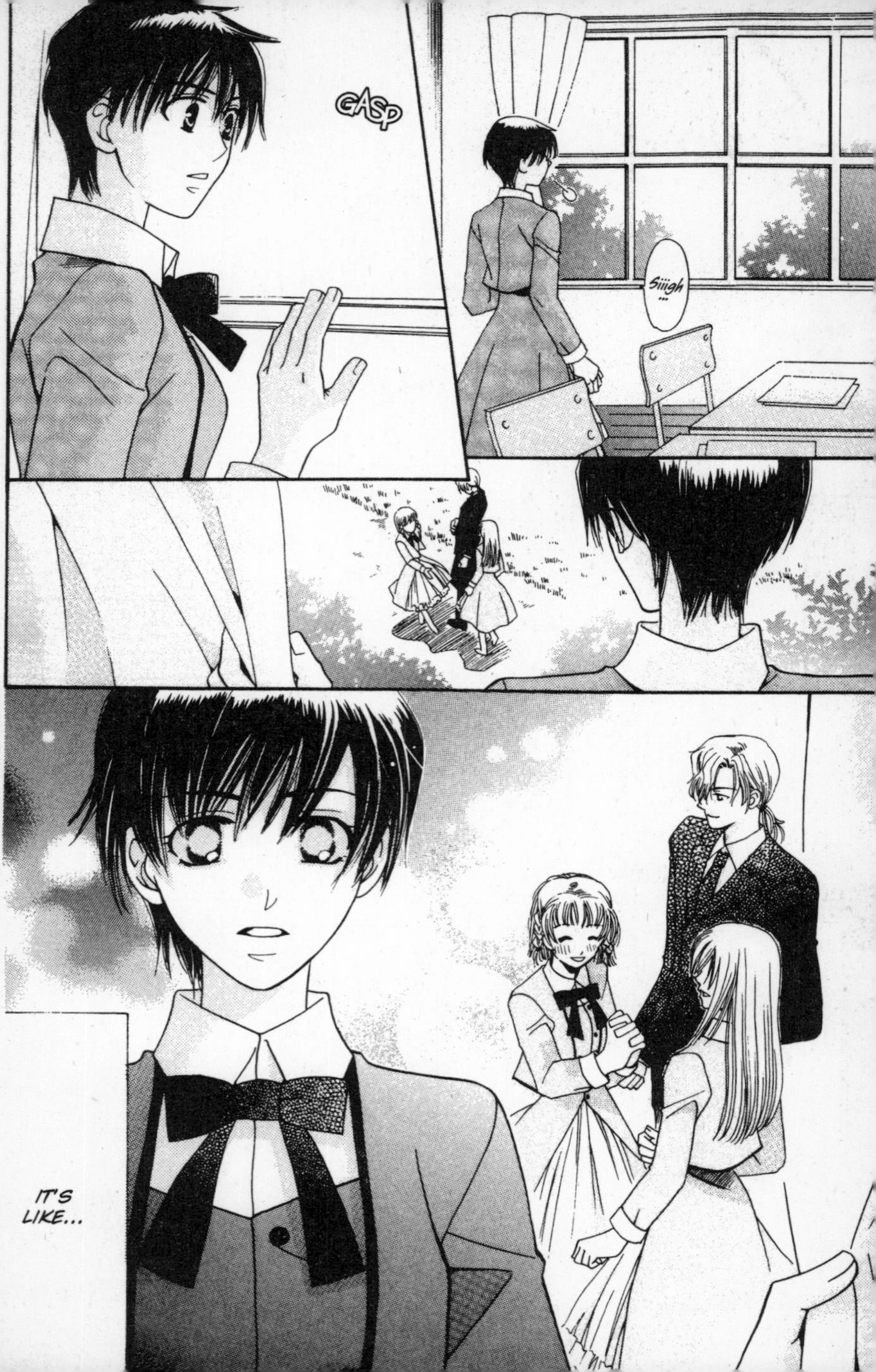
Siiigh...
GASP
IT'S LIKE...

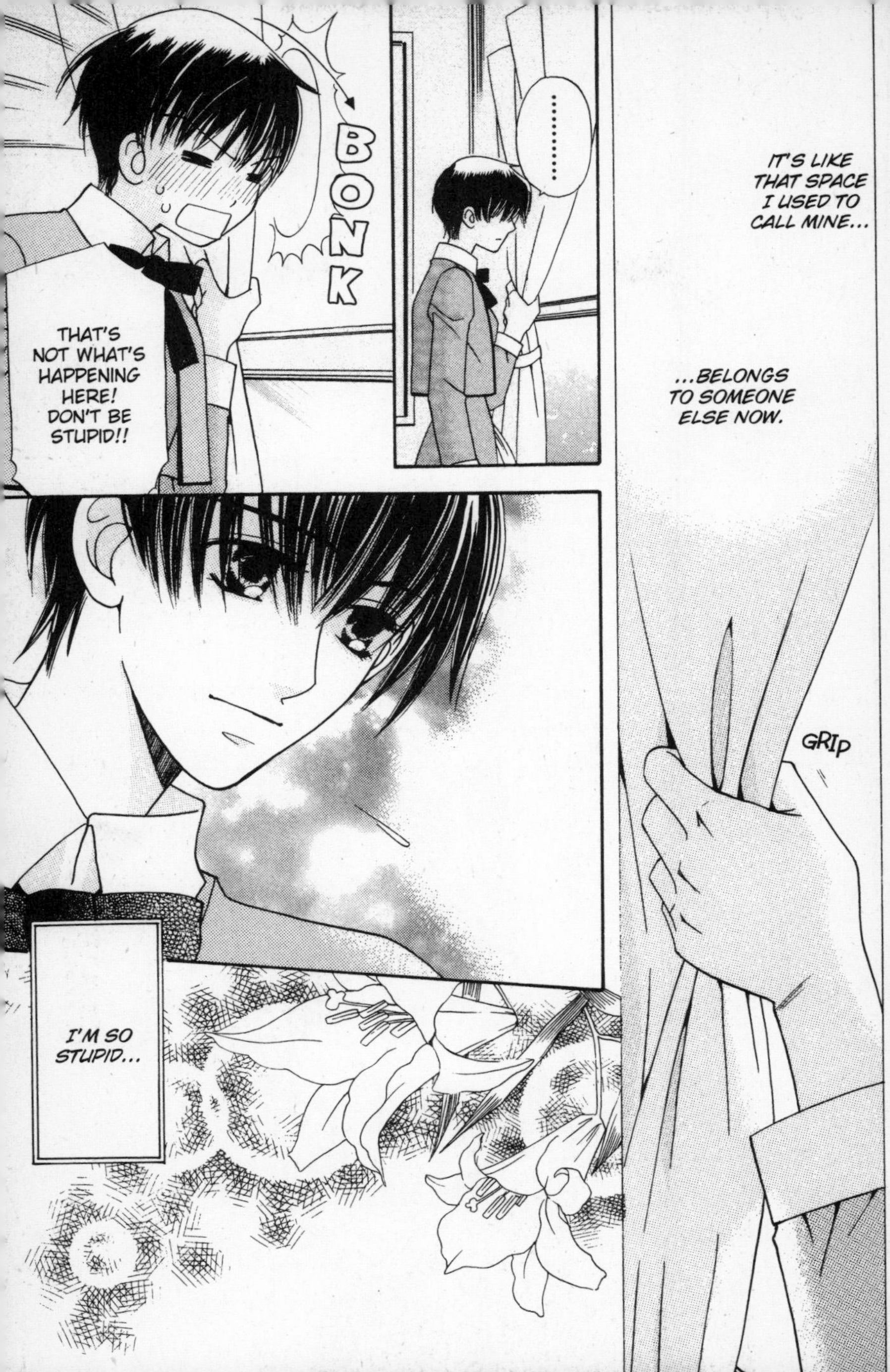
IT'S LIKE THAT SPACE I USED TO CALL MINE...
...BELONGS TO SOMEONE ELSE NOW.
GRIP
....
BONK
THAT'S NOT WHAT'S HAPPENING HERE! DON'T BE STUPID!!
I'M SO STUPID...

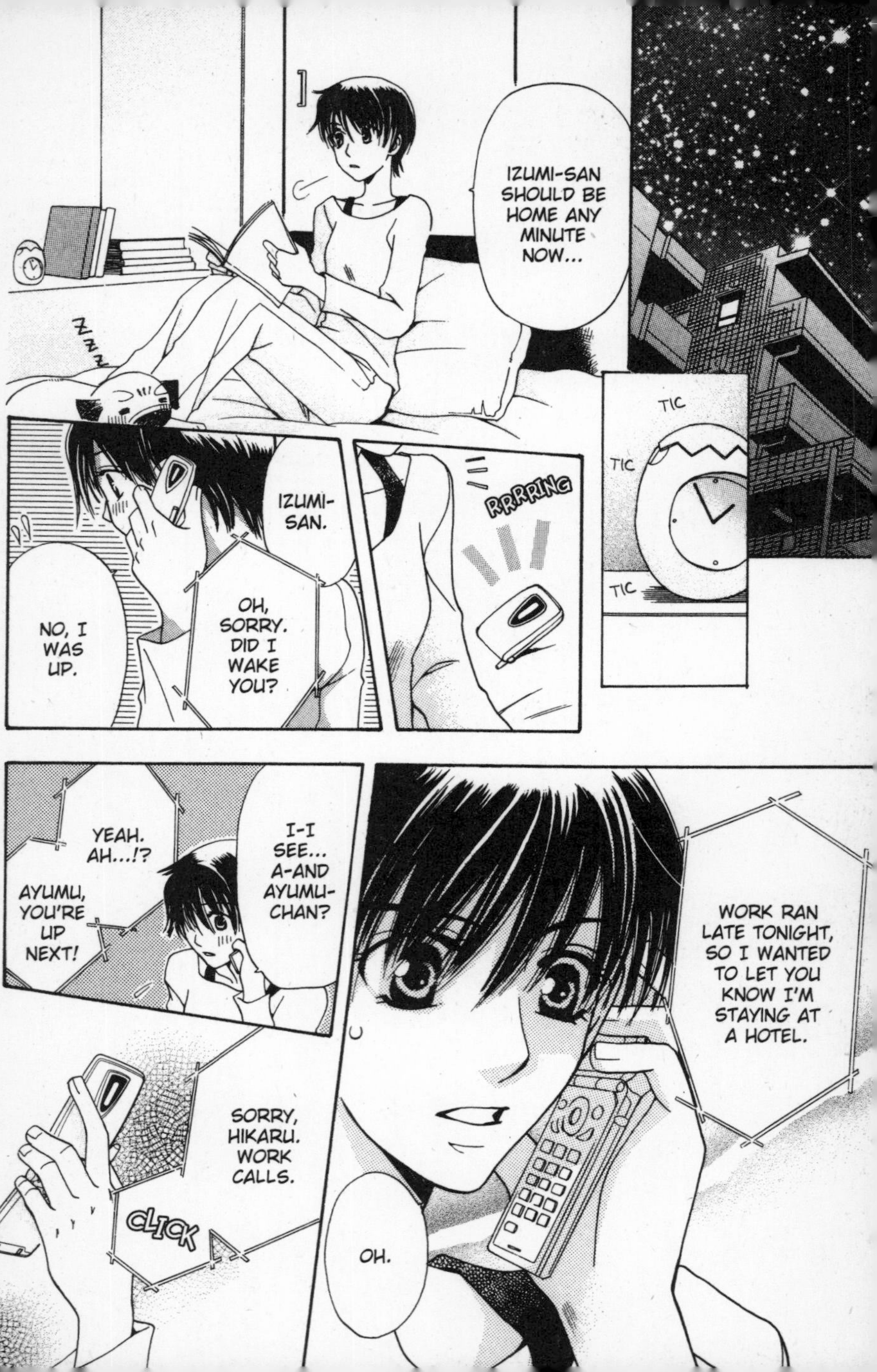
IZUMI-SAN SHOULD BE HOME ANY MINUTE NOW...
ZZZ
TIC
TIC
TIC
RRRRING
IZUMI-SAN.
OH, SORRY. DID I WAKE YOU?
NO, I WAS UP.
WORK RAN LATE TONIGHT, SO I WANTED TO LET YOU KNOW I'M STAYING AT A HOTEL.
I-I SEE... A-AND AYUMU-CHAN?
YEAH. AH...!?
AYUMU, YOU'RE UP NEXT!
SORRY, HIKARU. WORK CALLS.
CLICK
OH.

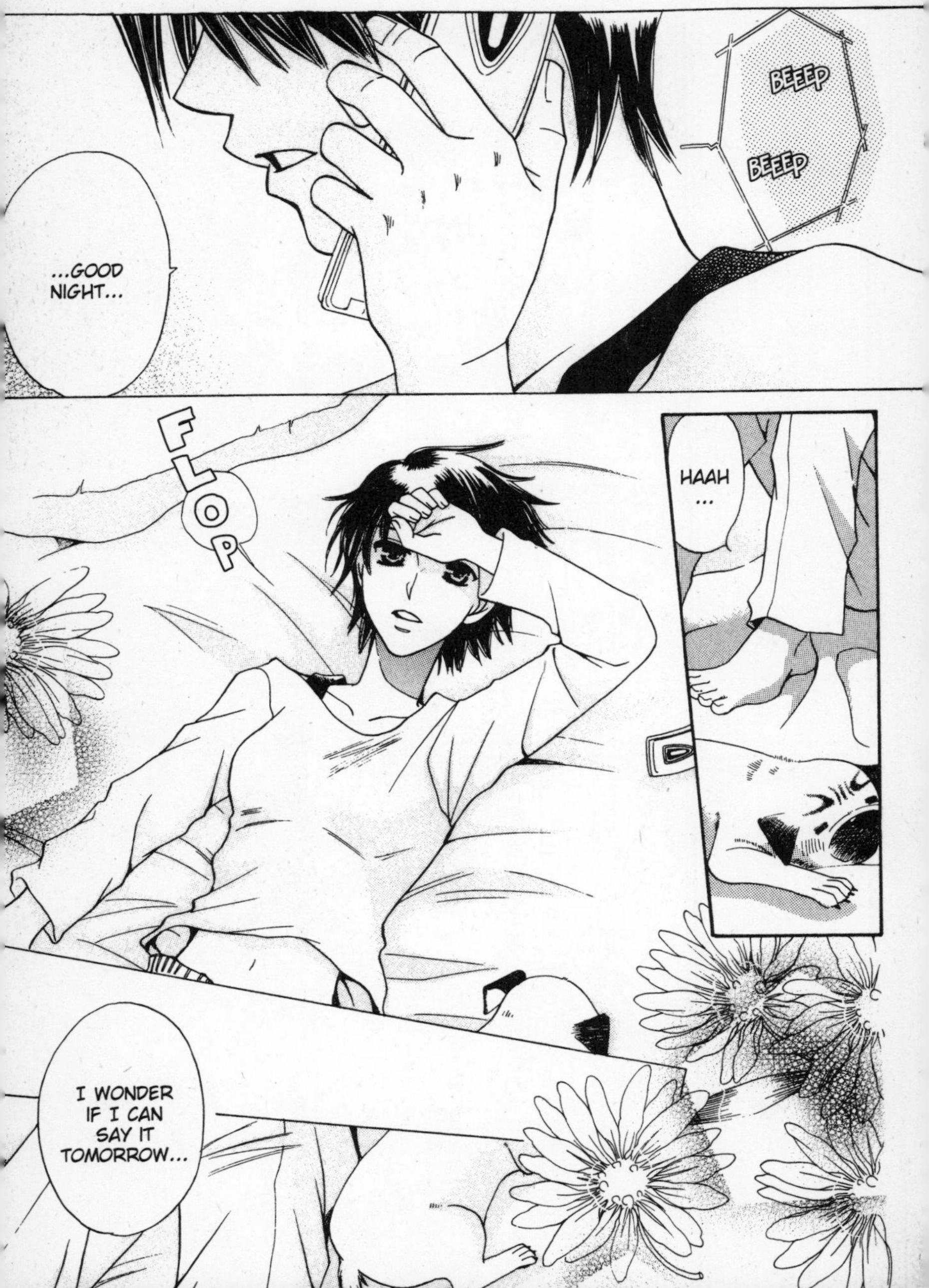
BEEEP
BEEEP
...GOOD NIGHT...
HAAH ...
FLOP
I WONDER IF I CAN SAY IT TOMORROW...

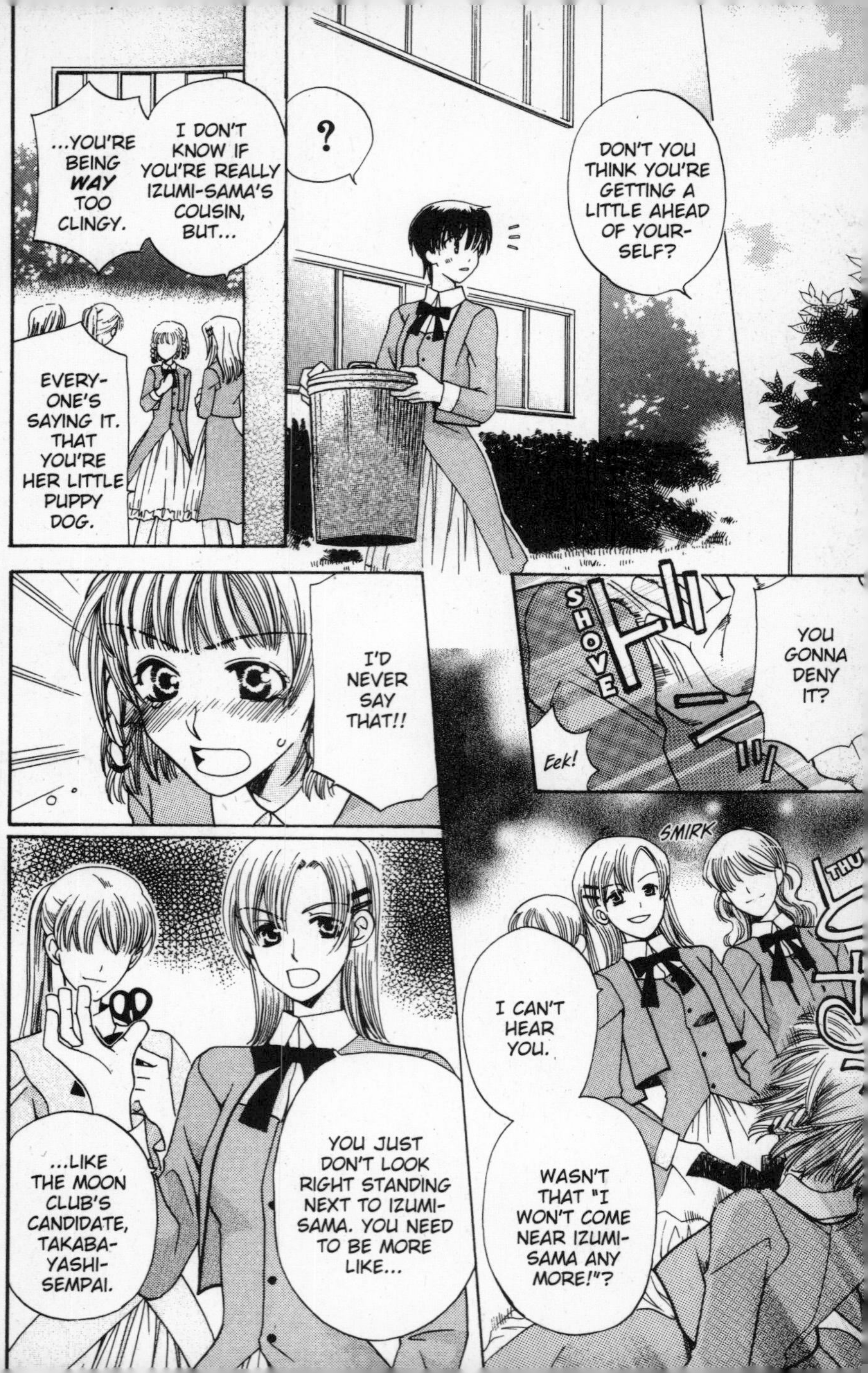
DON'T YOU THINK YOU'RE GETTING A LITTLE AHEAD OF YOURSELF?
?
I DON'T KNOW IF YOU'RE REALLY IZUMI-SAMA'S COUSIN, BUT...
...YOU'RE BEING WAY TOO CLINGY.
EVERYONE'S SAYING IT. THAT YOU'RE HER LITTLE PUPPY DOG.
SHOVE
YOU GONNA DENY IT?
Eek!
I'D NEVER SAY THAT!!
SMIRK
WASN'T THAT "I WON'T COME NEAR IZUMI-SAMA ANY MORE!"?
I CAN'T HEAR YOU.
YOU JUST DON'T LOOK RIGHT STANDING NEXT TO IZUMI-SAMA. YOU NEED TO BE MORE LIKE...
...LIKE THE MOON CLUB'S CANDIDATE, TAKABAYASHI-SEMPAI.

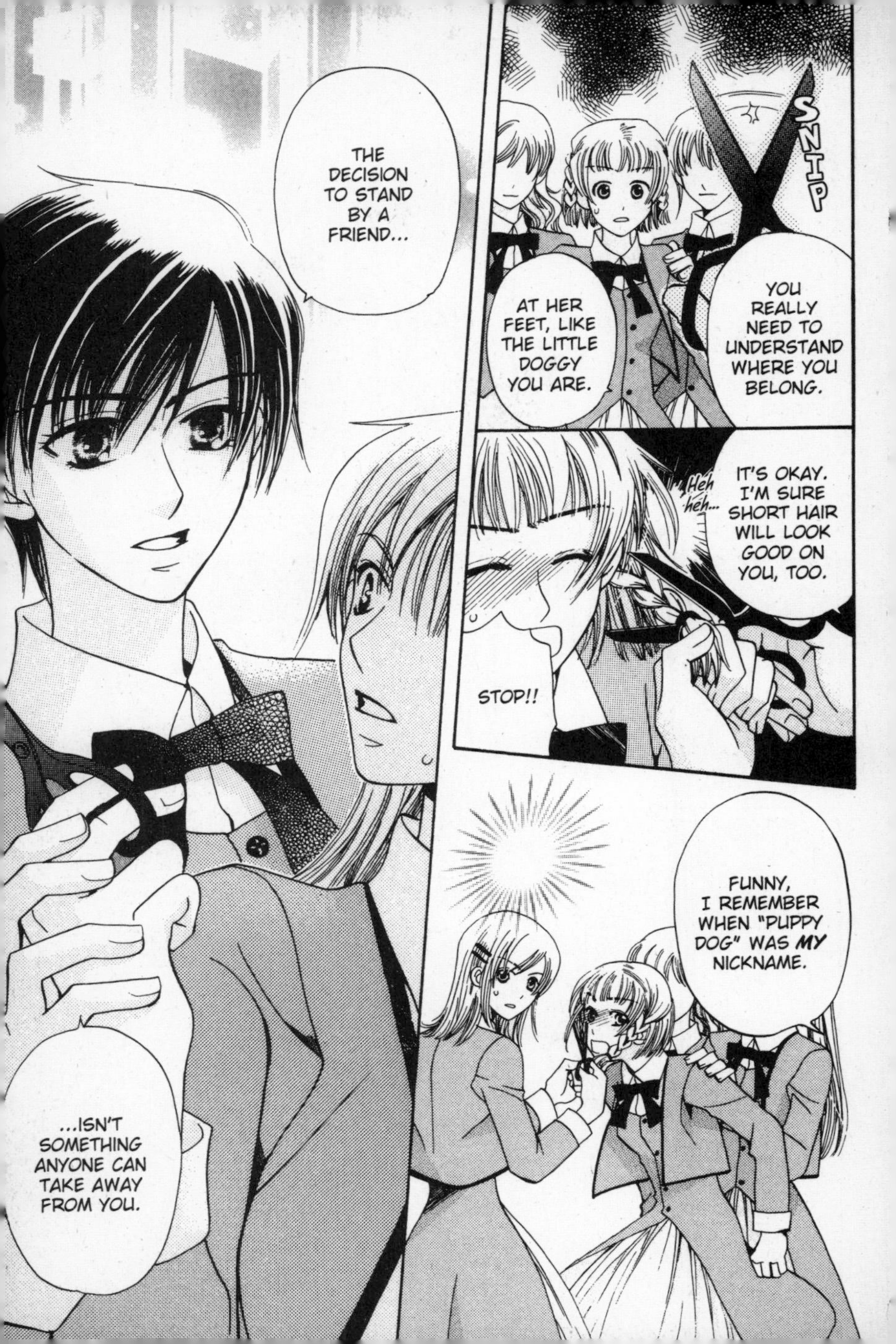
SNIP
YOU REALLY NEED TO UNDERSTAND WHERE YOU BELONG.
AT HER FEET, LIKE THE LITTLE DOGGY YOU ARE.
Heh heh...
IT'S OKAY. I'M SURE SHORT HAIR WILL LOOK GOOD ON YOU, TOO.
STOP!!
FUNNY, I REMEMBER WHEN "PUPPY DOG" WAS ***MY*** NICKNAME.
THE DECISION TO STAND BY A FRIEND...
...ISN'T SOMETHING ANYONE CAN TAKE AWAY FROM YOU.

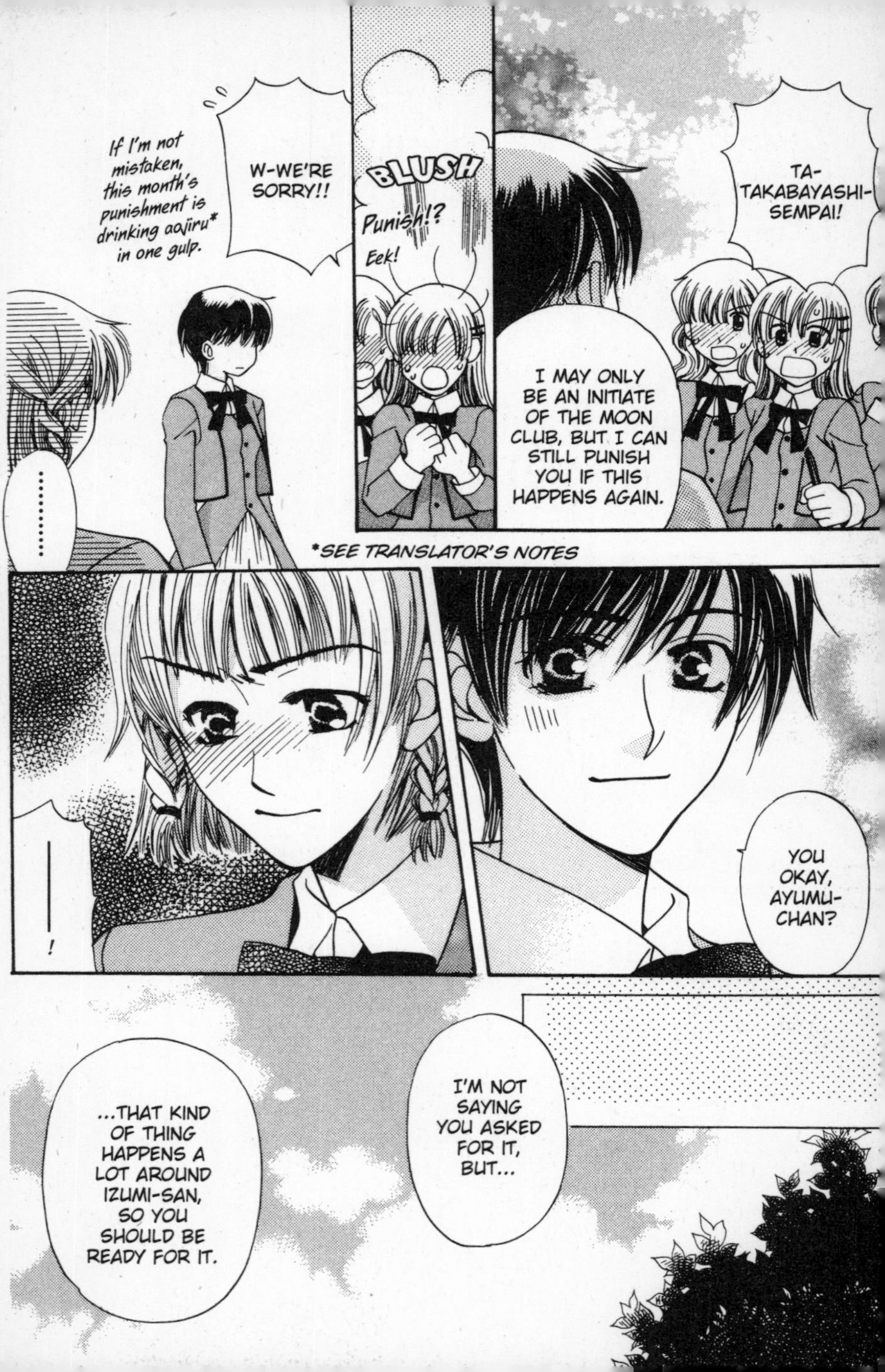
TA-TAKABAYASHI-SEMPAI!
I MAY ONLY BE AN INITIATE OF THE MOON CLUB, BUT I CAN STILL PUNISH YOU IF THIS HAPPENS AGAIN.
BLUSH
Punish!?
Eek!
W-WE'RE SORRY!!
If I'm not mistaken, this month's punishment is drinking aojiru* in one gulp.
......
YOU OKAY, AYUMU-CHAN?
—!
I'M NOT SAYING YOU ASKED FOR IT, BUT...
...THAT KIND OF THING HAPPENS A LOT AROUND IZUMI-SAN, SO YOU SHOULD BE READY FOR IT.
*SEE TRANSLATOR'S NOTES

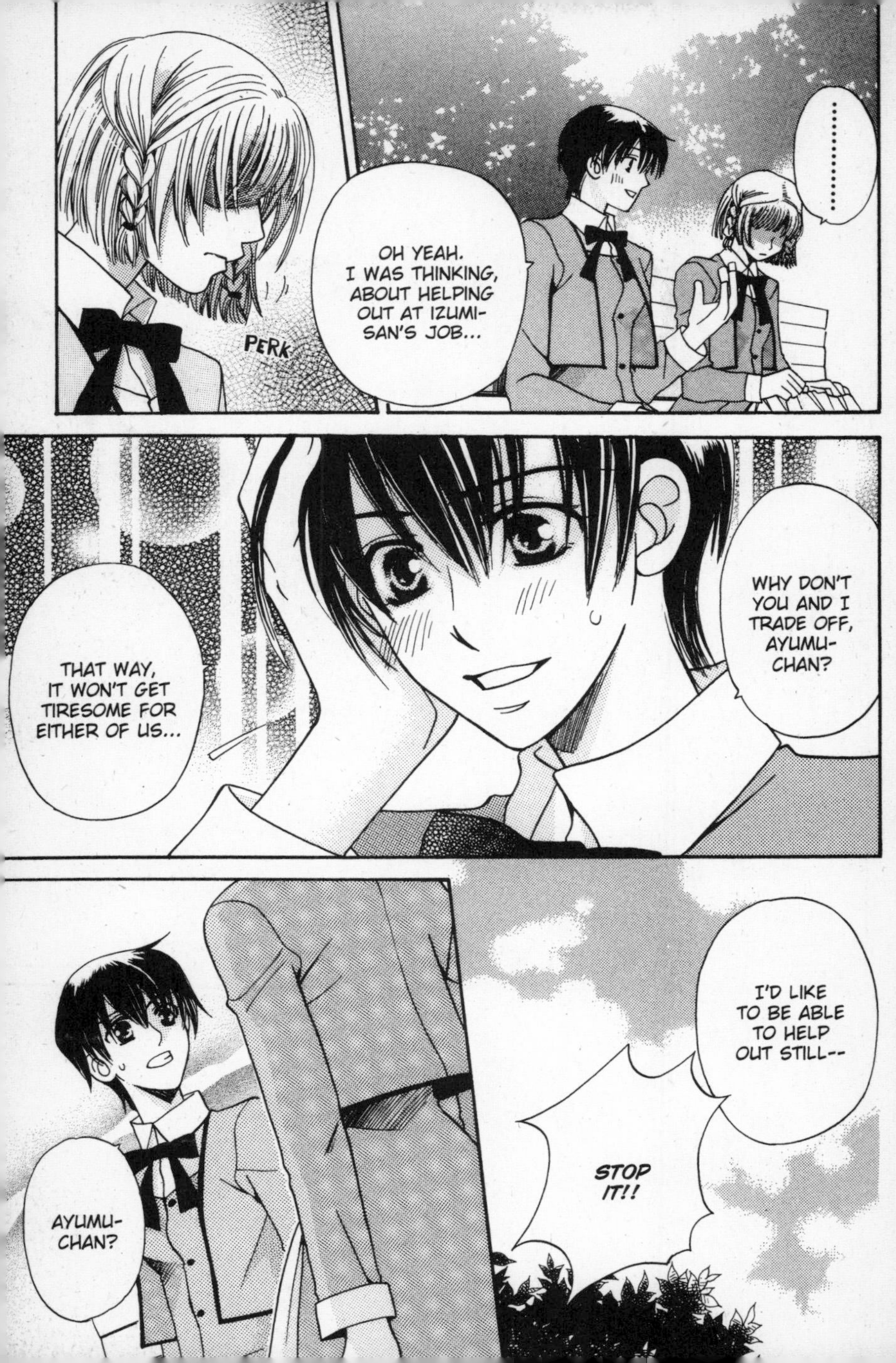
......
OH YEAH. I WAS THINKING, ABOUT HELPING OUT AT IZUMI-SAN'S JOB...
PERK
WHY DON'T YOU AND I TRADE OFF, AYUMU-CHAN?
THAT WAY, IT WON'T GET TIRESOME FOR EITHER OF US...
I'D LIKE TO BE ABLE TO HELP OUT STILL--
STOP IT!!
AYUMU-CHAN?

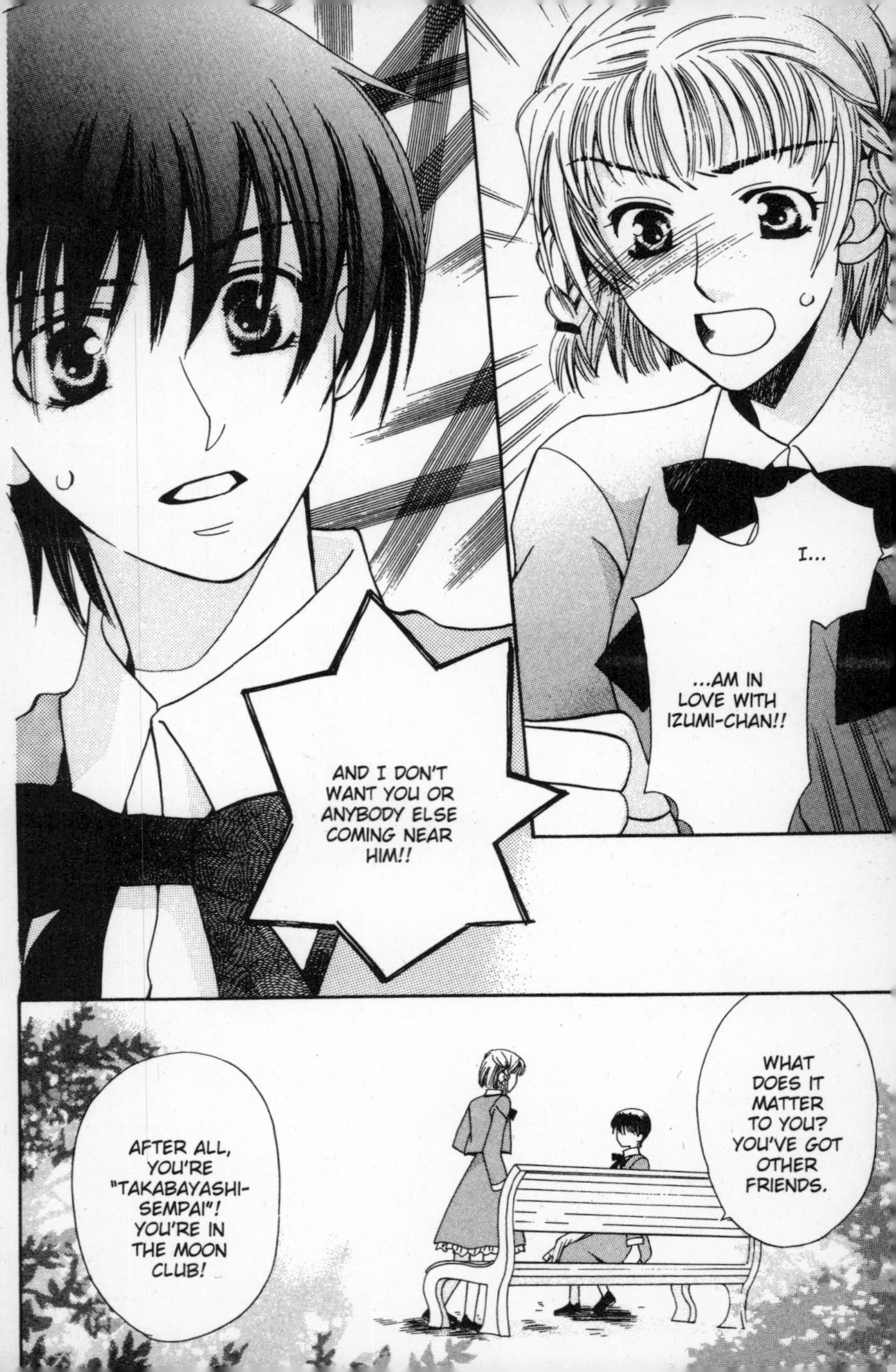
I...
...AM IN LOVE WITH IZUMI-CHAN!!
AND I DON'T WANT YOU OR ANYBODY ELSE COMING NEAR HIM!!
WHAT DOES IT MATTER TO YOU? YOU'VE GOT OTHER FRIENDS.
AFTER ALL, YOU'RE "TAKABAYASHI-SEMPAI"! YOU'RE IN THE MOON CLUB!

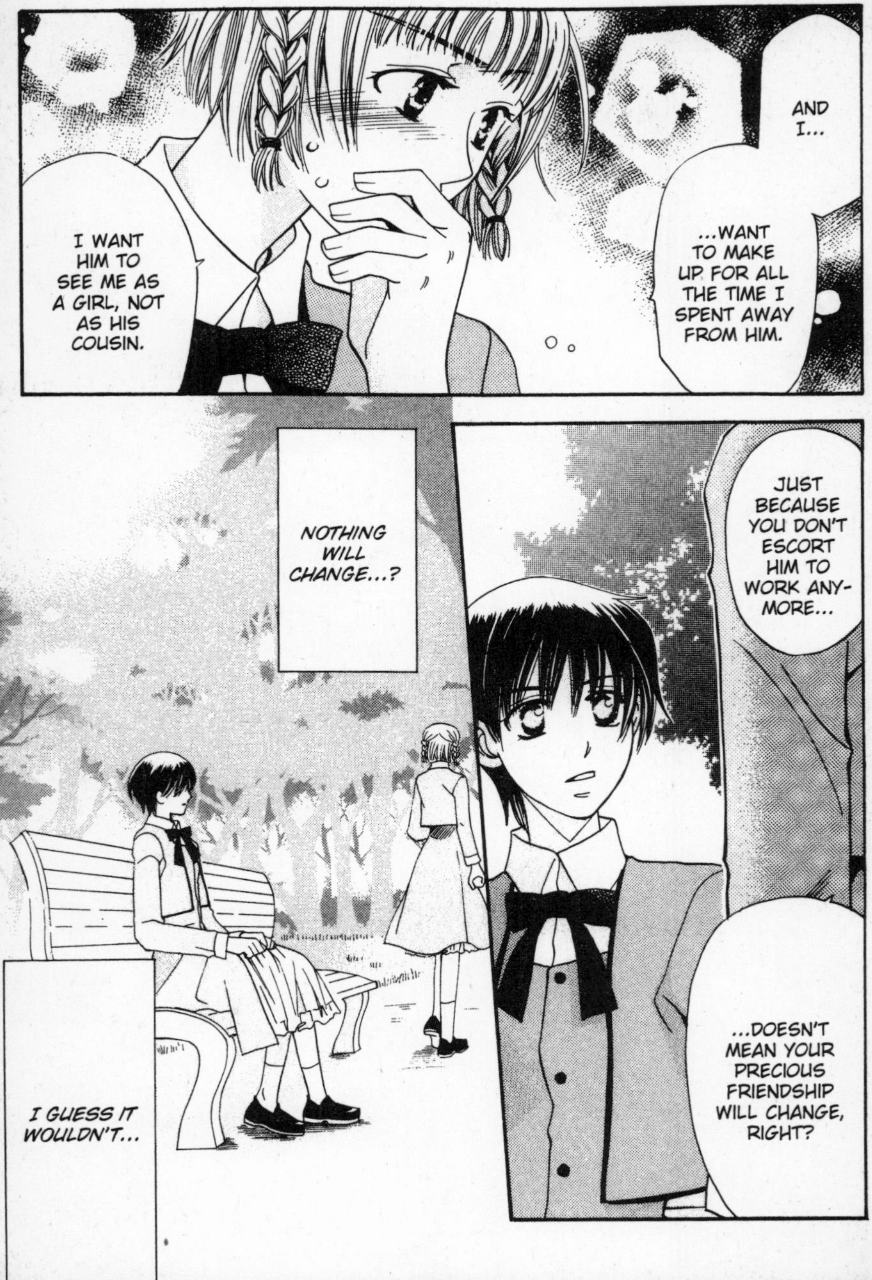
AND I...
...WANT TO MAKE UP FOR ALL THE TIME I SPENT AWAY FROM HIM.
I WANT HIM TO SEE ME AS A GIRL, NOT AS HIS COUSIN.
JUST BECAUSE YOU DON'T ESCORT HIM TO WORK ANY-MORE...
...DOESN'T MEAN YOUR PRECIOUS FRIENDSHIP WILL CHANGE, RIGHT?
NOTHING WILL CHANGE...?
I GUESS IT WOULDN'T...

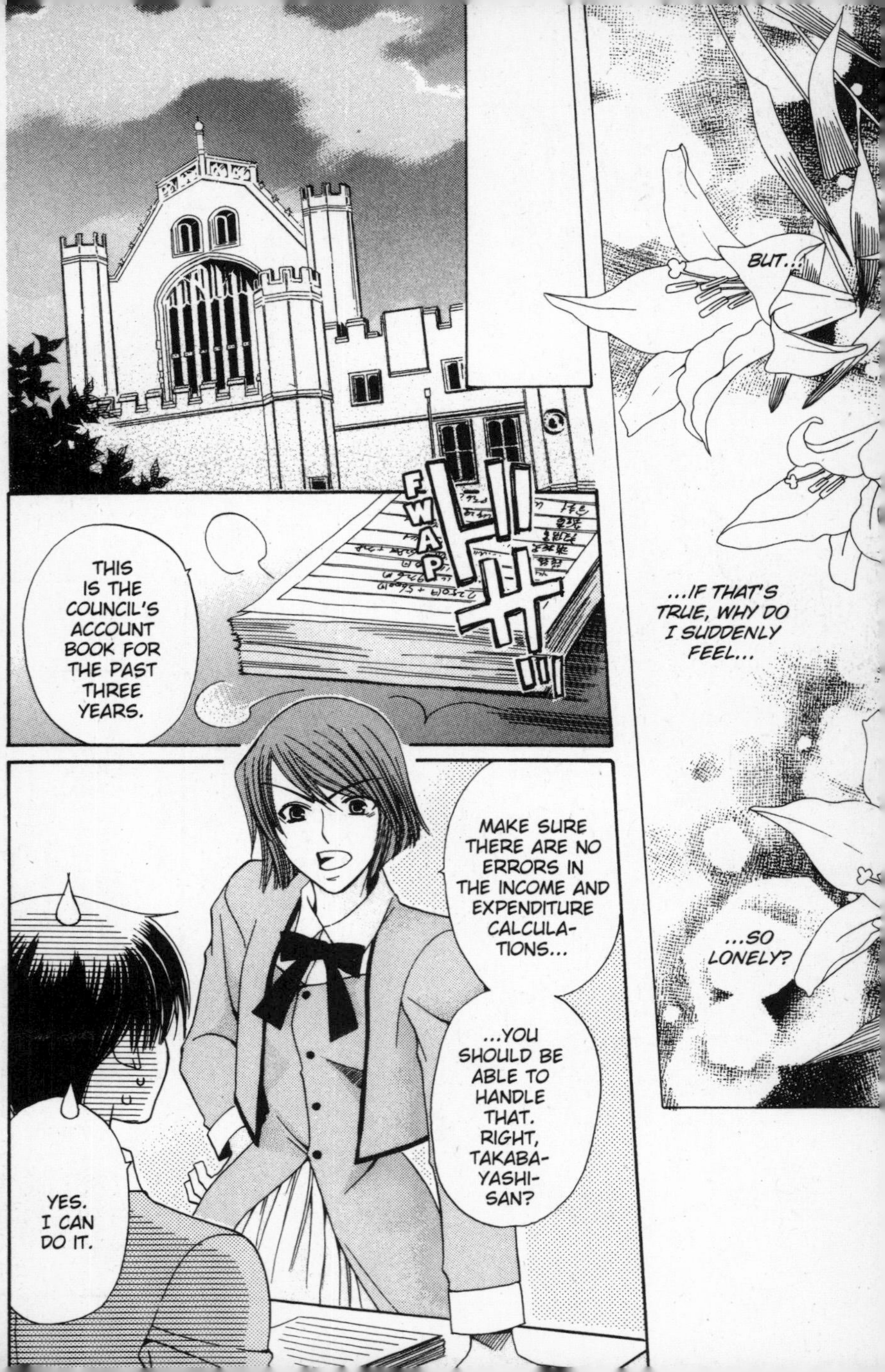
BUT...
...IF THAT'S TRUE, WHY DO I SUDDENLY FEEL...
...SO LONELY?
FWAP
THIS IS THE COUNCIL'S ACCOUNT BOOK FOR THE PAST THREE YEARS.
MAKE SURE THERE ARE NO ERRORS IN THE INCOME AND EXPENDITURE CALCULATIONS...
...YOU SHOULD BE ABLE TO HANDLE THAT. RIGHT, TAKABAYASHI-SAN?
YES. I CAN DO IT.

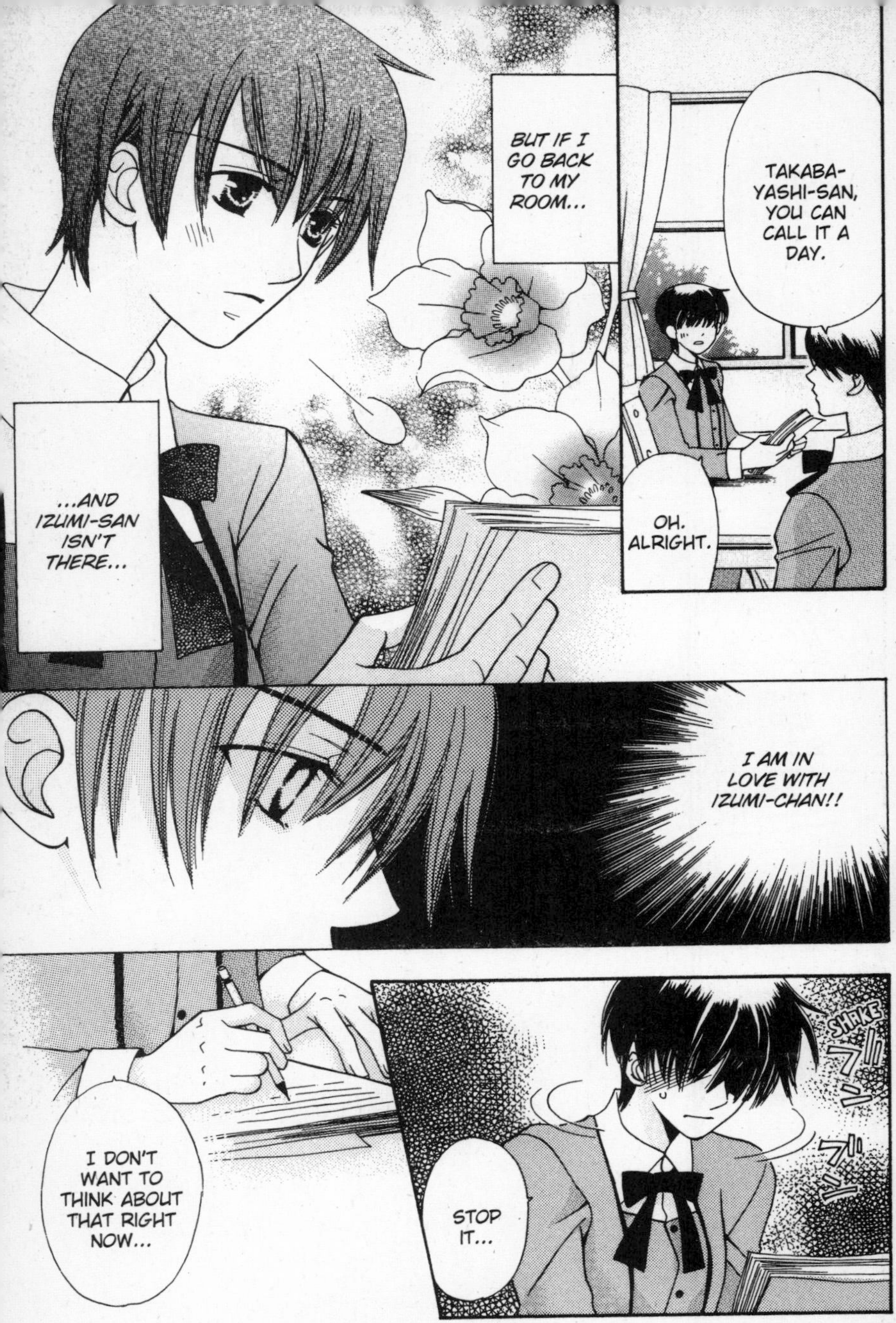
TAKABA-YASHI-SAN, YOU CAN CALL IT A DAY.
OH. ALRIGHT.
BUT IF I GO BACK TO MY ROOM...
...AND IZUMI-SAN ISN'T THERE...
I AM IN LOVE WITH IZUMI-CHAN!!
SHAKE
STOP IT...
I DON'T WANT TO THINK ABOUT THAT RIGHT NOW...

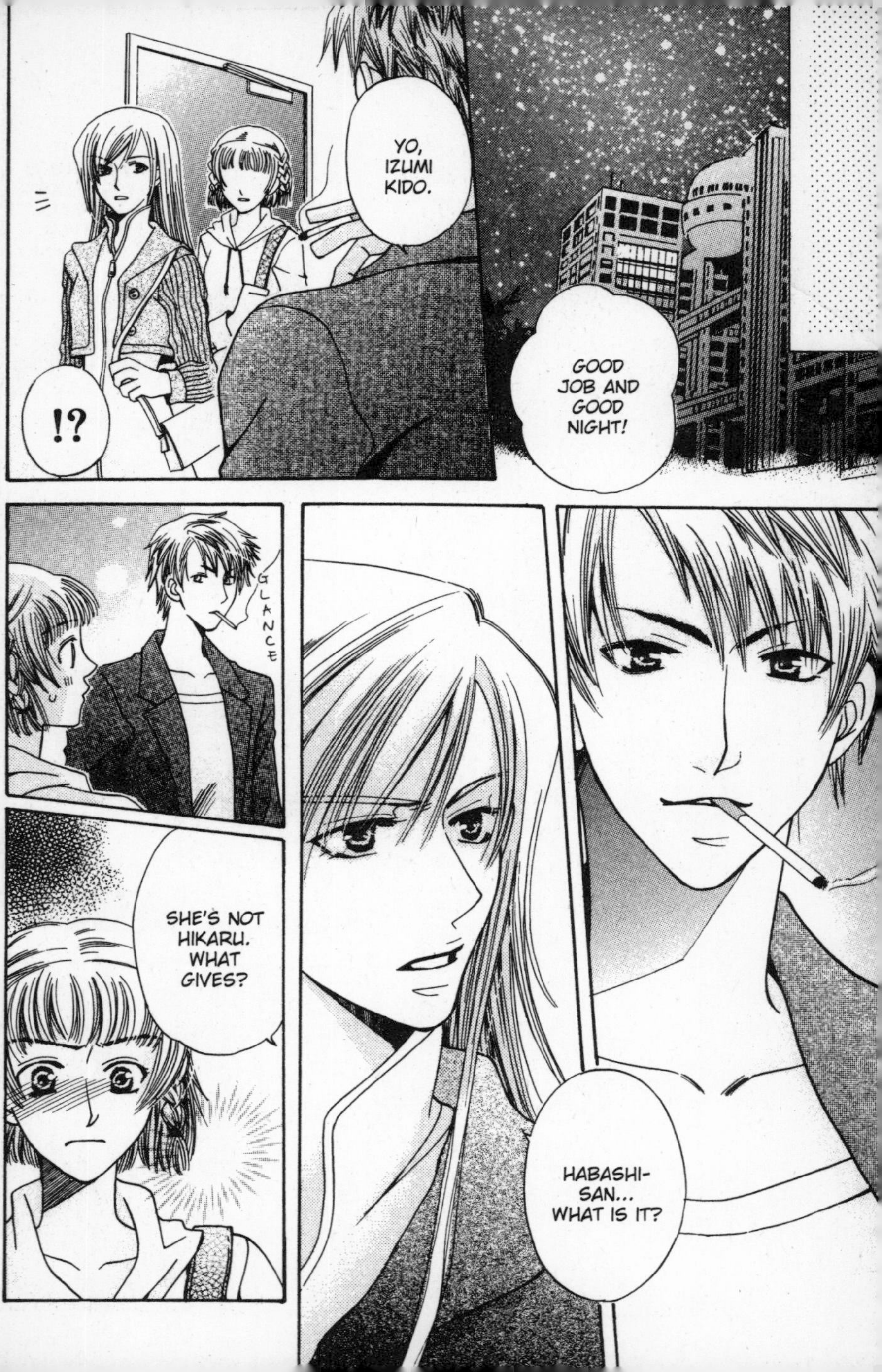
GOOD JOB AND GOOD NIGHT!
YO, IZUMI KIDO.
!?
HABASHI-SAN... WHAT IS IT?
GLANCE
SHE'S NOT HIKARU. WHAT GIVES?

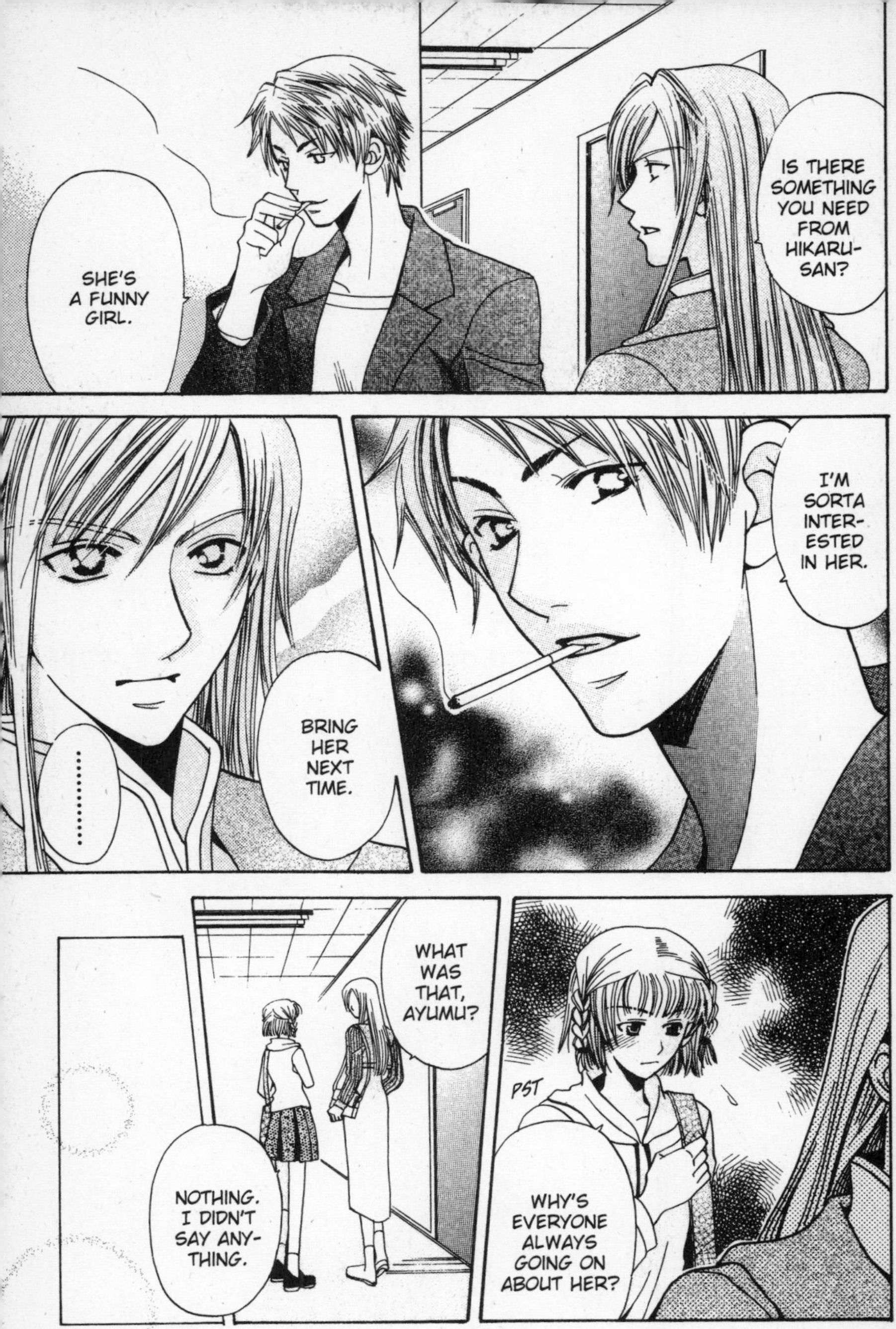
IS THERE SOMETHING YOU NEED FROM HIKARU-SAN?
SHE'S A FUNNY GIRL.
I'M SORTA INTER-ESTED IN HER.
BRING HER NEXT TIME.
……
PST
WHY'S EVERYONE ALWAYS GOING ON ABOUT HER?
WHAT WAS THAT, AYUMU?
NOTHING. I DIDN'T SAY ANY-THING.

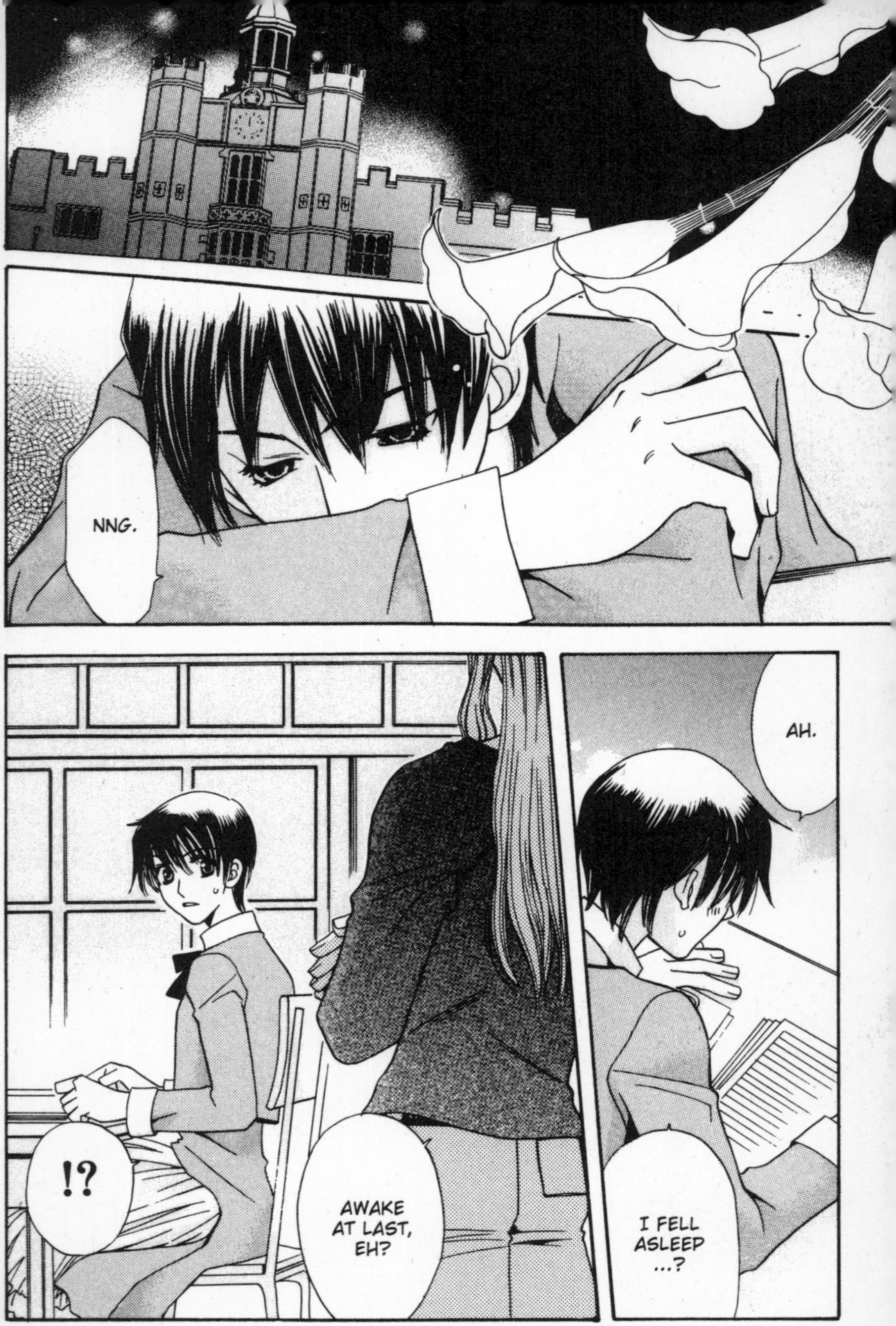
NNG.
AH.
I FELL ASLEEP ...?
AWAKE AT LAST, EH?
!?

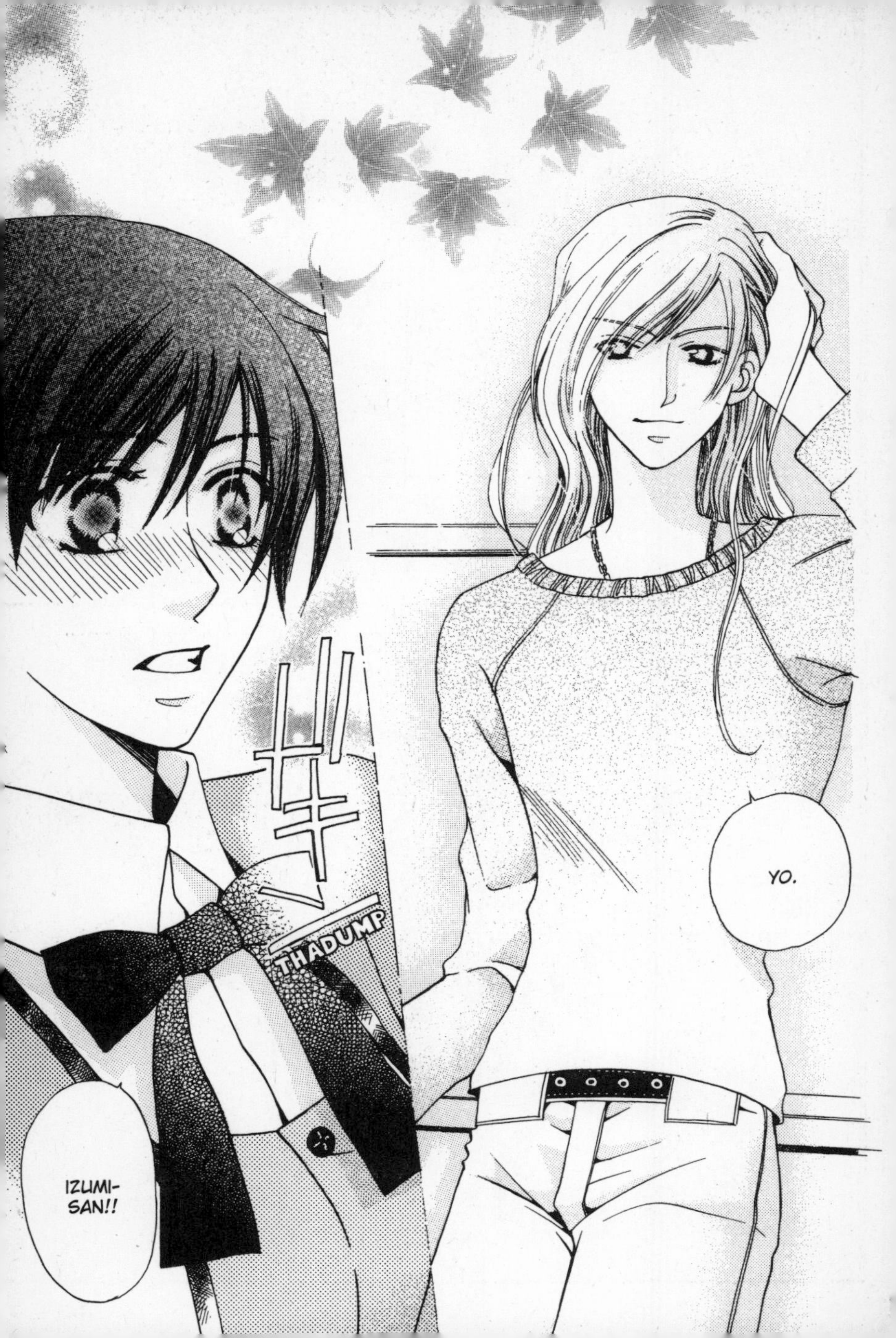
YO.
THADUMP
IZUMI-SAN!!

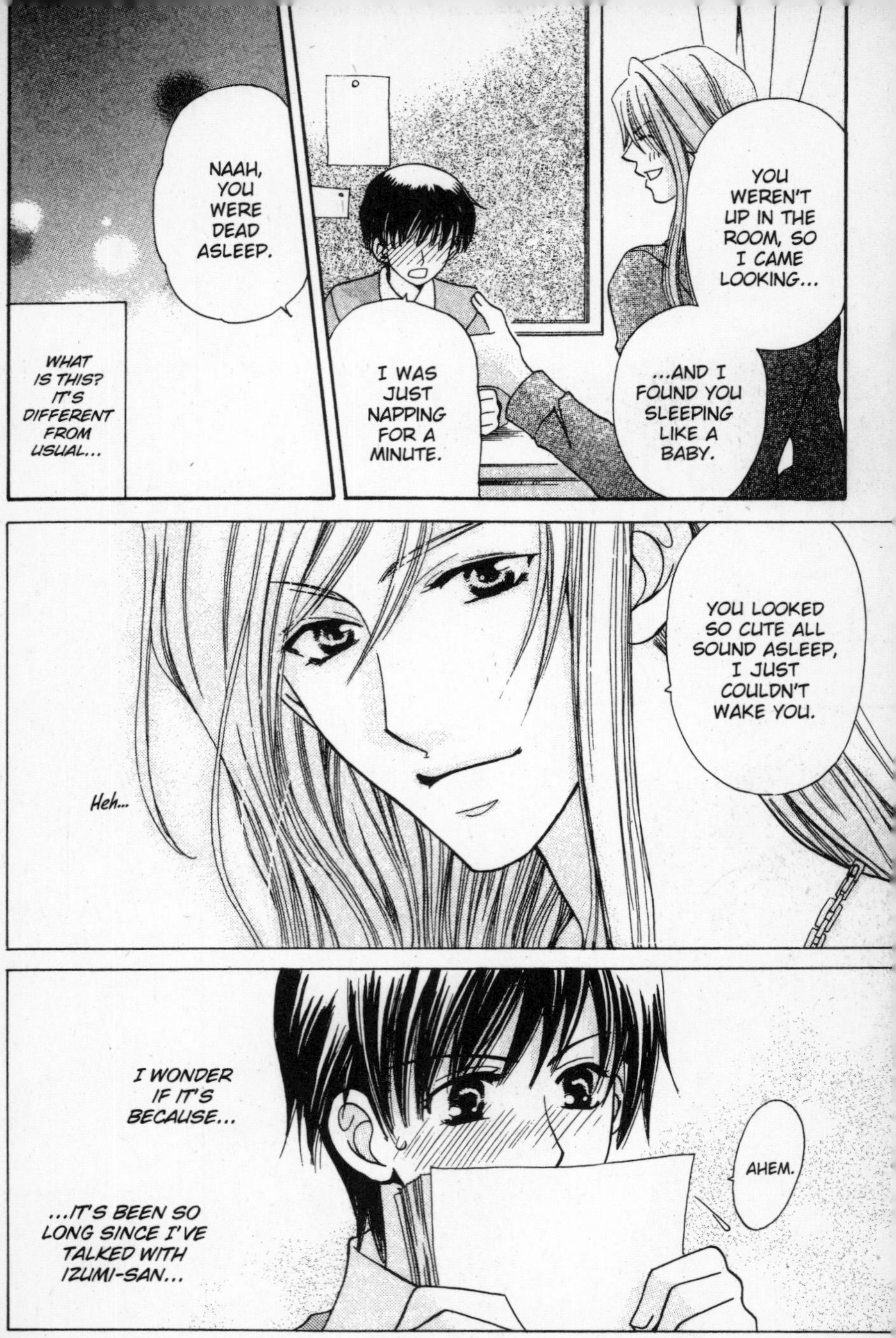
YOU WEREN'T UP IN THE ROOM, SO I CAME LOOKING...
...AND I FOUND YOU SLEEPING LIKE A BABY.
I WAS JUST NAPPING FOR A MINUTE.
NAAH, YOU WERE DEAD ASLEEP.
WHAT IS THIS? IT'S DIFFERENT FROM USUAL...
YOU LOOKED SO CUTE ALL SOUND ASLEEP, I JUST COULDN'T WAKE YOU.
Heh...
AHEM.
I WONDER IF IT'S BECAUSE...
...IT'S BEEN SO LONG SINCE I'VE TALKED WITH IZUMI-SAN...

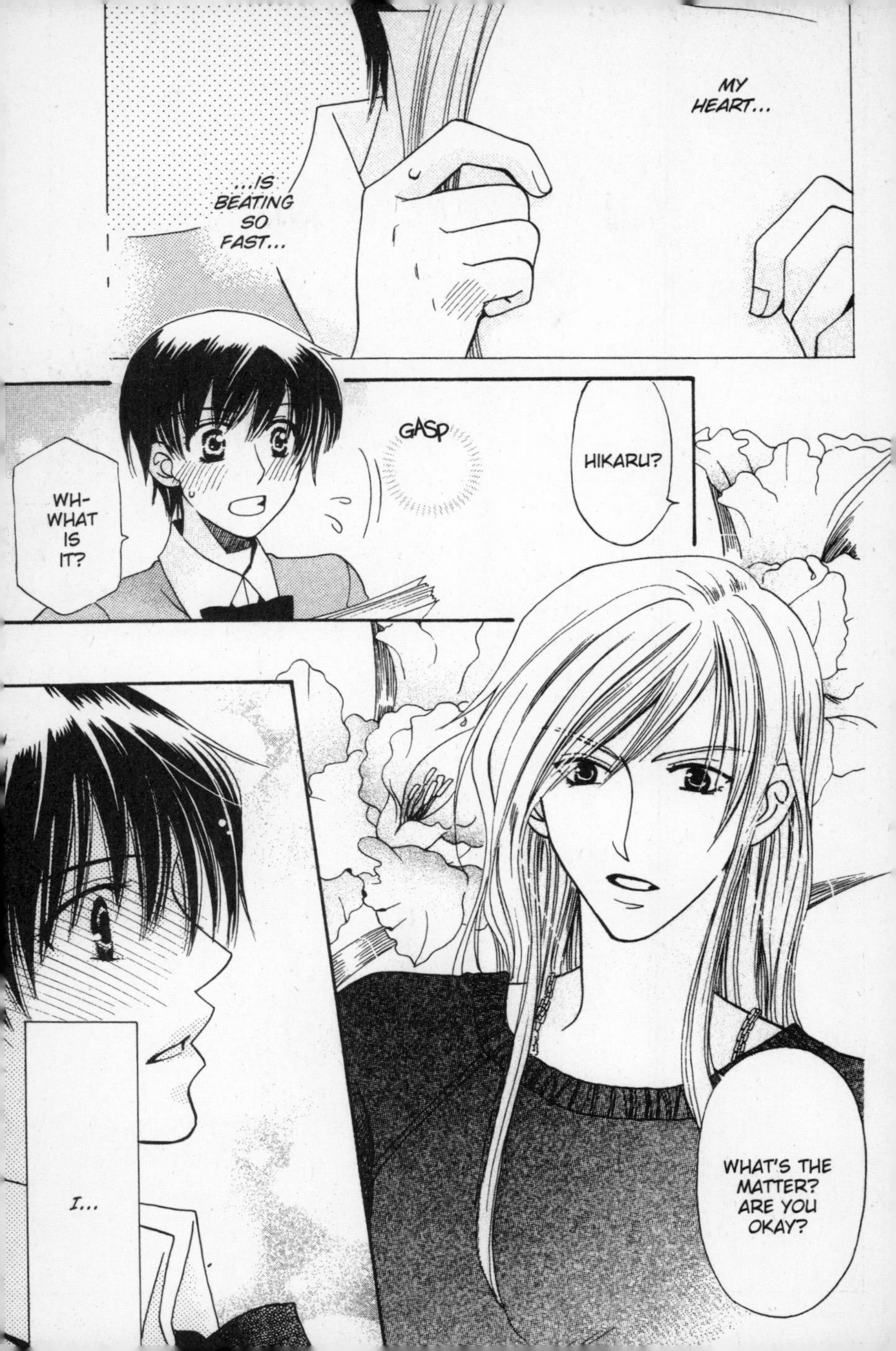
MY HEART...
...IS BEATING SO FAST...
HIKARU?
GASP
WH-WHAT IS IT?
WHAT'S THE MATTER? ARE YOU OKAY?
I...

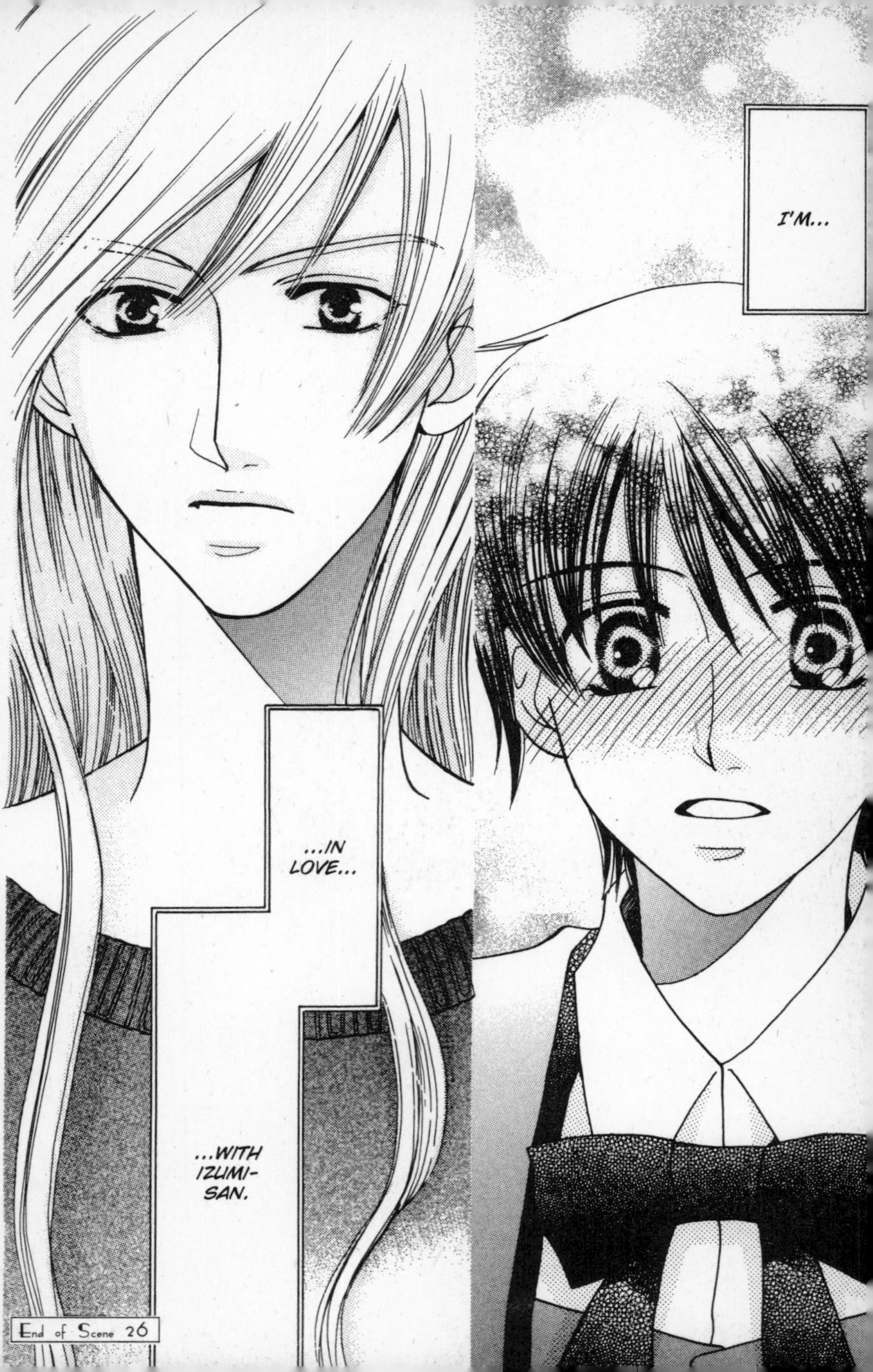
I'M...
...IN LOVE...
...WITH IZUMI-SAN.
End of Scene 26

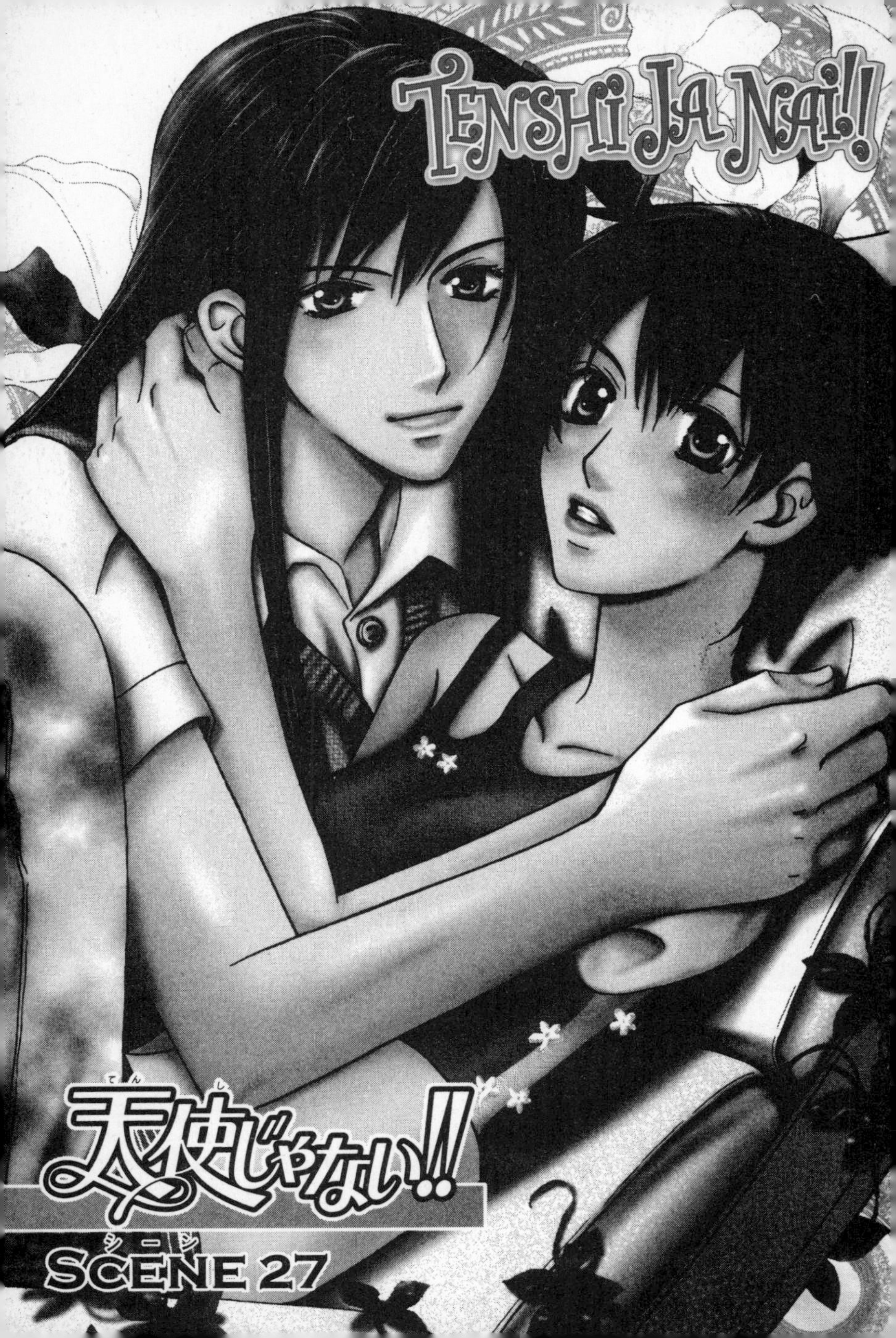
TENSHI JA NAI!!
天使じゃない!!
SCENE 27

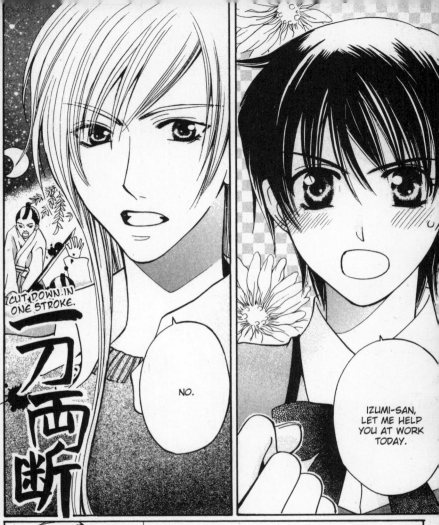

IZUMI-SAN, LET ME HELP YOU AT WORK TODAY.
NO.
CUT DOWN IN ONE STROKE.
一刀両断

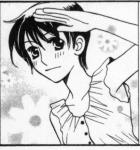

Greetings.

To those I'm meeting for the first time and those I've met before, hello! Thank you for picking up "Tenshi Ja Nai!!" volume 6!! I really hope you enjoy it to the very last page! I'll be so happy when we make it there together!

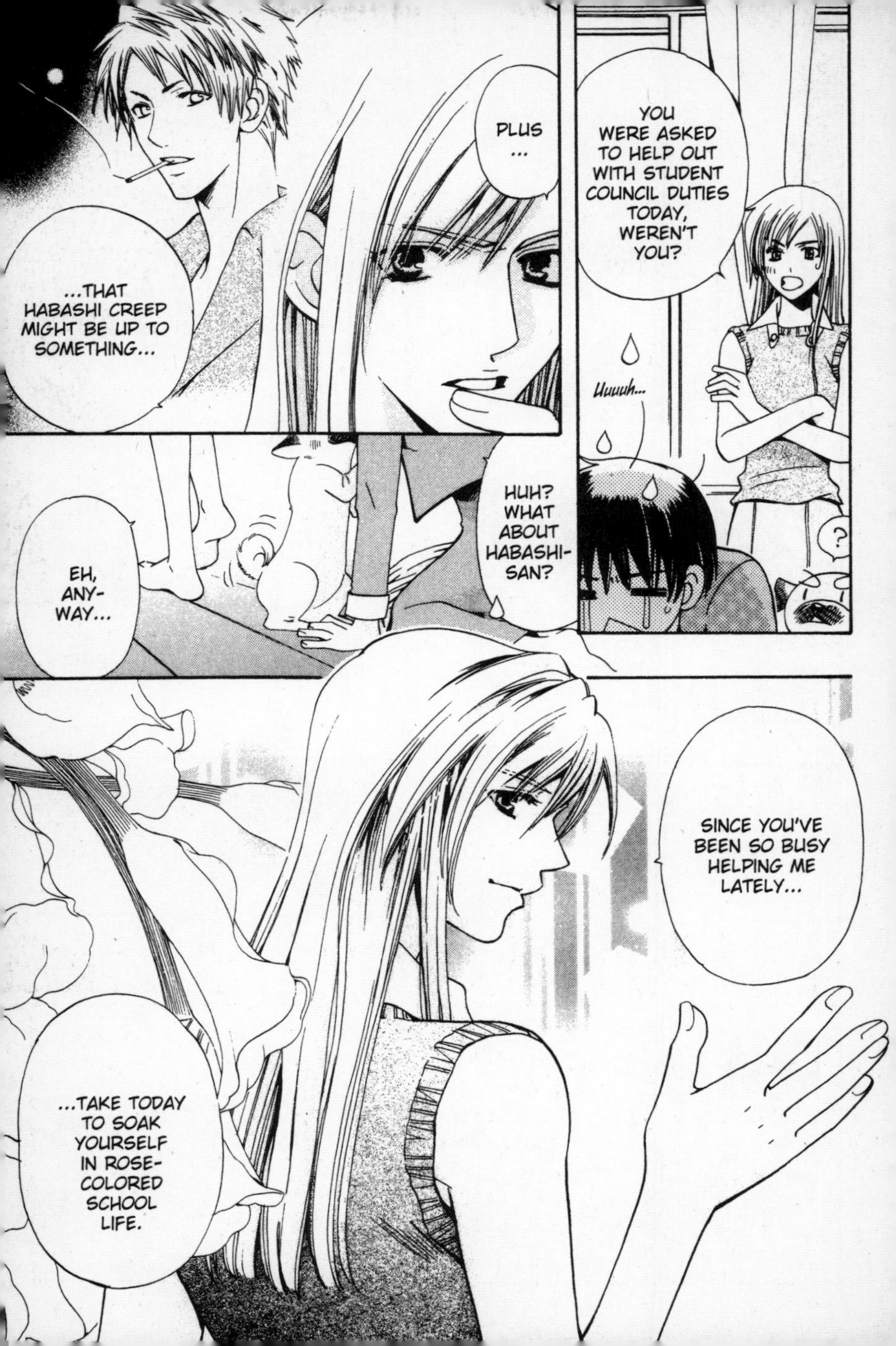
YOU WERE ASKED TO HELP OUT WITH STUDENT COUNCIL DUTIES TODAY, WEREN'T YOU?
Uuuuh...
?
PLUS ...
...THAT HABASHI CREEP MIGHT BE UP TO SOMETHING...
HUH? WHAT ABOUT HABASHI-SAN?
EH, ANY-WAY...
SINCE YOU'VE BEEN SO BUSY HELPING ME LATELY...
...TAKE TODAY TO SOAK YOURSELF IN ROSE-COLORED SCHOOL LIFE.

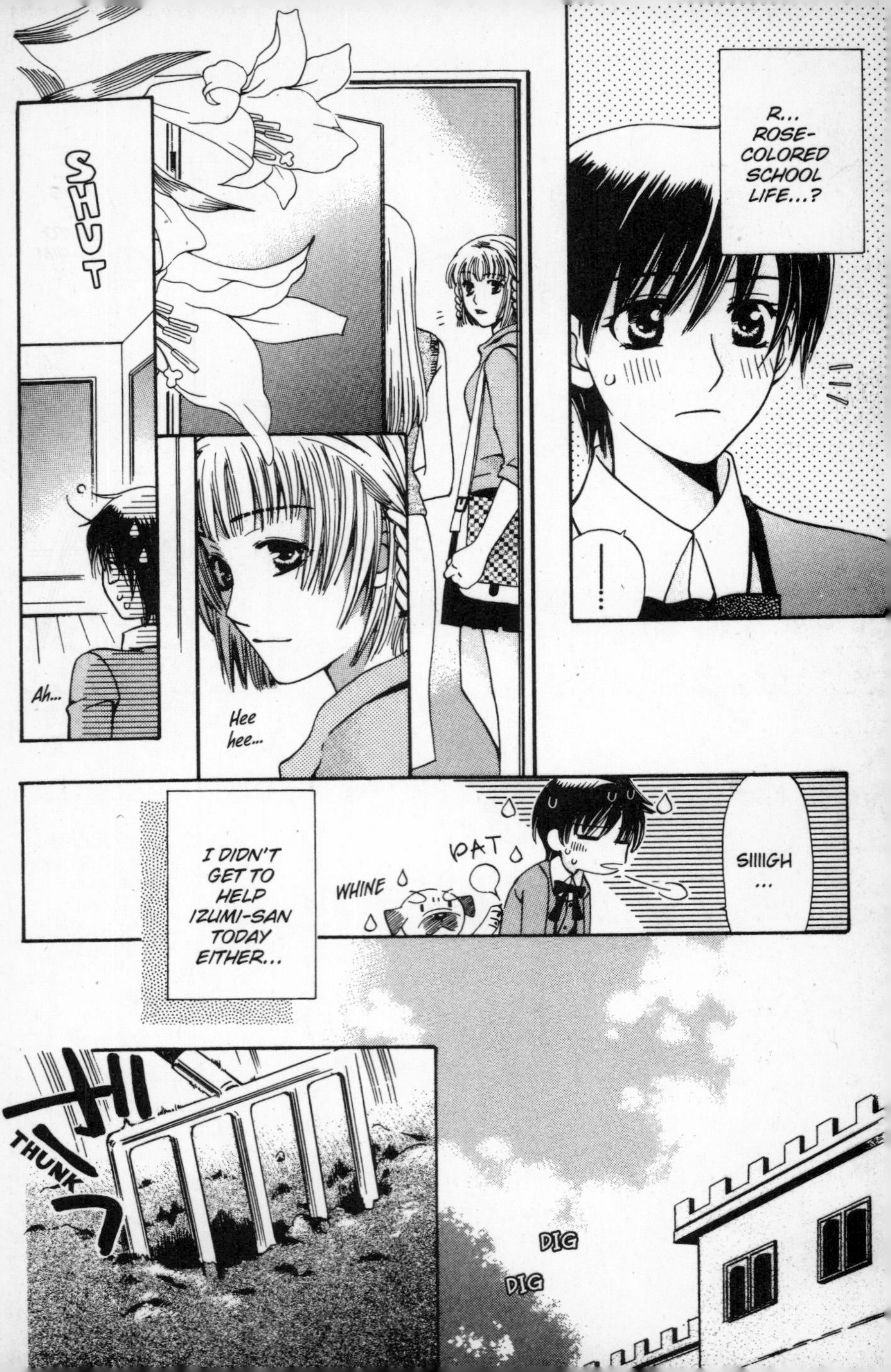
R... ROSE-COLORED SCHOOL LIFE...?
SHUT
Hee hee...
Ah...
SIIIGH ...
PAT
WHINE
I DIDN'T GET TO HELP IZUMI-SAN TODAY EITHER...
DIG
DIG
THUNK

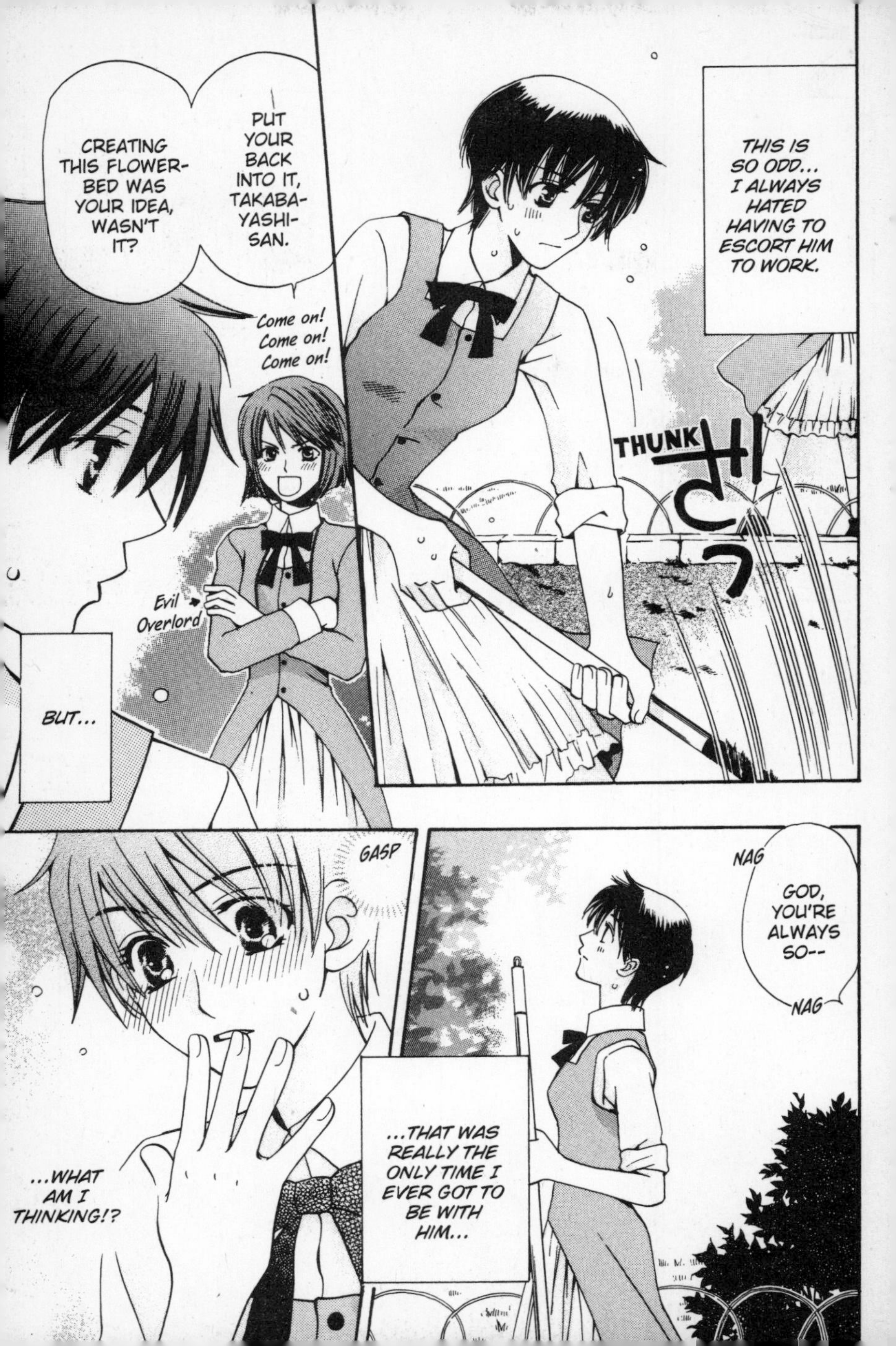
THIS IS SO ODD... I ALWAYS HATED HAVING TO ESCORT HIM TO WORK.
THUNK
PUT YOUR BACK INTO IT, TAKABAYASHI-SAN.
CREATING THIS FLOWER-BED WAS YOUR IDEA, WASN'T IT?
Come on! Come on! Come on!
Evil Overlord
BUT...
NAG
GOD, YOU'RE ALWAYS SO--
NAG
...THAT WAS REALLY THE ONLY TIME I EVER GOT TO BE WITH HIM...
GASP
...WHAT AM I THINKING!?

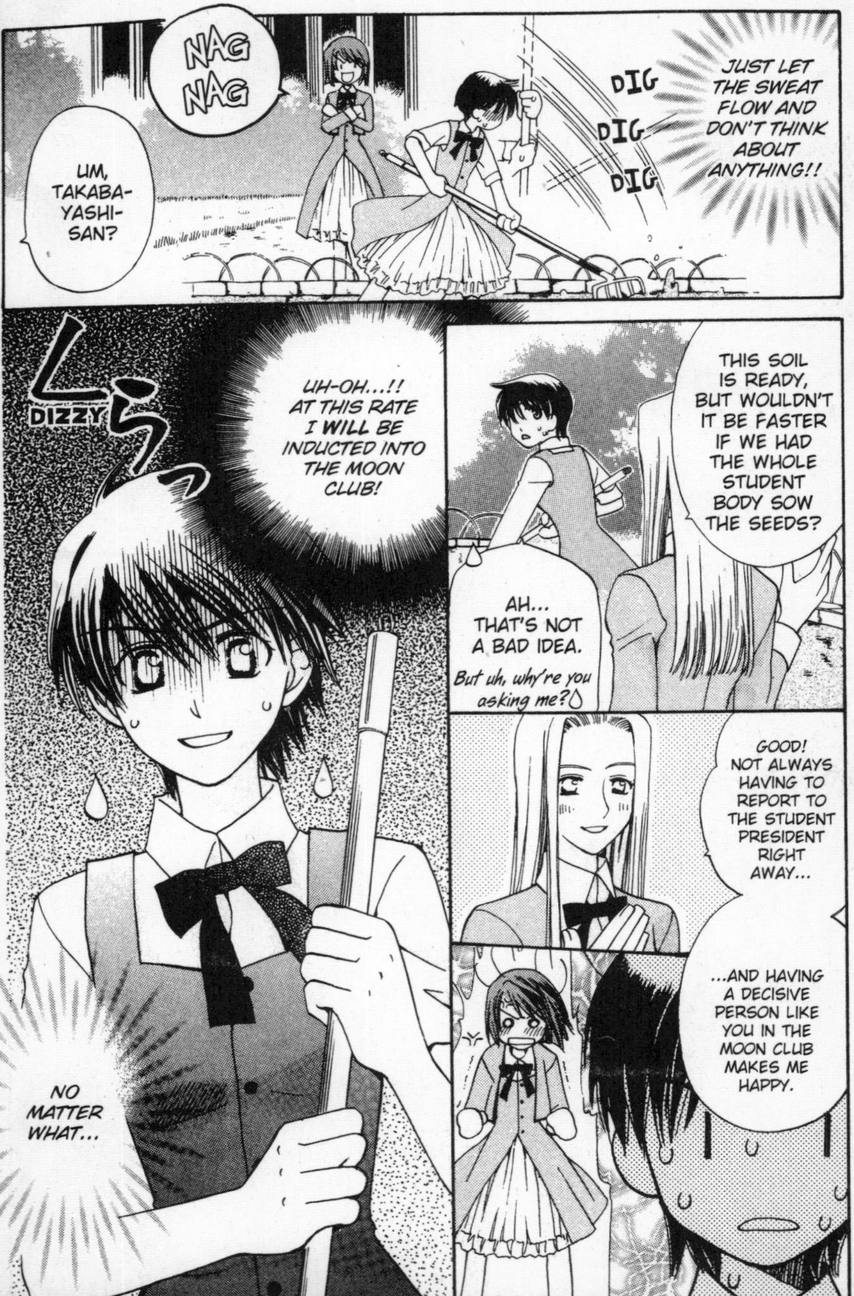
JUST LET THE SWEAT FLOW AND DON'T THINK ABOUT ANYTHING!!
DIG
DIG
DIG
NAG NAG
UM, TAKABAYASHI-SAN?
THIS SOIL IS READY, BUT WOULDN'T IT BE FASTER IF WE HAD THE WHOLE STUDENT BODY SOW THE SEEDS?
AH... THAT'S NOT A BAD IDEA.
But uh, why're you asking me?
GOOD! NOT ALWAYS HAVING TO REPORT TO THE STUDENT PRESIDENT RIGHT AWAY...
...AND HAVING A DECISIVE PERSON LIKE YOU IN THE MOON CLUB MAKES ME HAPPY.
くら
DIZZY
UH-OH...!! AT THIS RATE I WILL BE INDUCTED INTO THE MOON CLUB!
NO MATTER WHAT...

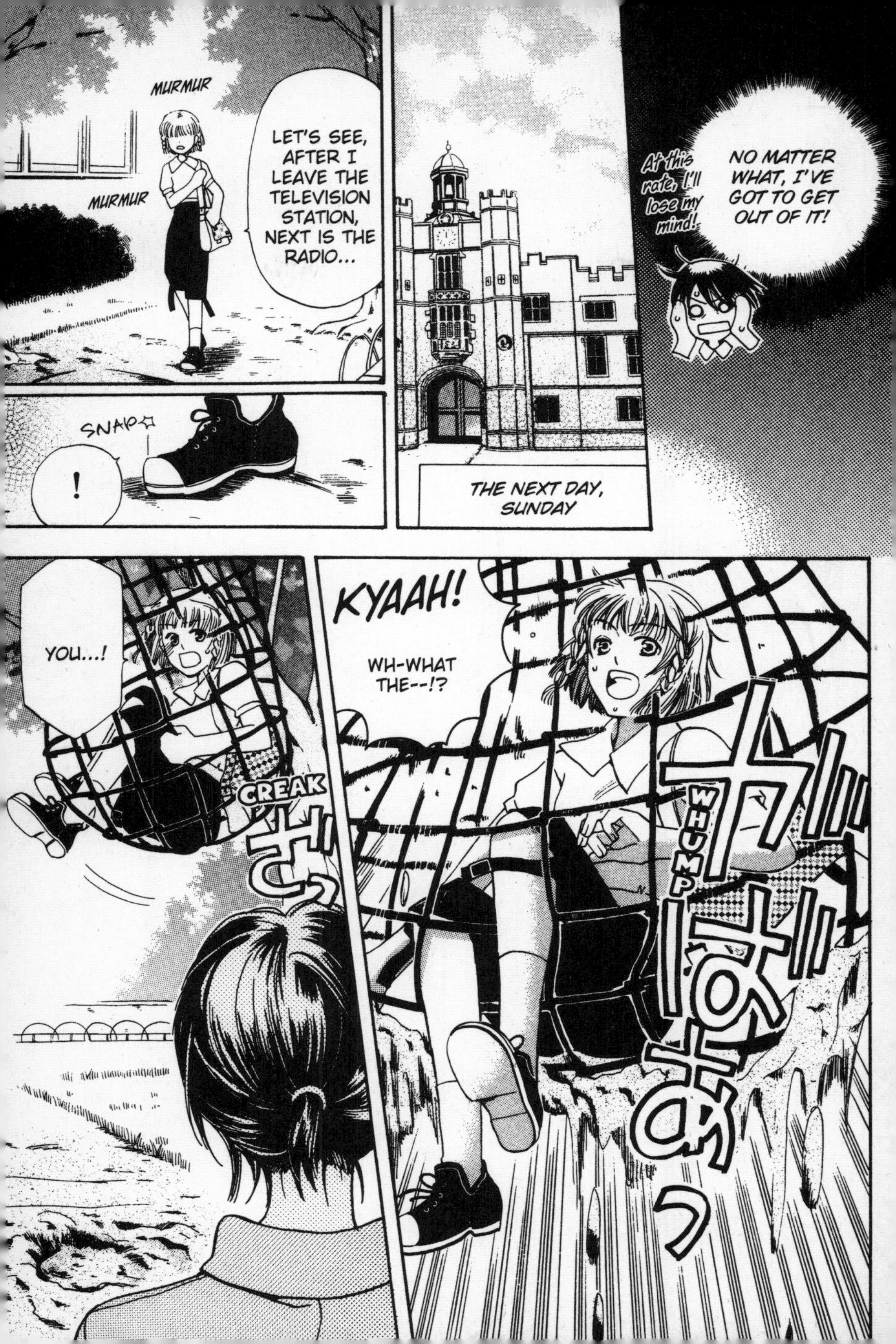
NO MATTER WHAT, I'VE GOT TO GET OUT OF IT!
At this rate, I'll lose my mind!
THE NEXT DAY, SUNDAY
LET'S SEE, AFTER I LEAVE THE TELEVISION STATION, NEXT IS THE RADIO...
MURMUR
MURMUR
SNAP☆
!
KYAAH!
WH-WHAT THE--!?
WHUMP!
YOU...!
CREAK

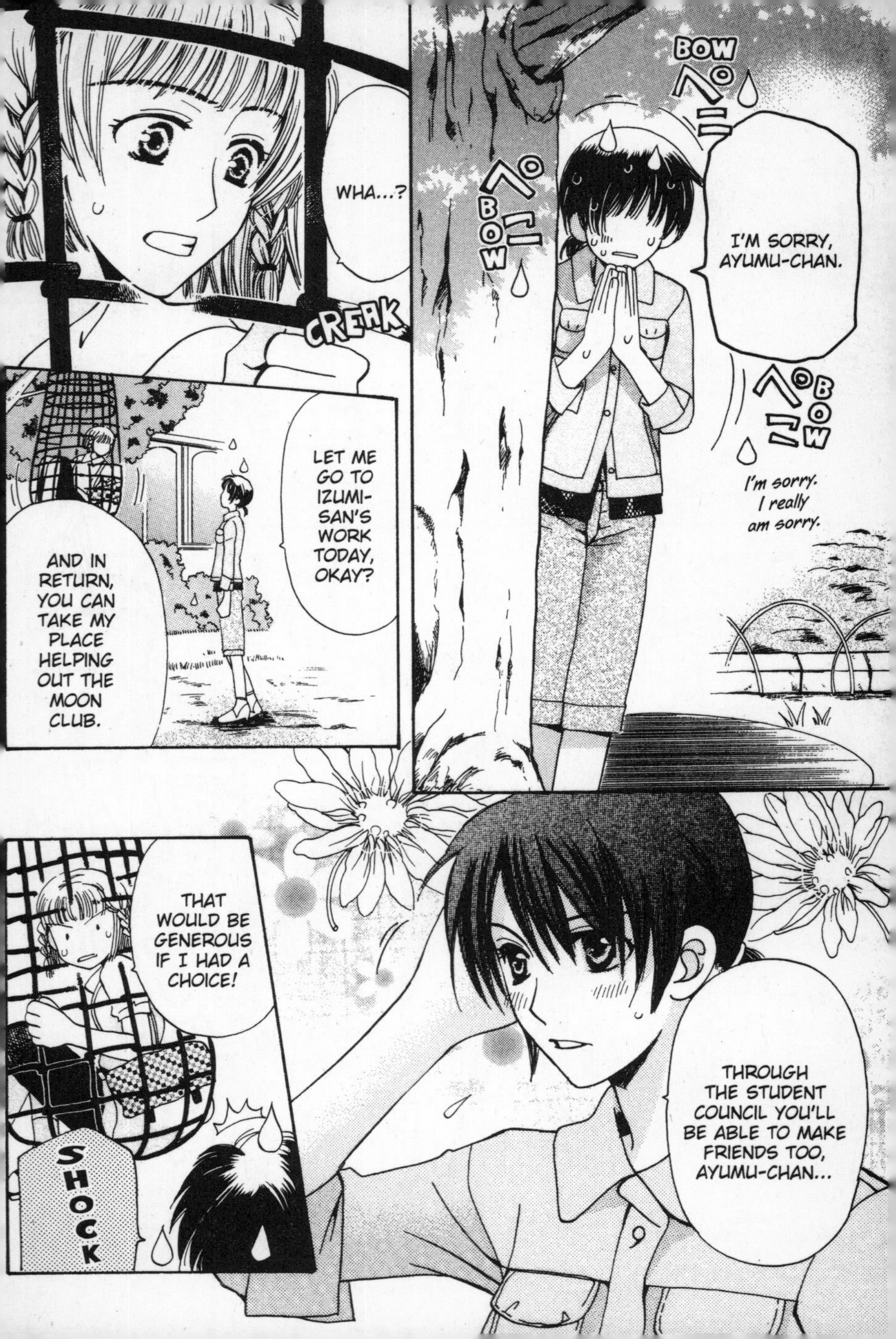
BOW
BOW
I'M SORRY, AYUMU-CHAN.
BOW
I'm sorry. I really am sorry.
WHA...?
CREAK
LET ME GO TO IZUMI-SAN'S WORK TODAY, OKAY?
AND IN RETURN, YOU CAN TAKE MY PLACE HELPING OUT THE MOON CLUB.
THROUGH THE STUDENT COUNCIL YOU'LL BE ABLE TO MAKE FRIENDS TOO, AYUMU-CHAN...
THAT WOULD BE GENEROUS IF I HAD A CHOICE!
SHOCK

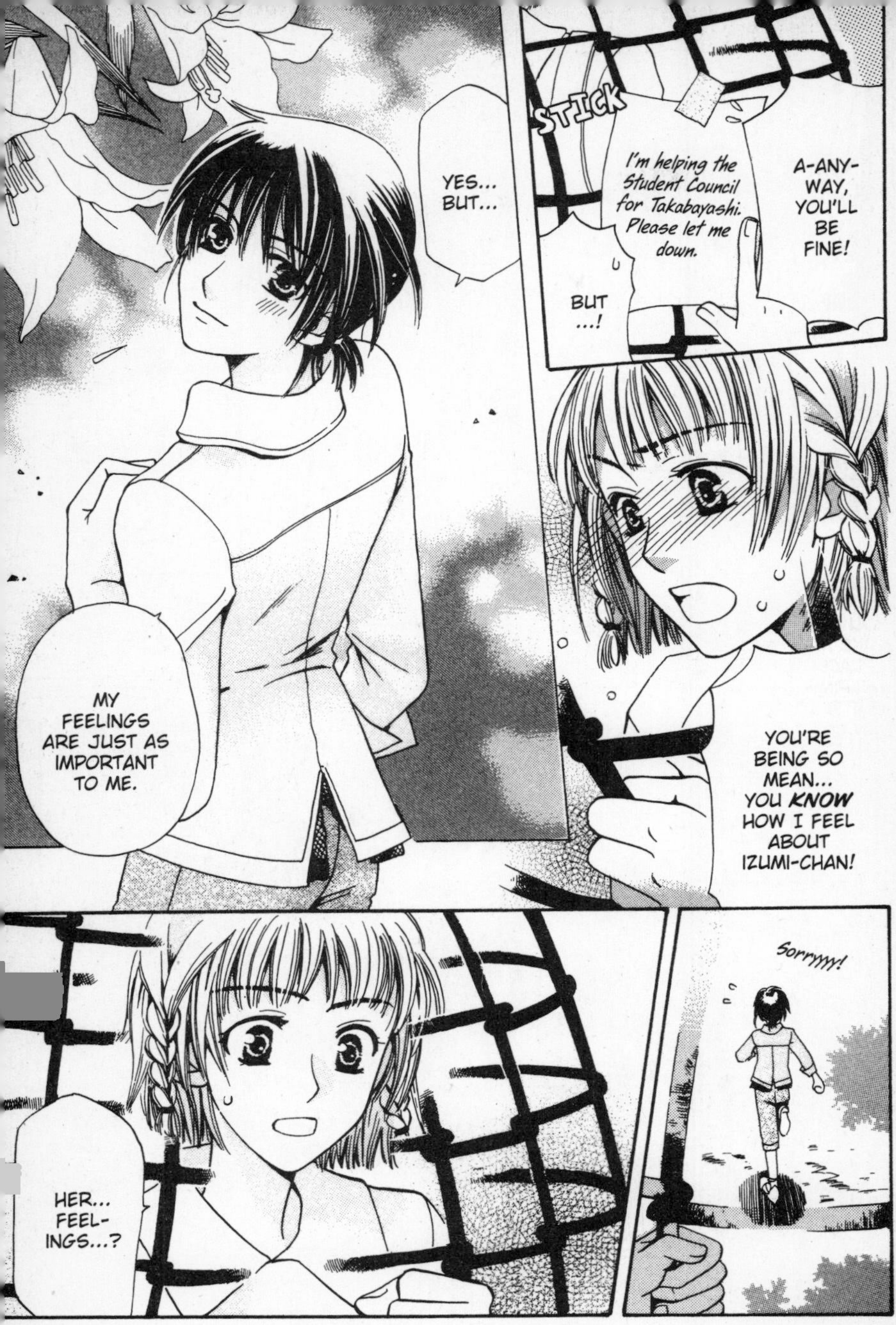
A-ANY-WAY, YOU'LL BE FINE!
I'm helping the Student Council for Takabayashi. Please let me down.
STICK
BUT ...!
YOU'RE BEING SO MEAN... YOU **KNOW** HOW I FEEL ABOUT IZUMI-CHAN!
YES... BUT...
MY FEELINGS ARE JUST AS IMPORTANT TO ME.
Sorryyyy!
HER... FEEL-INGS...?

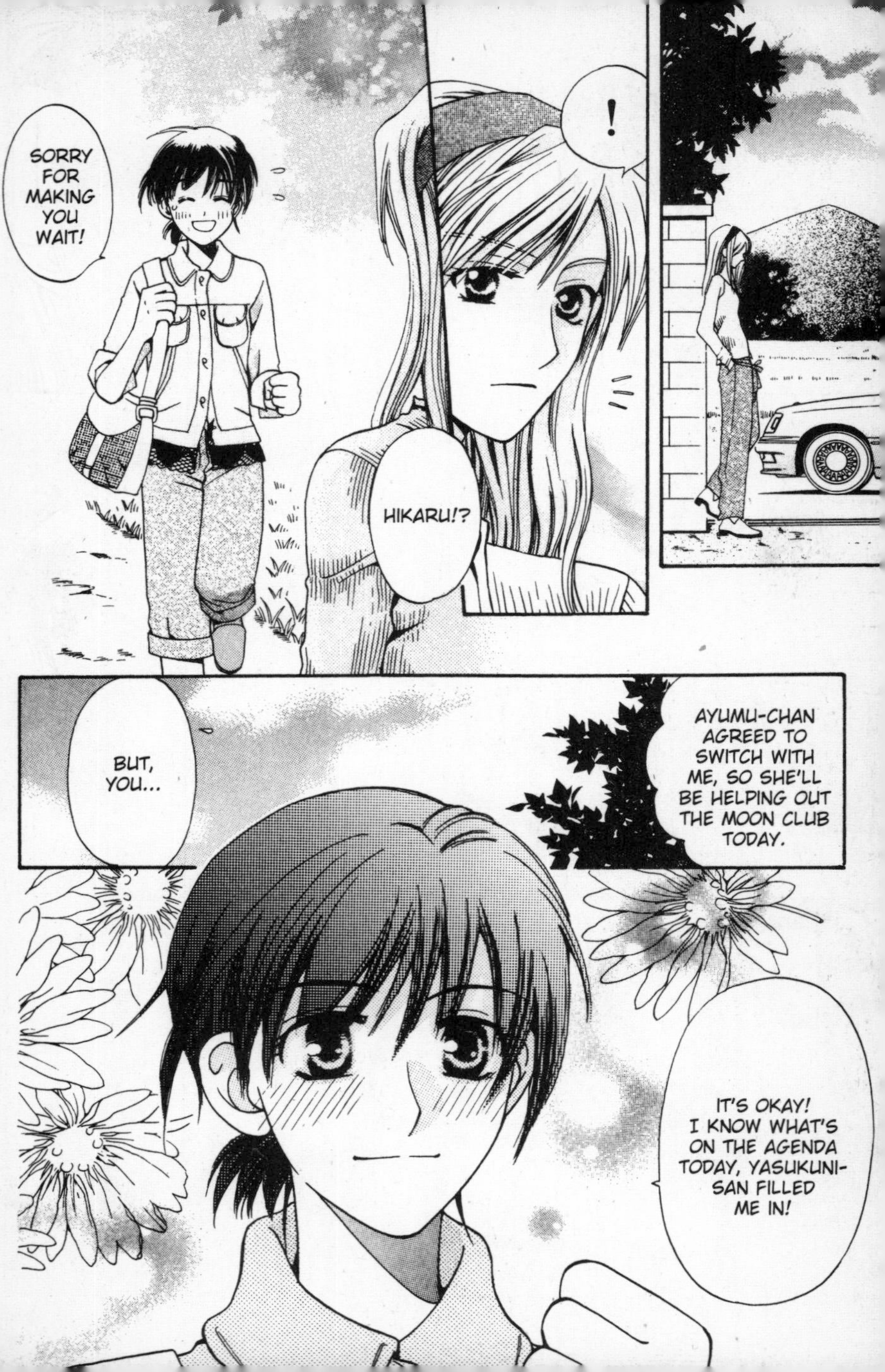
!
HIKARU!?
SORRY FOR MAKING YOU WAIT!
AYUMU-CHAN AGREED TO SWITCH WITH ME, SO SHE'LL BE HELPING OUT THE MOON CLUB TODAY.
BUT, YOU...
IT'S OKAY! I KNOW WHAT'S ON THE AGENDA TODAY, YASUKUNI-SAN FILLED ME IN!

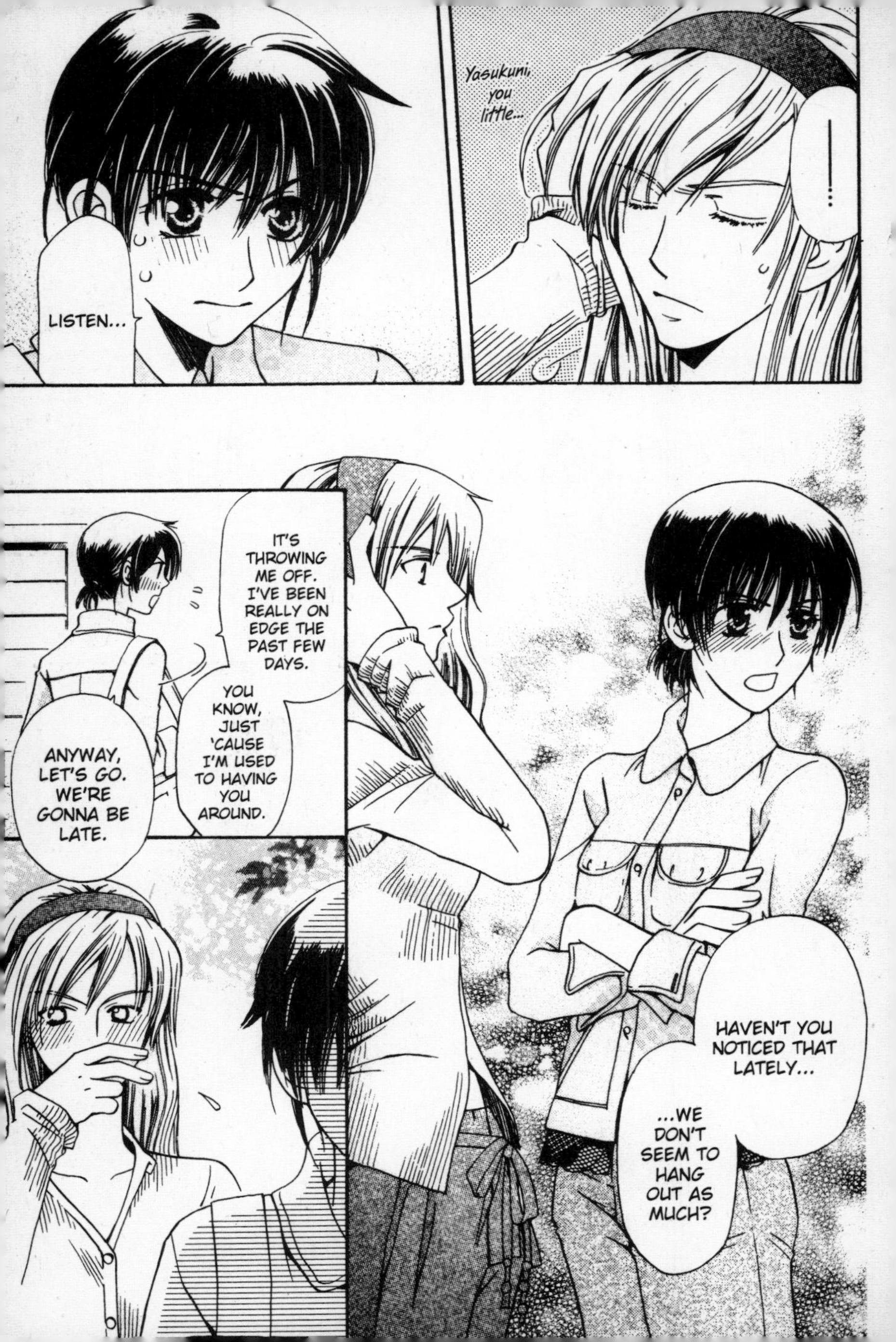
Yasukuni, you little...
LISTEN...
HAVEN'T YOU NOTICED THAT LATELY...
...WE DON'T SEEM TO HANG OUT AS MUCH?
IT'S THROWING ME OFF. I'VE BEEN REALLY ON EDGE THE PAST FEW DAYS.
YOU KNOW, JUST 'CAUSE I'M USED TO HAVING YOU AROUND.
ANYWAY, LET'S GO. WE'RE GONNA BE LATE.

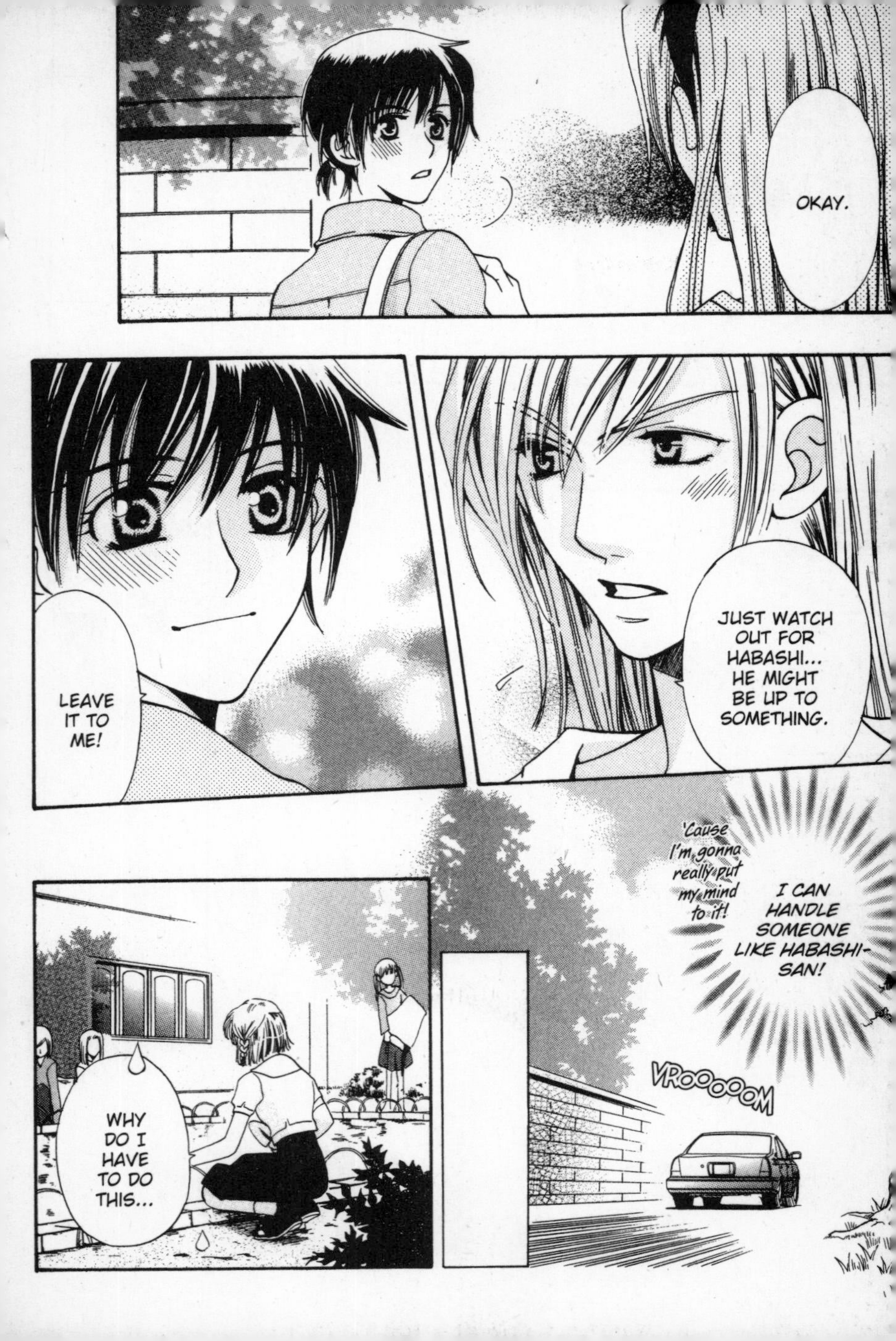
OKAY.
JUST WATCH OUT FOR HABASHI... HE MIGHT BE UP TO SOMETHING.
LEAVE IT TO ME!
I CAN HANDLE SOMEONE LIKE HABASHI-SAN!
'Cause I'm gonna really put my mind to it!
VROOOOOOM
WHY DO I HAVE TO DO THIS...

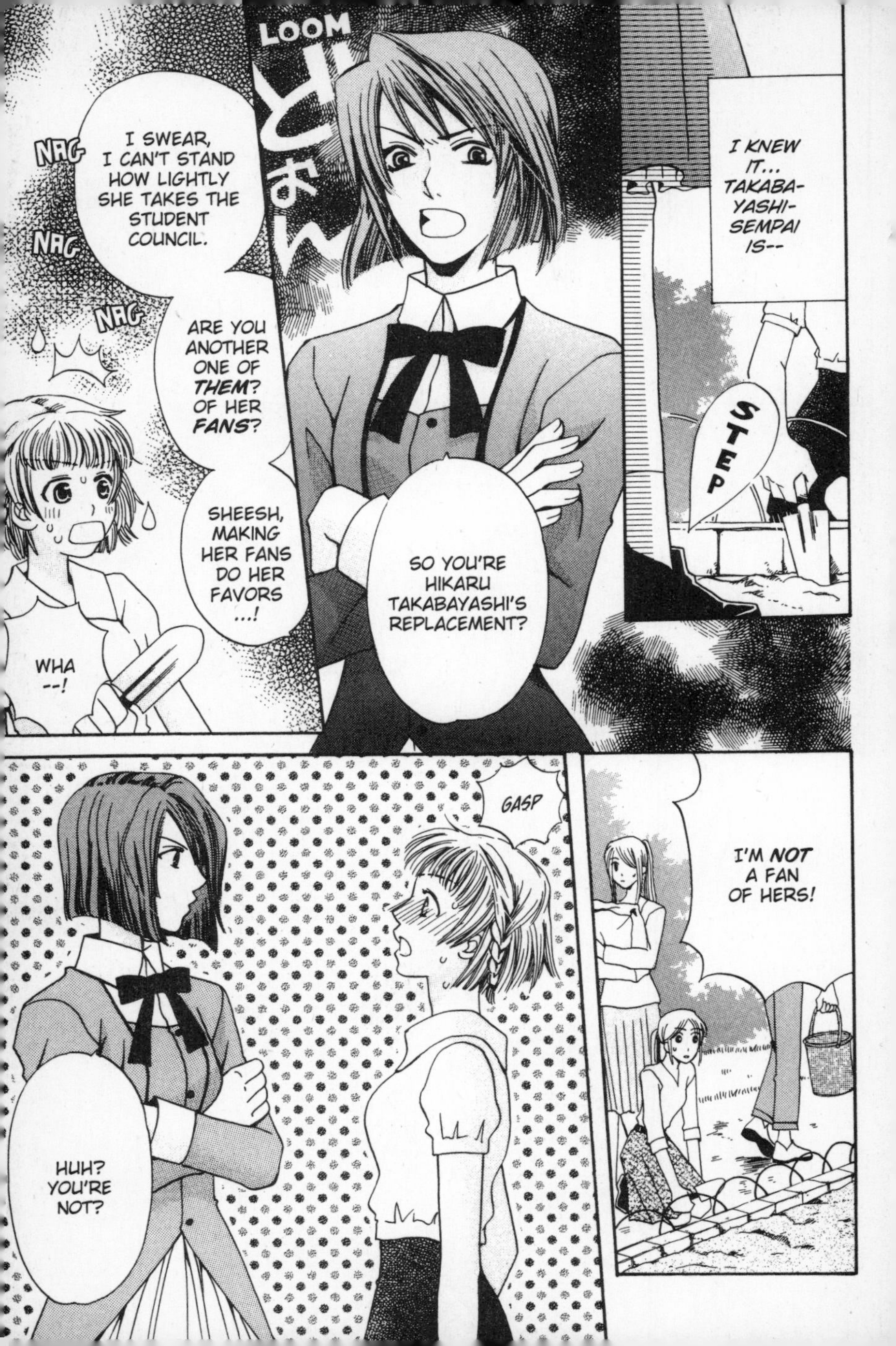
I KNEW IT... TAKABAYASHI-SEMPAI IS--
STEP
LOOM
どぉん
SO YOU'RE HIKARU TAKABAYASHI'S REPLACEMENT?
WHA --!
I SWEAR, I CAN'T STAND HOW LIGHTLY SHE TAKES THE STUDENT COUNCIL.
NAG
NAG
NAG
ARE YOU ANOTHER ONE OF ***THEM***? OF HER ***FANS***?
SHEESH, MAKING HER FANS DO HER FAVORS ...!
I'M ***NOT*** A FAN OF HERS!
GASP
HUH? YOU'RE NOT?

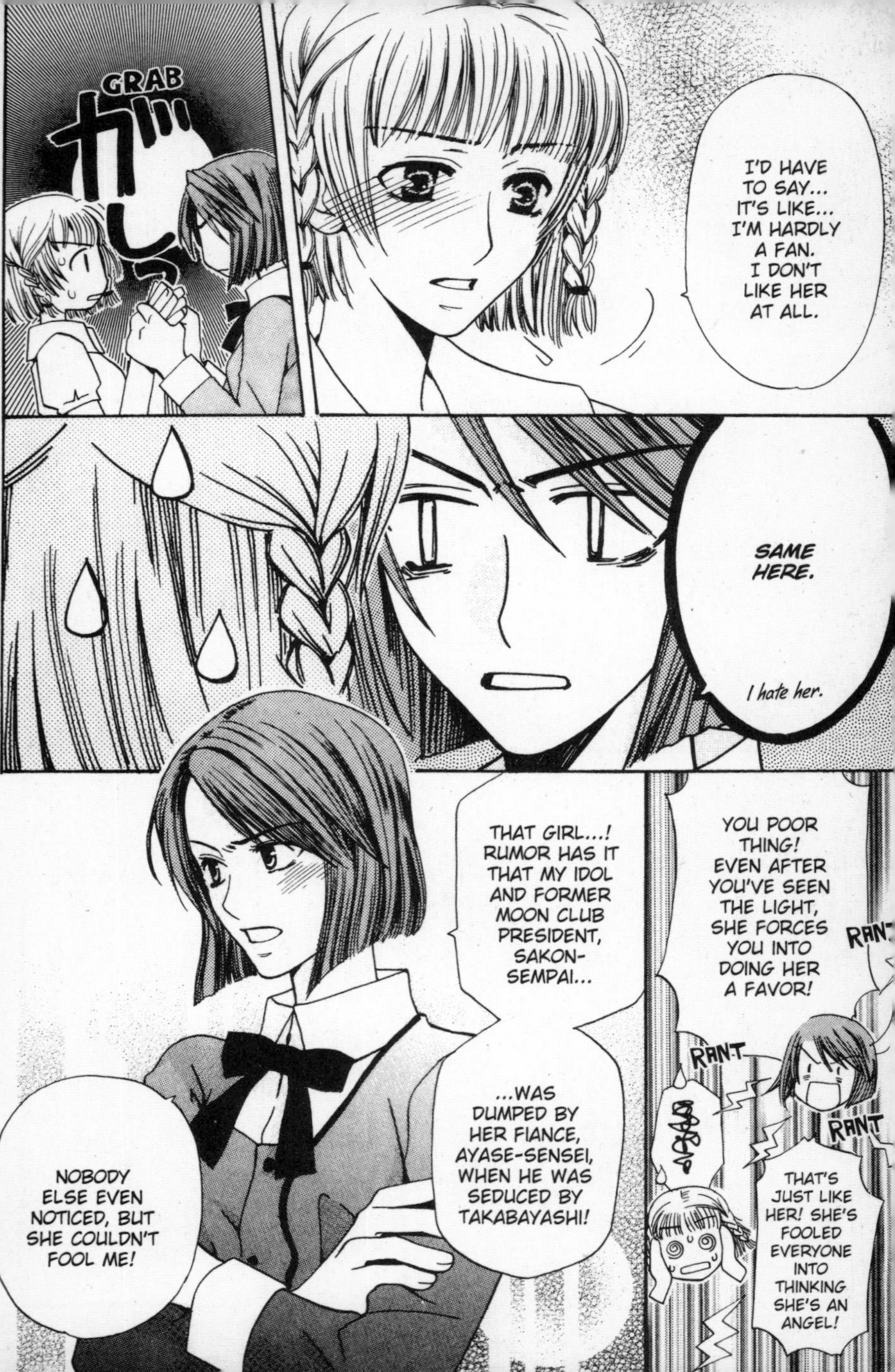
I'D HAVE TO SAY... IT'S LIKE... I'M HARDLY A FAN. I DON'T LIKE HER AT ALL.
GRAB
SAME HERE.
I hate her.
YOU POOR THING! EVEN AFTER YOU'VE SEEN THE LIGHT, SHE FORCES YOU INTO DOING HER A FAVOR!
RANT
RANT
RANT
THAT'S JUST LIKE HER! SHE'S FOOLED EVERYONE INTO THINKING SHE'S AN ANGEL!
THAT GIRL...! RUMOR HAS IT THAT MY IDOL AND FORMER MOON CLUB PRESIDENT, SAKON-SEMPAI...
...WAS DUMPED BY HER FIANCE, AYASE-SENSEI, WHEN HE WAS SEDUCED BY TAKABAYASHI!
NOBODY ELSE EVEN NOTICED, BUT SHE COULDN'T FOOL ME!

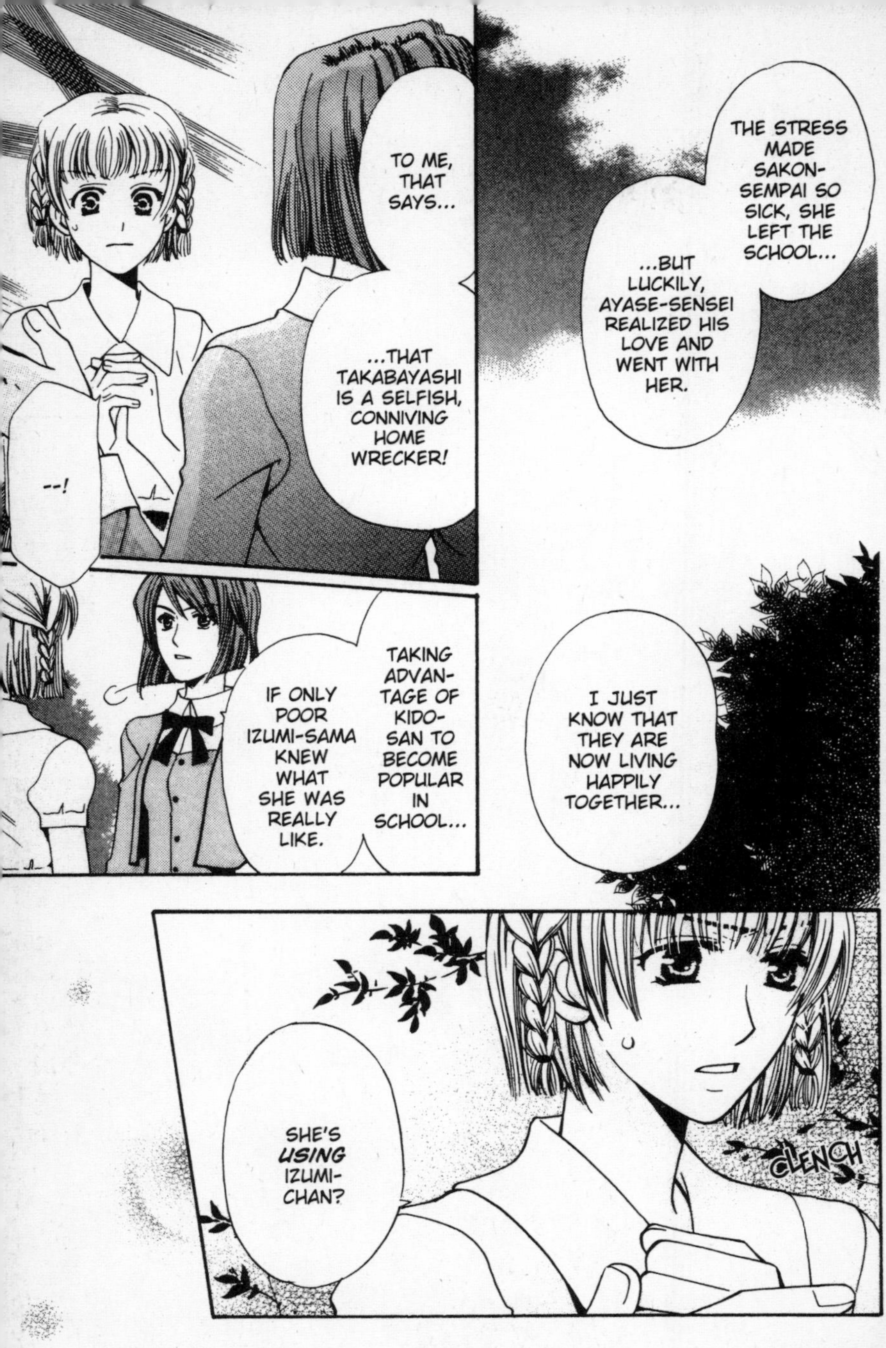
THE STRESS MADE SAKON-SEMPAI SO SICK, SHE LEFT THE SCHOOL...
...BUT LUCKILY, AYASE-SENSEI REALIZED HIS LOVE AND WENT WITH HER.
TO ME, THAT SAYS...
...THAT TAKABAYASHI IS A SELFISH, CONNIVING HOME WRECKER!
--!
I JUST KNOW THAT THEY ARE NOW LIVING HAPPILY TOGETHER...
TAKING ADVANTAGE OF KIDO-SAN TO BECOME POPULAR IN SCHOOL...
IF ONLY POOR IZUMI-SAMA KNEW WHAT SHE WAS REALLY LIKE.
CLENCH
SHE'S *USING* IZUMI-CHAN?

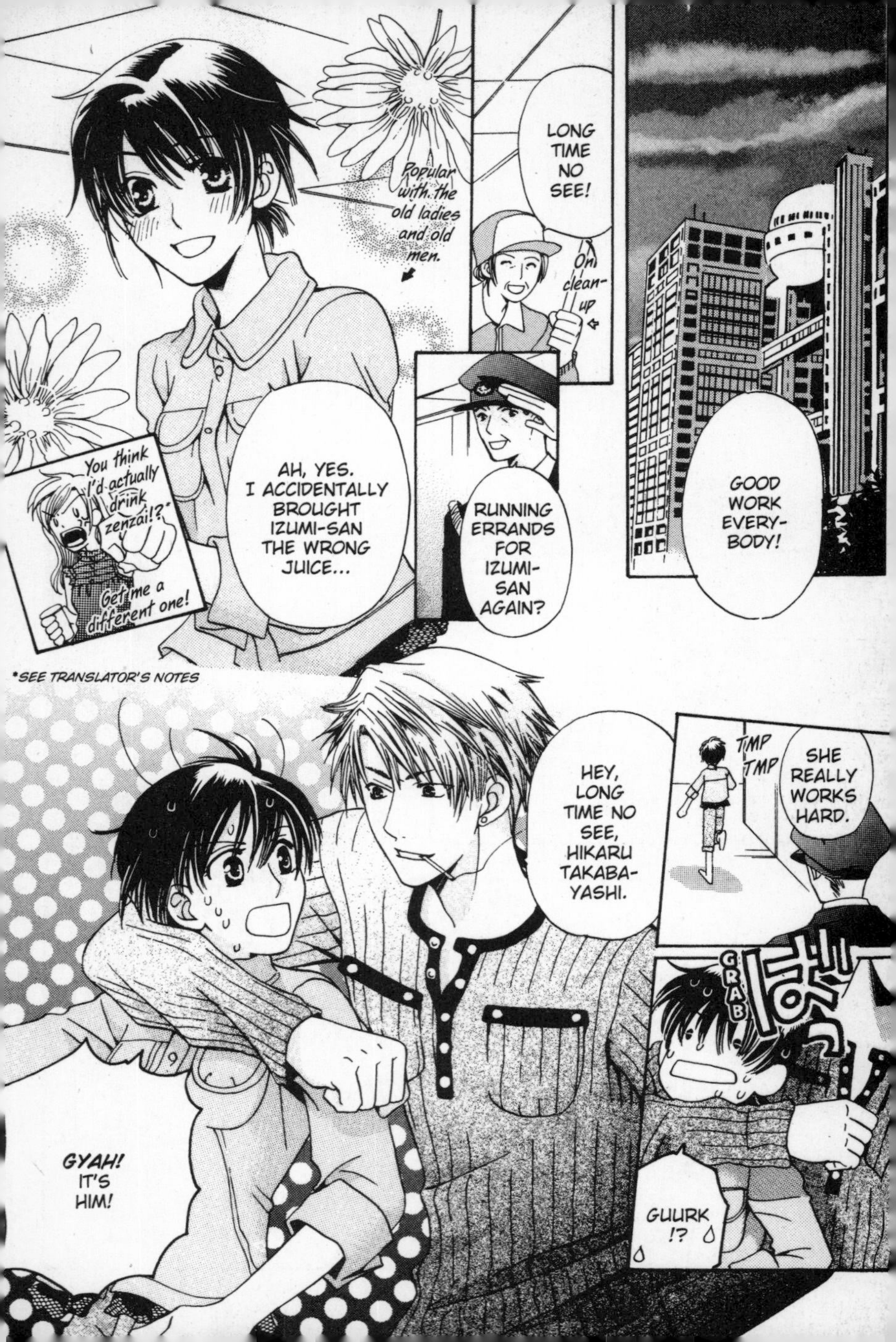
GOOD WORK EVERY-BODY!
LONG TIME NO SEE!
On clean-up
RUNNING ERRANDS FOR IZUMI-SAN AGAIN?
Popular with the old ladies and old men.
AH, YES. I ACCIDENTALLY BROUGHT IZUMI-SAN THE WRONG JUICE...
You think I'd actually drink zenzai!?*
Get me a different one!
TMP TMP
SHE REALLY WORKS HARD.
GRAB
ぱっ
GUURK !?
HEY, LONG TIME NO SEE, HIKARU TAKABA-YASHI.
GYAH! IT'S HIM!

*SEE TRANSLATOR'S NOTES

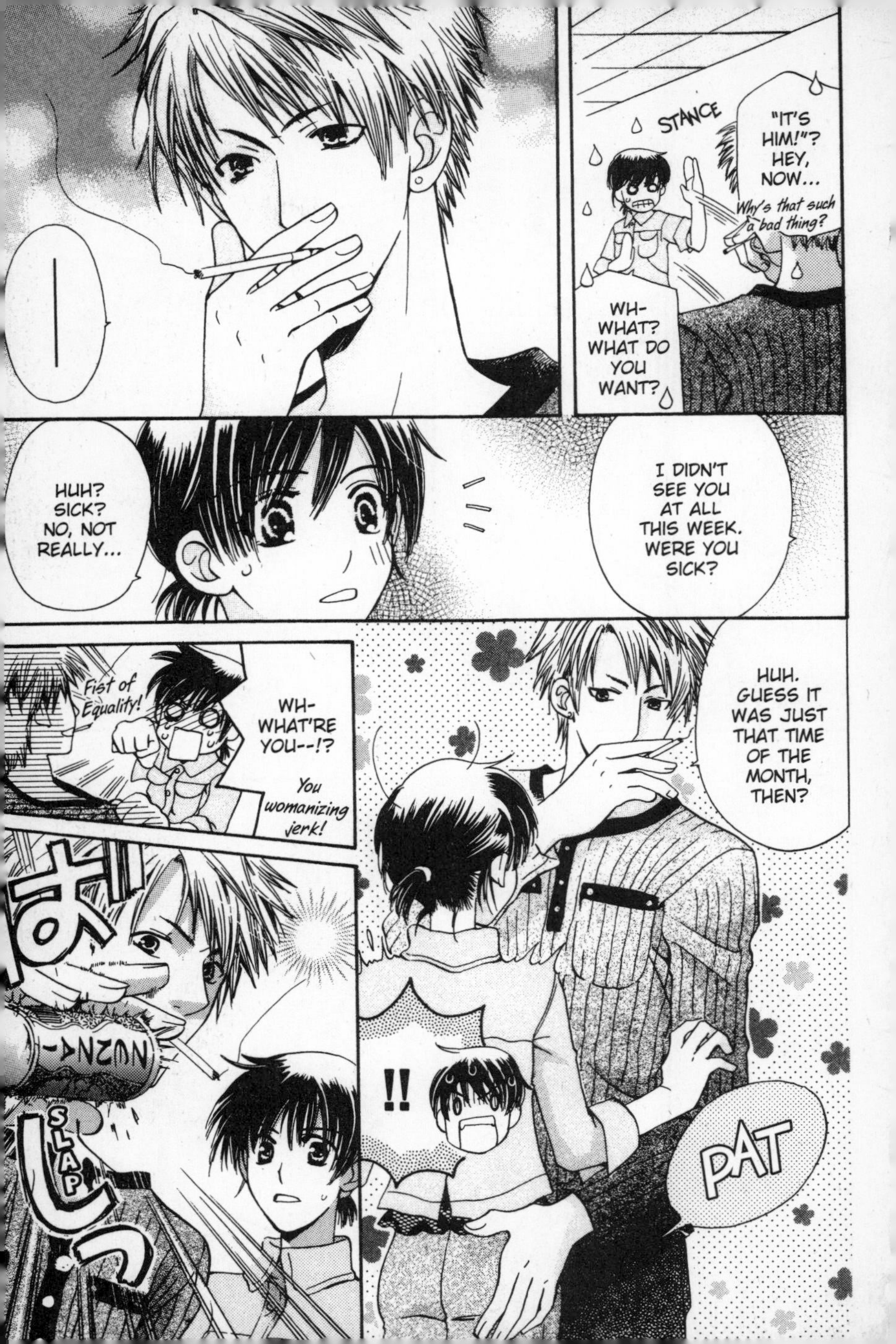
"IT'S HIM!"? HEY, NOW...
Why's that such a bad thing?
STANCE
WH- WHAT? WHAT DO YOU WANT?
I DIDN'T SEE YOU AT ALL THIS WEEK. WERE YOU SICK?
HUH? SICK? NO, NOT REALLY...
HUH. GUESS IT WAS JUST THAT TIME OF THE MONTH, THEN?
PAT
!!
WH- WHAT'RE YOU--!?
You womanizing jerk!
Fist of Equality!
SLAP

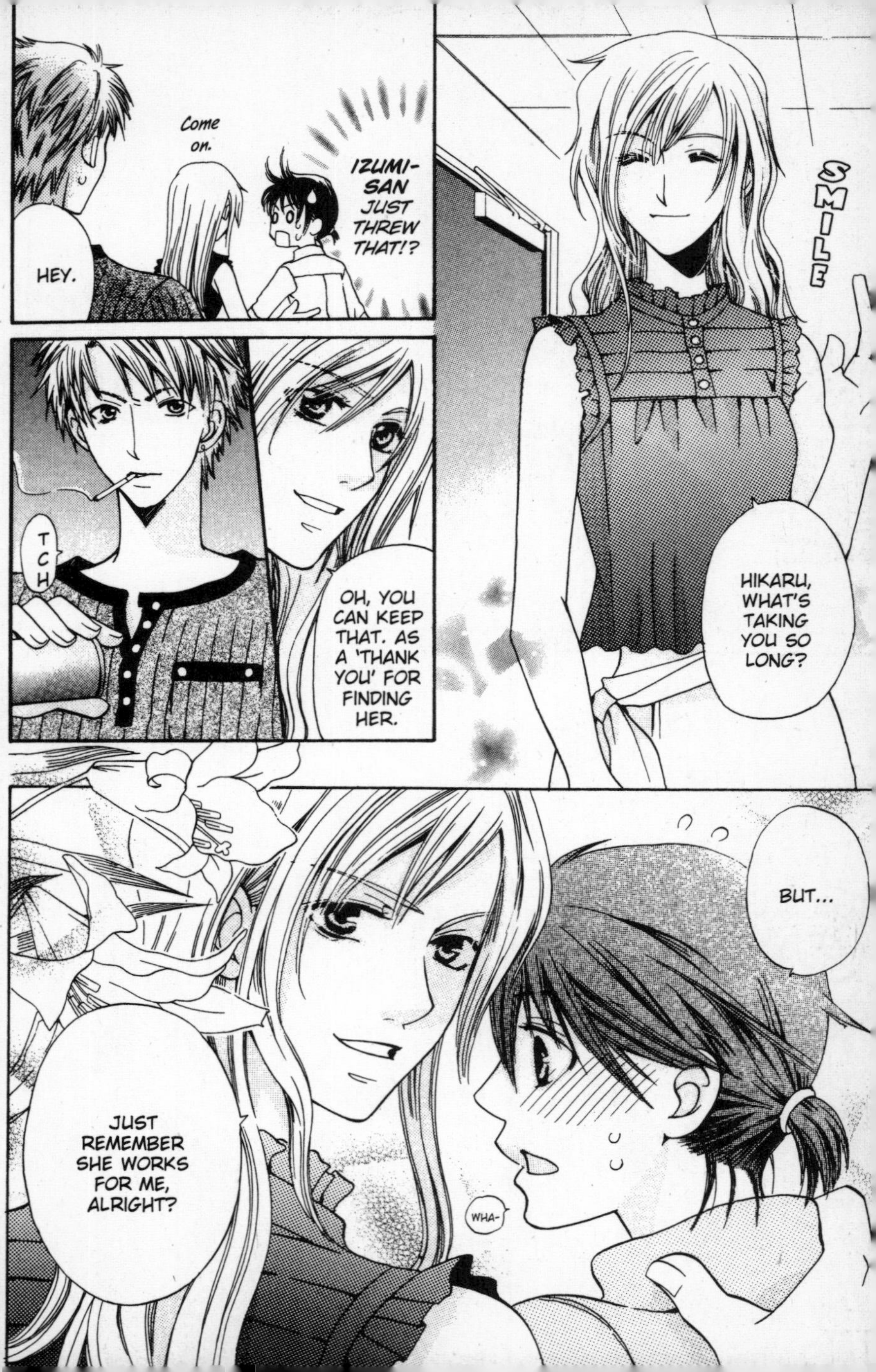
SMILE
HIKARU, WHAT'S TAKING YOU SO LONG?
IZUMI-SAN JUST THREW THAT!?
Come on.
HEY.
OH, YOU CAN KEEP THAT. AS A 'THANK YOU' FOR FINDING HER.
TCH
BUT...
JUST REMEMBER SHE WORKS FOR ME, ALRIGHT?
WHA-

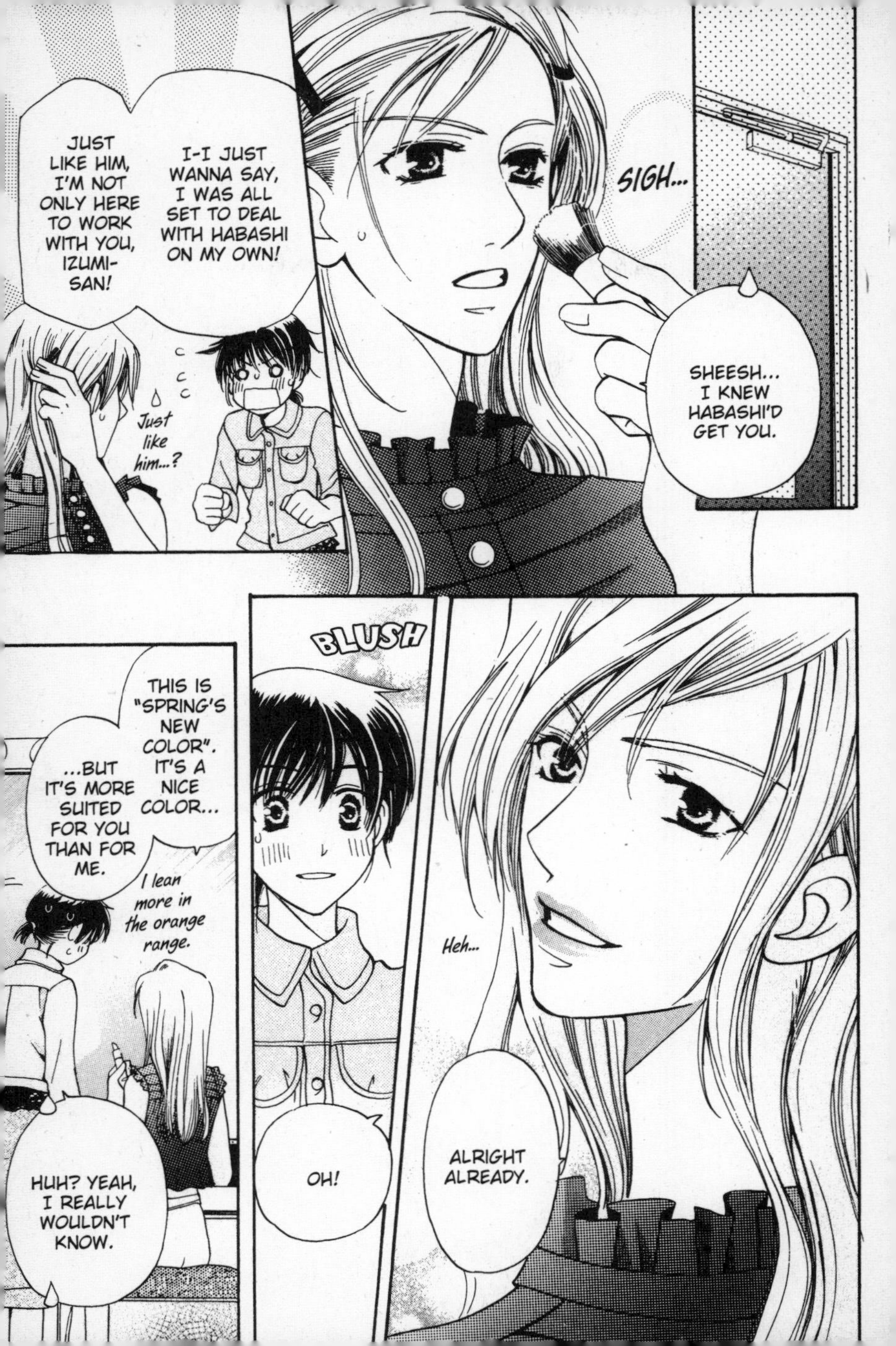
SIGH...
SHEESH... I KNEW HABASHI'D GET YOU.
I-I JUST WANNA SAY, I WAS ALL SET TO DEAL WITH HABASHI ON MY OWN!
JUST LIKE HIM, I'M NOT ONLY HERE TO WORK WITH YOU, IZUMI-SAN!
Just like him...?
Heh...
ALRIGHT ALREADY.
BLUSH
OH!
THIS IS "SPRING'S NEW COLOR". IT'S A NICE COLOR...
...BUT IT'S MORE SUITED FOR YOU THAN FOR ME.
I lean more in the orange range.
HUH? YEAH, I REALLY WOULDN'T KNOW.

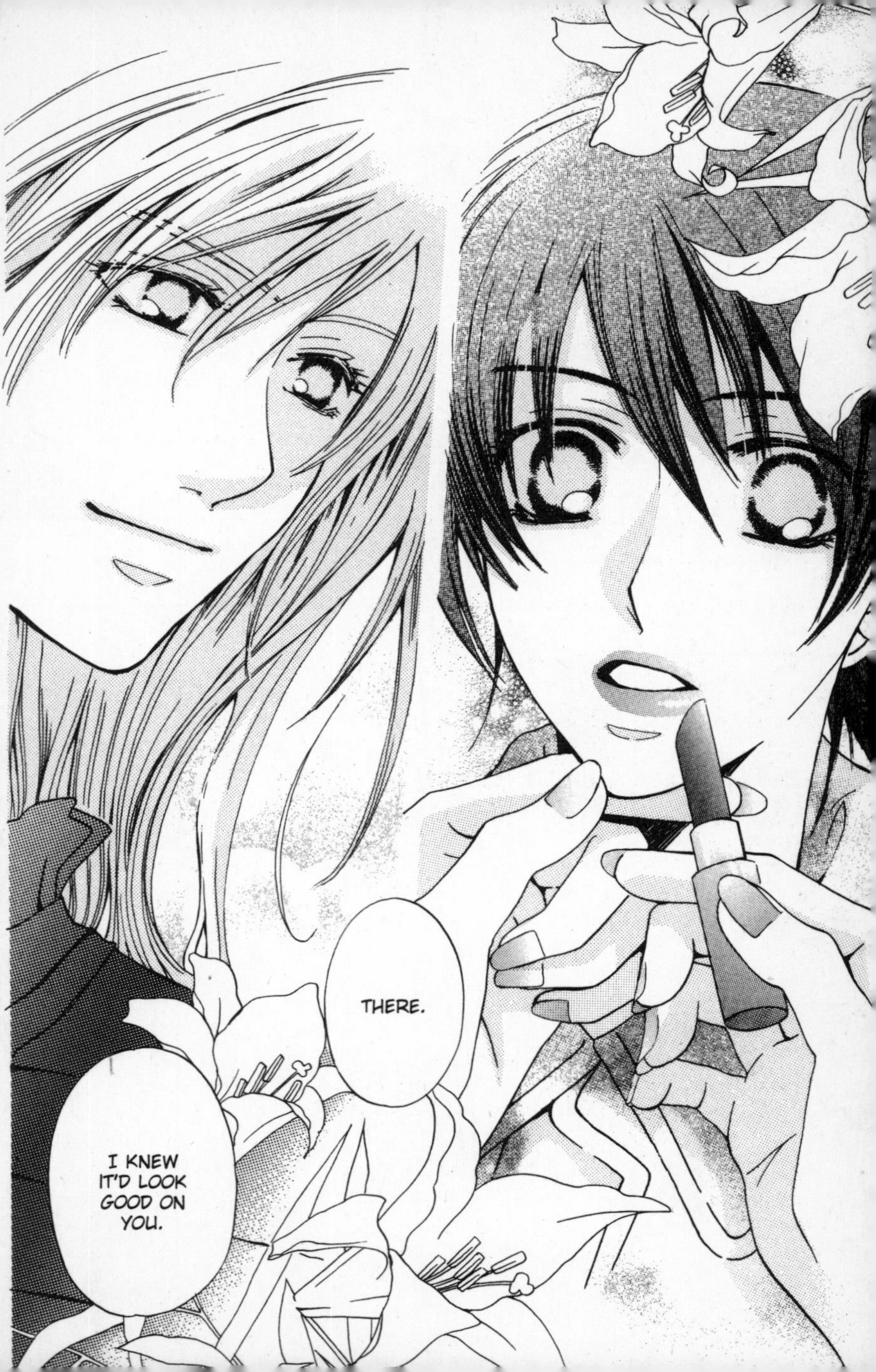
THERE.
I KNEW IT'D LOOK GOOD ON YOU.

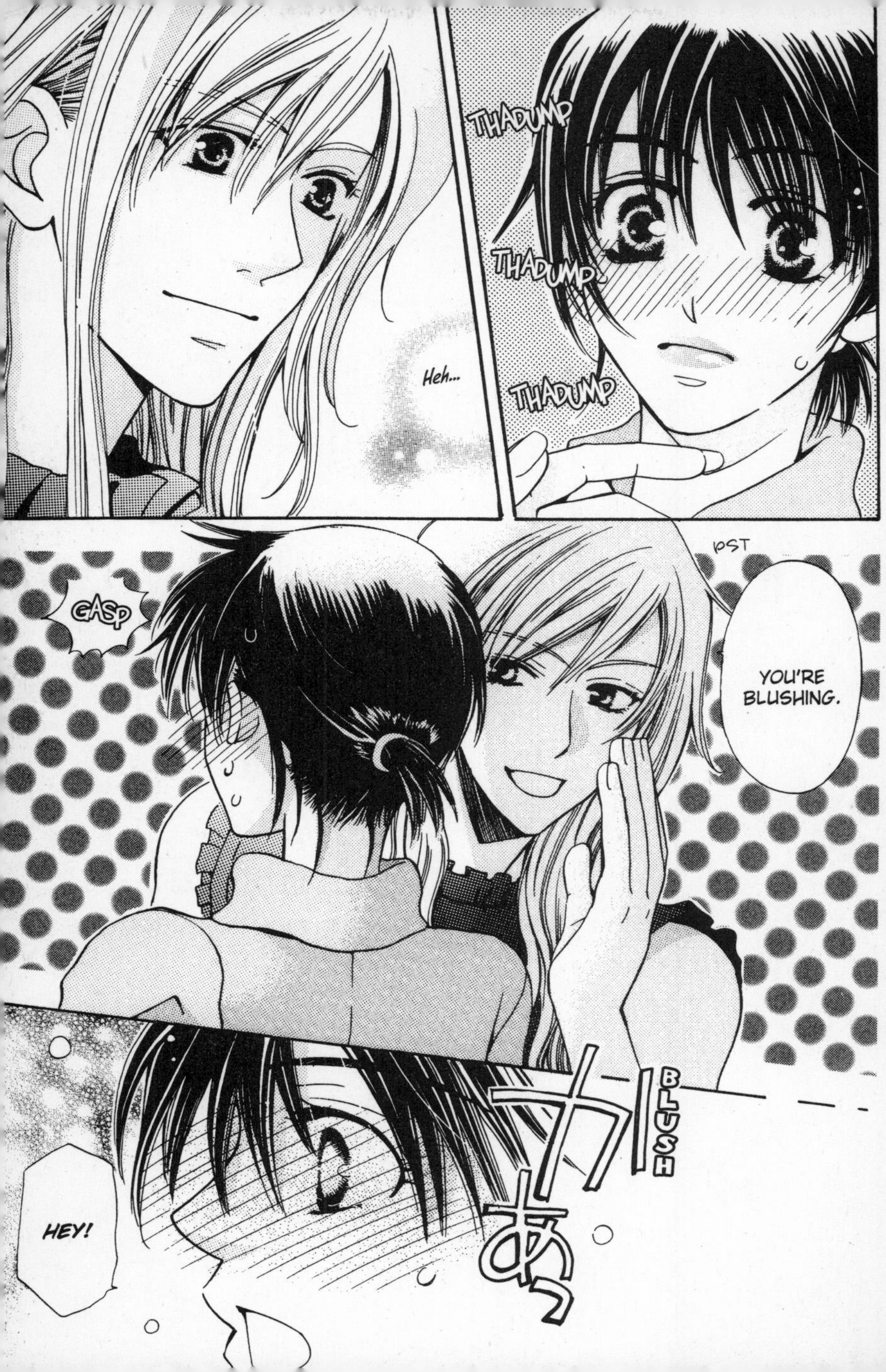
THADUMP
THADUMP
THADUMP
Heh...
PST
YOU'RE BLUSHING.
GASP
BLUSH
カあっ
HEY!

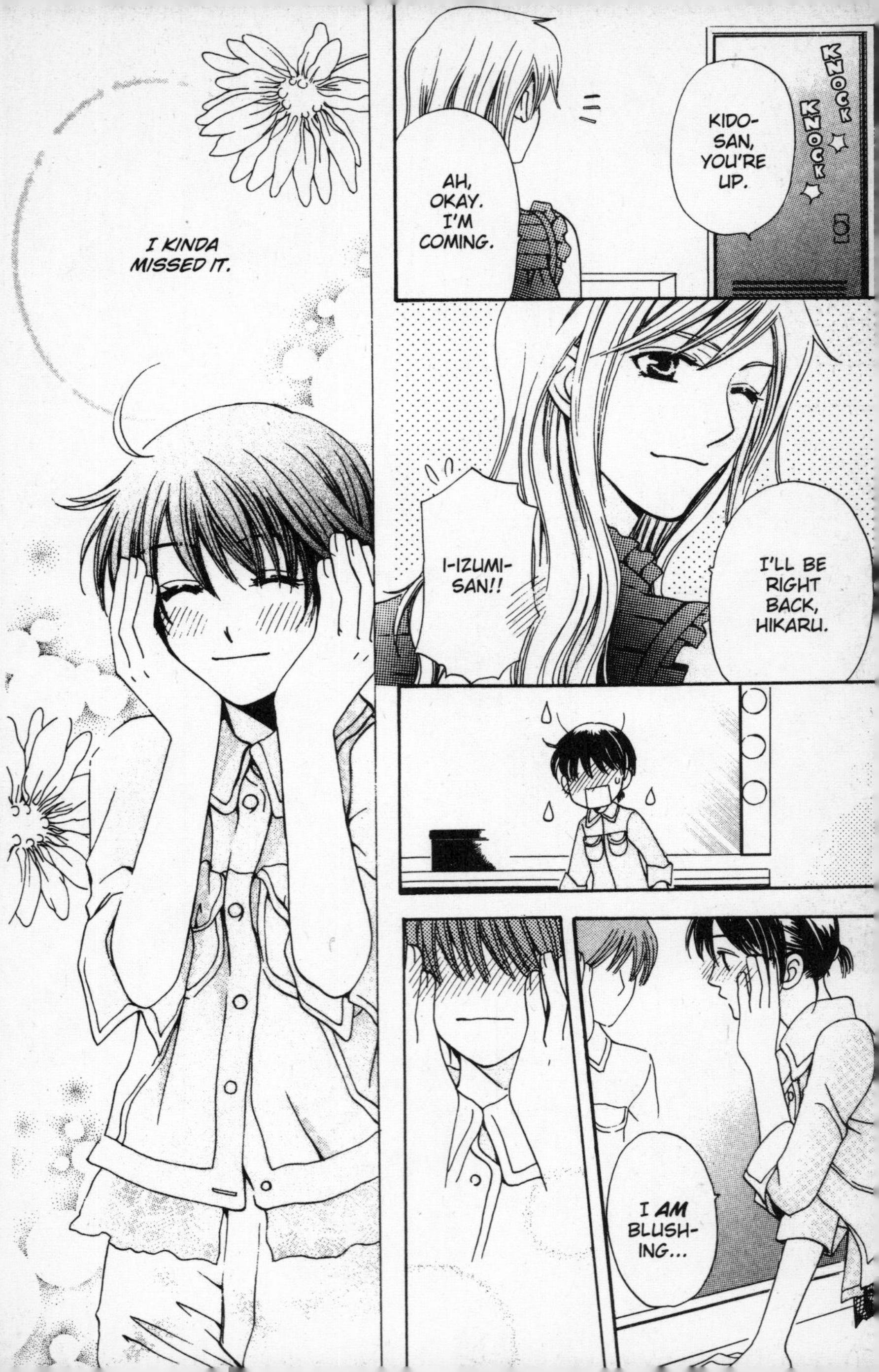

KNOCK KNOCK
KIDO-SAN, YOU'RE UP.
AH, OKAY. I'M COMING.
I'LL BE RIGHT BACK, HIKARU.
I-IZUMI-SAN!!
I AM BLUSHING...
I KINDA MISSED IT.

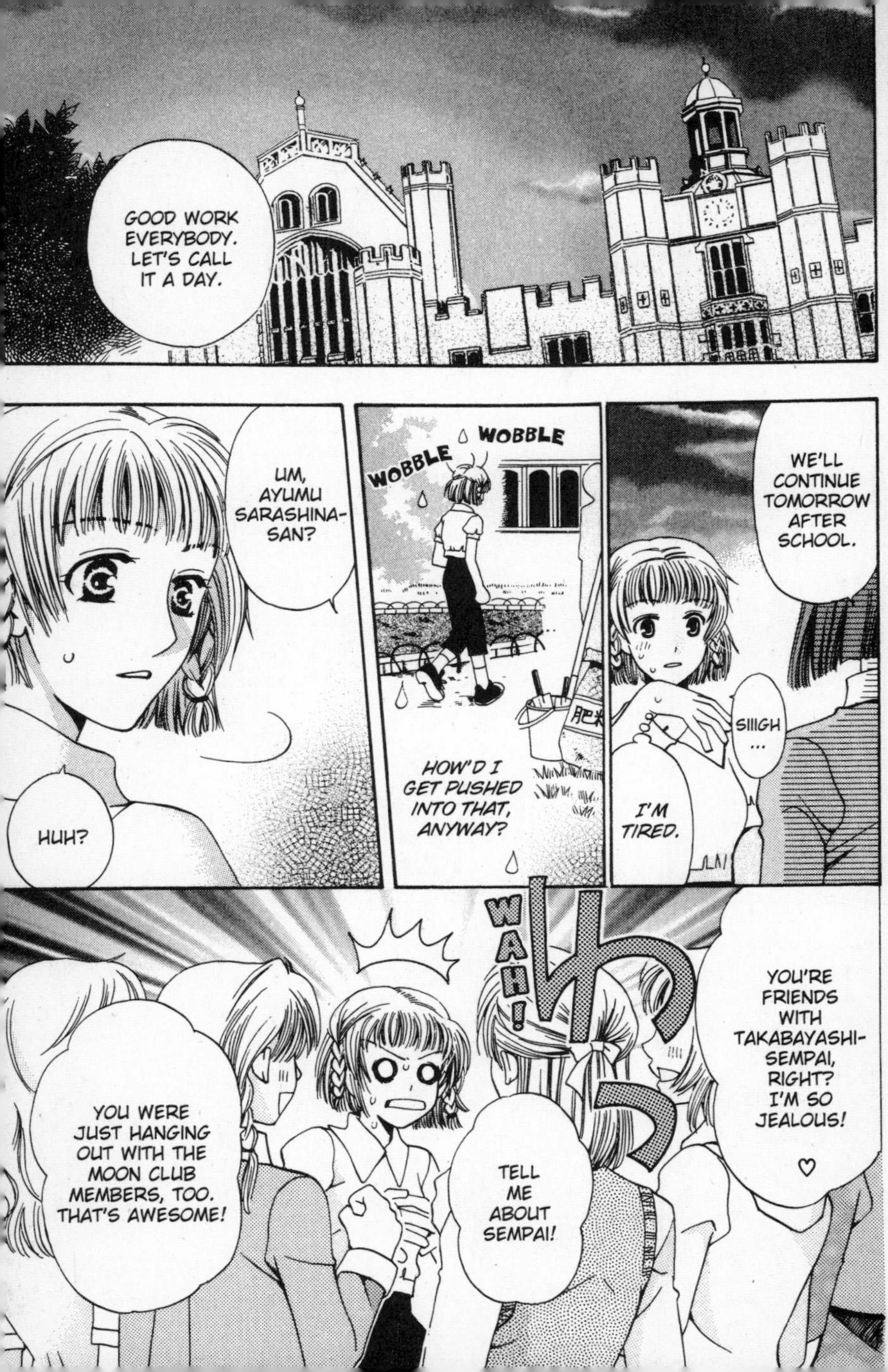
GOOD WORK EVERYBODY. LET'S CALL IT A DAY.
WE'LL CONTINUE TOMORROW AFTER SCHOOL.
SIIIGH...
I'M TIRED.
WOBBLE WOBBLE
HOW'D I GET PUSHED INTO THAT, ANYWAY?
UM, AYUMU SARASHINA-SAN?
HUH?
WAH!
YOU'RE FRIENDS WITH TAKABAYASHI-SEMPAI, RIGHT? I'M SO JEALOUS! ♡
TELL ME ABOUT SEMPAI!
YOU WERE JUST HANGING OUT WITH THE MOON CLUB MEMBERS, TOO. THAT'S AWESOME!

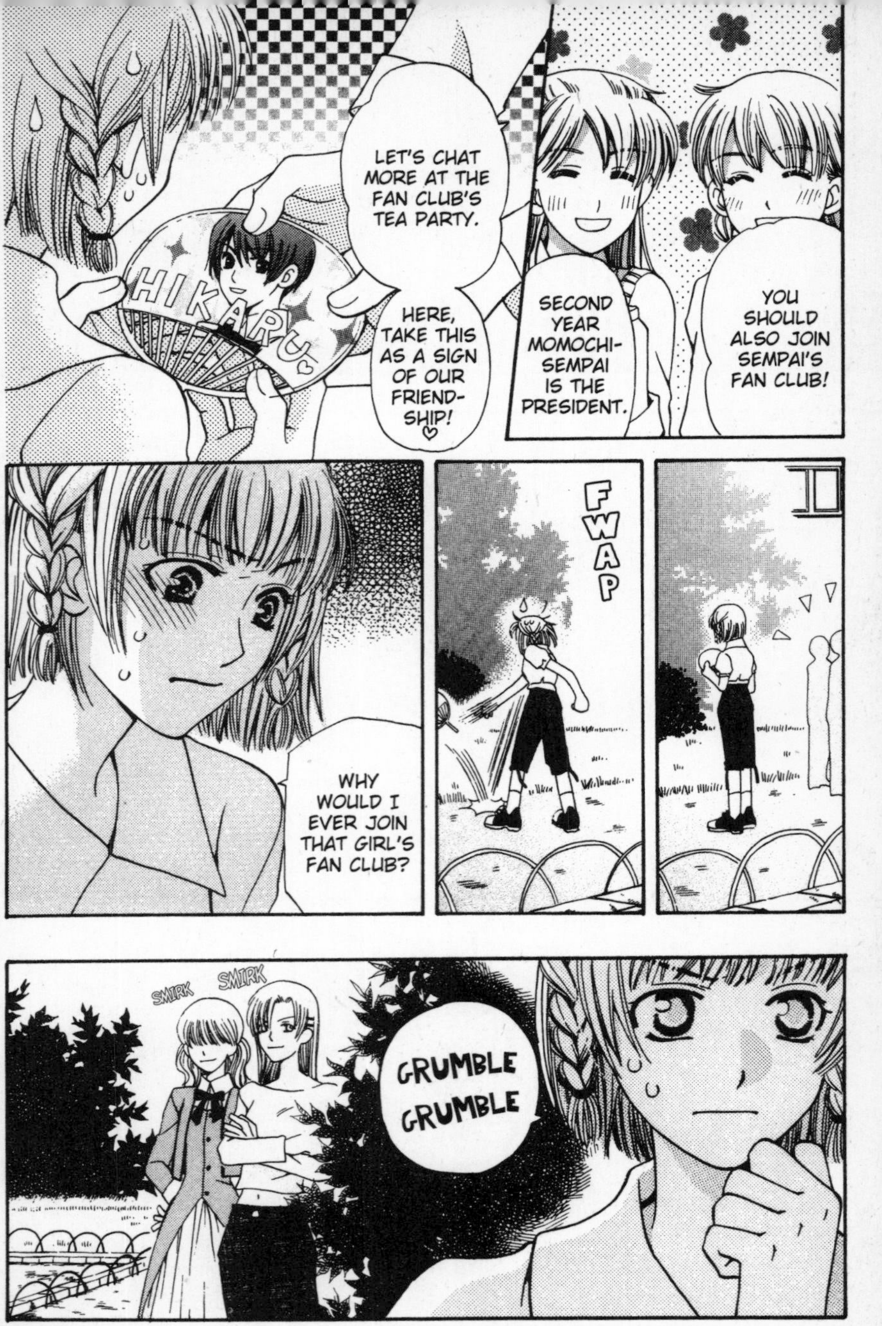
YOU SHOULD ALSO JOIN SEMPAI'S FAN CLUB!
SECOND YEAR MOMOCHI-SEMPAI IS THE PRESIDENT.
LET'S CHAT MORE AT THE FAN CLUB'S TEA PARTY.
HIKARU
HERE, TAKE THIS AS A SIGN OF OUR FRIEND-SHIP! ♡
FWAP
WHY WOULD I EVER JOIN THAT GIRL'S FAN CLUB?
GRUMBLE GRUMBLE
SMIRK
SMIRK

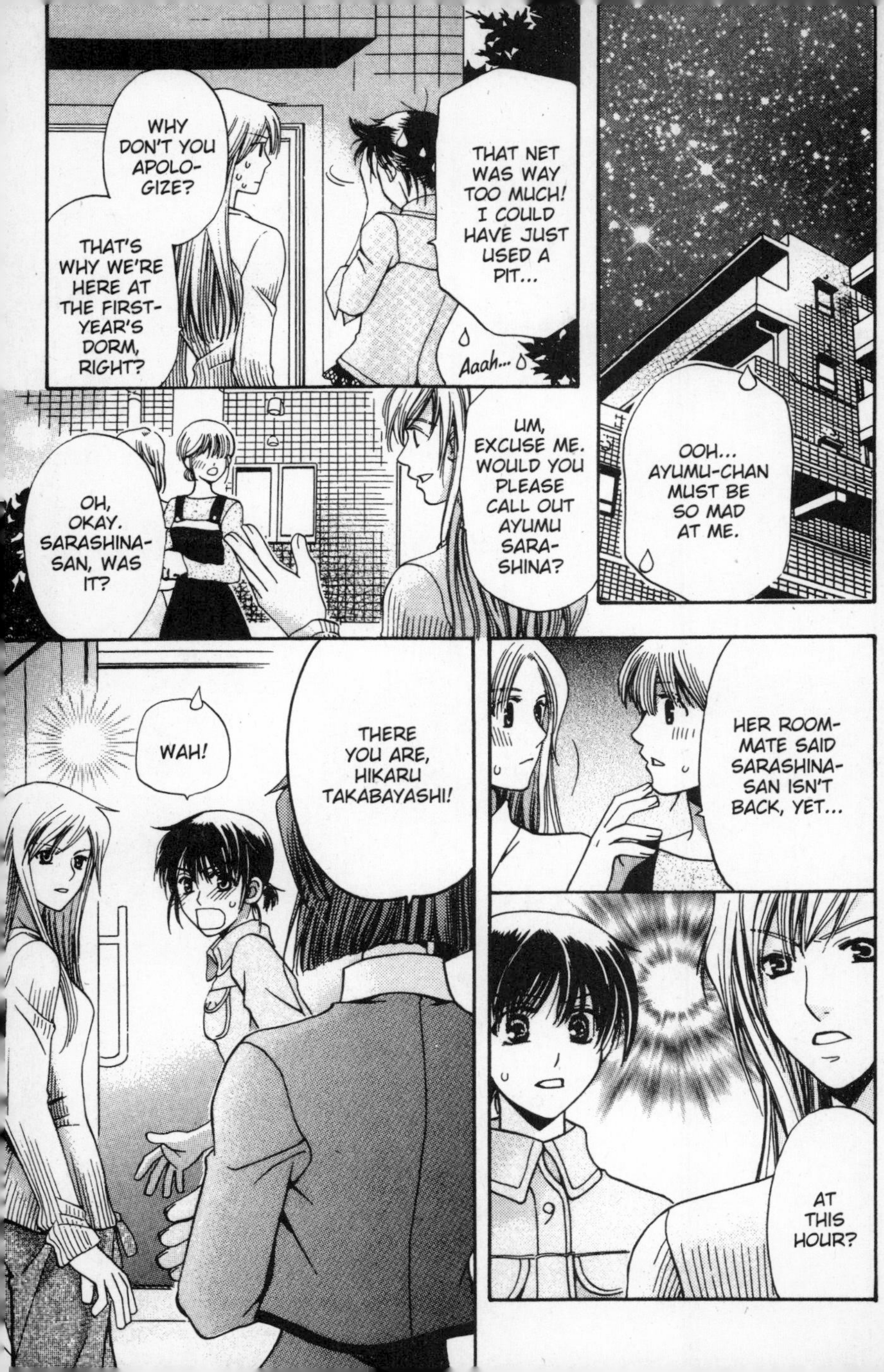
OOH... AYUMU-CHAN MUST BE SO MAD AT ME.
THAT NET WAS WAY TOO MUCH! I COULD HAVE JUST USED A PIT...
Aaah...
WHY DON'T YOU APOLOGIZE?
THAT'S WHY WE'RE HERE AT THE FIRST-YEAR'S DORM, RIGHT?
UM, EXCUSE ME. WOULD YOU PLEASE CALL OUT AYUMU SARASHINA?
OH, OKAY. SARASHINA-SAN, WAS IT?
HER ROOMMATE SAID SARASHINA-SAN ISN'T BACK, YET...
AT THIS HOUR?
THERE YOU ARE, HIKARU TAKABAYASHI!
WAH!

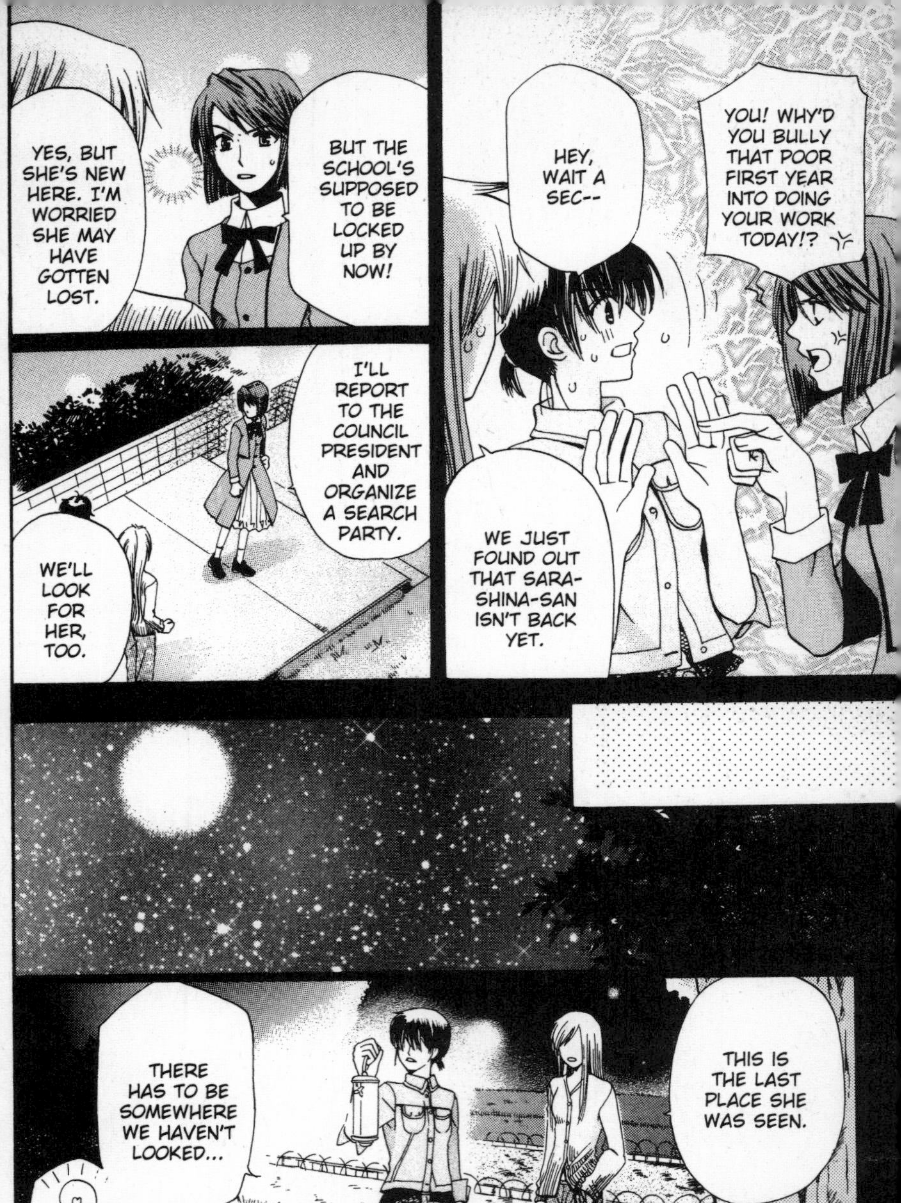
YOU! WHY'D YOU BULLY THAT POOR FIRST YEAR INTO DOING YOUR WORK TODAY!?
HEY, WAIT A SEC--
WE JUST FOUND OUT THAT SARA-SHINA-SAN ISN'T BACK YET.
BUT THE SCHOOL'S SUPPOSED TO BE LOCKED UP BY NOW!
YES, BUT SHE'S NEW HERE. I'M WORRIED SHE MAY HAVE GOTTEN LOST.
I'LL REPORT TO THE COUNCIL PRESIDENT AND ORGANIZE A SEARCH PARTY.
WE'LL LOOK FOR HER, TOO.
THIS IS THE LAST PLACE SHE WAS SEEN.
THERE HAS TO BE SOMEWHERE WE HAVEN'T LOOKED...

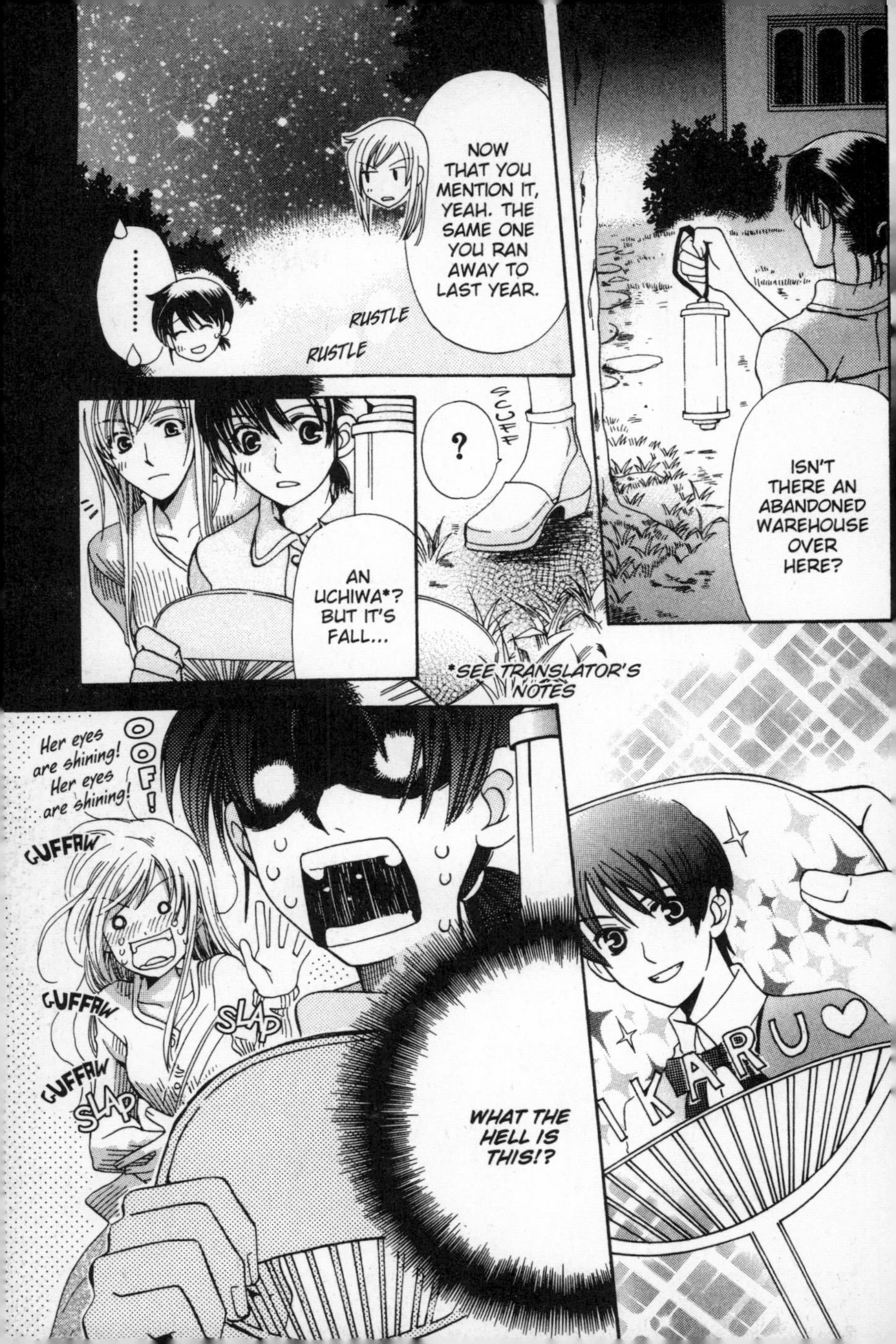
ISN'T THERE AN ABANDONED WAREHOUSE OVER HERE?
……
NOW THAT YOU MENTION IT, YEAH. THE SAME ONE YOU RAN AWAY TO LAST YEAR.
RUSTLE
RUSTLE
SCUFF
?
AN UCHIWA*? BUT IT'S FALL...
*SEE TRANSLATOR'S NOTES
IKARU♡
WHAT THE HELL IS THIS!?
OOF!
Her eyes are shining! Her eyes are shining!
GUFFAW
GUFFAW
SLAP
GUFFAW
SLAP

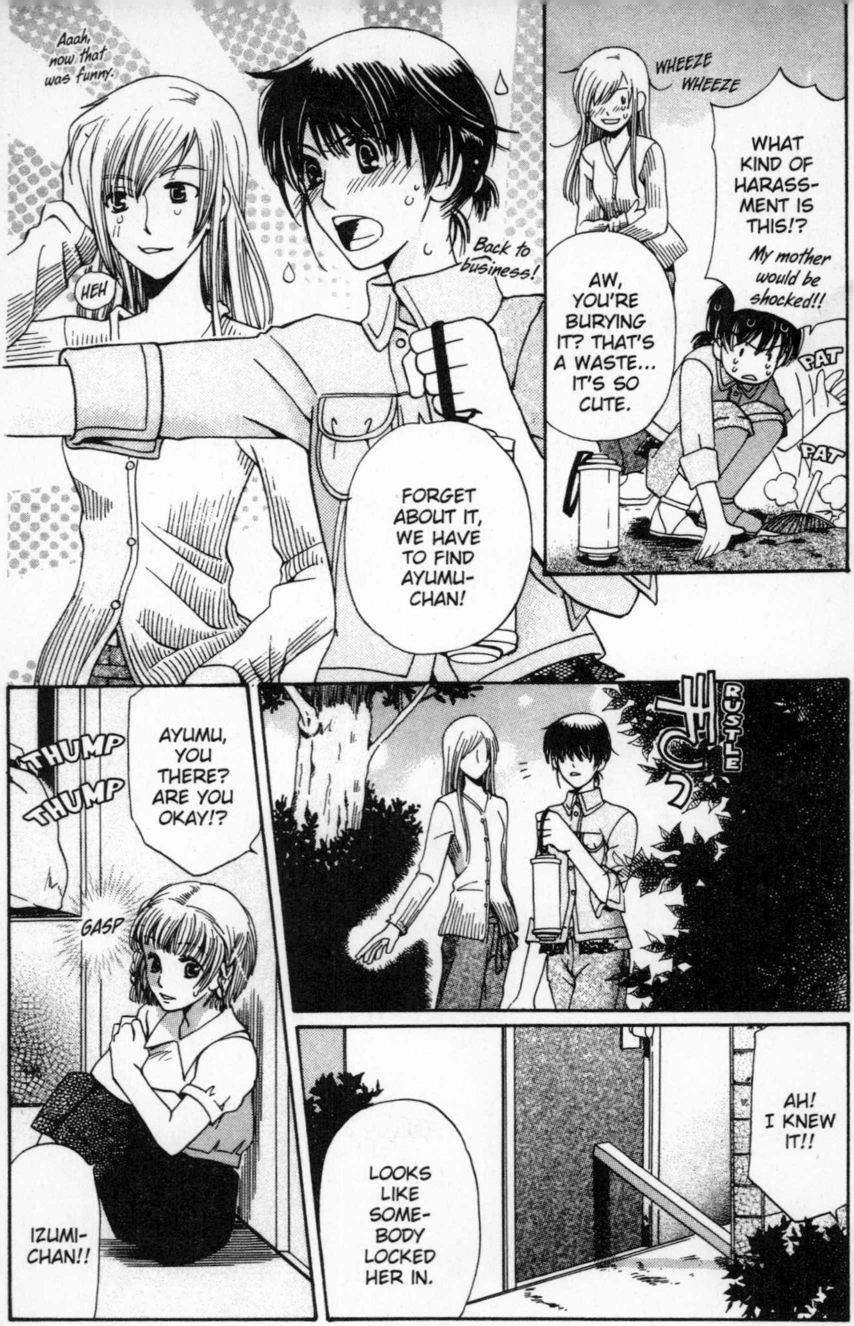
WHEEZE WHEEZE
WHAT KIND OF HARASS-MENT IS THIS!?
My mother would be shocked!!
AW, YOU'RE BURYING IT? THAT'S A WASTE... IT'S SO CUTE.
PAT
PAT
Aaah, now that was funny.
HEH
Back to business!
FORGET ABOUT IT, WE HAVE TO FIND AYUMU-CHAN!
RUSTLE
AH! I KNEW IT!!
LOOKS LIKE SOME-BODY LOCKED HER IN.
AYUMU, YOU THERE? ARE YOU OKAY!?
THUMP
THUMP
GASP
IZUMI-CHAN!!

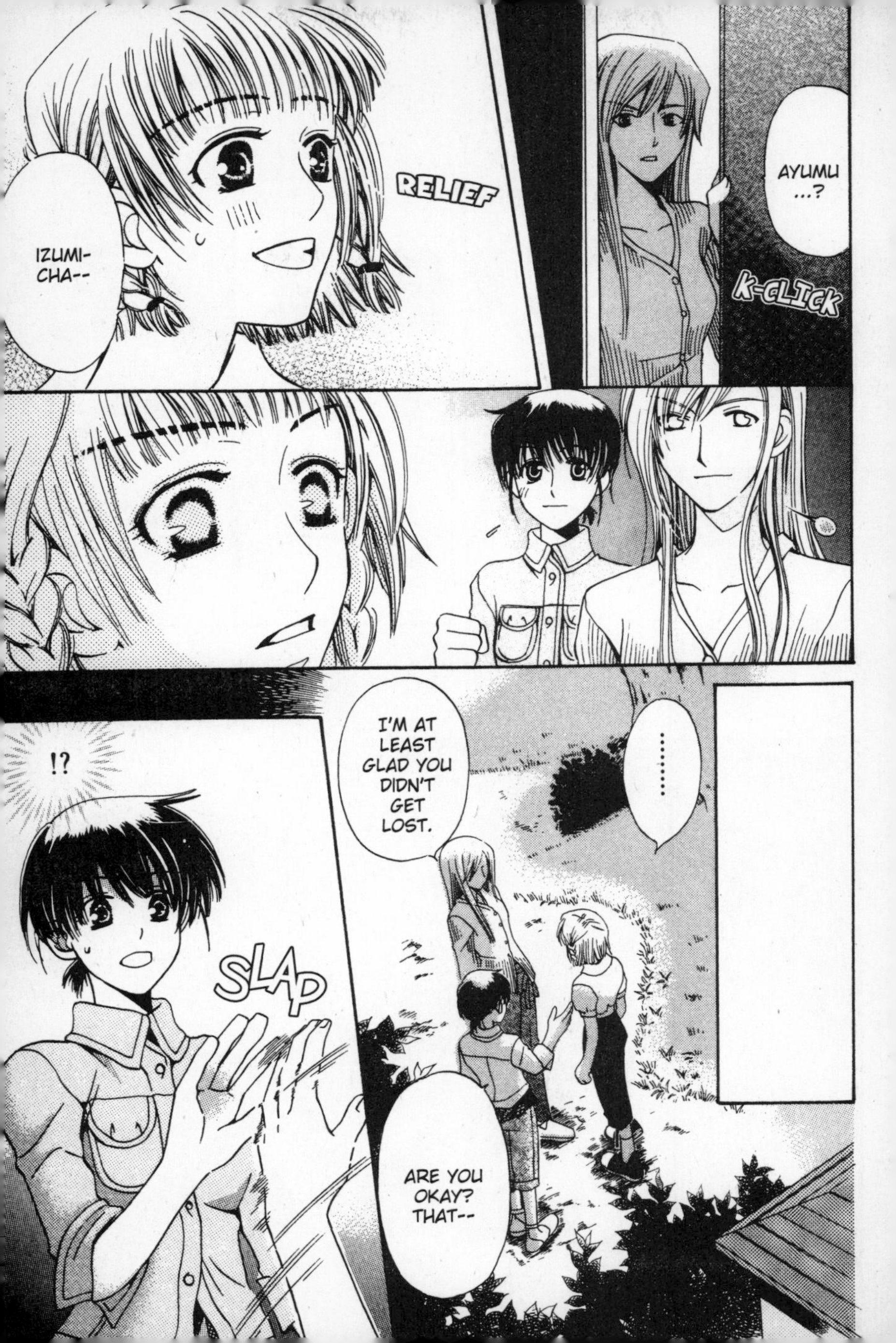
AYUMU ...?
K-CLICK
RELIEF
IZUMI-CHA--
......
I'M AT LEAST GLAD YOU DIDN'T GET LOST.
ARE YOU OKAY? THAT--
!?
SLAP

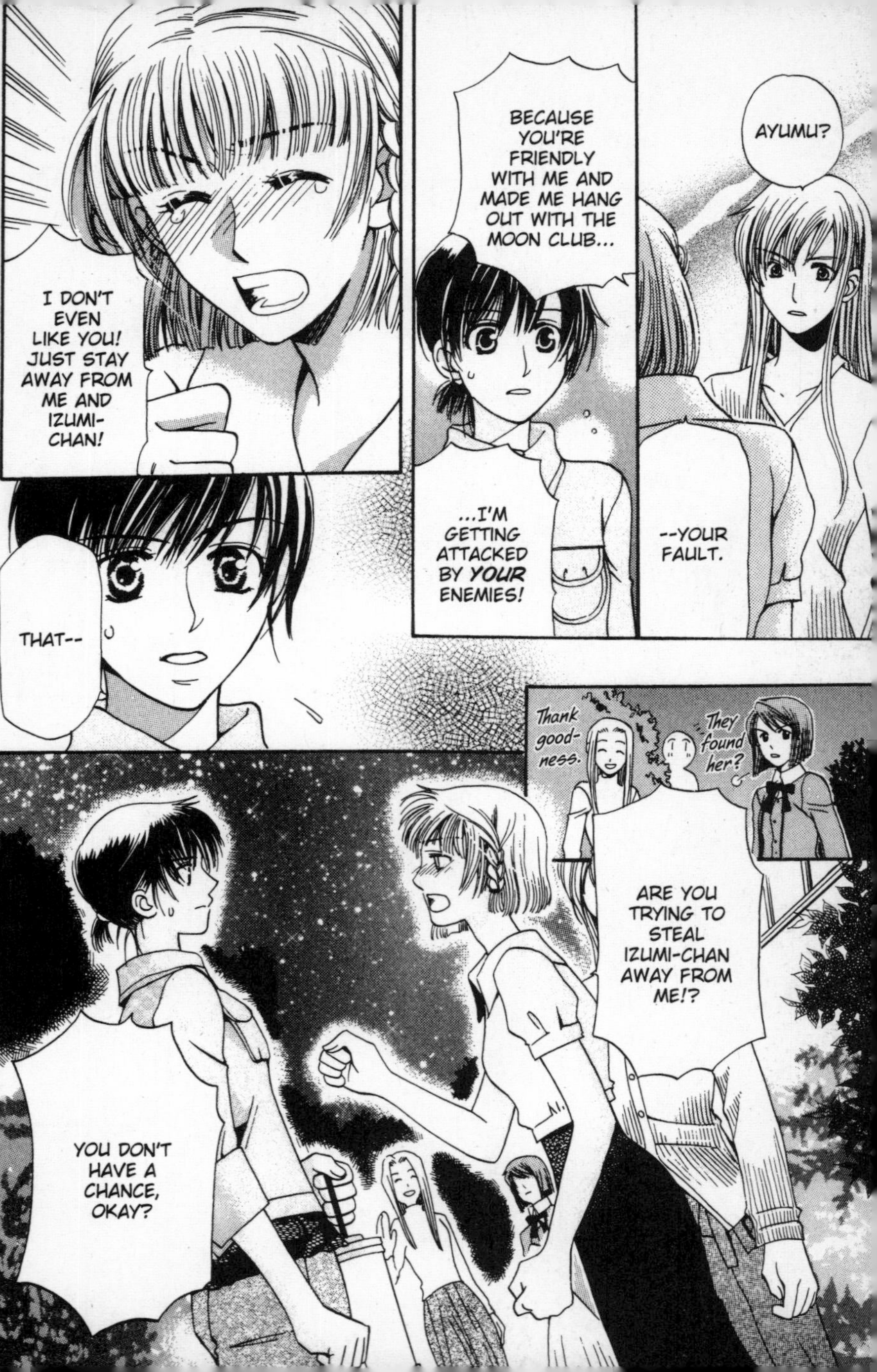
AYUMU?
--YOUR FAULT.
BECAUSE YOU'RE FRIENDLY WITH ME AND MADE ME HANG OUT WITH THE MOON CLUB...
...I'M GETTING ATTACKED BY *YOUR* ENEMIES!
I DON'T EVEN LIKE YOU! JUST STAY AWAY FROM ME AND IZUMI-CHAN!
THAT--
They found her?
Thank goodness.
ARE YOU TRYING TO STEAL IZUMI-CHAN AWAY FROM ME!?
YOU DON'T HAVE A CHANCE, OKAY?

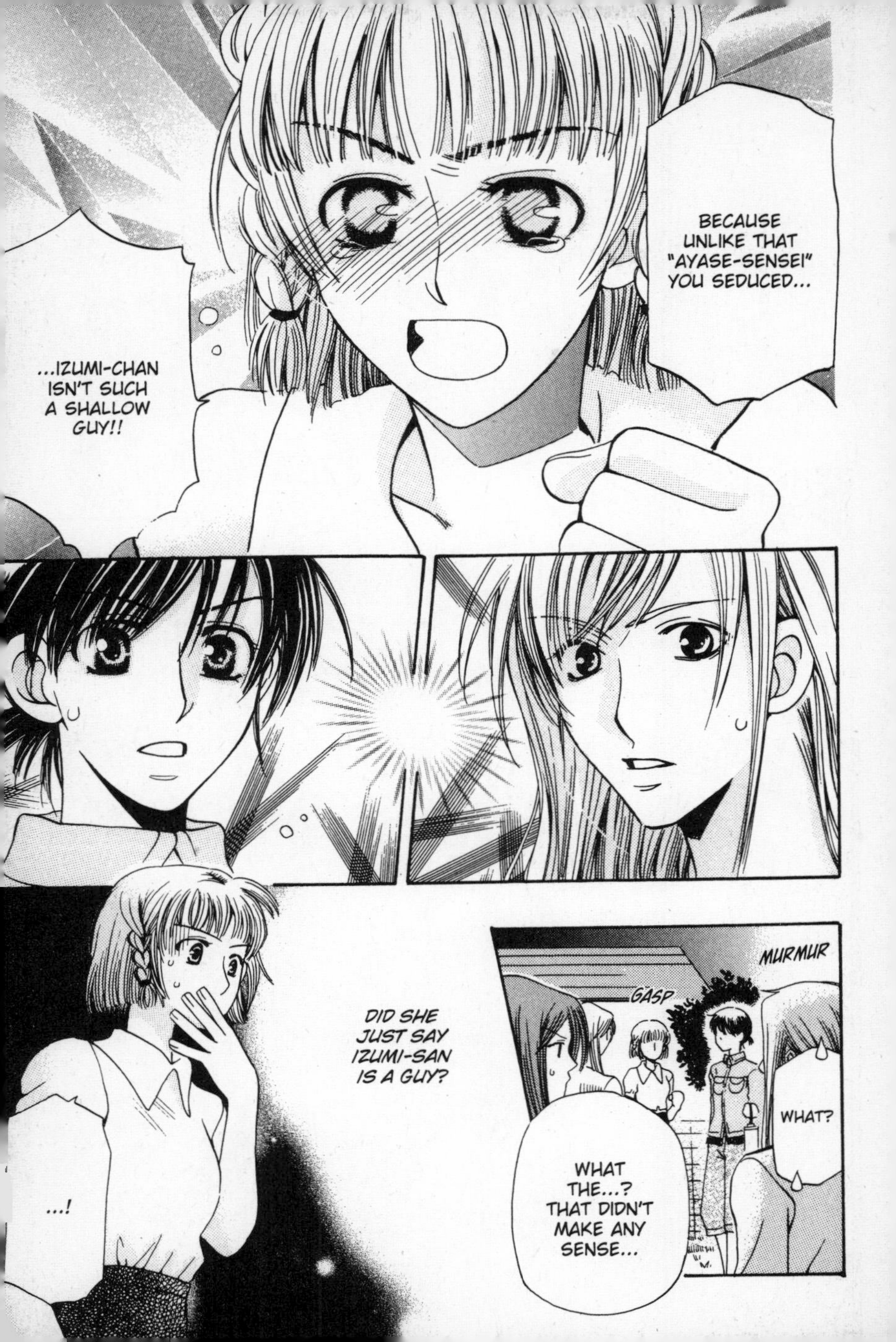
BECAUSE UNLIKE THAT "AYASE-SENSEI" YOU SEDUCED...
...IZUMI-CHAN ISN'T SUCH A SHALLOW GUY!!
MURMUR
GASP
WHAT?
WHAT THE...? THAT DIDN'T MAKE ANY SENSE...
DID SHE JUST SAY IZUMI-SAN IS A GUY?
...!

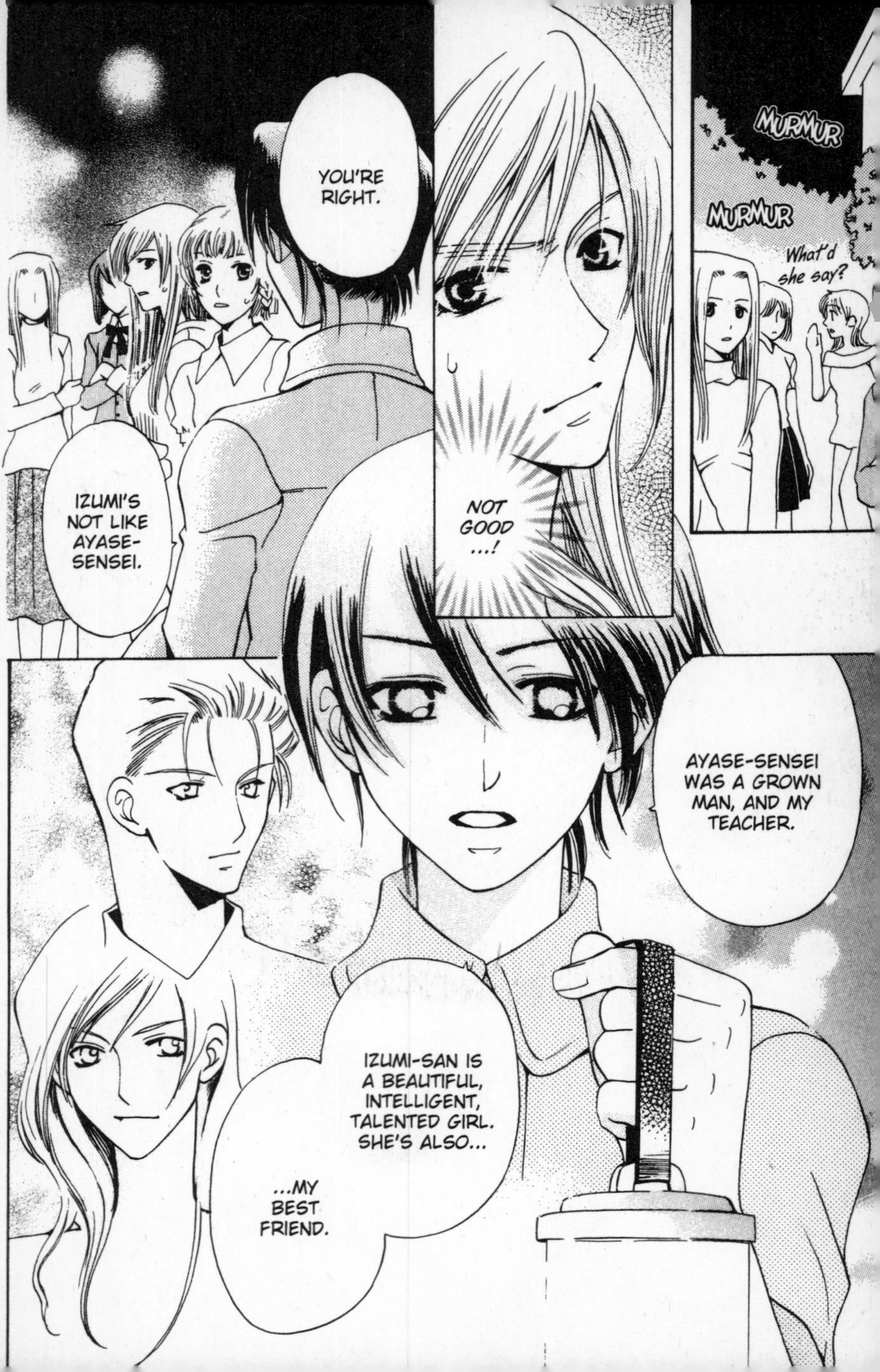
MURMUR
MURMUR
What'd she say?
NOT GOOD ...!
YOU'RE RIGHT.
IZUMI'S NOT LIKE AYASE-SENSEI.
AYASE-SENSEI WAS A GROWN MAN, AND MY TEACHER.
IZUMI-SAN IS A BEAUTIFUL, INTELLIGENT, TALENTED GIRL. SHE'S ALSO...
...MY BEST FRIEND.

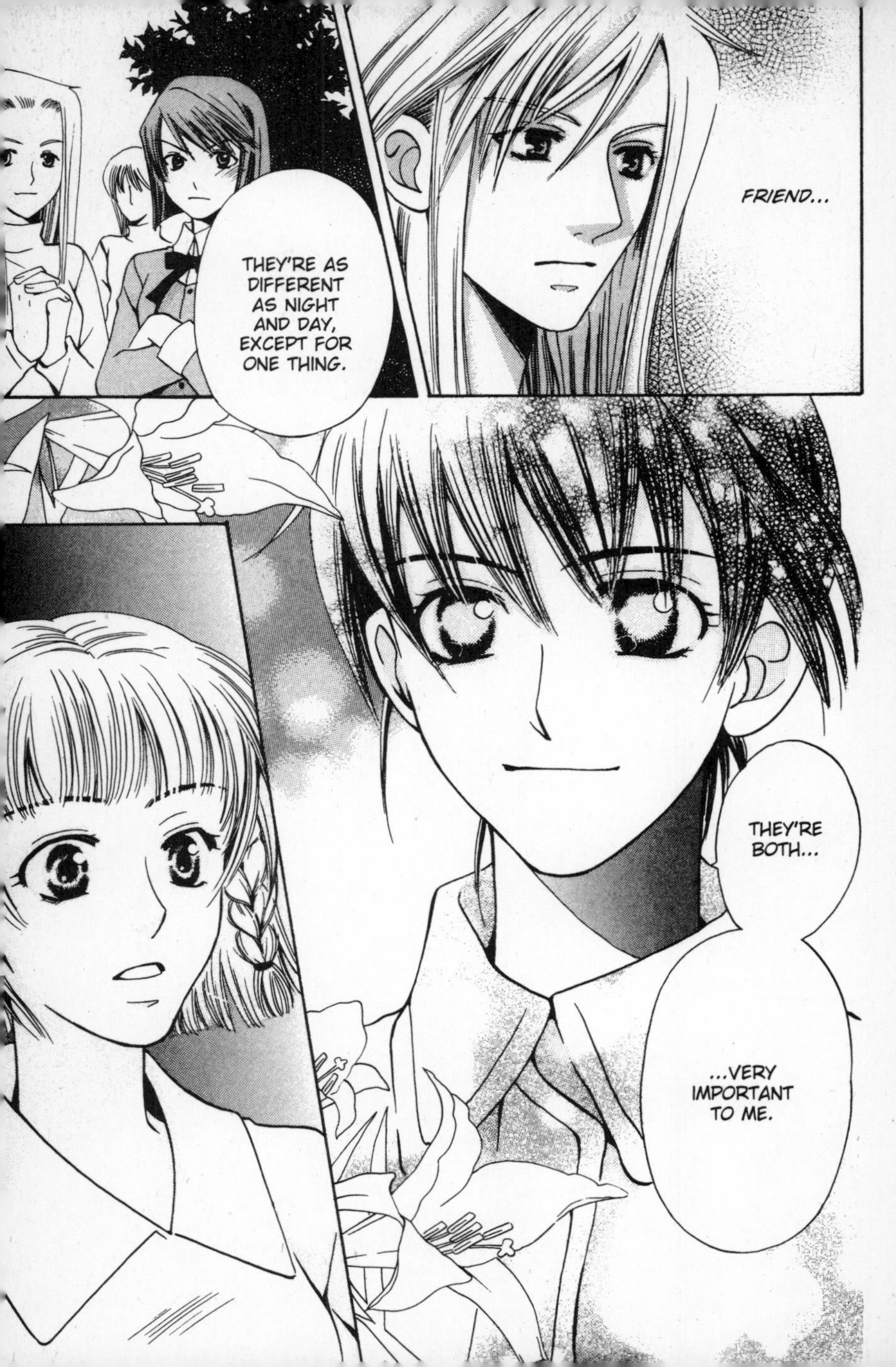
FRIEND...
THEY'RE AS DIFFERENT AS NIGHT AND DAY, EXCEPT FOR ONE THING.
THEY'RE BOTH...
...VERY IMPORTANT TO ME.

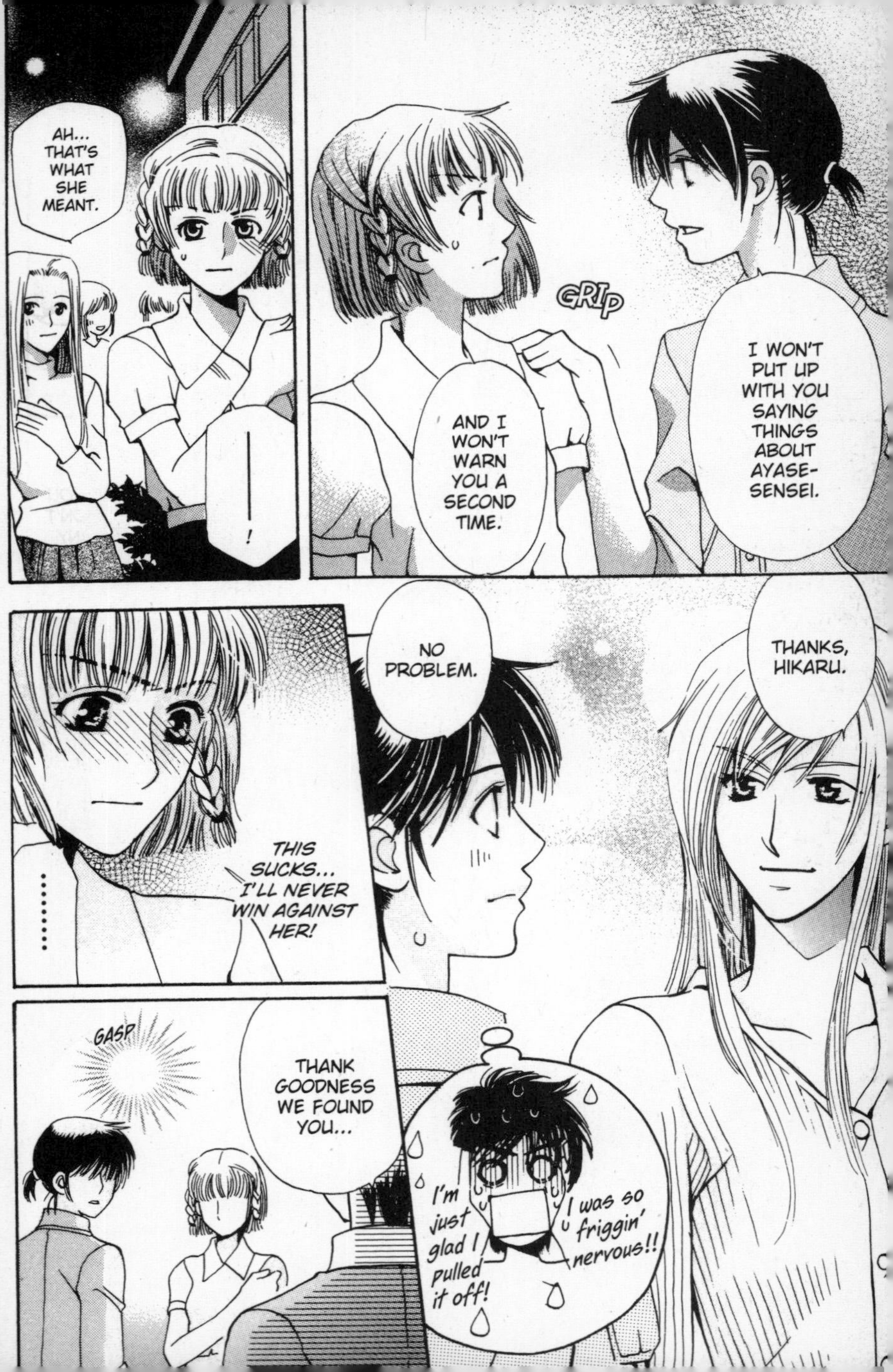
I WON'T PUT UP WITH YOU SAYING THINGS ABOUT AYASE-SENSEI.
GRIP
AND I WON'T WARN YOU A SECOND TIME.
AH... THAT'S WHAT SHE MEANT.
...!
THANKS, HIKARU.
NO PROBLEM.
I was so friggin' nervous!!
I'm just glad I pulled it off!
THIS SUCKS... I'LL NEVER WIN AGAINST HER!
....
GASP
THANK GOODNESS WE FOUND YOU...

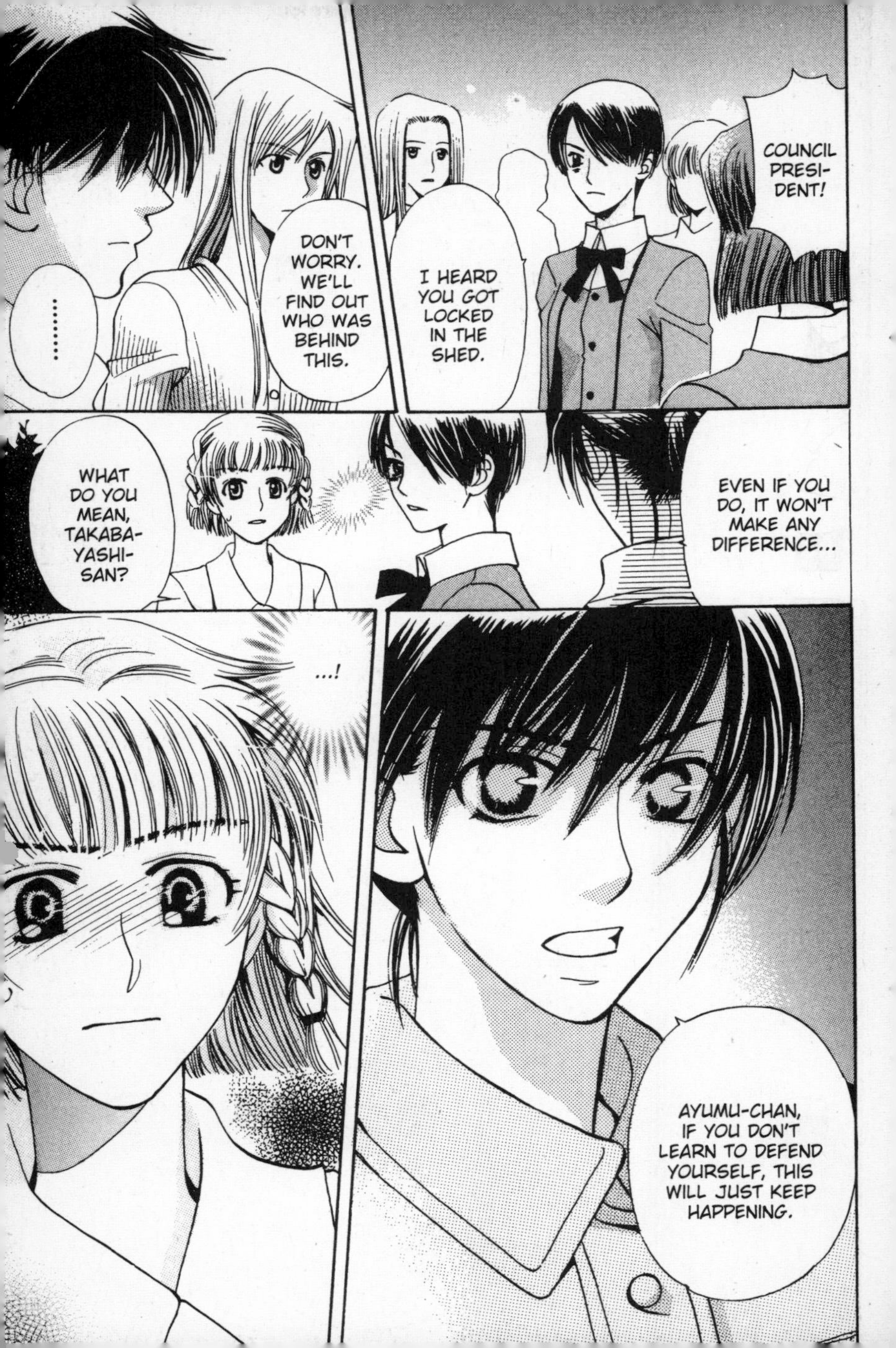
COUNCIL PRESIDENT!
I HEARD YOU GOT LOCKED IN THE SHED.
DON'T WORRY. WE'LL FIND OUT WHO WAS BEHIND THIS.
......
EVEN IF YOU DO, IT WON'T MAKE ANY DIFFERENCE...
WHAT DO YOU MEAN, TAKABAYASHI-SAN?
AYUMU-CHAN, IF YOU DON'T LEARN TO DEFEND YOURSELF, THIS WILL JUST KEEP HAPPENING.
...!

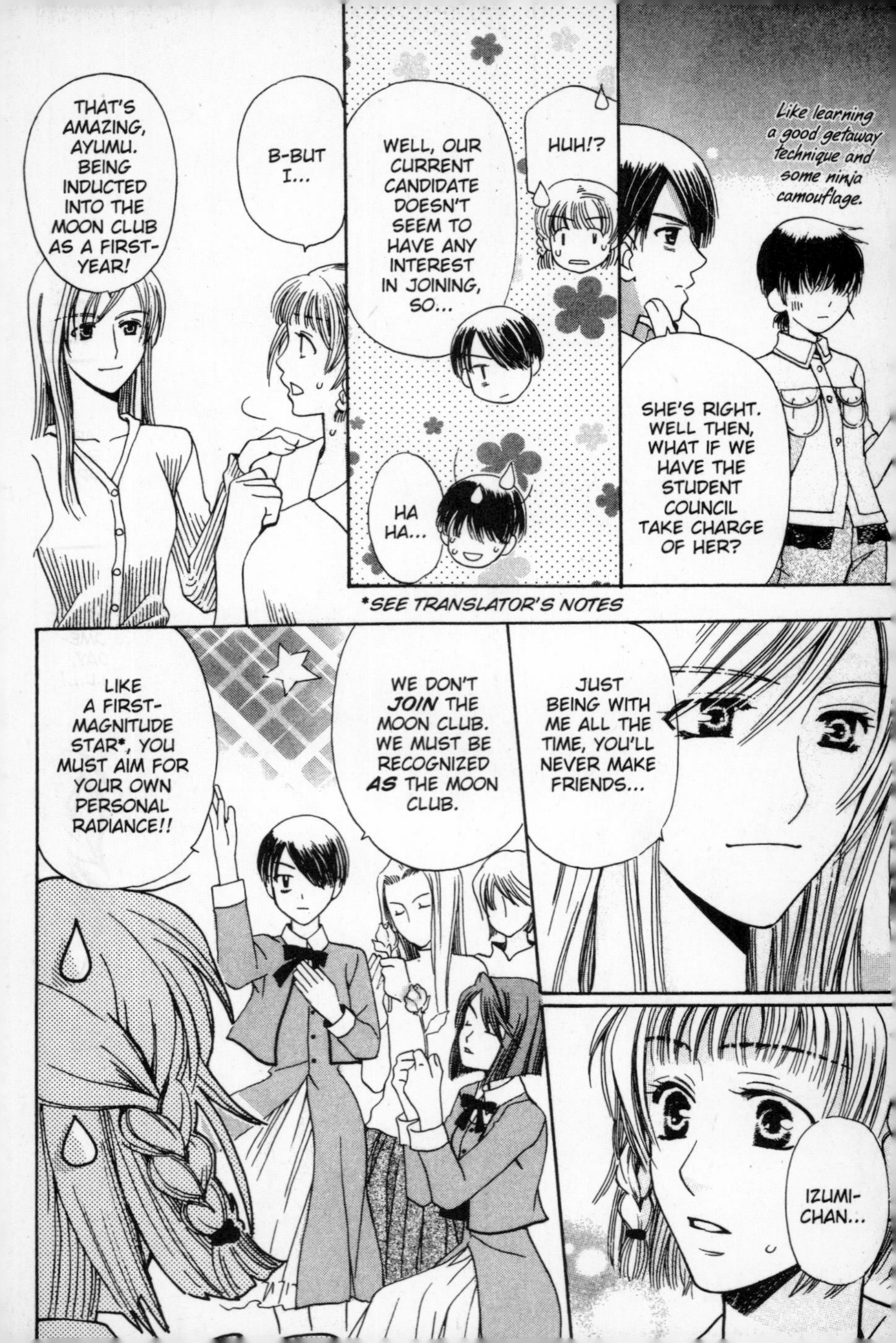
Like learning a good getaway technique and some ninja camouflage.
SHE'S RIGHT. WELL THEN, WHAT IF WE HAVE THE STUDENT COUNCIL TAKE CHARGE OF HER?
WELL, OUR CURRENT CANDIDATE DOESN'T SEEM TO HAVE ANY INTEREST IN JOINING, SO...
HUH!?
HA HA...
THAT'S AMAZING, AYUMU. BEING INDUCTED INTO THE MOON CLUB AS A FIRST-YEAR!
B-BUT I...
*SEE TRANSLATOR'S NOTES
JUST BEING WITH ME ALL THE TIME, YOU'LL NEVER MAKE FRIENDS...
IZUMI-CHAN...
WE DON'T JOIN THE MOON CLUB. WE MUST BE RECOGNIZED AS THE MOON CLUB.
LIKE A FIRST-MAGNITUDE STAR*, YOU MUST AIM FOR YOUR OWN PERSONAL RADIANCE!!

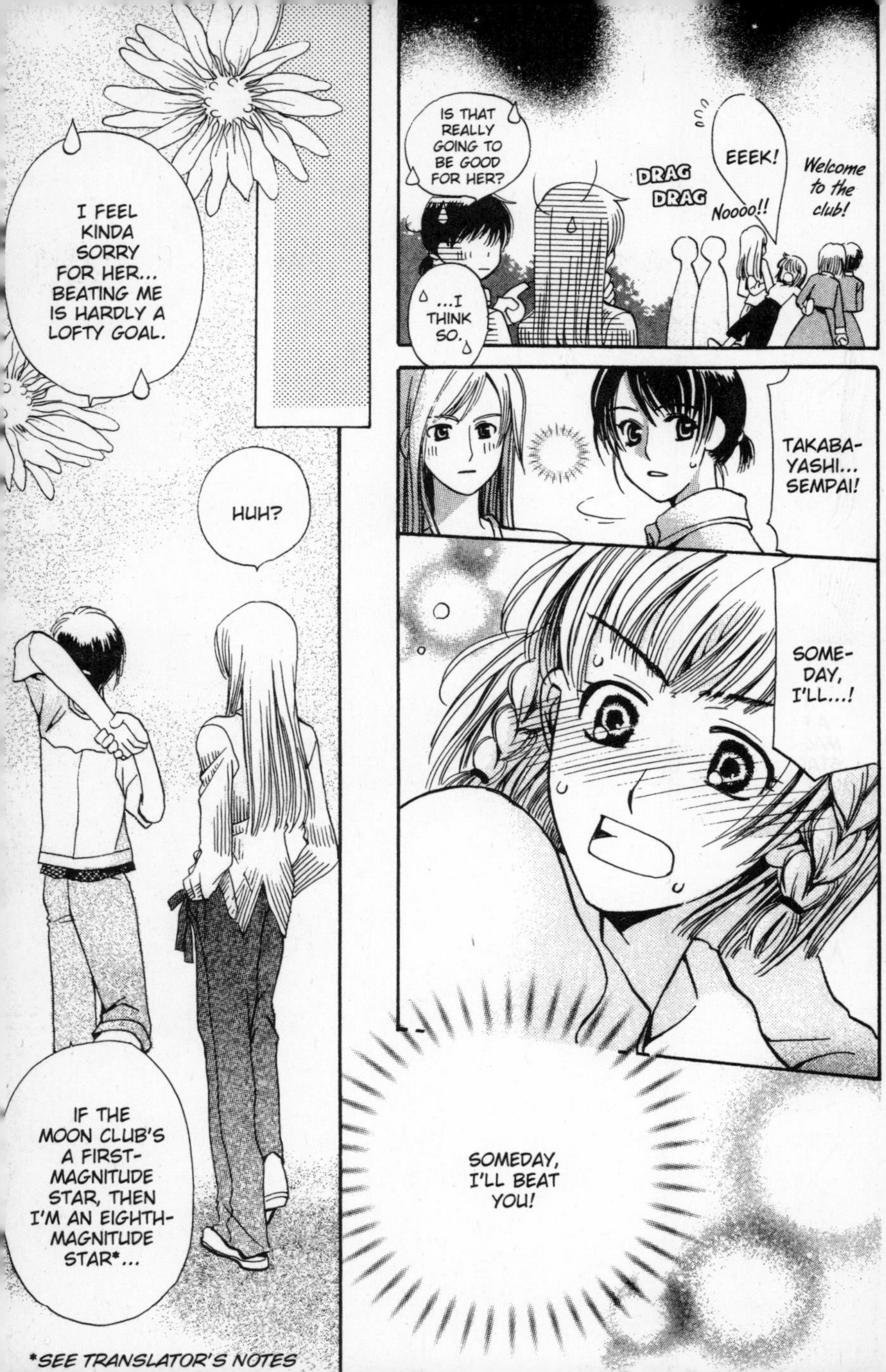
Welcome to the club!
EEEK! Noooo!!
DRAG DRAG
IS THAT REALLY GOING TO BE GOOD FOR HER?
...I THINK SO.
TAKABA-YASHI... SEMPAI!
SOME-DAY, I'LL...!
SOMEDAY, I'LL BEAT YOU!
I FEEL KINDA SORRY FOR HER... BEATING ME IS HARDLY A LOFTY GOAL.
HUH?
IF THE MOON CLUB'S A FIRST-MAGNITUDE STAR, THEN I'M AN EIGHTH-MAGNITUDE STAR*...

*SEE TRANSLATOR'S NOTES

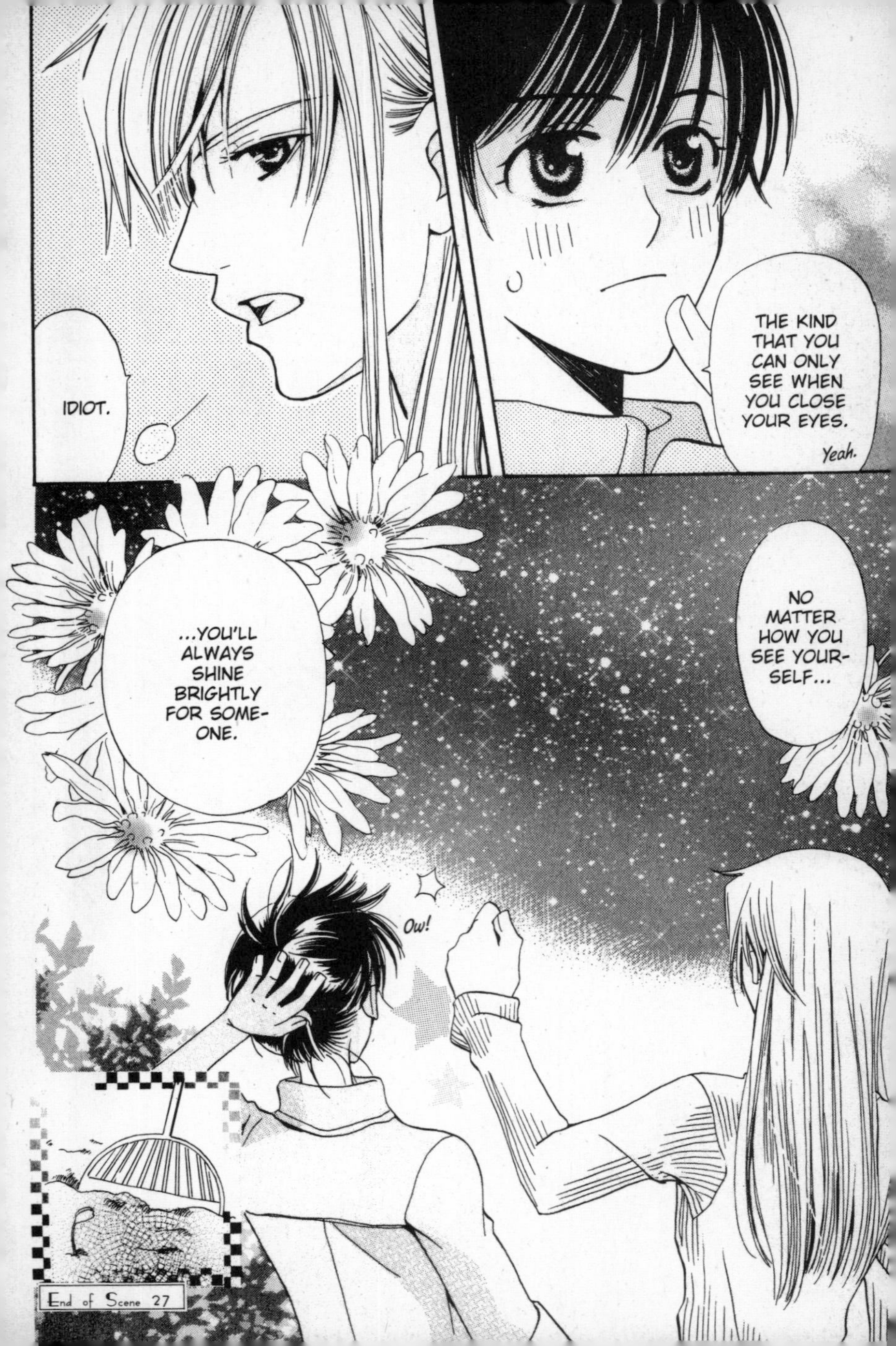
THE KIND THAT YOU CAN ONLY SEE WHEN YOU CLOSE YOUR EYES.
Yeah.
IDIOT.
NO MATTER HOW YOU SEE YOUR-SELF...
...YOU'LL ALWAYS SHINE BRIGHTLY FOR SOME-ONE.
Ow!
End of Scene 27

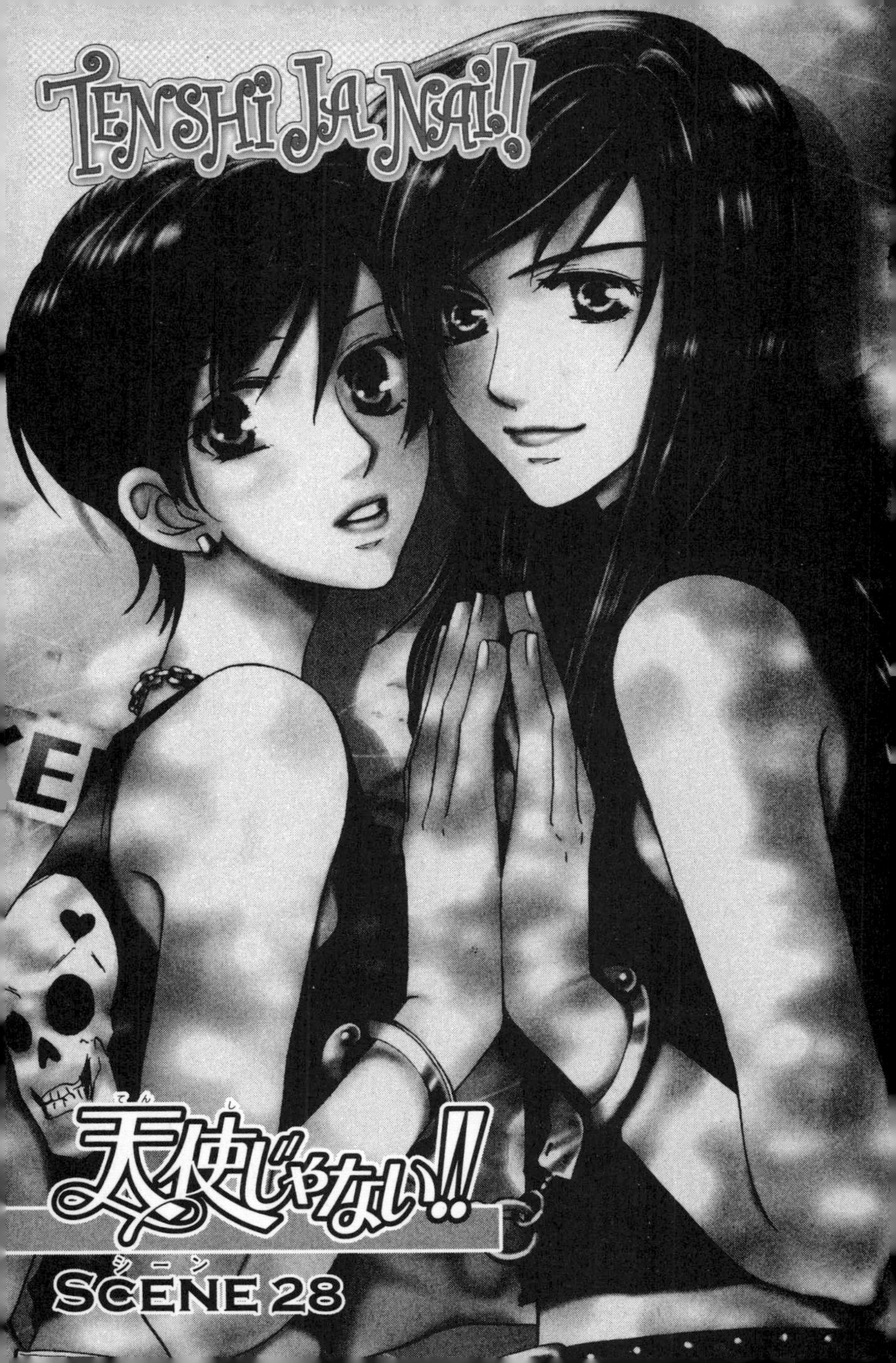
TENSHI JA NAI!!
天使じゃない!!
SCENE 28

EVEN THOUGH I'D FINALLY ESCAPED THE CLUTCHES OF THE STUDENT COUNCIL...

...AND RETURNED TO MY NORMAL ROUTINE WITH IZUMI-SAN...

...DUE TO SOME UNAVOID-ABLE CIRCUM-STANCES...

I THOUGHT YOU KNEW ME BETTER THAN THAT, IZUMI-SAN!

IS THAT SO!? WELL SOR-RY FOR DISAPPOINTING YOU!

HMPH

Kikyo Izuki (16 years old)
Born: July 18
Blood Type: AB

Her name hasn't really come out at all yet. She's totally the athletic type. For some reason, she's decided she just doesn't like Hikaru. She had a bad experience with love when she was younger, which is why she's so hard on herself.

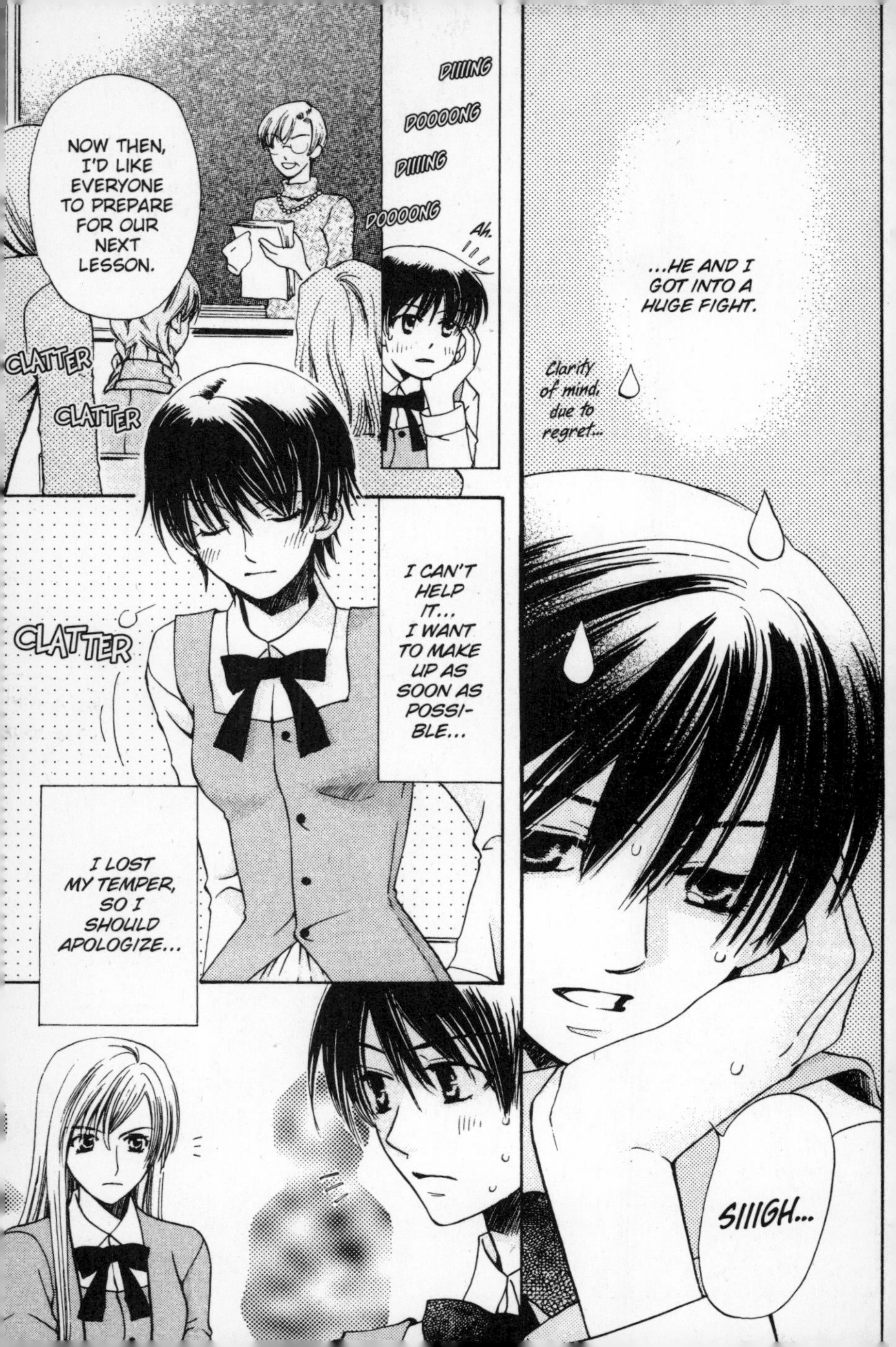
...HE AND I GOT INTO A HUGE FIGHT.
Clarity of mind, due to regret...
SIIIGH...
DIIIING
DOOOONG
DIIIING
DOOOONG
Ah.
NOW THEN, I'D LIKE EVERYONE TO PREPARE FOR OUR NEXT LESSON.
CLATTER
CLATTER
I CAN'T HELP IT... I WANT TO MAKE UP AS SOON AS POSSI-BLE...
CLATTER
I LOST MY TEMPER, SO I SHOULD APOLOGIZE...

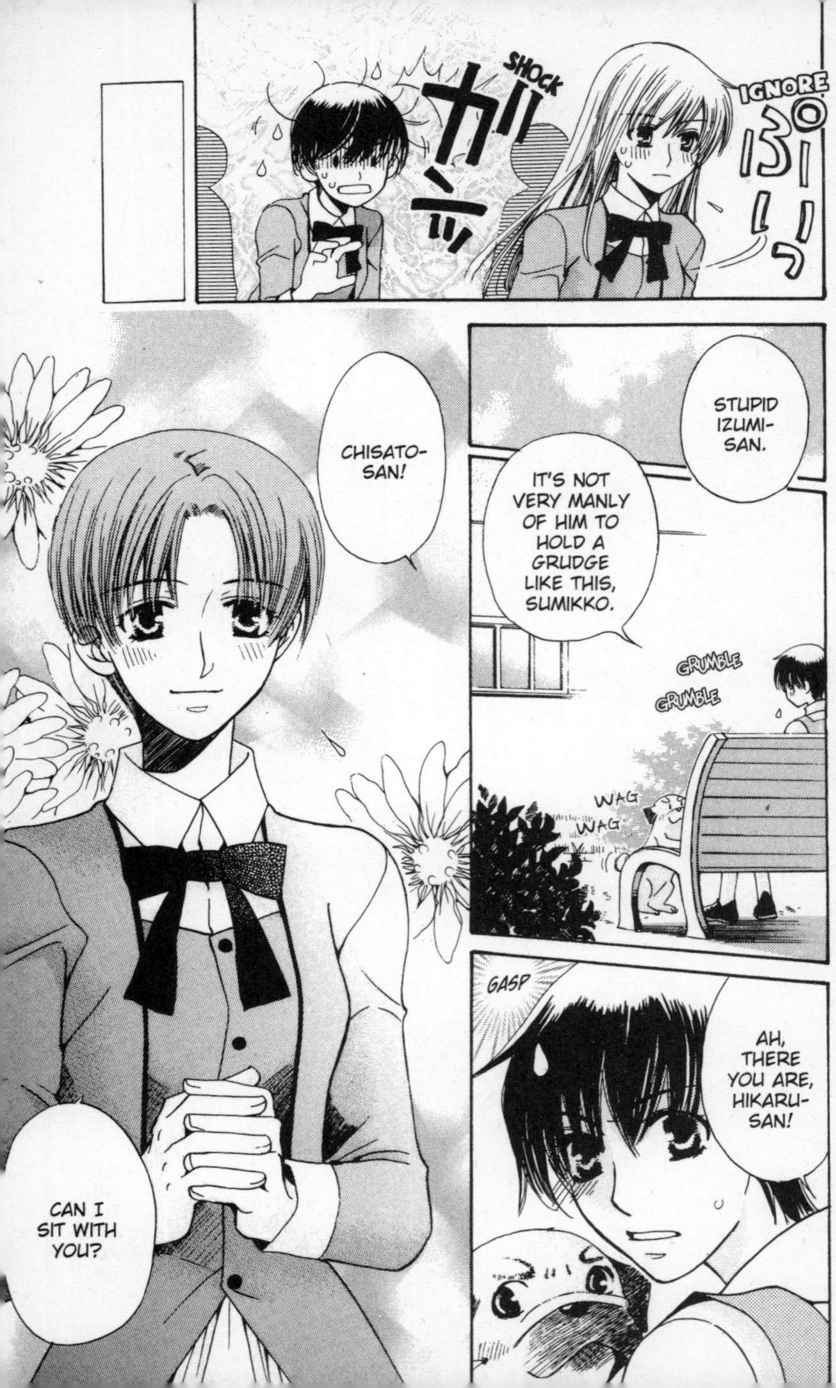
IGNORE
SHOCK
STUPID IZUMI-SAN.
IT'S NOT VERY MANLY OF HIM TO HOLD A GRUDGE LIKE THIS, SUMIKKO.
GRUMBLE
GRUMBLE
WAG
WAG
GASP
AH, THERE YOU ARE, HIKARU-SAN!
CHISATO-SAN!
CAN I SIT WITH YOU?

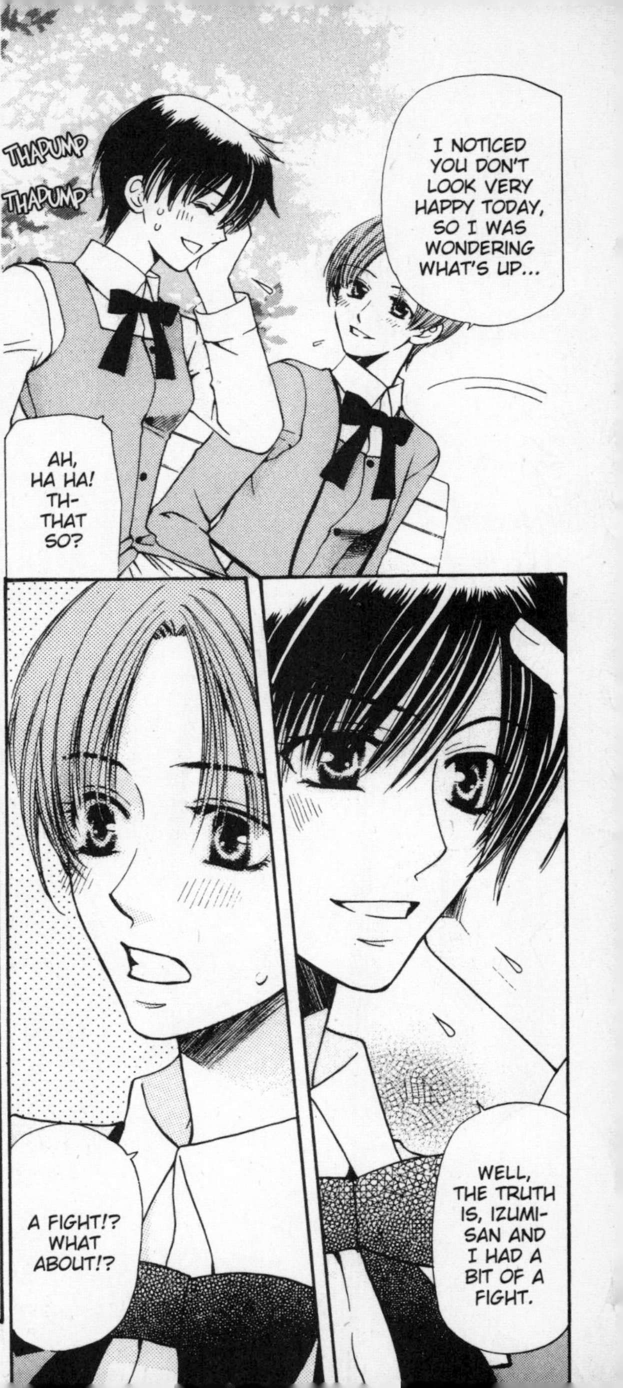
I NOTICED YOU DON'T LOOK VERY HAPPY TODAY, SO I WAS WONDERING WHAT'S UP...
THAPUMP
THAPUMP
AH, HA HA! TH- THAT SO?
WELL, THE TRUTH IS, IZUMI-SAN AND I HAD A BIT OF A FIGHT.
A FIGHT!? WHAT ABOUT!?

A Day in the Life

When I'm tired, people's kindness really hits home for me. At the beginning of the year, T-san came to help me as an assistant. Her house is near the studio, so the day before deadlines she stays up late working for me.

But, T-san!! I'm begging you!! When I say, "I'm going to go take a nap. Wake me up in an hour and a half, 'kay?" Don't just let me sleep as long as I want.

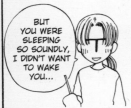

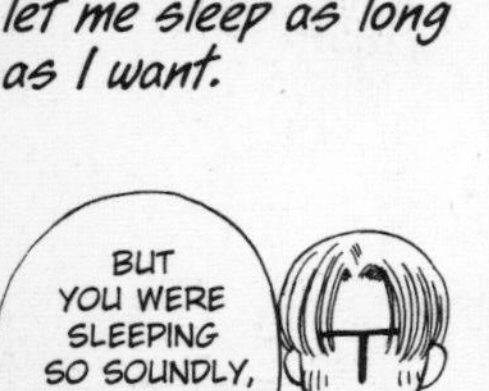
BUT YOU WERE SLEEPING SO SOUNDLY, I DIDN'T WANT TO WAKE YOU...

Yeah, but the deadline's tomorrow! I've got to hand in the roughs! But this just is another sign of T-san's kindness... or should I even call it kindness?

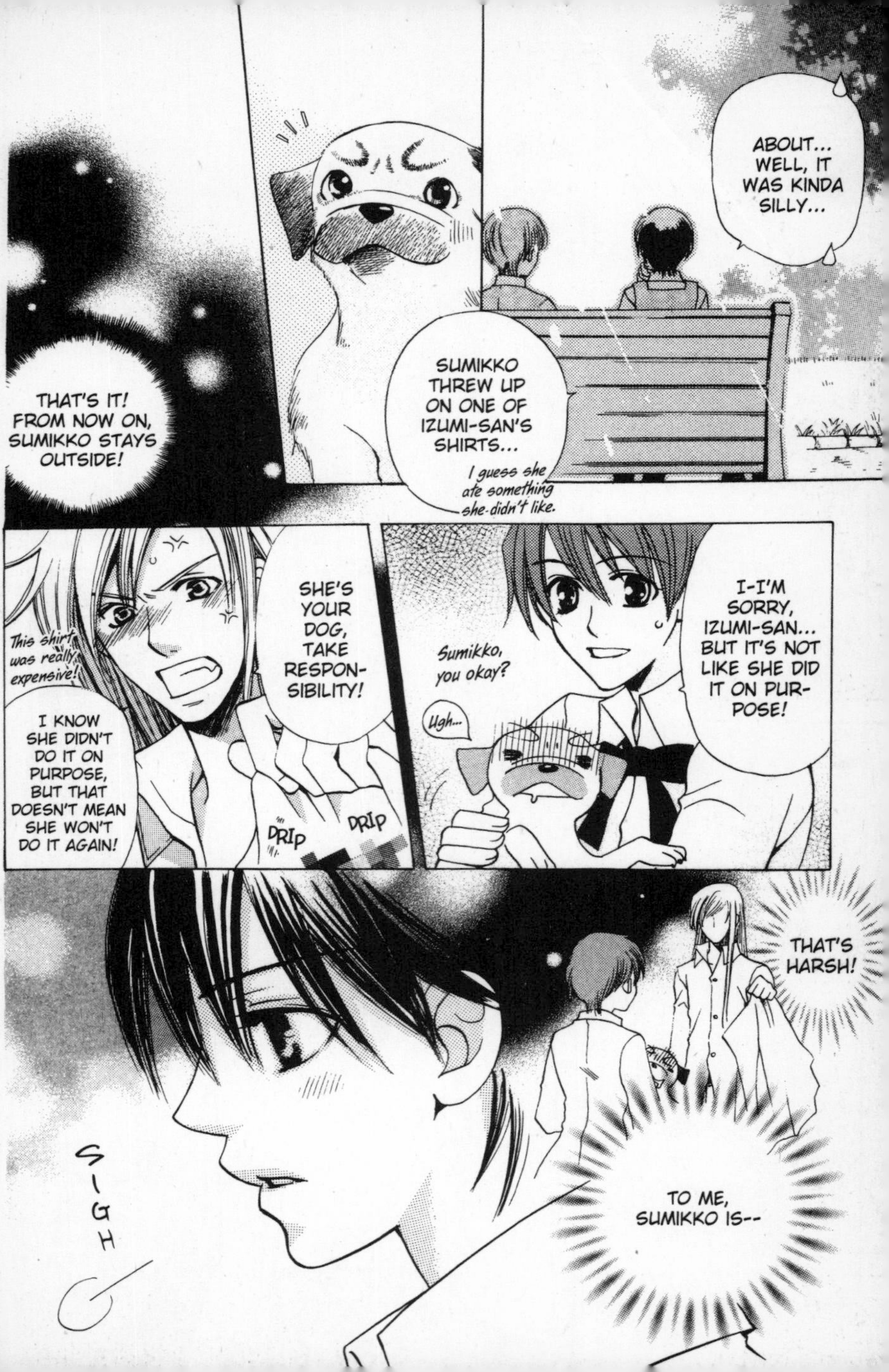
ABOUT... WELL, IT WAS KINDA SILLY...
SUMIKKO THREW UP ON ONE OF IZUMI-SAN'S SHIRTS...
I guess she ate something she didn't like.
THAT'S IT! FROM NOW ON, SUMIKKO STAYS OUTSIDE!
I-I'M SORRY, IZUMI-SAN... BUT IT'S NOT LIKE SHE DID IT ON PURPOSE!
Sumikko, you okay?
Ugh...
SHE'S YOUR DOG, TAKE RESPON-SIBILITY!
This shirt was really expensive!
I KNOW SHE DIDN'T DO IT ON PURPOSE, BUT THAT DOESN'T MEAN SHE WON'T DO IT AGAIN!
DRIP
DRIP
THAT'S HARSH!
TO ME, SUMIKKO IS--
SIGH

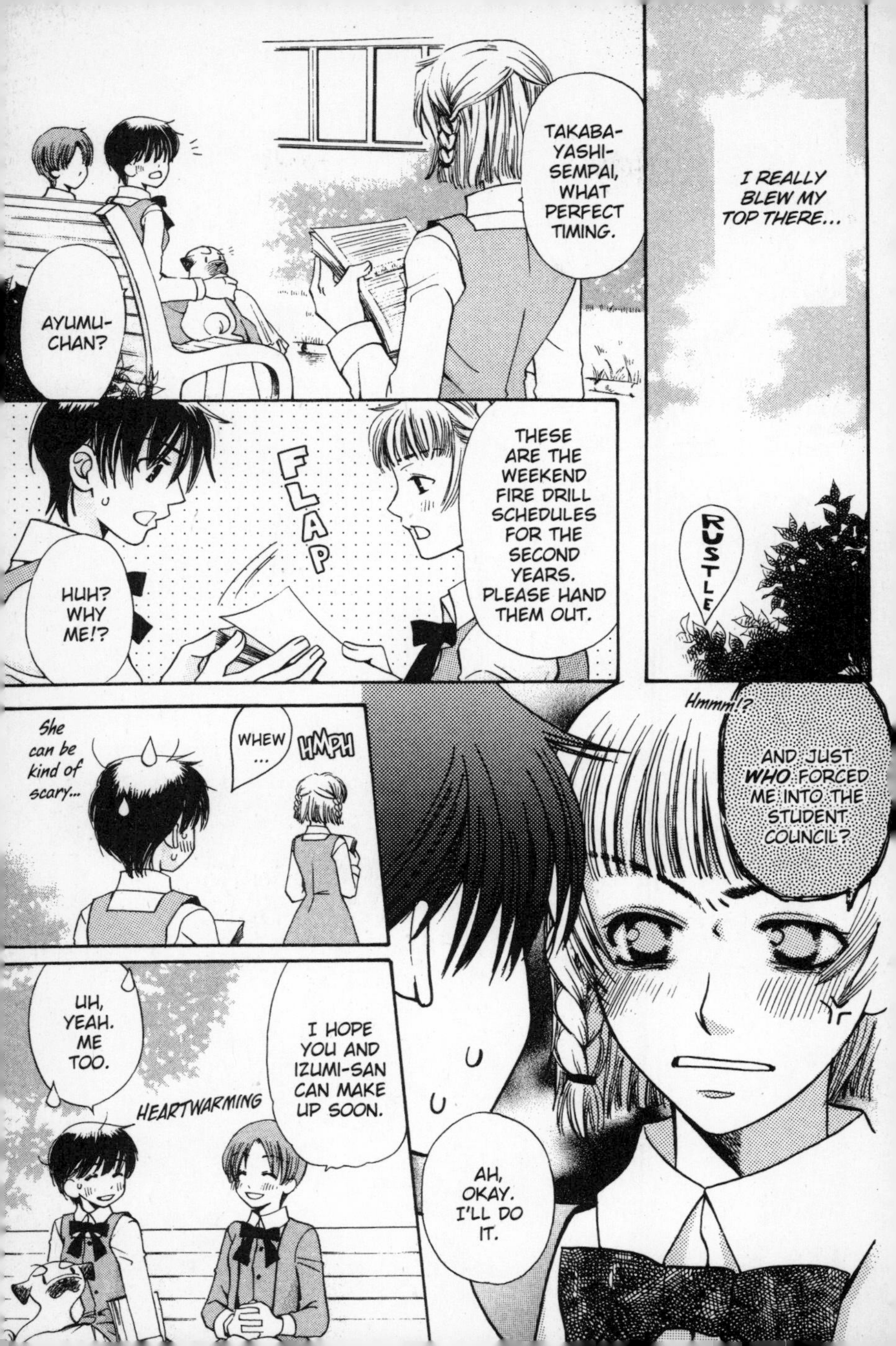

I REALLY BLEW MY TOP THERE...
RUSTLE
TAKABAYASHI-SEMPAI, WHAT PERFECT TIMING.
AYUMU-CHAN?
THESE ARE THE WEEKEND FIRE DRILL SCHEDULES FOR THE SECOND YEARS. PLEASE HAND THEM OUT.
FLAP
HUH? WHY ME!?
Hmmm!?
AND JUST WHO FORCED ME INTO THE STUDENT COUNCIL?
AH, OKAY. I'LL DO IT.
WHEW ...
HMPH
She can be kind of scary...
I HOPE YOU AND IZUMI-SAN CAN MAKE UP SOON.
HEARTWARMING
UH, YEAH. ME TOO.

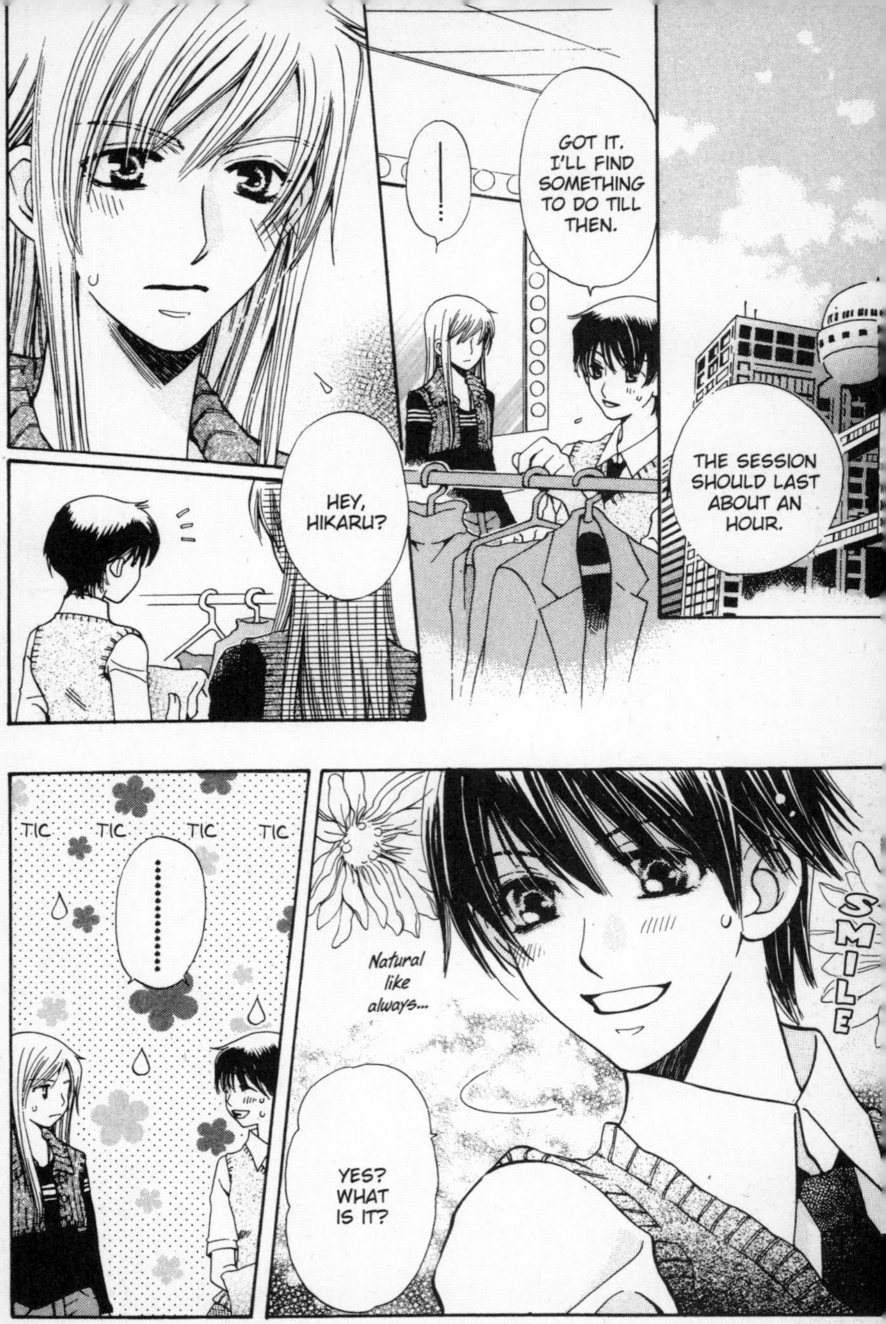
THE SESSION SHOULD LAST ABOUT AN HOUR.
GOT IT. I'LL FIND SOMETHING TO DO TILL THEN.
……
HEY, HIKARU?
SMILE
Natural like always...
YES? WHAT IS IT?
TIC TIC TIC TIC
……

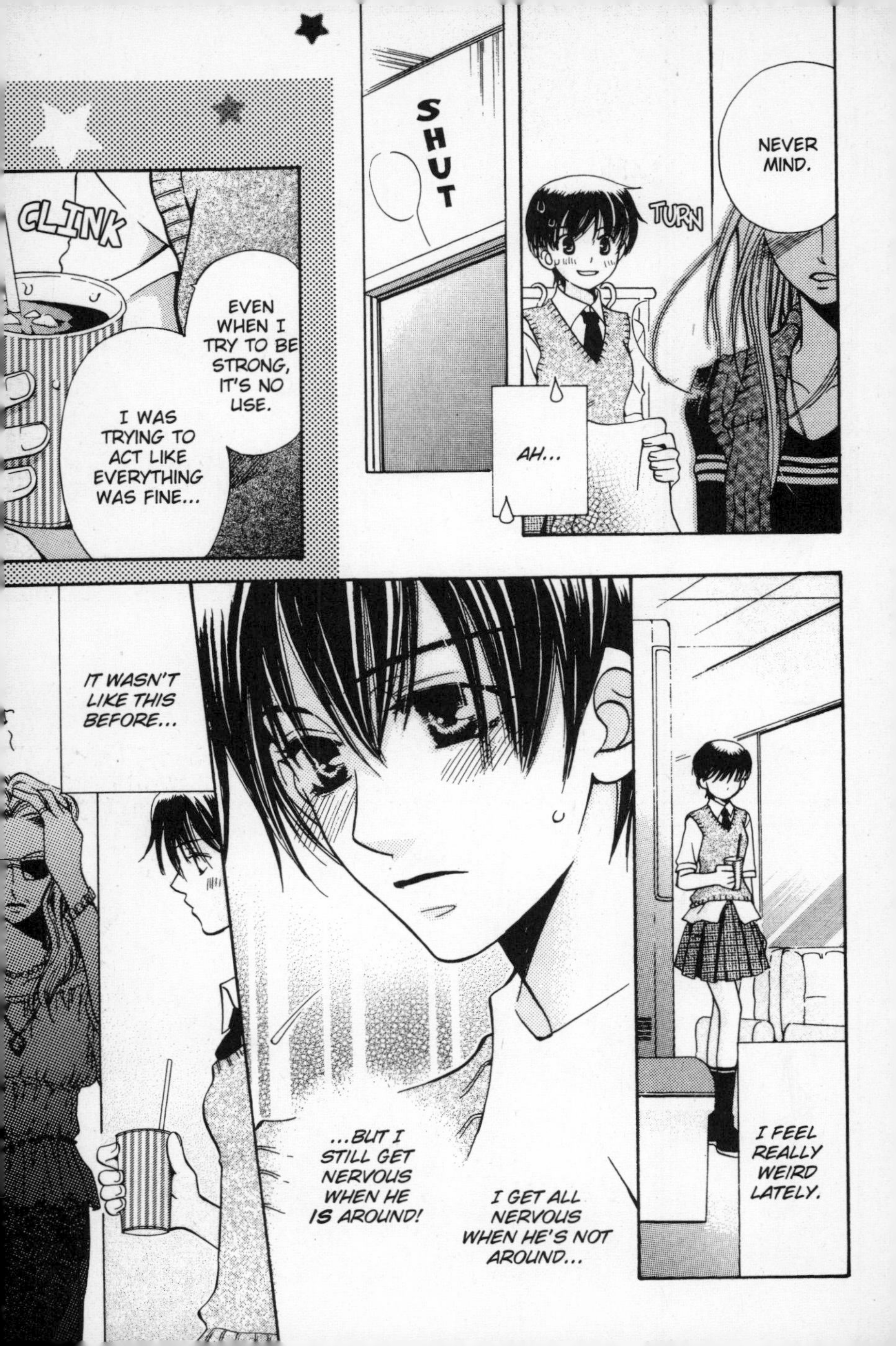
NEVER MIND.
TURN
AH...
SHUT
CLINK
EVEN WHEN I TRY TO BE STRONG, IT'S NO USE.
I WAS TRYING TO ACT LIKE EVERYTHING WAS FINE...
I FEEL REALLY WEIRD LATELY.
I GET ALL NERVOUS WHEN HE'S NOT AROUND...
...BUT I STILL GET NERVOUS WHEN HE IS AROUND!
IT WASN'T LIKE THIS BEFORE...

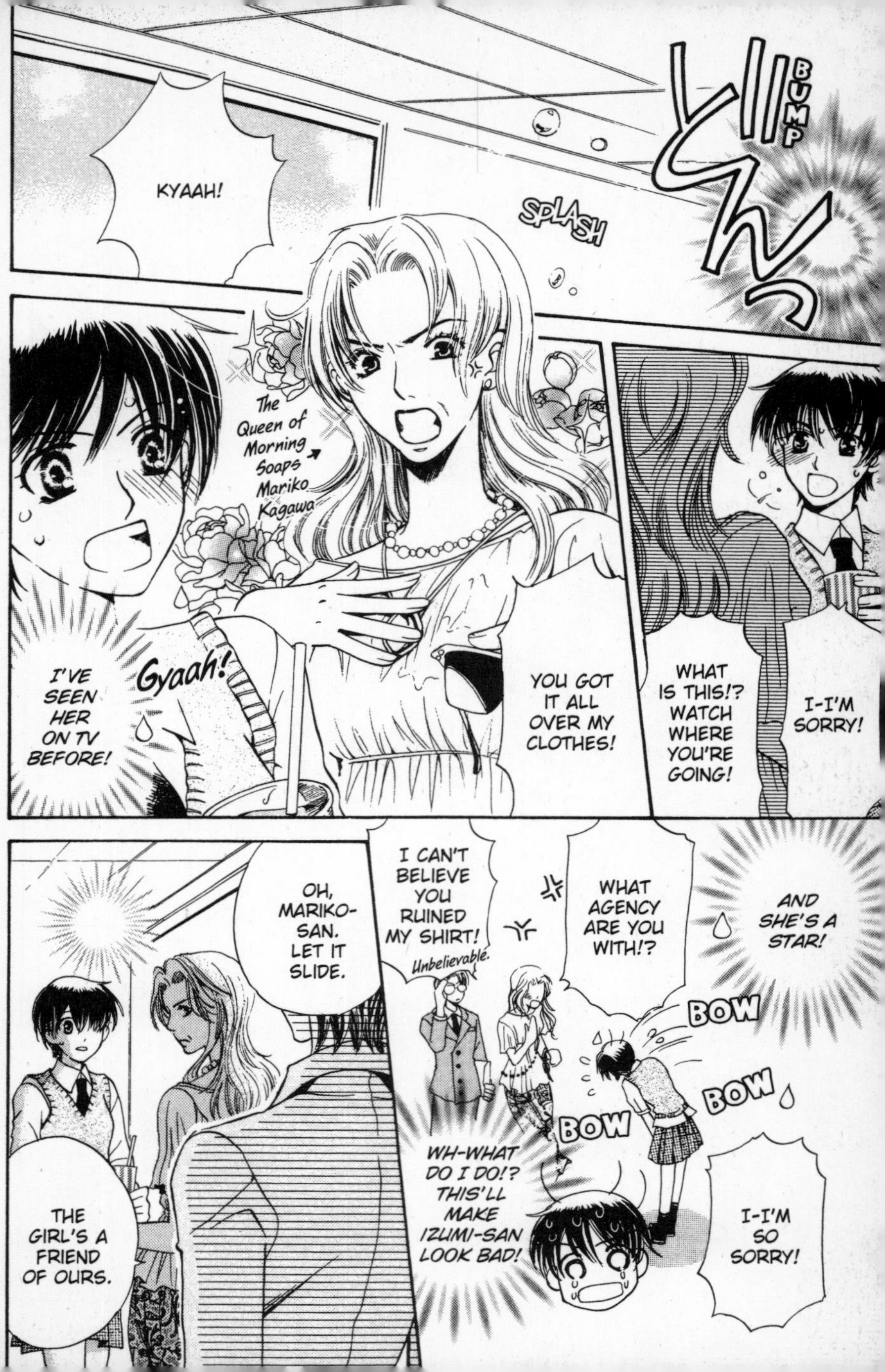
BUMP
SPLASH
KYAAH!
I-I'M SORRY!
WHAT IS THIS!? WATCH WHERE YOU'RE GOING!
YOU GOT IT ALL OVER MY CLOTHES!
The Queen of Morning Soaps → Mariko Kagawa
Gyaah!
I'VE SEEN HER ON TV BEFORE!
AND SHE'S A STAR!
WHAT AGENCY ARE YOU WITH!?
I CAN'T BELIEVE YOU RUINED MY SHIRT!
Unbelievable.
BOW
BOW
BOW
I-I'M SO SORRY!
WH-WHAT DO I DO!? THIS'LL MAKE IZUMI-SAN LOOK BAD!
OH, MARIKO-SAN. LET IT SLIDE.
THE GIRL'S A FRIEND OF OURS.

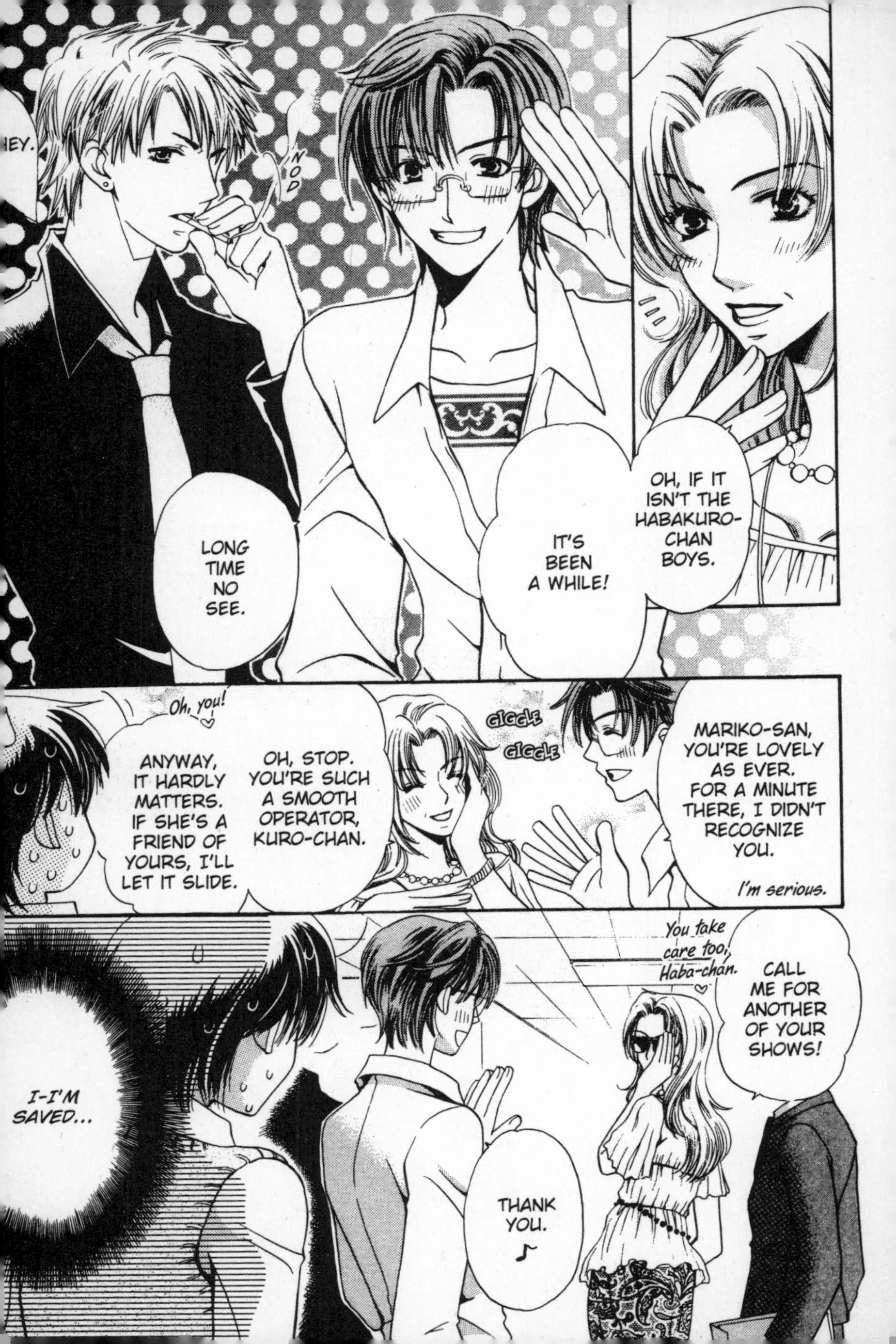
OH, IF IT ISN'T THE HABAKURO-CHAN BOYS.
IT'S BEEN A WHILE!
NOD
LONG TIME NO SEE.
HEY.
MARIKO-SAN, YOU'RE LOVELY AS EVER. FOR A MINUTE THERE, I DIDN'T RECOGNIZE YOU.
I'm serious.
GIGGLE
GIGGLE
OH, STOP. YOU'RE SUCH A SMOOTH OPERATOR, KURO-CHAN.
Oh, you!
ANYWAY, IT HARDLY MATTERS. IF SHE'S A FRIEND OF YOURS, I'LL LET IT SLIDE.
CALL ME FOR ANOTHER OF YOUR SHOWS!
You take care too, Haba-chan.
THANK YOU.
I-I'M SAVED...

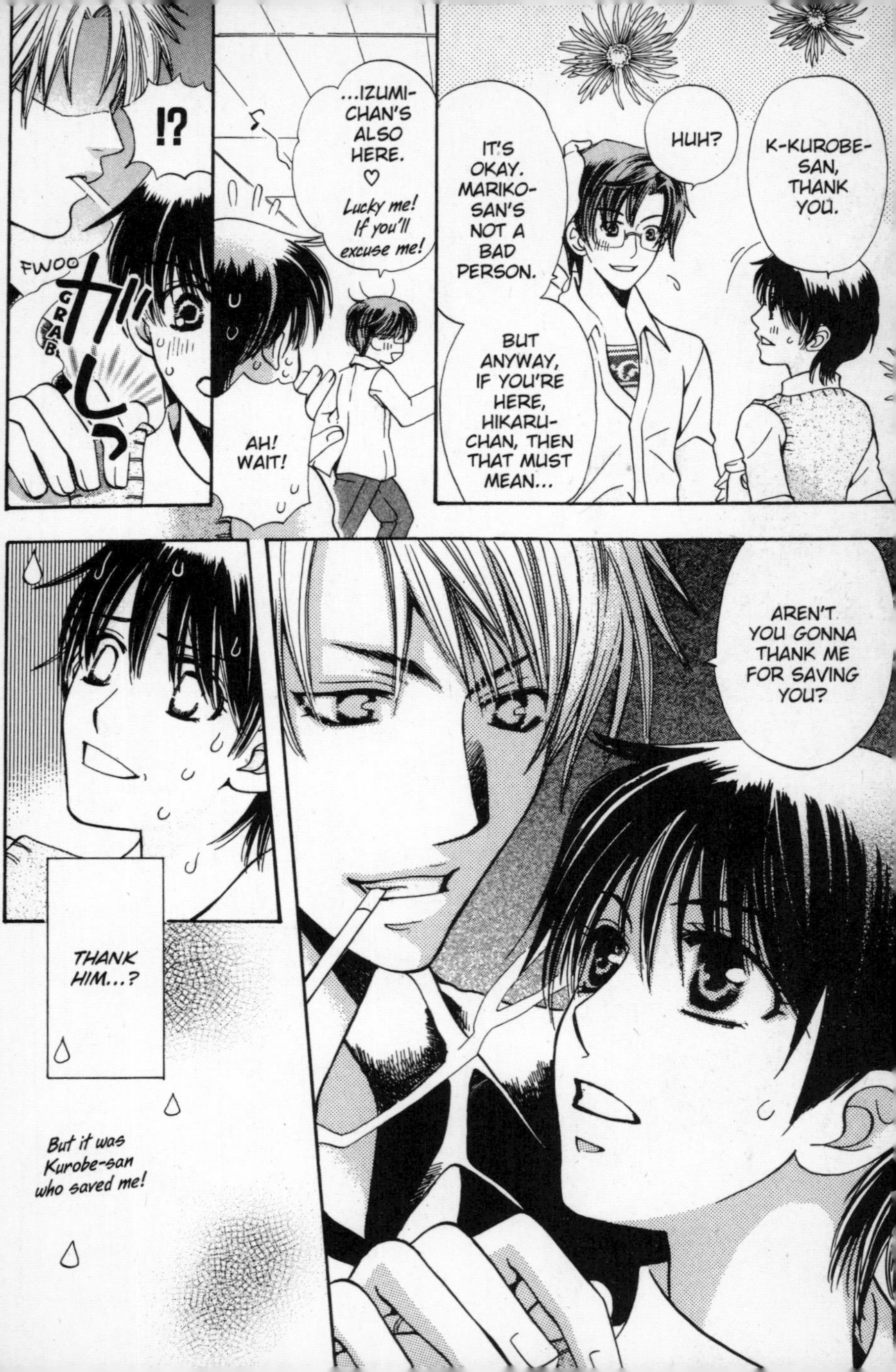
K-KUROBE-SAN, THANK YOU.
HUH?
IT'S OKAY. MARIKO-SAN'S NOT A BAD PERSON.
BUT ANYWAY, IF YOU'RE HERE, HIKARU-CHAN, THEN THAT MUST MEAN...
...IZUMI-CHAN'S ALSO HERE. ♡
Lucky me! If you'll excuse me!
AH! WAIT!
!?
FWOO
GRAB
AREN'T YOU GONNA THANK ME FOR SAVING YOU?
THANK HIM...?
But it was Kurobe-san who saved me!

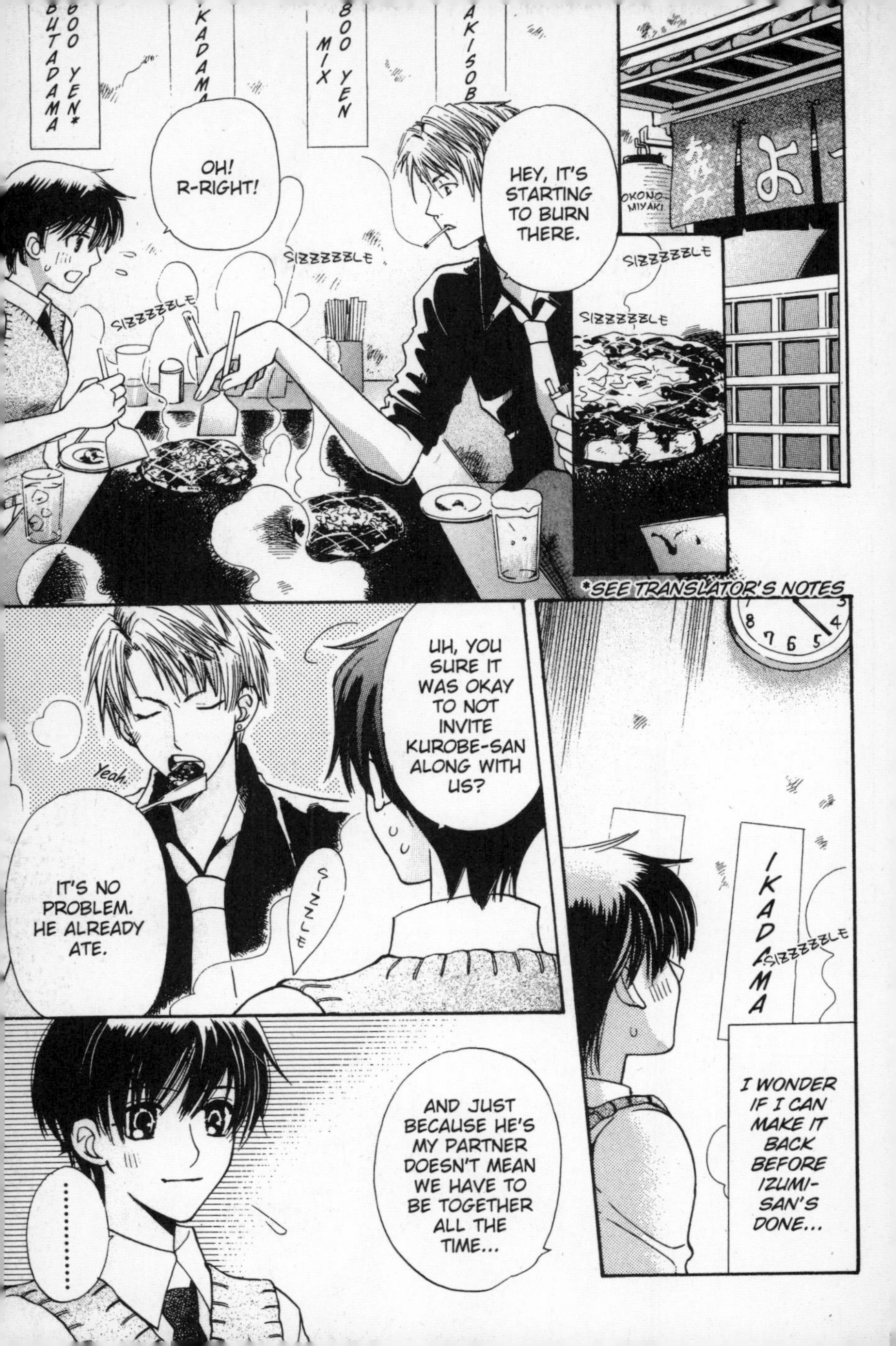
OKONOMIYAKI
AKISOB
800 YEN
MIX
KADAMA
BUTADAMA
600 YEN*
HEY, IT'S STARTING TO BURN THERE.
OH! R-RIGHT!
SIZZZZZLE
SIZZZZZLE
SIZZZZZLE
SIZZZZZLE
*SEE TRANSLATOR'S NOTES
IKADAMA
SIZZZZZLE
I WONDER IF I CAN MAKE IT BACK BEFORE IZUMI-SAN'S DONE...
UH, YOU SURE IT WAS OKAY TO NOT INVITE KUROBE-SAN ALONG WITH US?
Yeah.
IT'S NO PROBLEM. HE ALREADY ATE.
SIZZLE
AND JUST BECAUSE HE'S MY PARTNER DOESN'T MEAN WE HAVE TO BE TOGETHER ALL THE TIME...
....

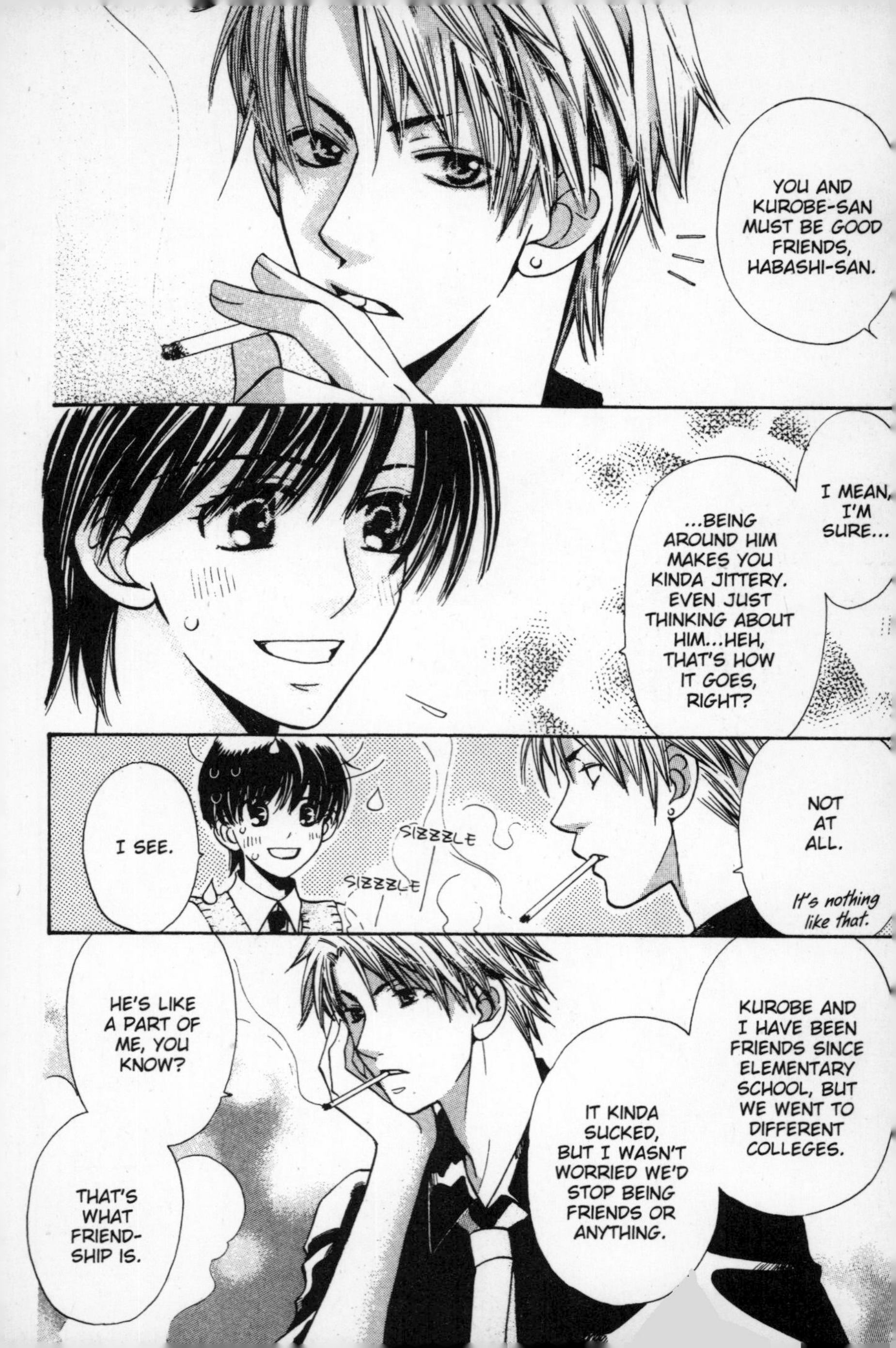
YOU AND KUROBE-SAN MUST BE GOOD FRIENDS, HABASHI-SAN.
I MEAN, I'M SURE...
...BEING AROUND HIM MAKES YOU KINDA JITTERY. EVEN JUST THINKING ABOUT HIM...HEH, THAT'S HOW IT GOES, RIGHT?
NOT AT ALL.
It's nothing like that.
SIZZZLE
SIZZZLE
I SEE.
KUROBE AND I HAVE BEEN FRIENDS SINCE ELEMENTARY SCHOOL, BUT WE WENT TO DIFFERENT COLLEGES.
IT KINDA SUCKED, BUT I WASN'T WORRIED WE'D STOP BEING FRIENDS OR ANYTHING.
HE'S LIKE A PART OF ME, YOU KNOW?
THAT'S WHAT FRIEND-SHIP IS.

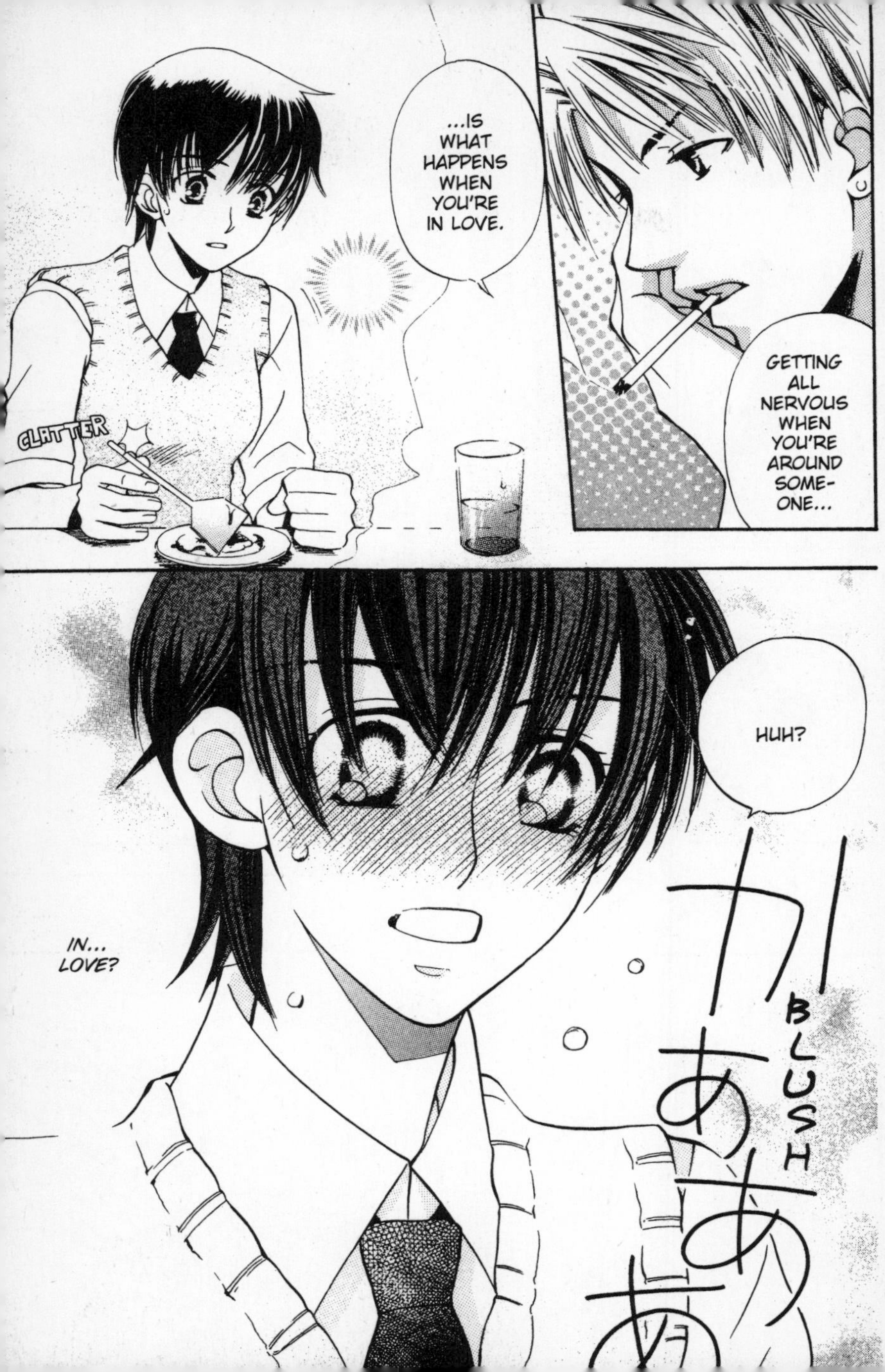
GETTING ALL NERVOUS WHEN YOU'RE AROUND SOME-ONE...
...IS WHAT HAPPENS WHEN YOU'RE IN LOVE.
CLATTER
HUH?
BLUSH
IN... LOVE?

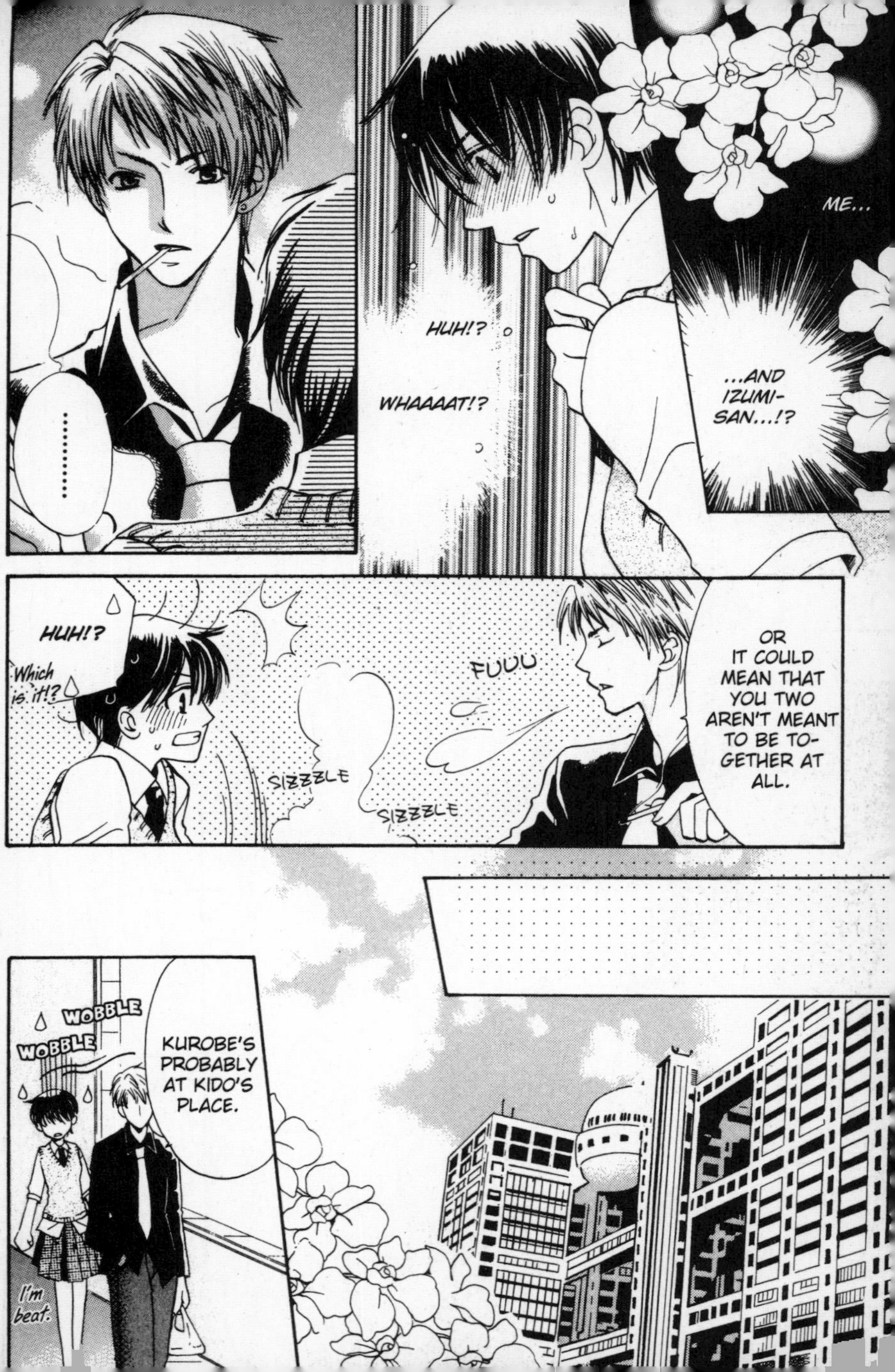
ME...
...AND IZUMI-SAN...!?
HUH!?
WHAAAAT!?
......
OR IT COULD MEAN THAT YOU TWO AREN'T MEANT TO BE TO-GETHER AT ALL.
FUUU
SIZZLE
SIZZLE
HUH!?
Which is it!?
KUROBE'S PROBABLY AT KIDO'S PLACE.
WOBBLE
WOBBLE
I'm beat.

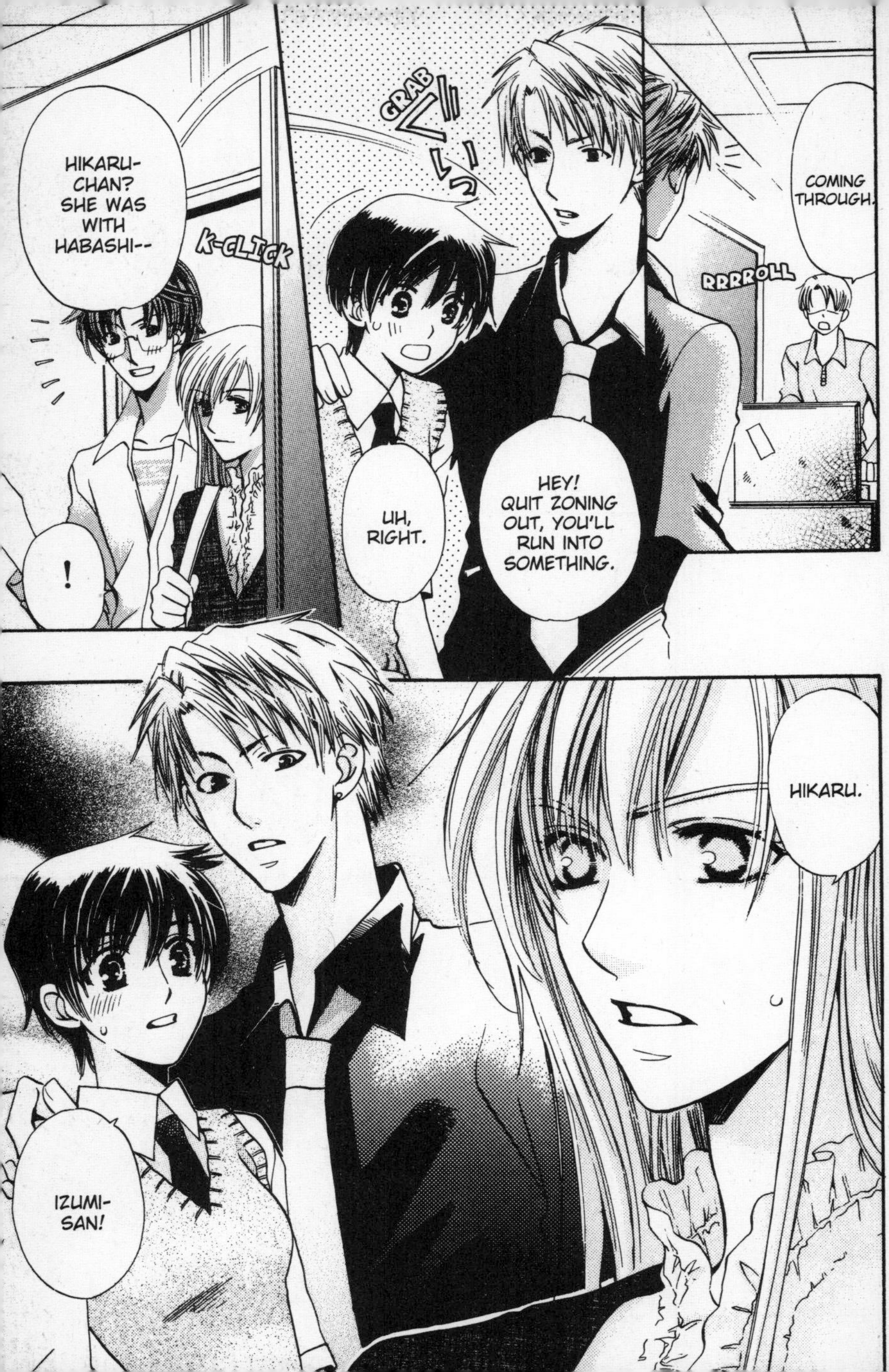
COMING THROUGH.
RRRROLL
GRAB
HEY! QUIT ZONING OUT, YOU'LL RUN INTO SOMETHING.
UH, RIGHT.
HIKARU-CHAN? SHE WAS WITH HABASHI--
K-CLICK
!
HIKARU.
IZUMI-SAN!

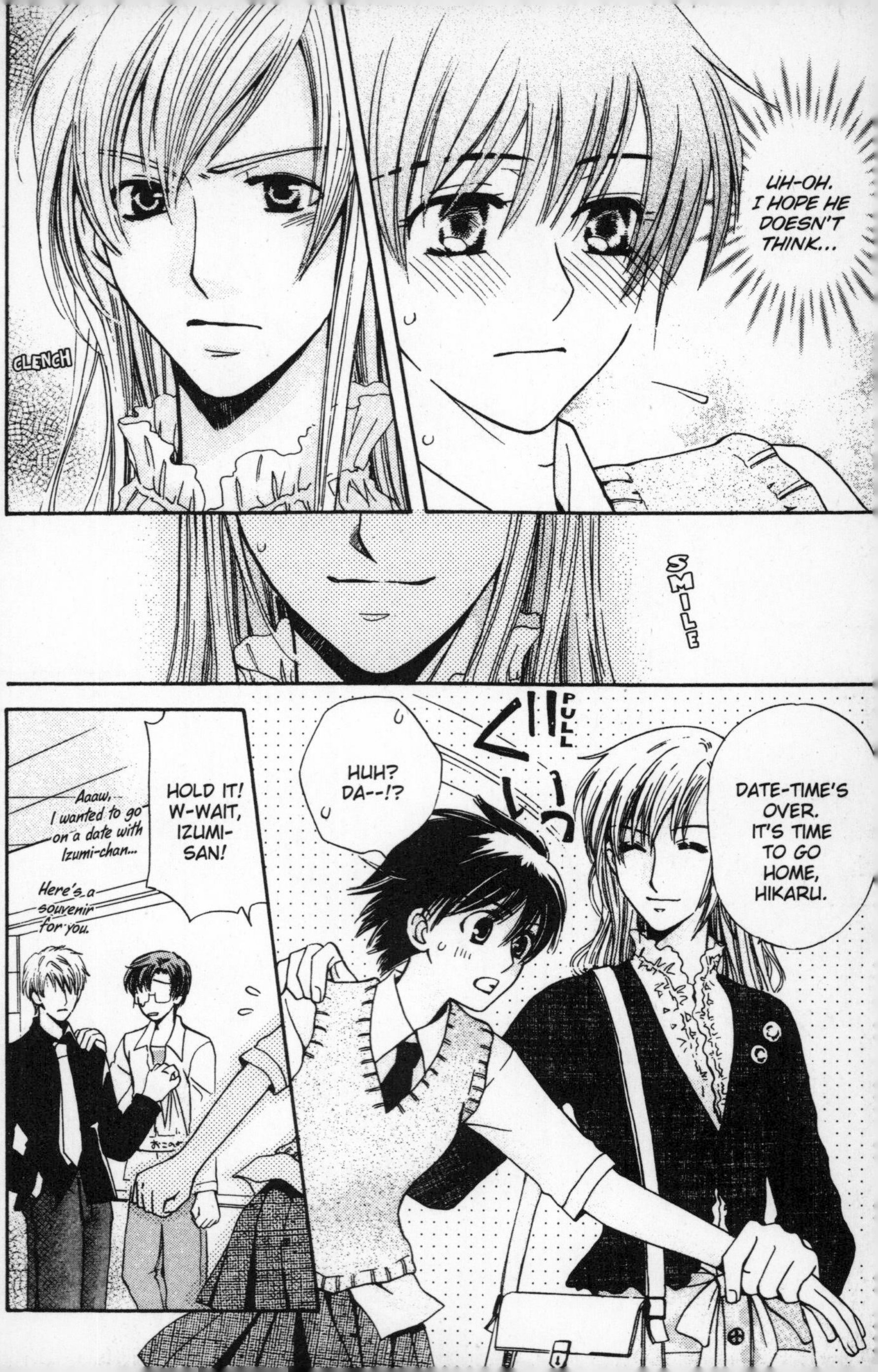
UH-OH. I HOPE HE DOESN'T THINK...
CLENCH
SMILE
DATE-TIME'S OVER. IT'S TIME TO GO HOME, HIKARU.
PULL
HUH? DA--!?
HOLD IT! W-WAIT, IZUMI-SAN!
Aaaw, I wanted to go on a date with Izumi-chan...
Here's a souvenir for you.

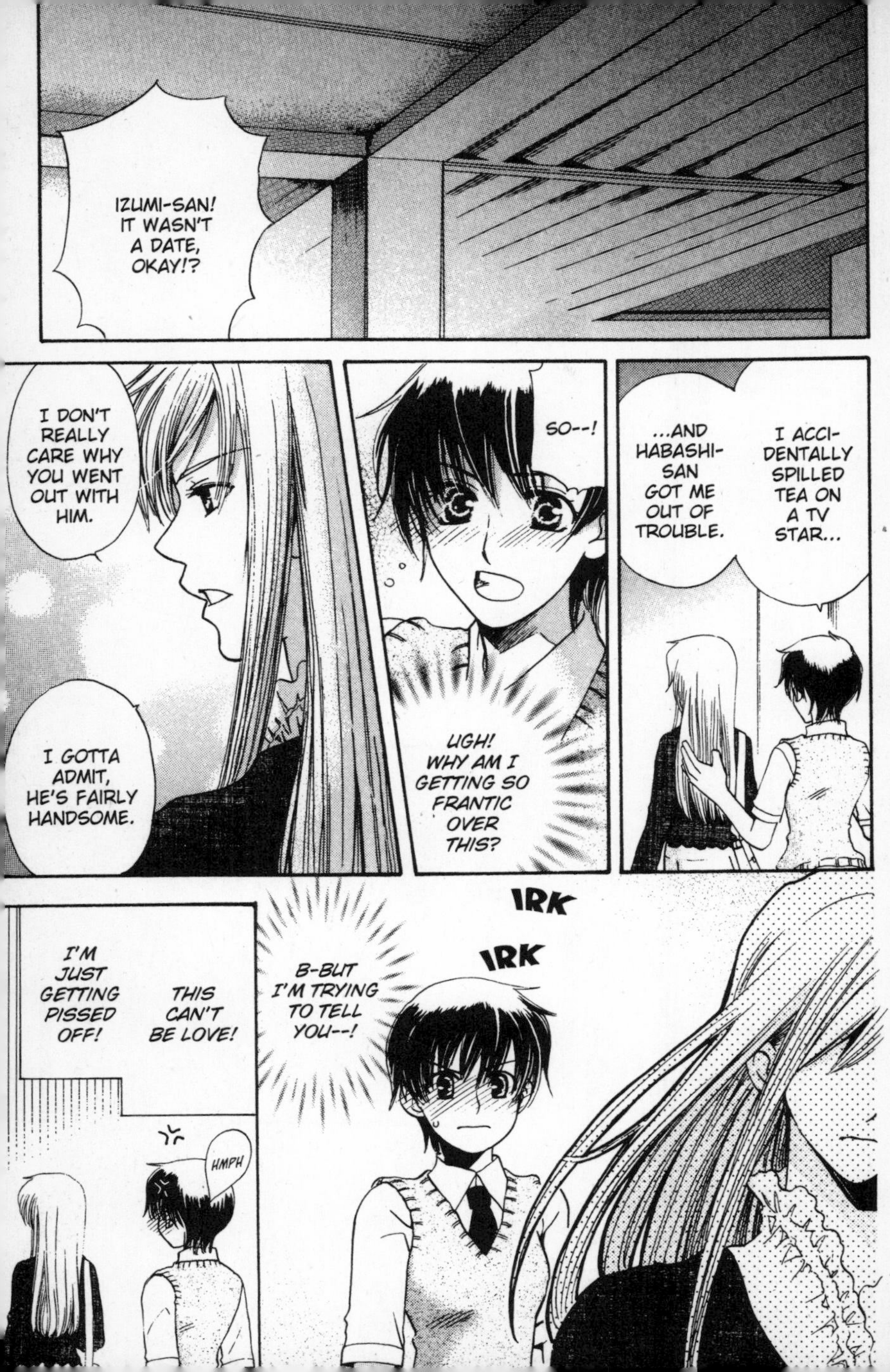

IZUMI-SAN! IT WASN'T A DATE, OKAY!?
I ACCI-DENTALLY SPILLED TEA ON A TV STAR...
...AND HABASHI-SAN GOT ME OUT OF TROUBLE.
SO--!
UGH! WHY AM I GETTING SO FRANTIC OVER THIS?
I DON'T REALLY CARE WHY YOU WENT OUT WITH HIM.
I GOTTA ADMIT, HE'S FAIRLY HANDSOME.
IRK
IRK
B-BUT I'M TRYING TO TELL YOU--!
THIS CAN'T BE LOVE!
I'M JUST GETTING PISSED OFF!
HMPH

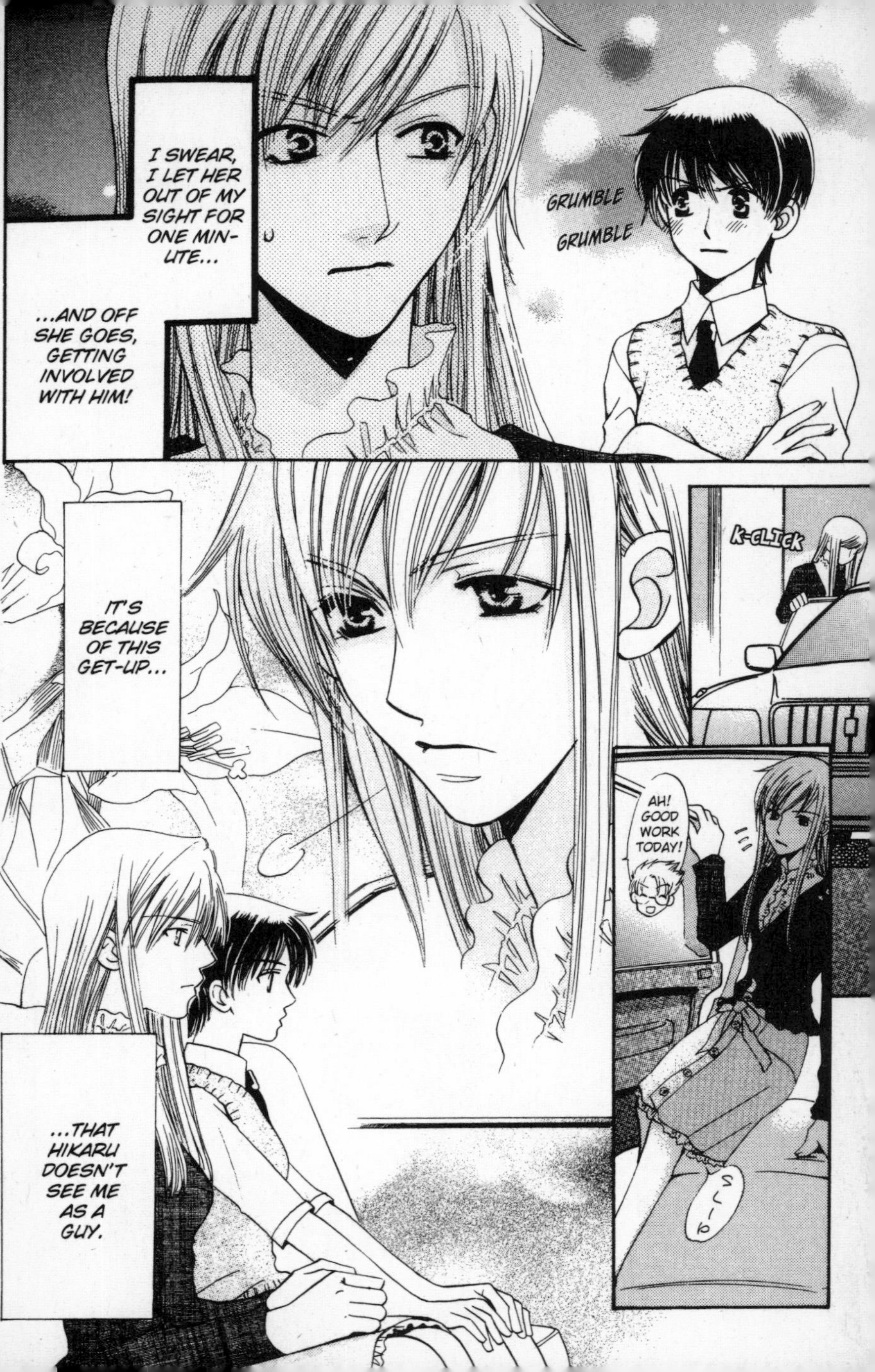
GRUMBLE
GRUMBLE
I SWEAR, I LET HER OUT OF MY SIGHT FOR ONE MIN-UTE...
...AND OFF SHE GOES, GETTING INVOLVED WITH HIM!
K-CLICK
AH! GOOD WORK TODAY!
IT'S BECAUSE OF THIS GET-UP...
...THAT HIKARU DOESN'T SEE ME AS A GUY.

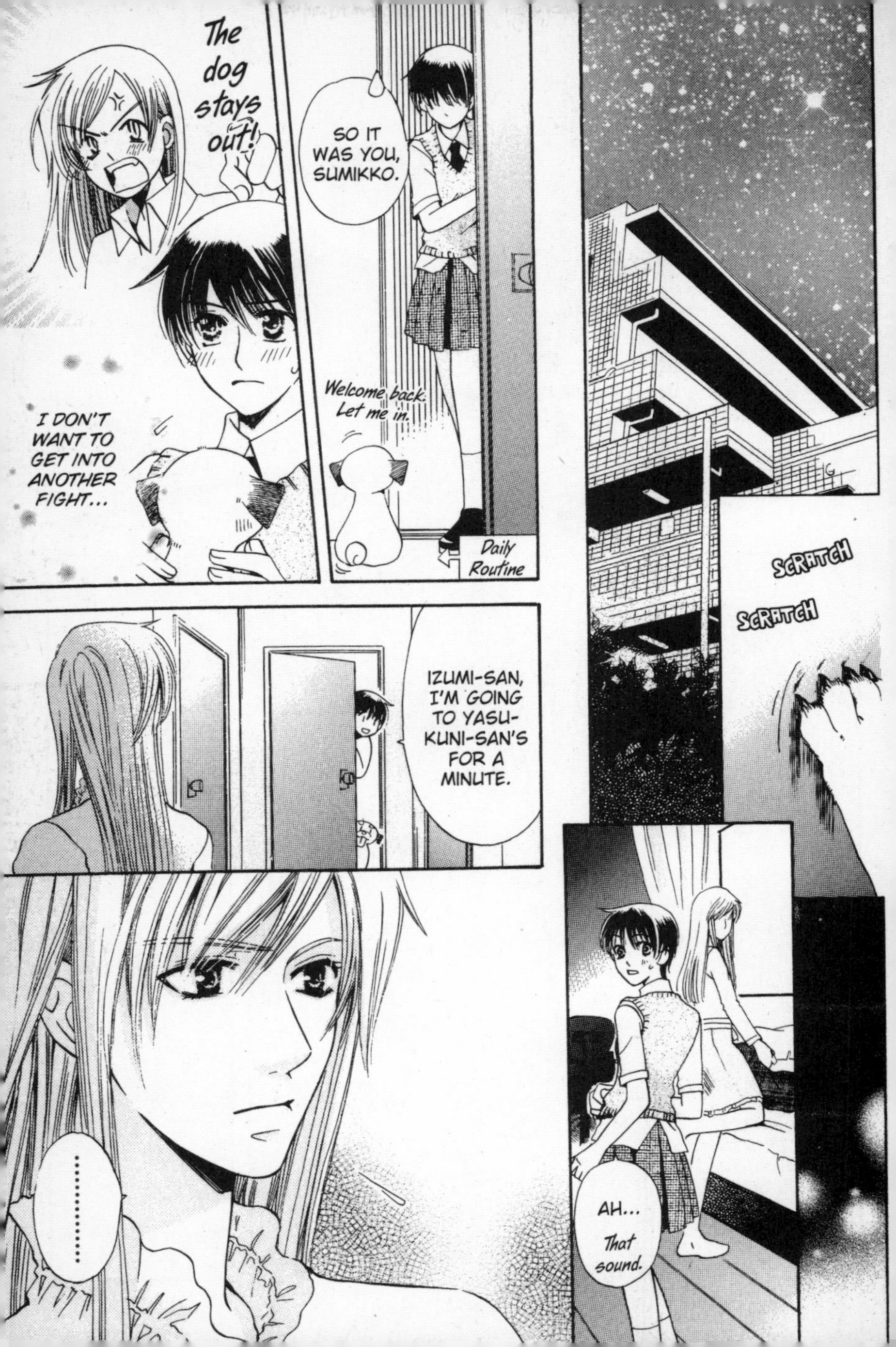
SCRATCH
SCRATCH
AH...
That sound.
SO IT WAS YOU, SUMIKKO.
Welcome back. Let me in.
Daily Routine
The dog stays out!
I DON'T WANT TO GET INTO ANOTHER FIGHT...
IZUMI-SAN, I'M GOING TO YASU-KUNI-SAN'S FOR A MINUTE.
......

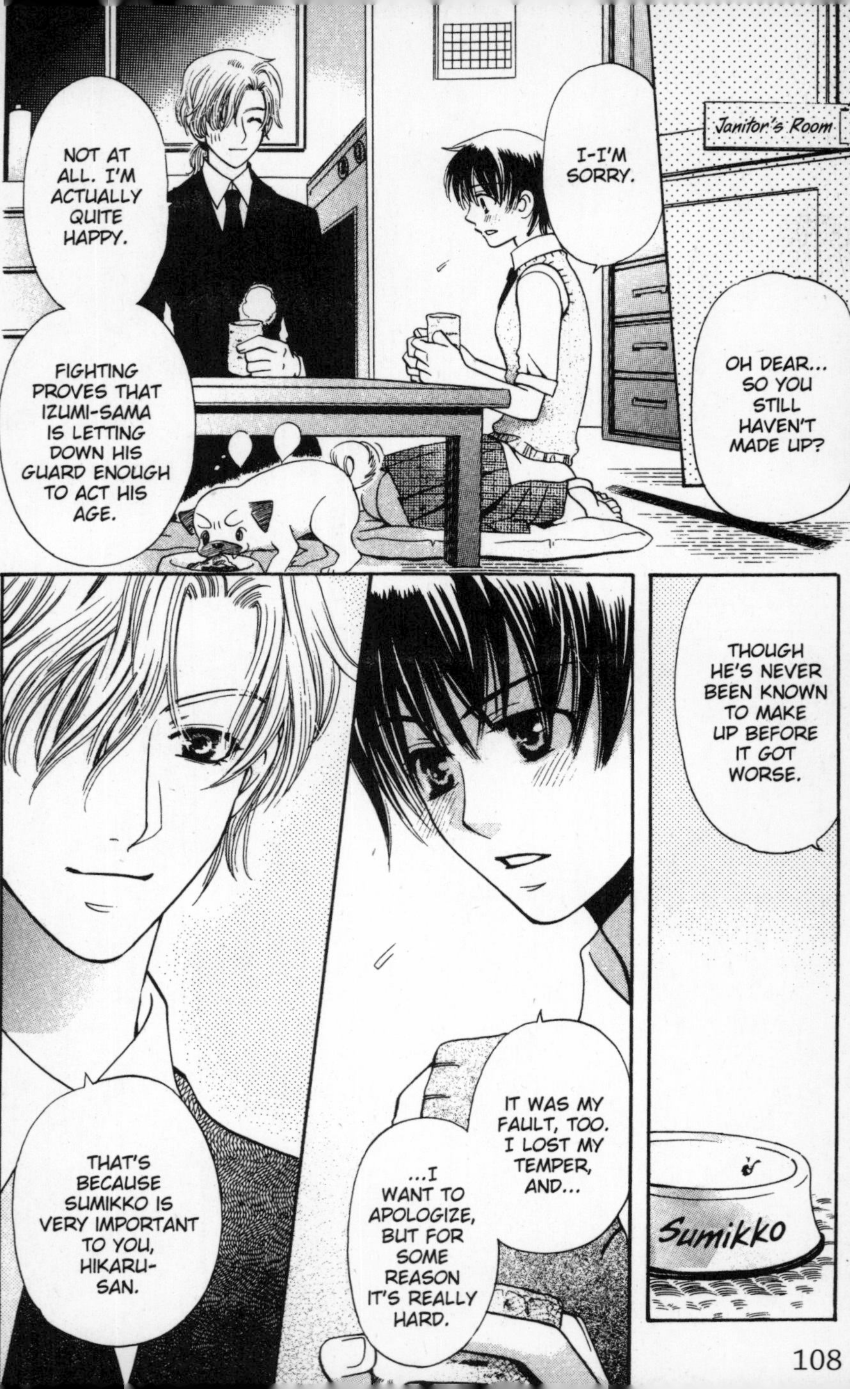
Janitor's Room
OH DEAR... SO YOU STILL HAVEN'T MADE UP?
I-I'M SORRY.
NOT AT ALL. I'M ACTUALLY QUITE HAPPY.
FIGHTING PROVES THAT IZUMI-SAMA IS LETTING DOWN HIS GUARD ENOUGH TO ACT HIS AGE.
THOUGH HE'S NEVER BEEN KNOWN TO MAKE UP BEFORE IT GOT WORSE.
Sumikko
IT WAS MY FAULT, TOO. I LOST MY TEMPER, AND...
...I WANT TO APOLOGIZE, BUT FOR SOME REASON IT'S REALLY HARD.
THAT'S BECAUSE SUMIKKO IS VERY IMPORTANT TO YOU, HIKARU-SAN.

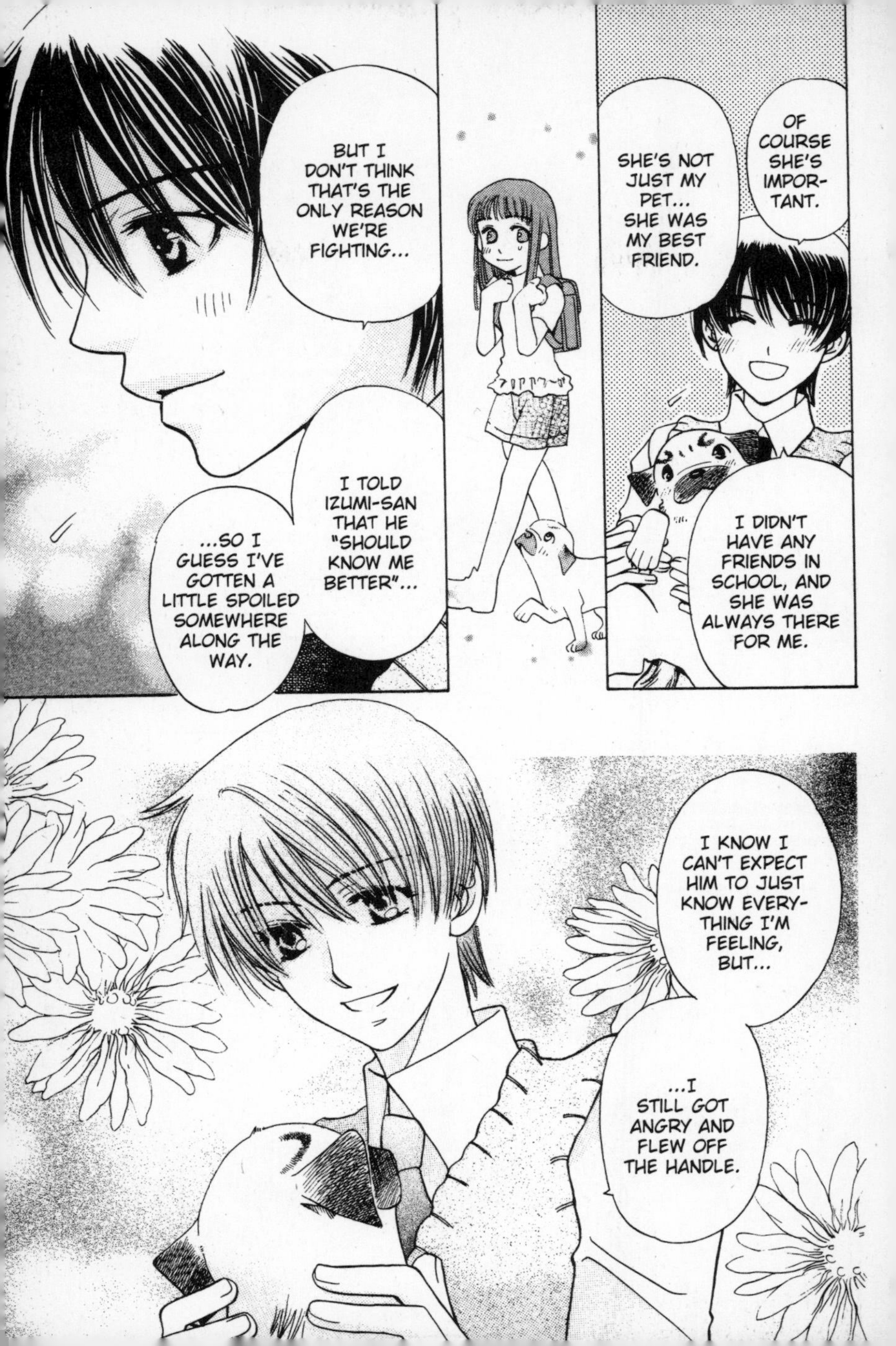

OF COURSE SHE'S IMPORTANT.
SHE'S NOT JUST MY PET... SHE WAS MY BEST FRIEND.
I DIDN'T HAVE ANY FRIENDS IN SCHOOL, AND SHE WAS ALWAYS THERE FOR ME.
BUT I DON'T THINK THAT'S THE ONLY REASON WE'RE FIGHTING...
I TOLD IZUMI-SAN THAT HE "SHOULD KNOW ME BETTER"...
...SO I GUESS I'VE GOTTEN A LITTLE SPOILED SOMEWHERE ALONG THE WAY.
I KNOW I CAN'T EXPECT HIM TO JUST KNOW EVERY-THING I'M FEELING, BUT...
...I STILL GOT ANGRY AND FLEW OFF THE HANDLE.

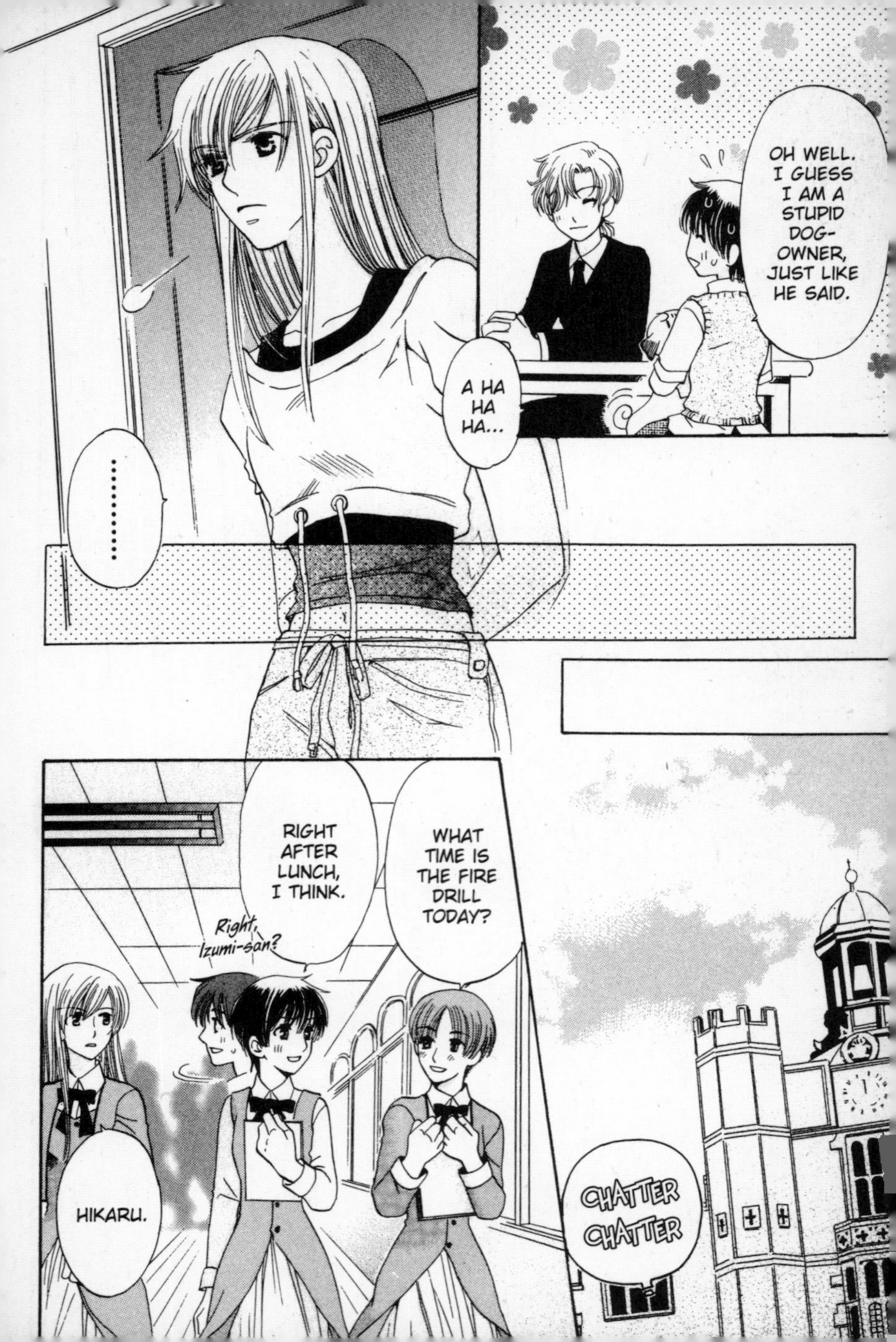

OH WELL. I GUESS I AM A STUPID DOG-OWNER, JUST LIKE HE SAID.
A HA HA HA...
....
CHATTER CHATTER
WHAT TIME IS THE FIRE DRILL TODAY?
RIGHT AFTER LUNCH, I THINK.
Right, Izumi-san?
HIKARU.

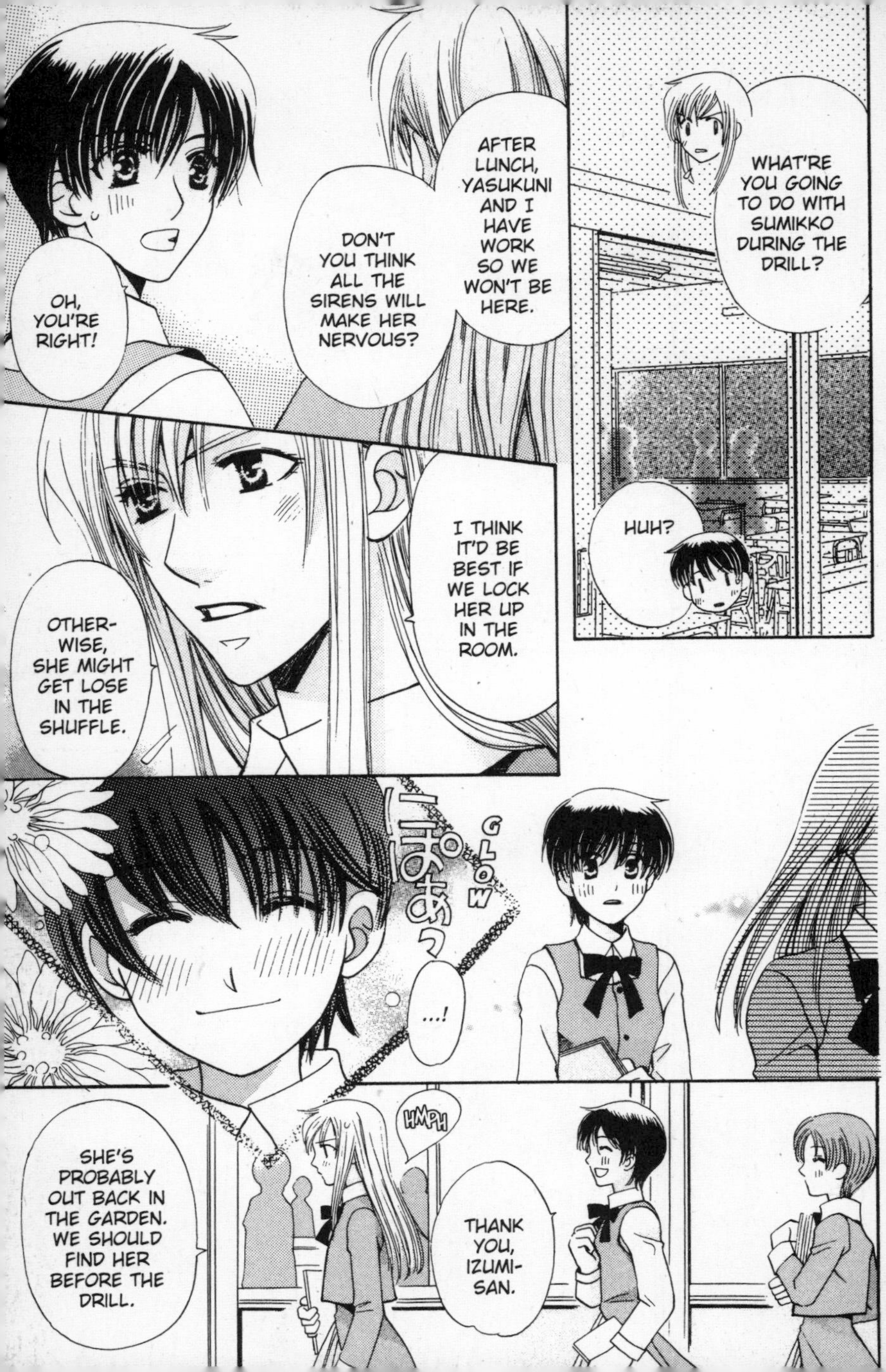
WHAT'RE YOU GOING TO DO WITH SUMIKKO DURING THE DRILL?
HUH?
AFTER LUNCH, YASUKUNI AND I HAVE WORK SO WE WON'T BE HERE.
DON'T YOU THINK ALL THE SIRENS WILL MAKE HER NERVOUS?
OH, YOU'RE RIGHT!
I THINK IT'D BE BEST IF WE LOCK HER UP IN THE ROOM.
OTHER-WISE, SHE MIGHT GET LOSE IN THE SHUFFLE.
...!
ぽあっ
GLOW
THANK YOU, IZUMI-SAN.
HMPH
SHE'S PROBABLY OUT BACK IN THE GARDEN. WE SHOULD FIND HER BEFORE THE DRILL.

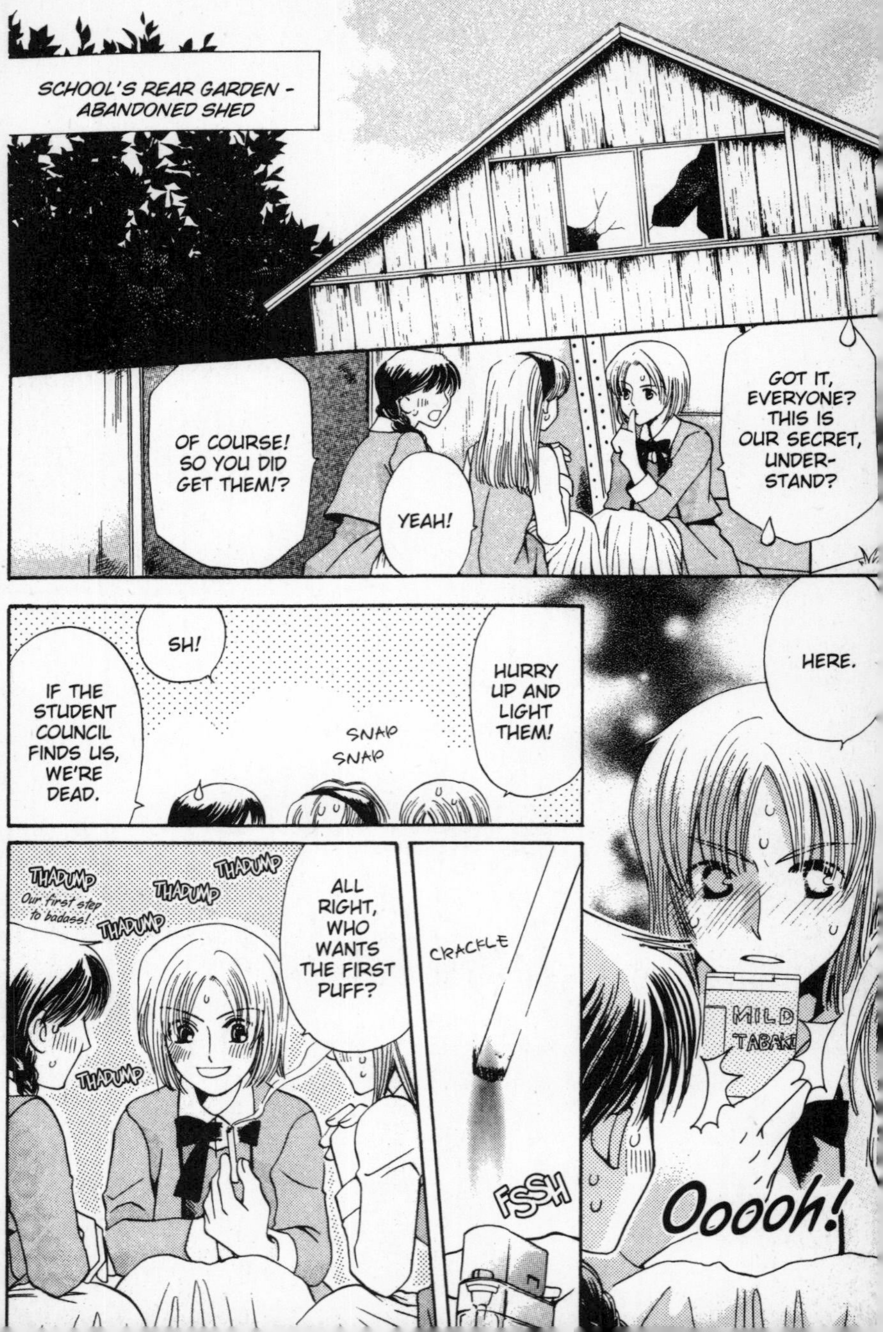
SCHOOL'S REAR GARDEN - ABANDONED SHED
GOT IT, EVERYONE? THIS IS OUR SECRET, UNDER-STAND?
YEAH!
OF COURSE! SO YOU DID GET THEM!?
HERE.
MILD TABAKI
Ooooh!
HURRY UP AND LIGHT THEM!
SNAP SNAP
SH!
IF THE STUDENT COUNCIL FINDS US, WE'RE DEAD.
CRACKLE
FSSH
ALL RIGHT, WHO WANTS THE FIRST PUFF?
THADUMP THADUMP THADUMP THADUMP THADUMP
Our first step to badass!

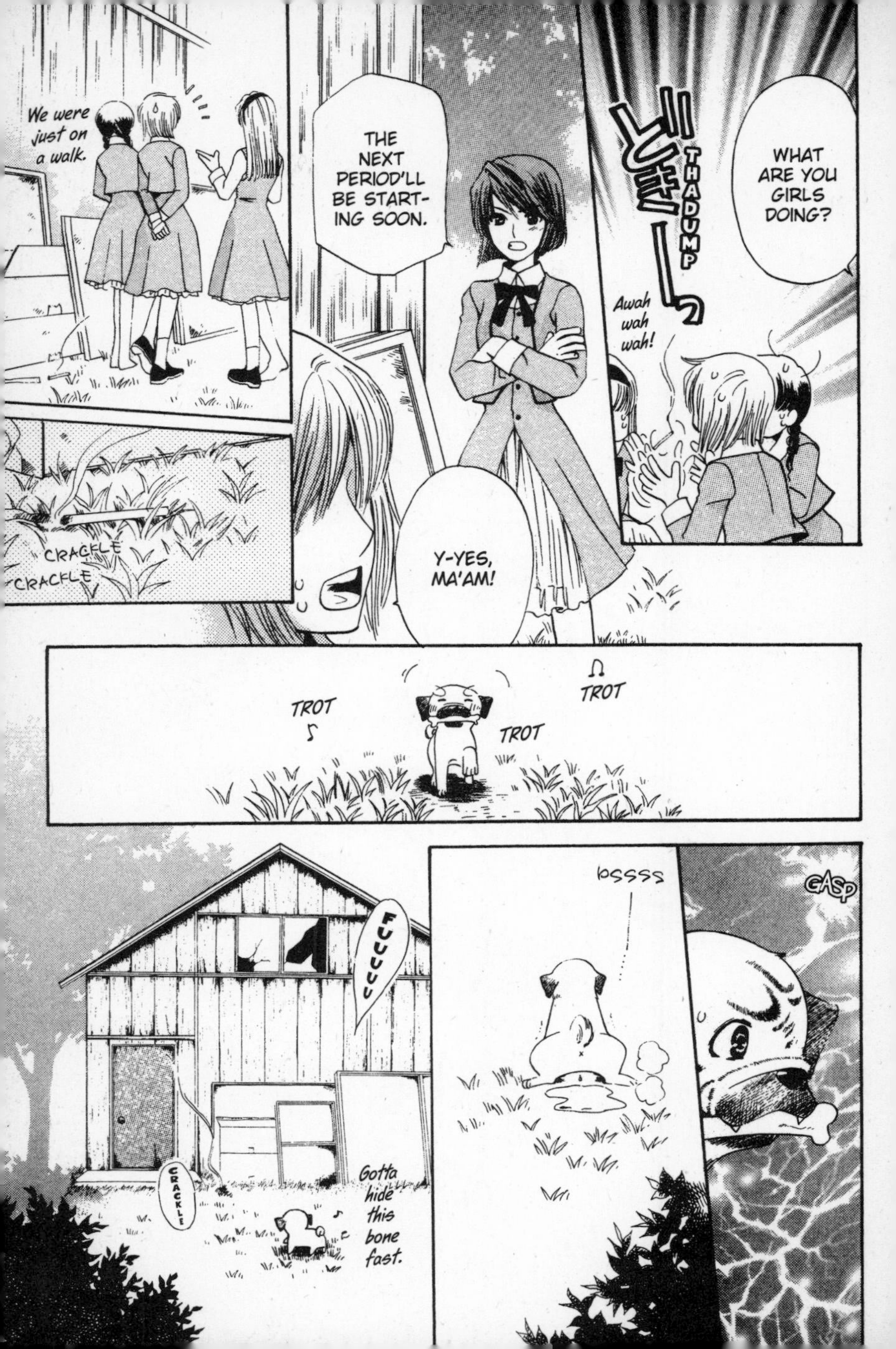
WHAT ARE YOU GIRLS DOING?
THADUMP
Awah wah wah!
THE NEXT PERIOD'LL BE STARTING SOON.
Y-YES, MA'AM!
We were just on a walk.
CRACKLE
CRACKLE
TROT
TROT
TROT
GASP
pssss
FUUUUU
CRACKLE
Gotta hide this bone fast.

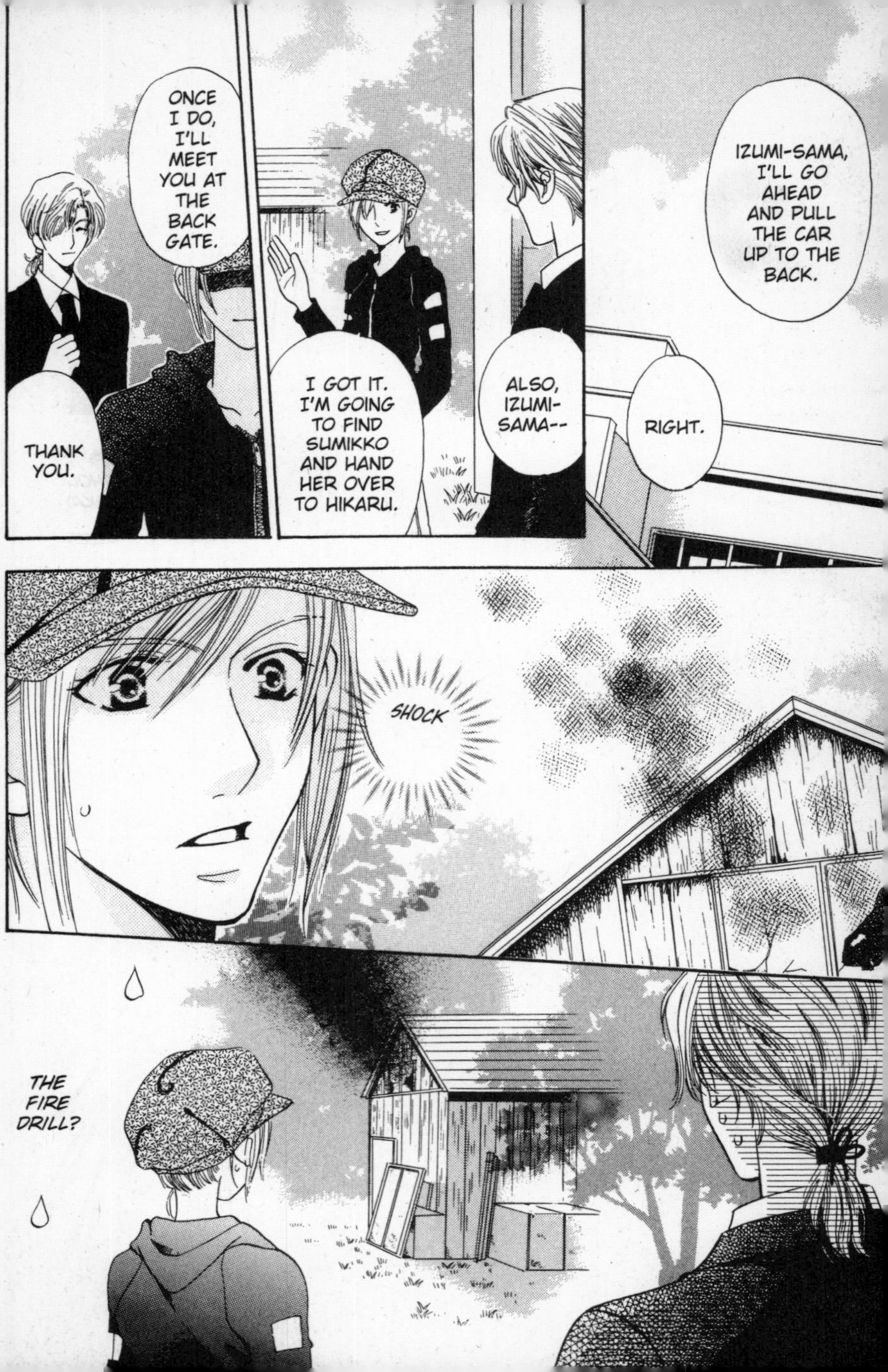
IZUMI-SAMA, I'LL GO AHEAD AND PULL THE CAR UP TO THE BACK.
RIGHT.
ALSO, IZUMI-SAMA--
I GOT IT. I'M GOING TO FIND SUMIKKO AND HAND HER OVER TO HIKARU.
ONCE I DO, I'LL MEET YOU AT THE BACK GATE.
THANK YOU.
SHOCK
THE FIRE DRILL?

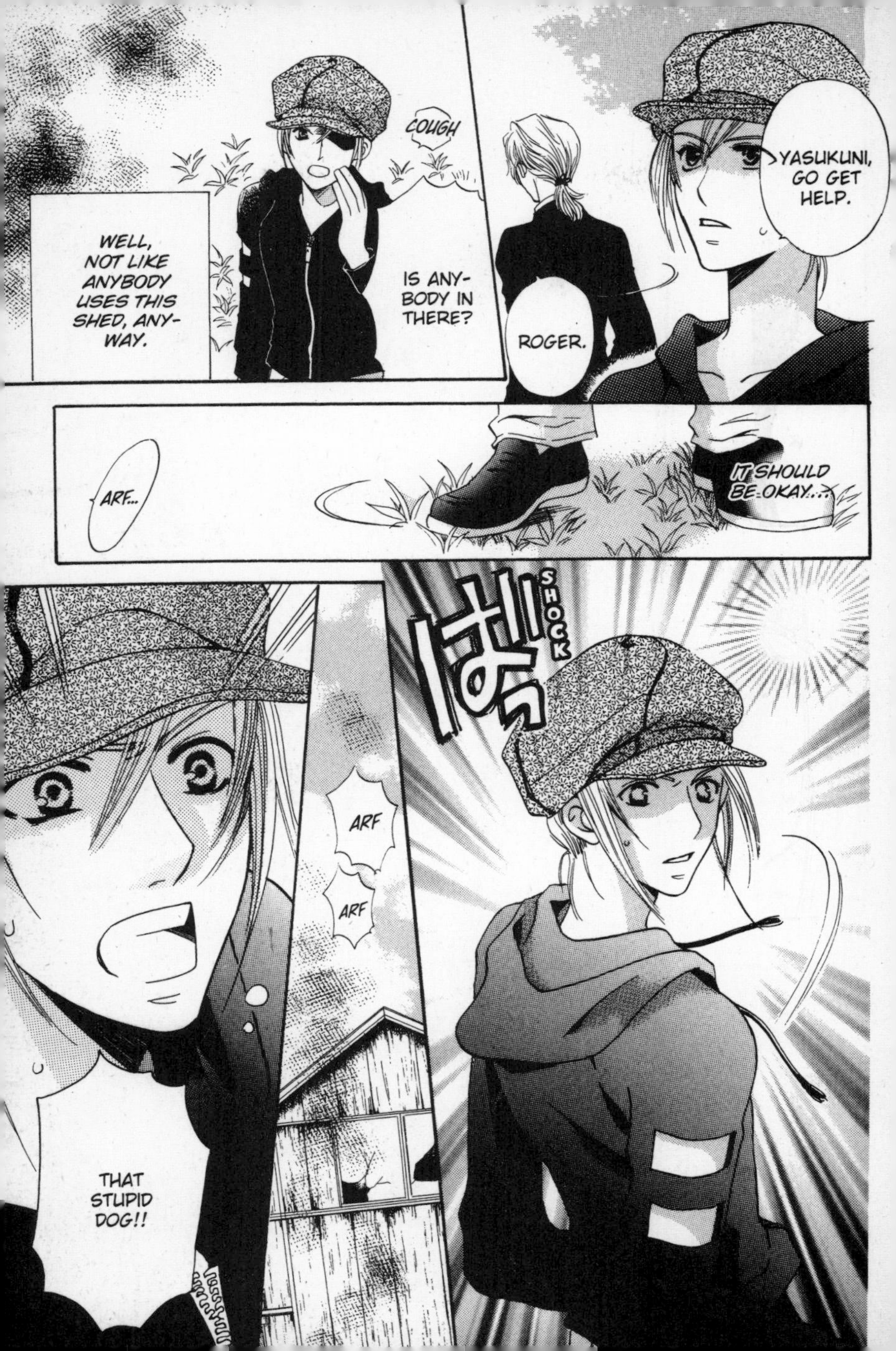
YASUKUNI, GO GET HELP.
ROGER.
COUGH
IS ANY-BODY IN THERE?
WELL, NOT LIKE ANYBODY USES THIS SHED, ANY-WAY.
IT SHOULD BE OKAY...
ARF...
はっ
SHOCK
ARF
ARF
THAT STUPID DOG!!

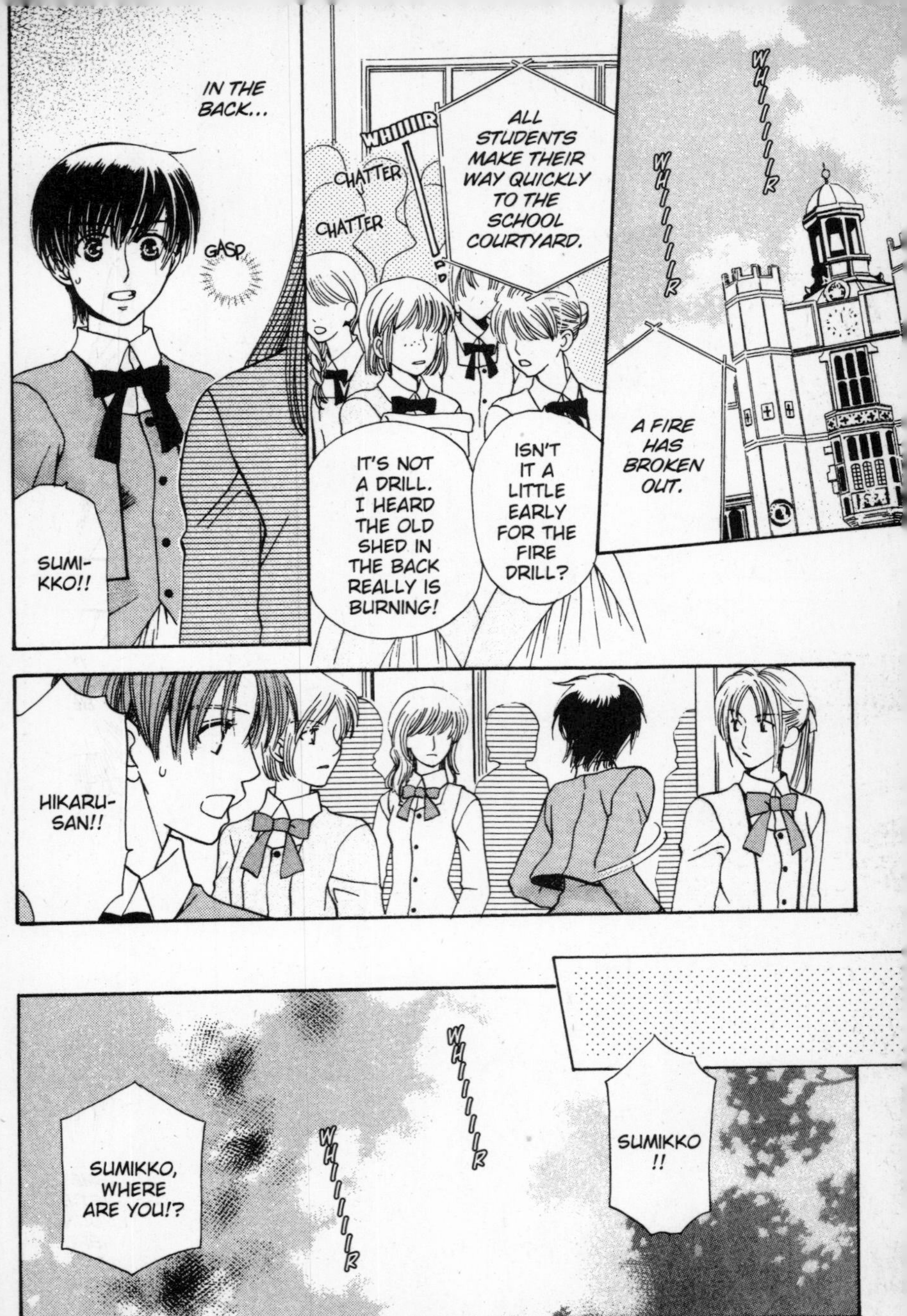
WHIIIIIR
WHIIIIIR
A FIRE HAS BROKEN OUT.
ALL STUDENTS MAKE THEIR WAY QUICKLY TO THE SCHOOL COURTYARD.
WHIIIIIR
CHATTER
CHATTER
ISN'T IT A LITTLE EARLY FOR THE FIRE DRILL?
IT'S NOT A DRILL. I HEARD THE OLD SHED IN THE BACK REALLY IS BURNING!
IN THE BACK...
GASP
SUMI-KKO!!
HIKARU-SAN!!
SUMIKKO !!
WHIIIIIR
WHIIIIIR
SUMIKKO, WHERE ARE YOU!?

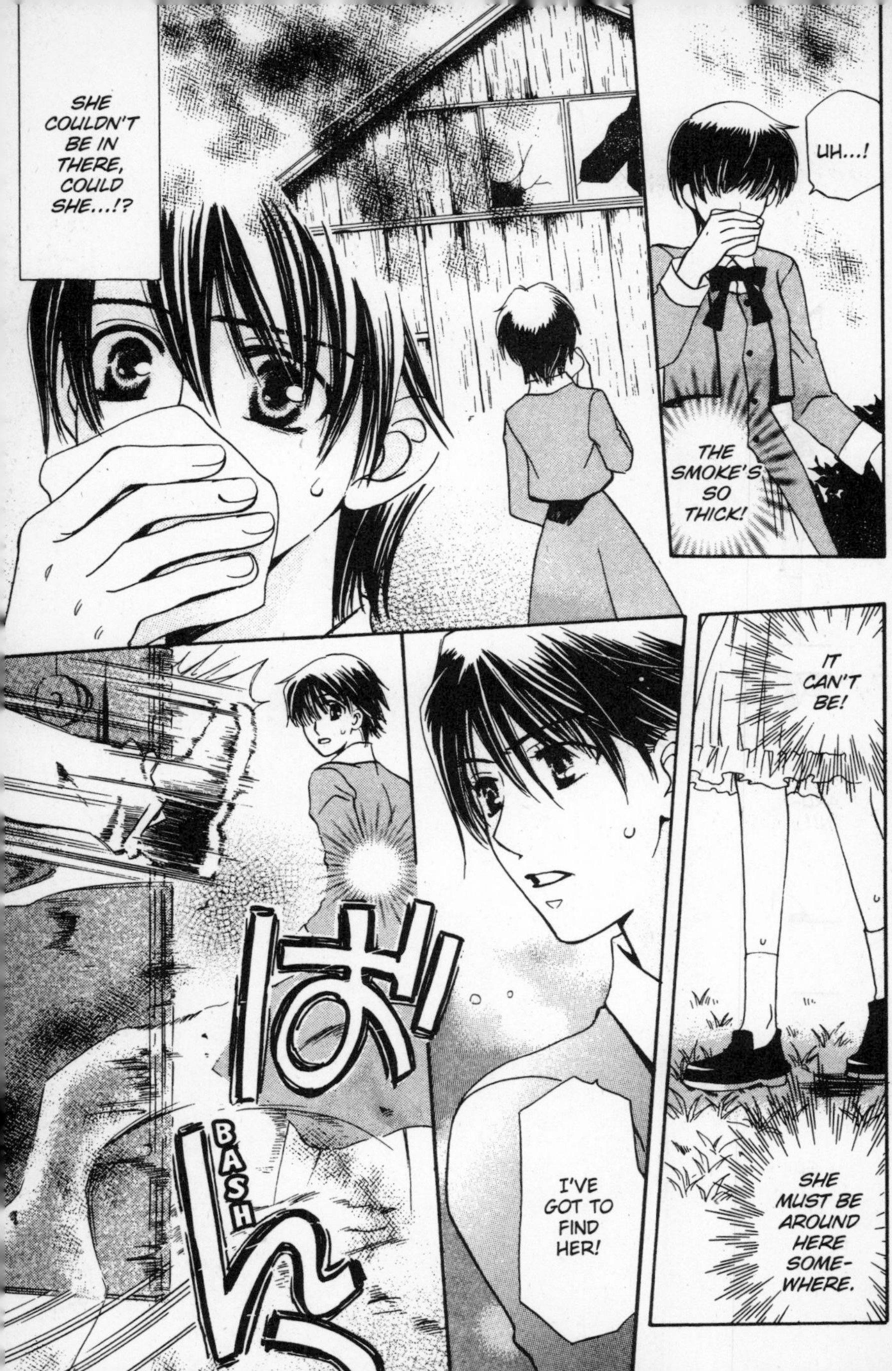
UH...!
THE SMOKE'S SO THICK!
SHE COULDN'T BE IN THERE, COULD SHE...!?
IT CAN'T BE!
SHE MUST BE AROUND HERE SOME-WHERE.
I'VE GOT TO FIND HER!
ばん
BASH

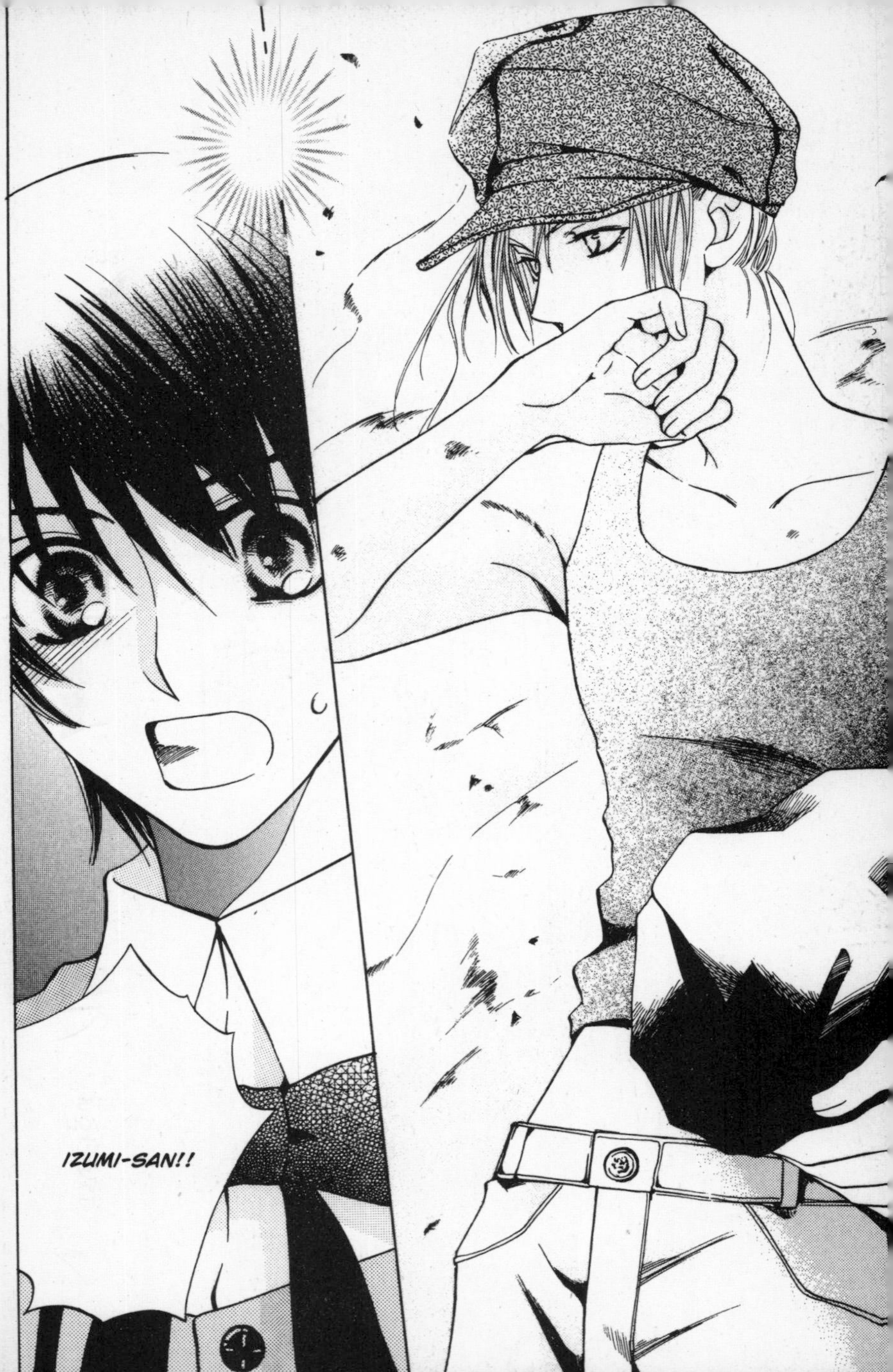
IZUMI-SAN!!

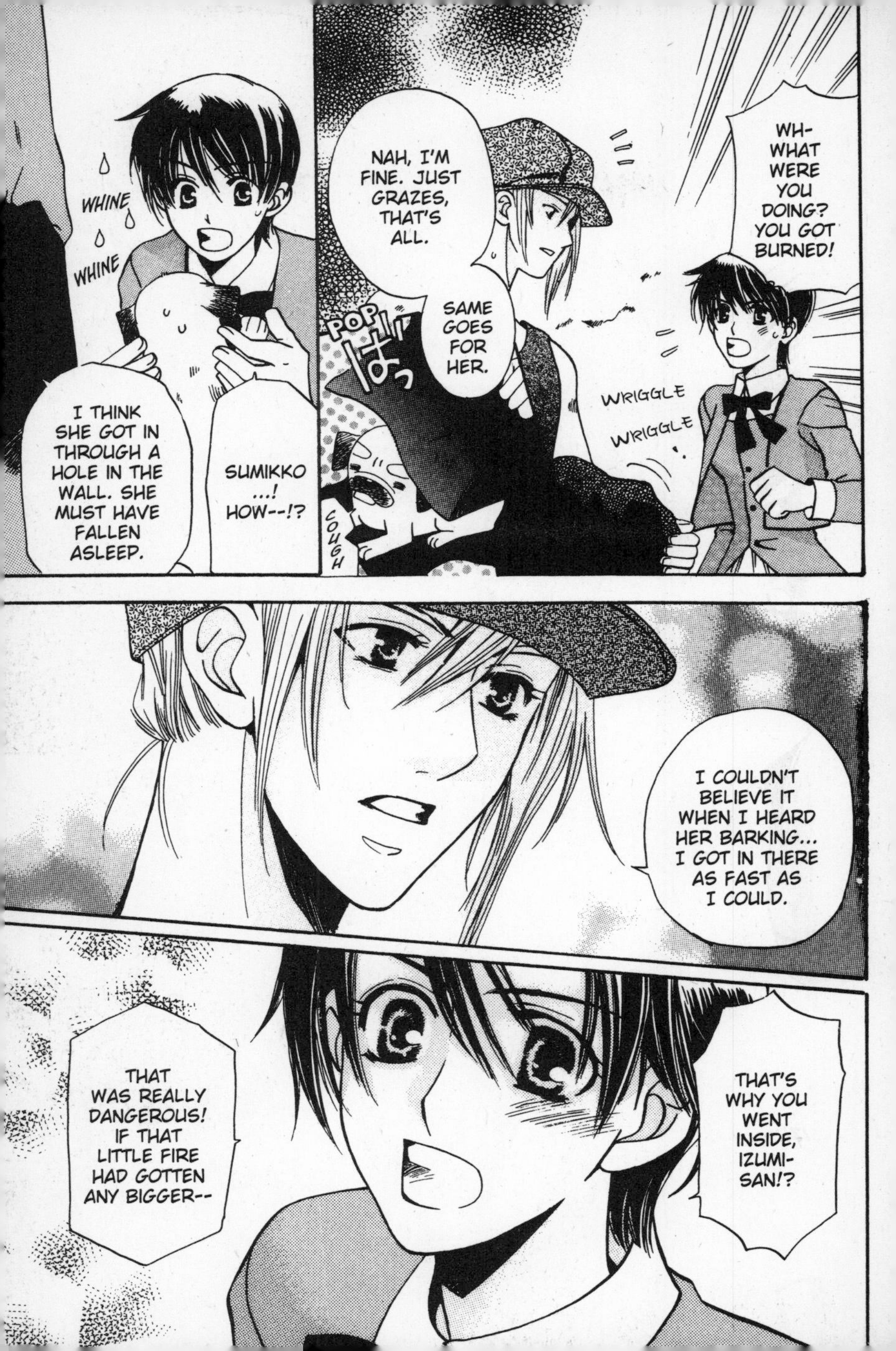
WH-WHAT WERE YOU DOING? YOU GOT BURNED!
NAH, I'M FINE. JUST GRAZES, THAT'S ALL.
SAME GOES FOR HER.
WRIGGLE WRIGGLE
POP ぱっ
COUGH
WHINE WHINE
SUMIKKO ...! HOW--!?
I THINK SHE GOT IN THROUGH A HOLE IN THE WALL. SHE MUST HAVE FALLEN ASLEEP.
I COULDN'T BELIEVE IT WHEN I HEARD HER BARKING... I GOT IN THERE AS FAST AS I COULD.
THAT'S WHY YOU WENT INSIDE, IZUMI-SAN!?
THAT WAS REALLY DANGEROUS! IF THAT LITTLE FIRE HAD GOTTEN ANY BIGGER--

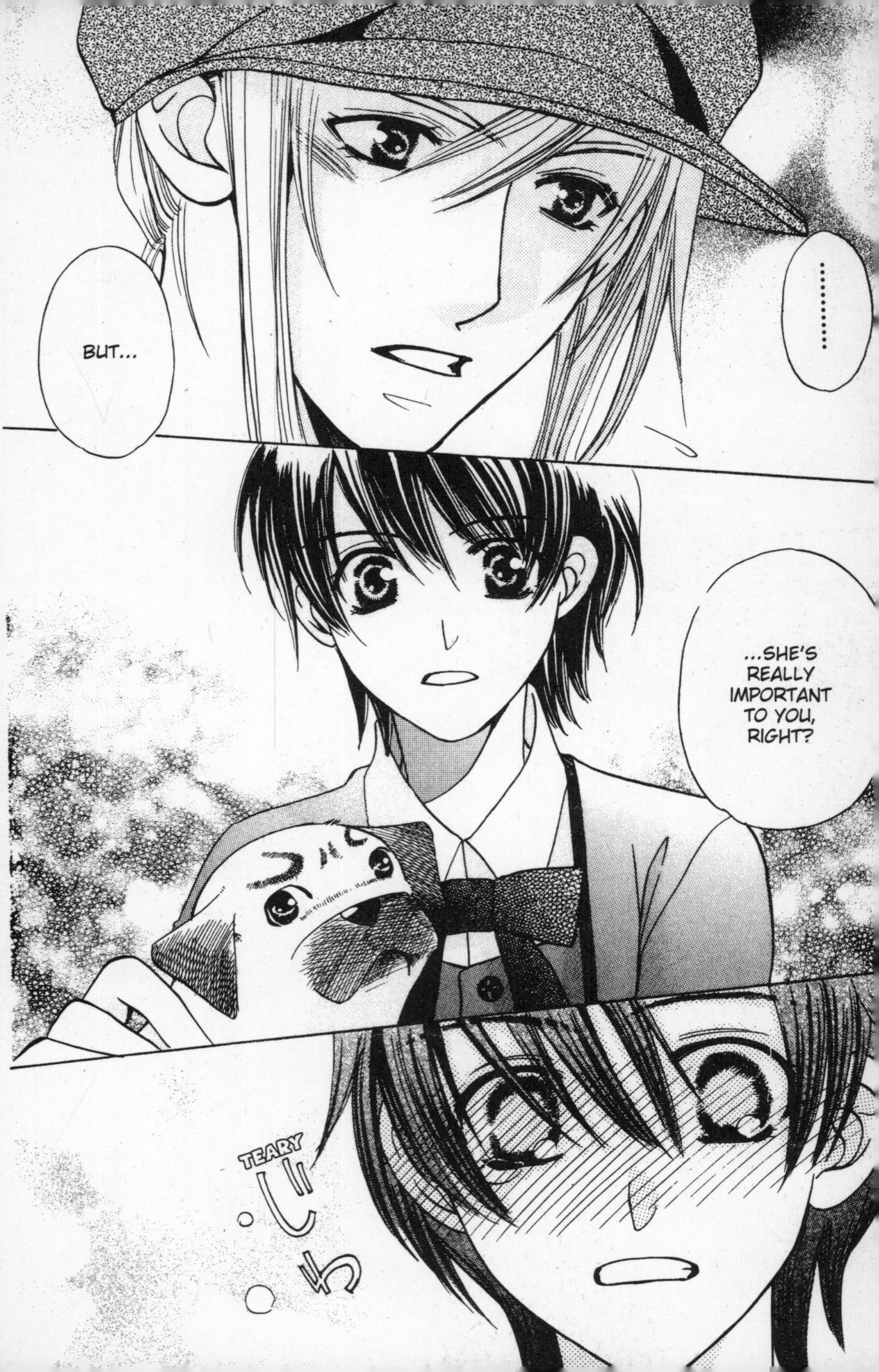
......
BUT...
...SHE'S REALLY IMPORTANT TO YOU, RIGHT?
TEARY

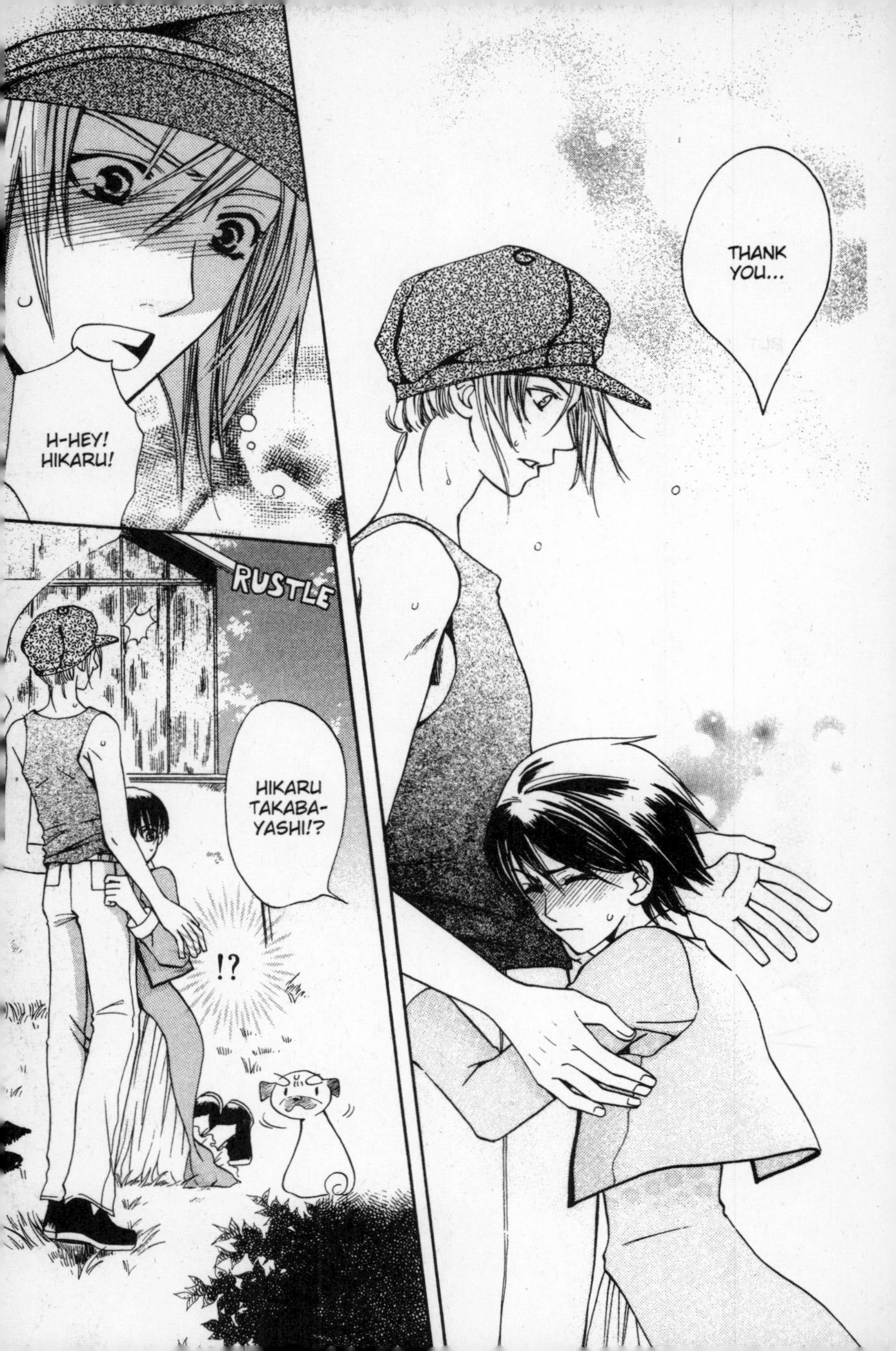

THANK YOU...
H-HEY! HIKARU!
RUSTLE
HIKARU TAKABA-YASHI!?
!?

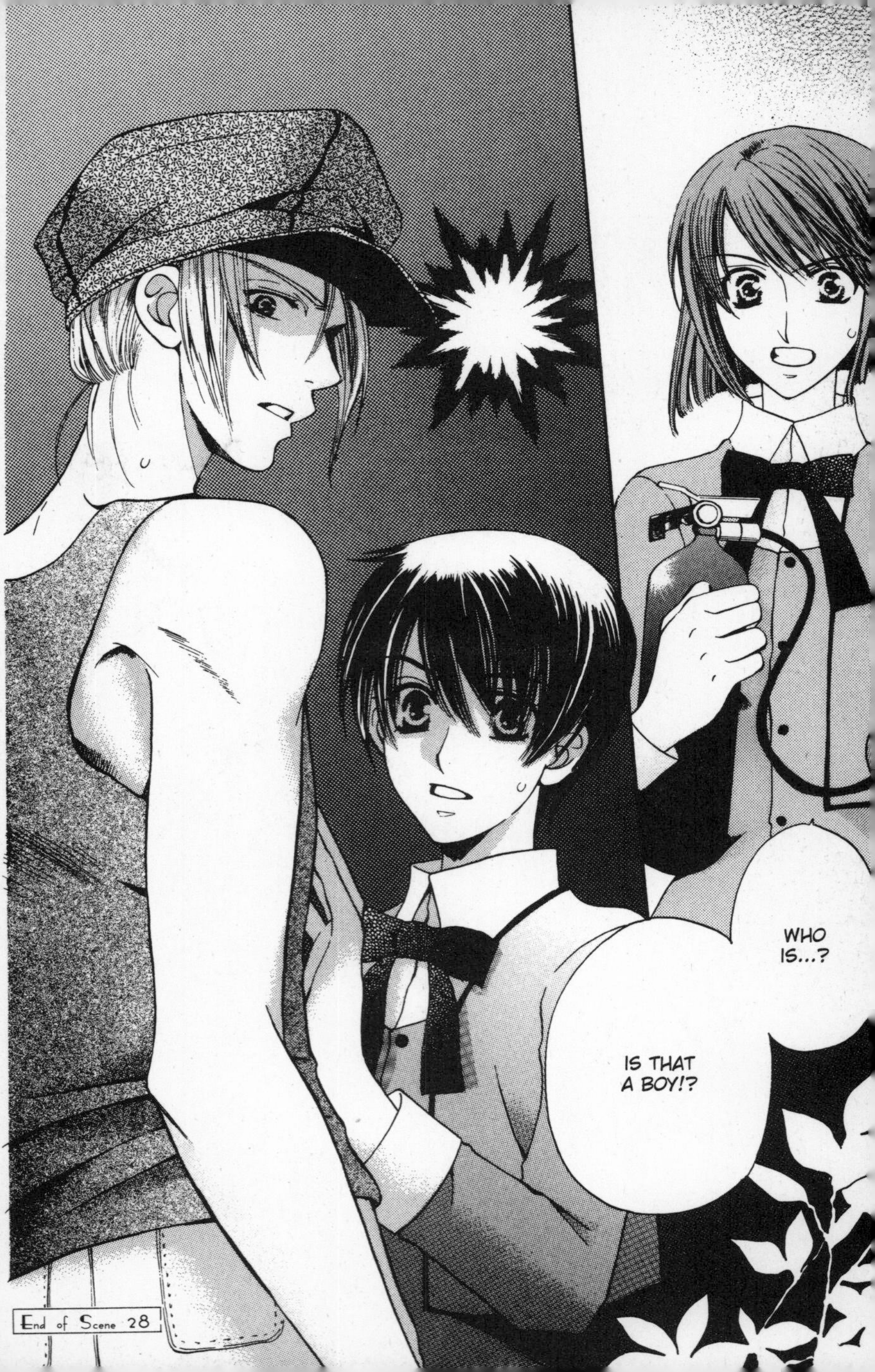
WHO IS...?
IS THAT A BOY!?

End of Scene 28

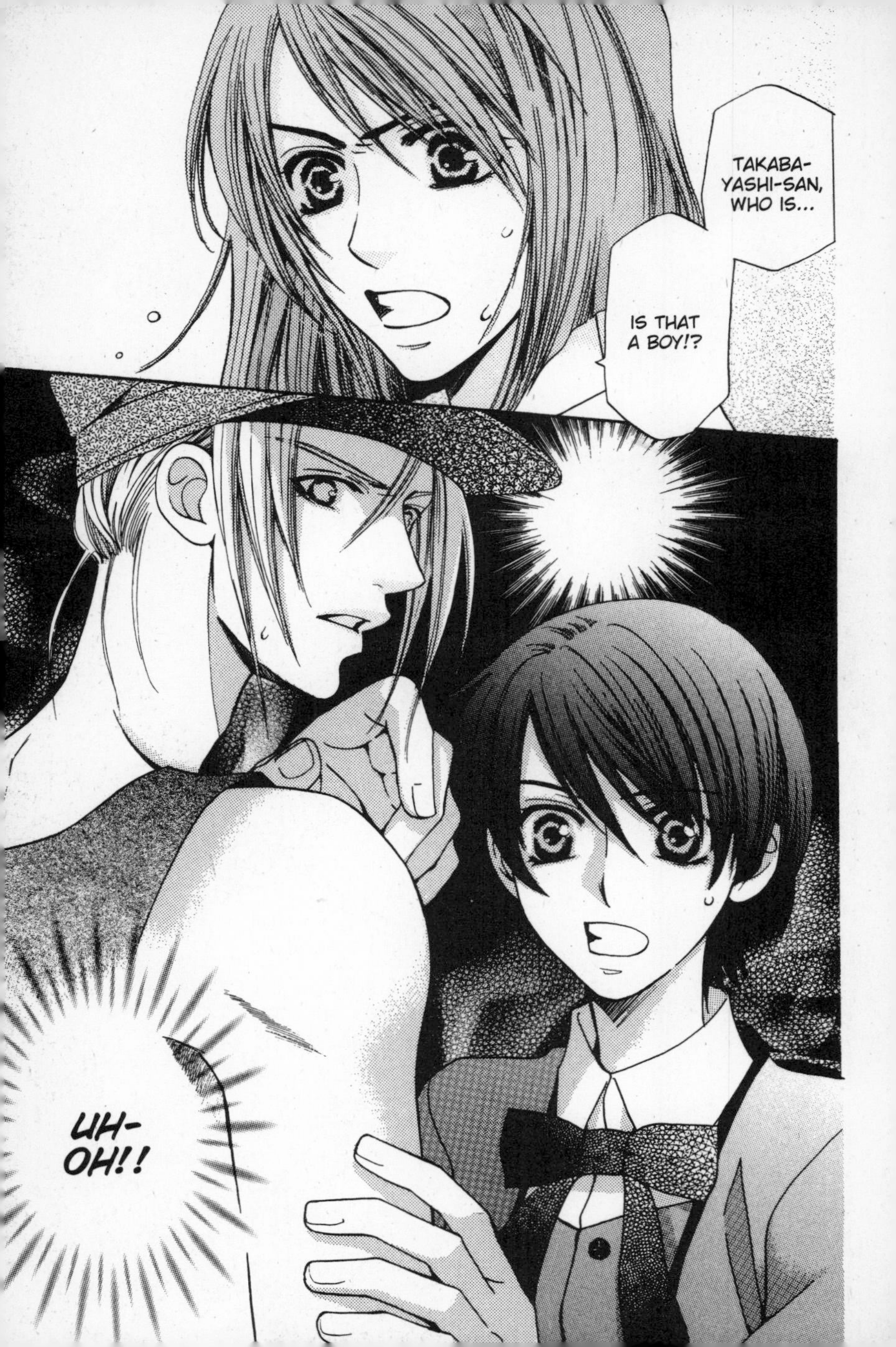
TAKABA-YASHI-SAN, WHO IS...
IS THAT A BOY!?
UH-OH!!

DASH

IZUMI-SAN! HURRY!

AH! HOLD IT!!

WHAT HAPPENED!?

T·M·P
T·M·P
T·M·P

HIKARU TAKABAYASHI WAS WITH A GUY--

AH! THE FIRE!!

!!

My Current Addictions #1

Since the year's started for some reason I've become really interested in a bunch of different things. Like gazing at books on antique jewelry (though I don't actually acquire any of it), researching motorcycles (but it seemed really difficult so I gave up halfway). collecting old books, etc...

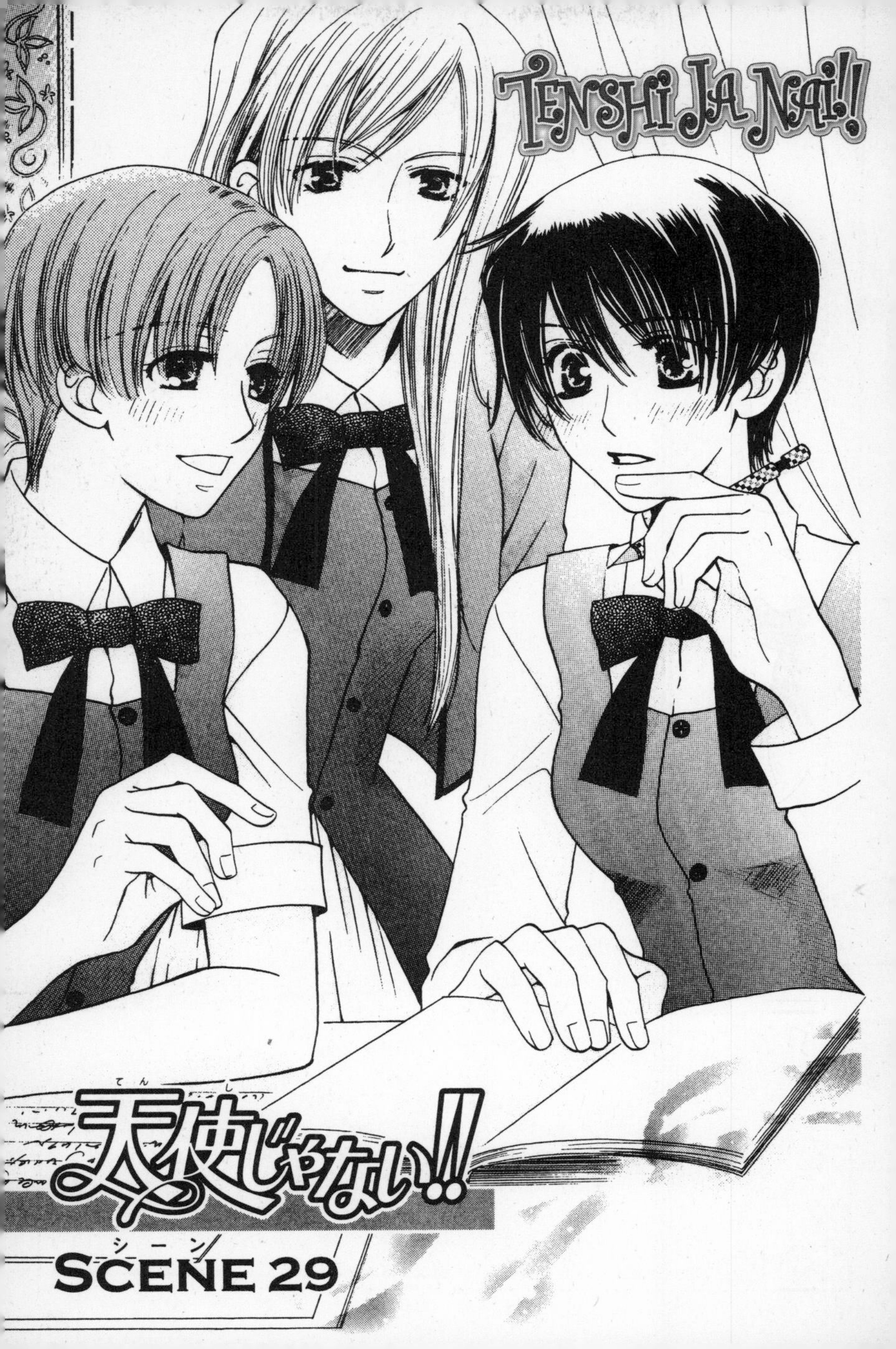
TENSHI JA NAI!!
天使じゃない!!
SCENE 29

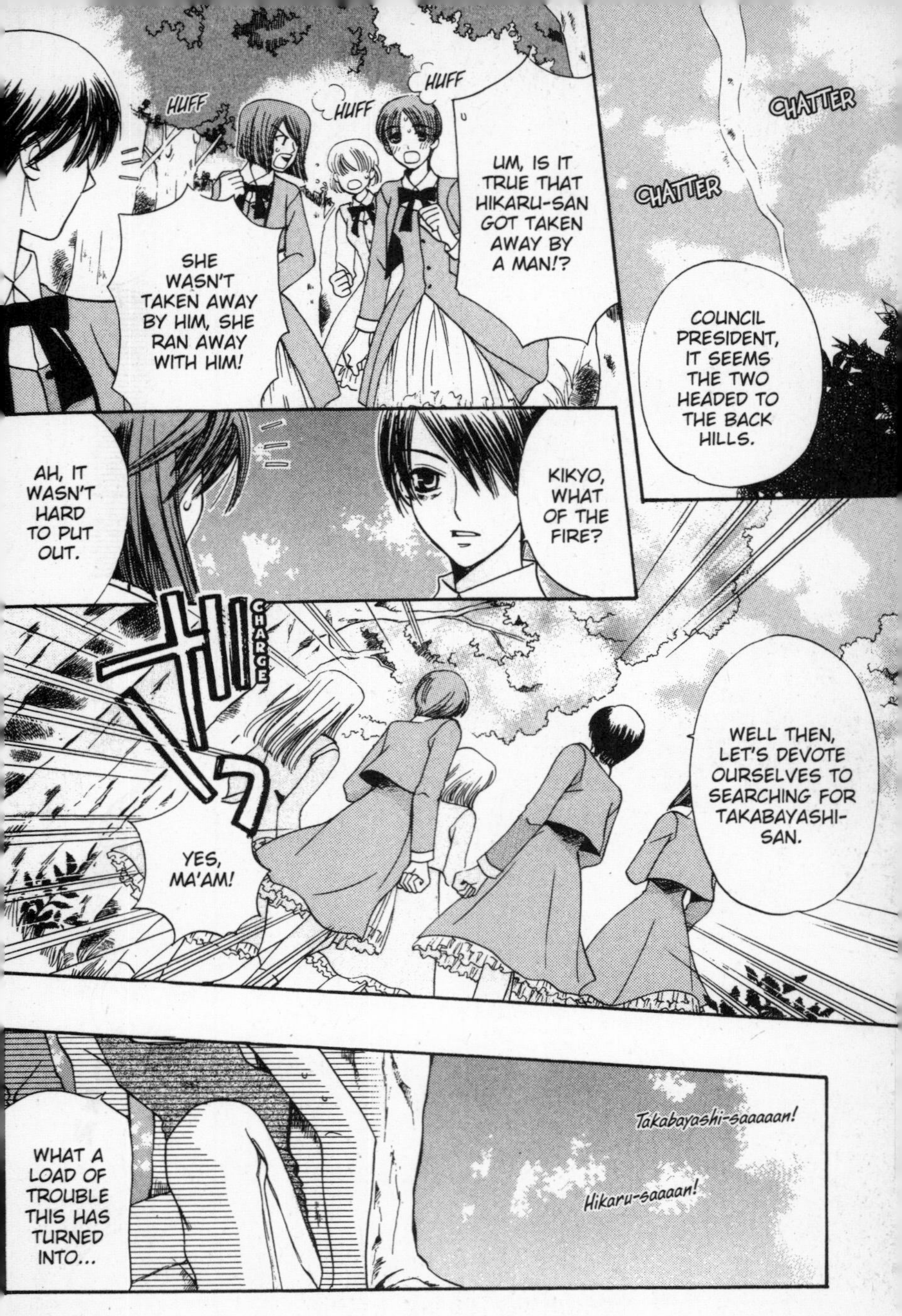

CHATTER
CHATTER
COUNCIL PRESIDENT, IT SEEMS THE TWO HEADED TO THE BACK HILLS.
HUFF
HUFF
HUFF
UM, IS IT TRUE THAT HIKARU-SAN GOT TAKEN AWAY BY A MAN!?
SHE WASN'T TAKEN AWAY BY HIM, SHE RAN AWAY WITH HIM!
KIKYO, WHAT OF THE FIRE?
AH, IT WASN'T HARD TO PUT OUT.
WELL THEN, LET'S DEVOTE OURSELVES TO SEARCHING FOR TAKABAYASHI-SAN.
CHARGE
YES, MA'AM!
Takabayashi-saaaaan!
Hikaru-saaaan!
WHAT A LOAD OF TROUBLE THIS HAS TURNED INTO...

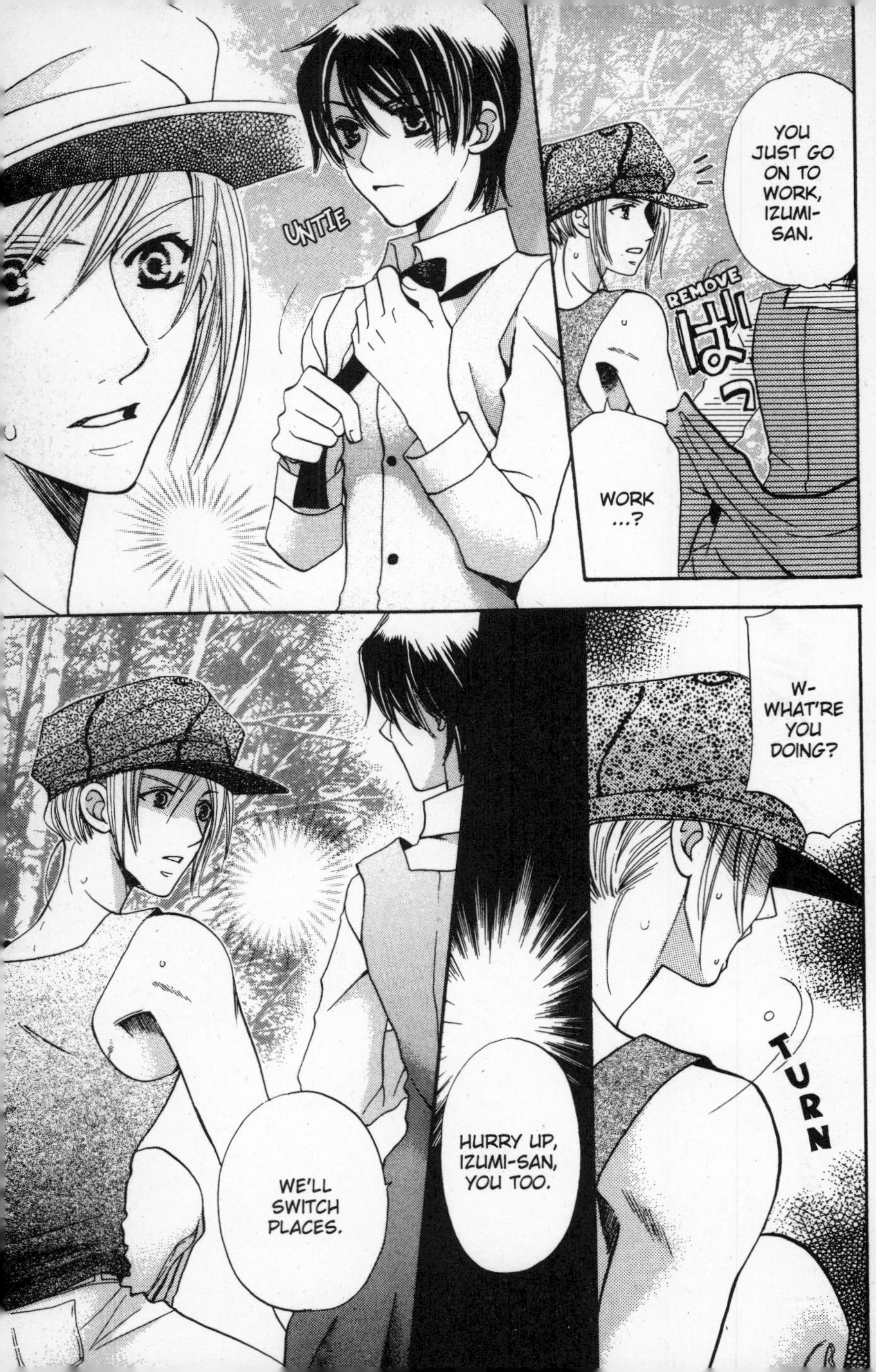
YOU JUST GO ON TO WORK, IZUMI-SAN.
REMOVE
ぱっ
WORK ...?
UNTIE
W-WHAT'RE YOU DOING?
TURN
HURRY UP, IZUMI-SAN, YOU TOO.
WE'LL SWITCH PLACES.

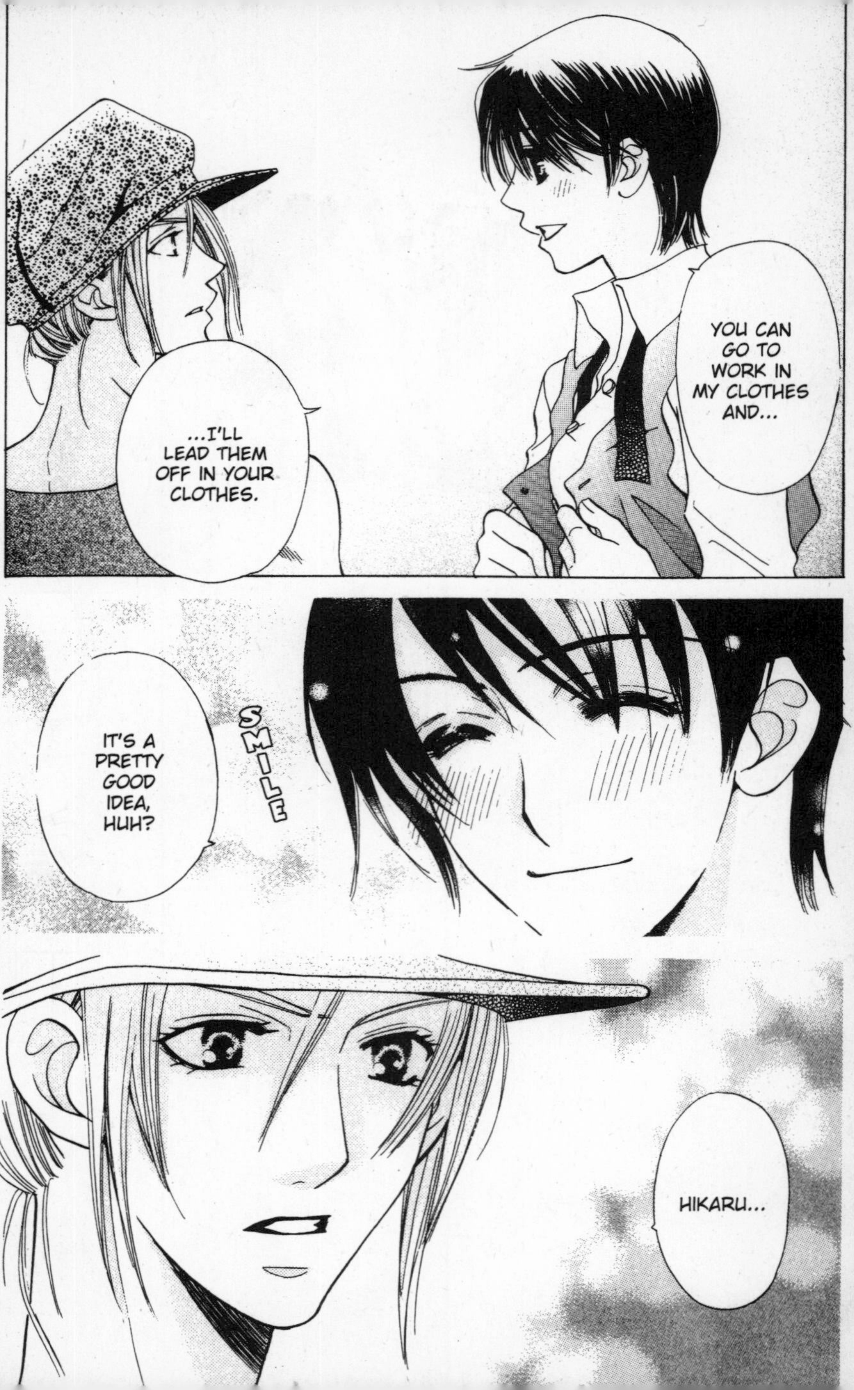
YOU CAN GO TO WORK IN MY CLOTHES AND...
...I'LL LEAD THEM OFF IN YOUR CLOTHES.
SMILE
IT'S A PRETTY GOOD IDEA, HUH?
HIKARU...

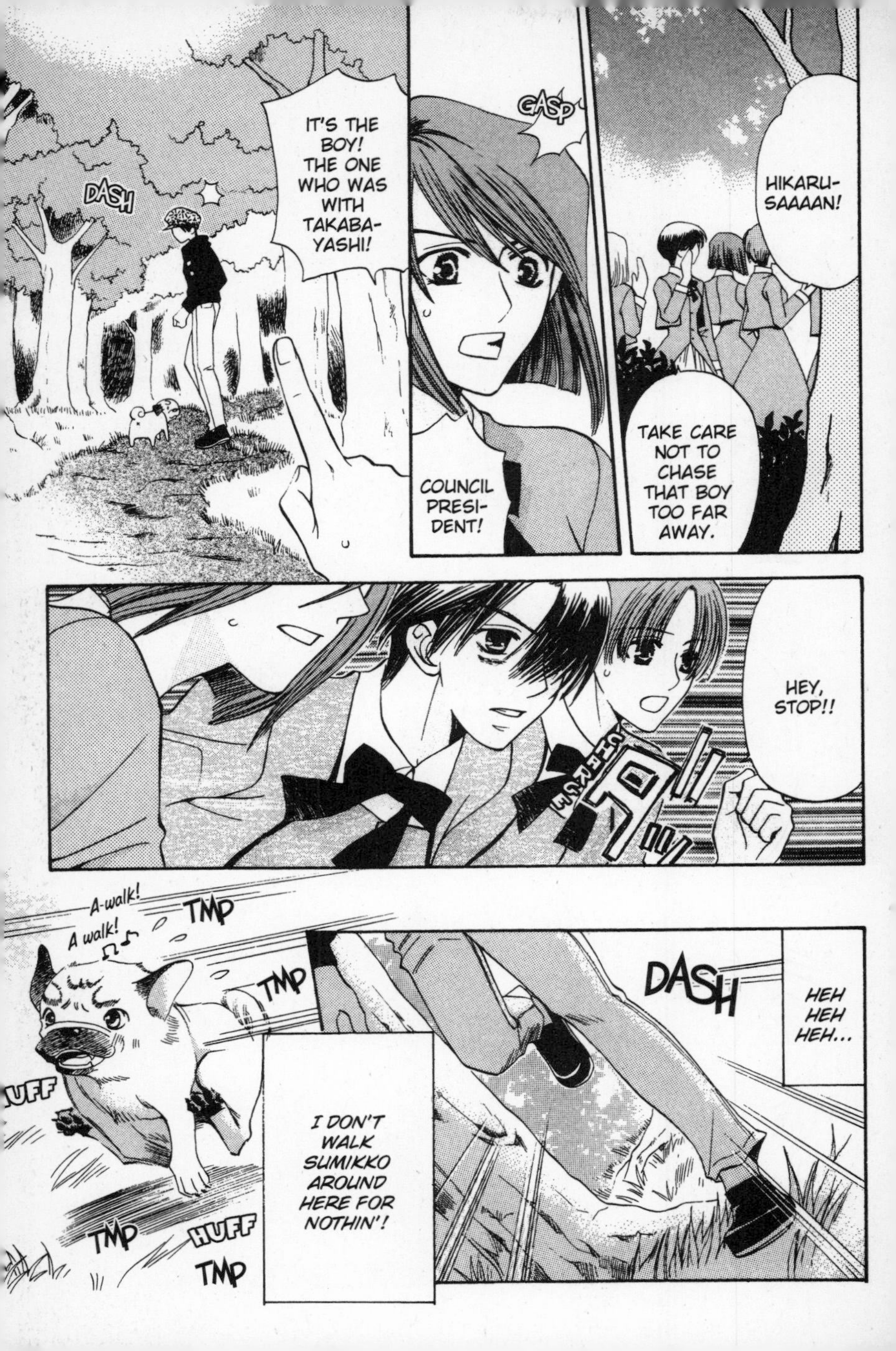
HIKARU-SAAAAN!
TAKE CARE NOT TO CHASE THAT BOY TOO FAR AWAY.
GASP
COUNCIL PRESI-DENT!
IT'S THE BOY! THE ONE WHO WAS WITH TAKABA-YASHI!
DASH
HEY, STOP!!
HEH HEH HEH...
DASH
I DON'T WALK SUMIKKO AROUND HERE FOR NOTHIN'!
A-walk!
A walk!
TMP
TMP
HUFF
TMP
HUFF
TMP

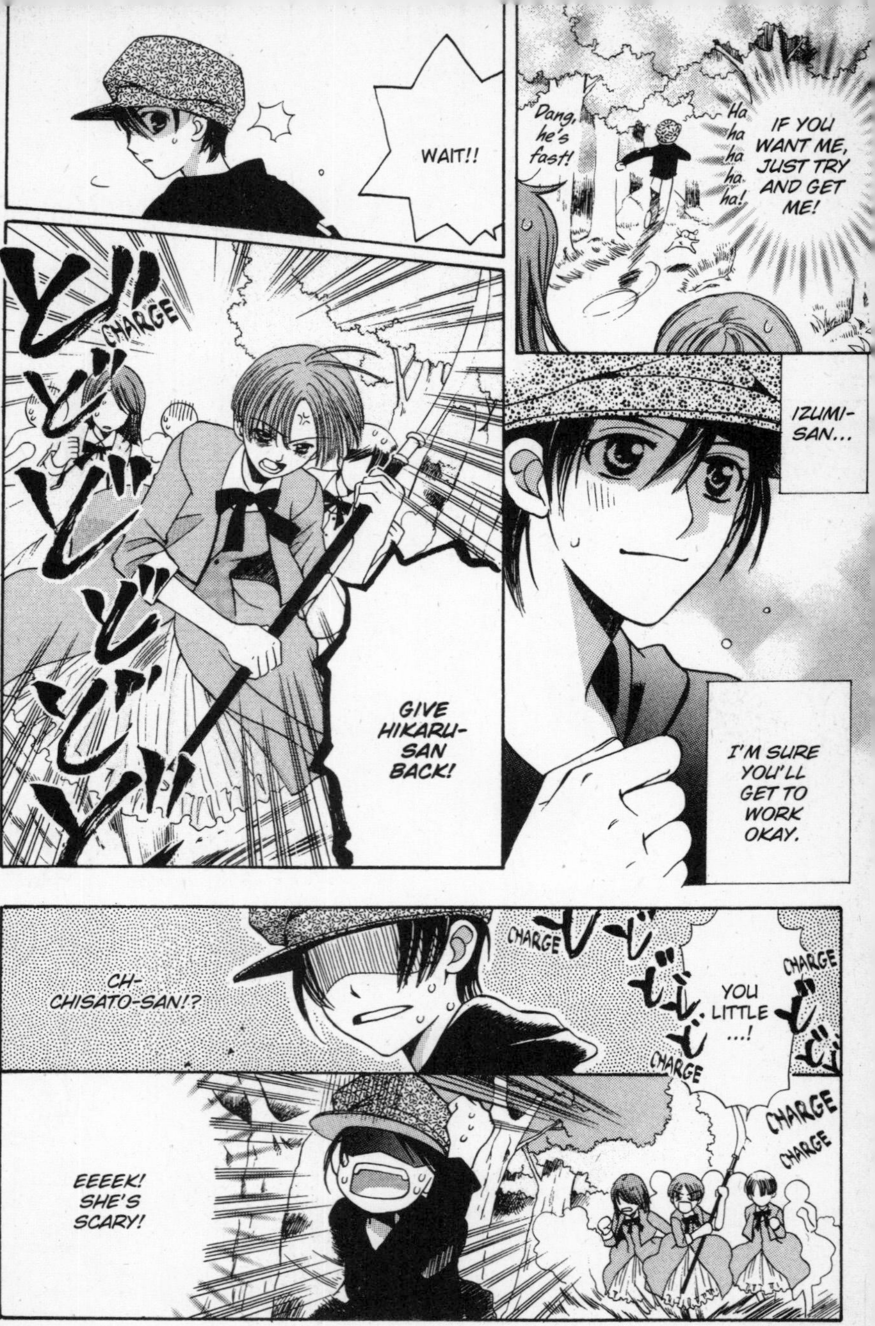
IF YOU WANT ME, JUST TRY AND GET ME!
Ha ha ha ha ha!
Dang, he's fast!
WAIT!!
IZUMI-SAN...
I'M SURE YOU'LL GET TO WORK OKAY.
CHARGE
GIVE HIKARU-SAN BACK!
CHARGE
CHARGE
YOU LITTLE ...!
CHARGE
CH-CHISATO-SAN!?
CHARGE
CHARGE
EEEEK! SHE'S SCARY!

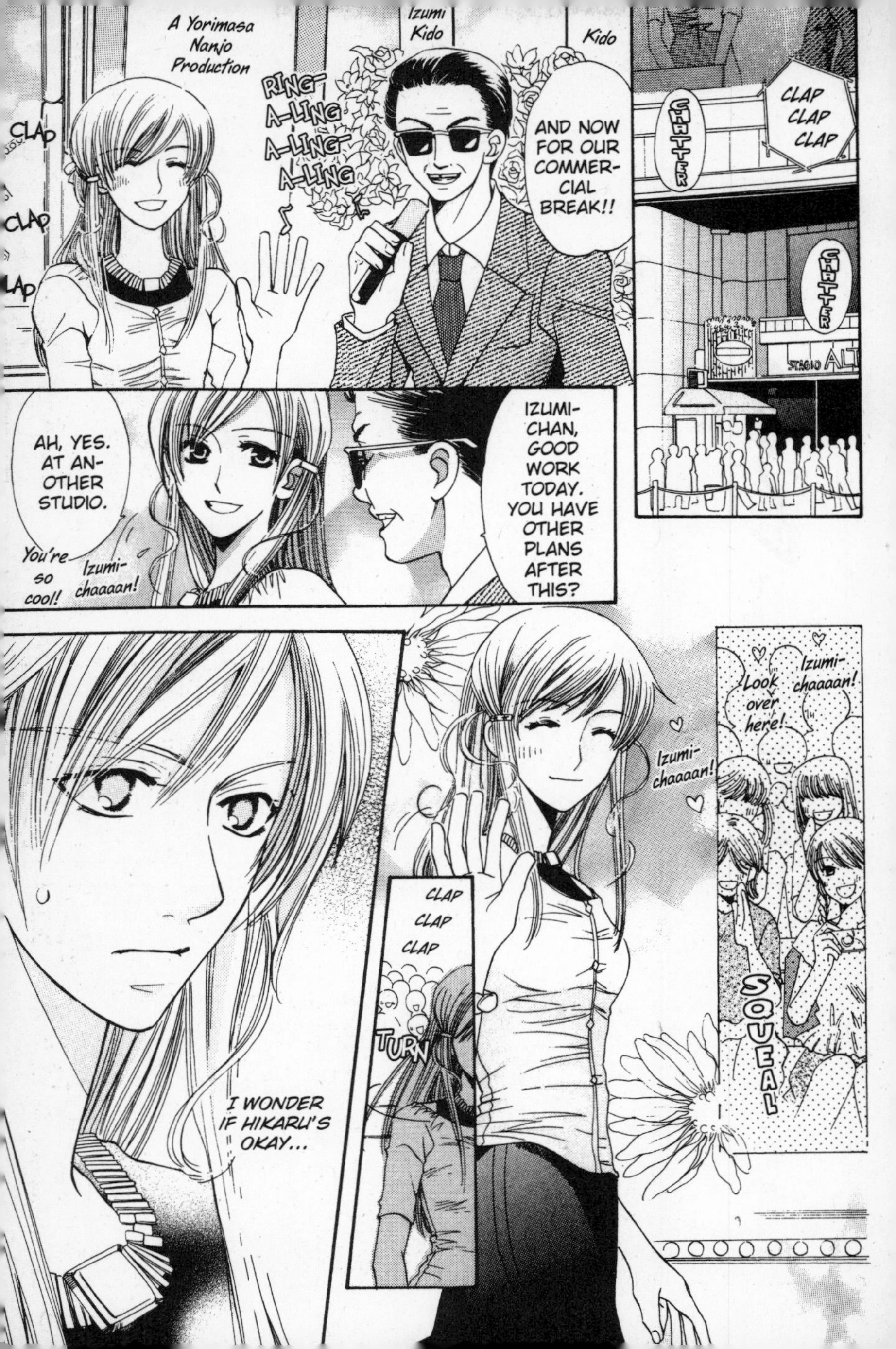
CLAP CLAP CLAP
CHATTER
CHATTER
Kido
AND NOW FOR OUR COMMERCIAL BREAK!!
Izumi Kido
RING-A-LING-A-LING-A-LING
A Yorimasa Nanjo Production
CLAP
CLAP
LAP
IZUMI-CHAN, GOOD WORK TODAY. YOU HAVE OTHER PLANS AFTER THIS?
AH, YES. AT ANOTHER STUDIO.
Izumi-chaaaan!
You're so cool!
Izumi-chaaaan!
Look over here!
Izumi-chaaaan!
SQUEAL
CLAP CLAP CLAP
TURN
I WONDER IF HIKARU'S OKAY...

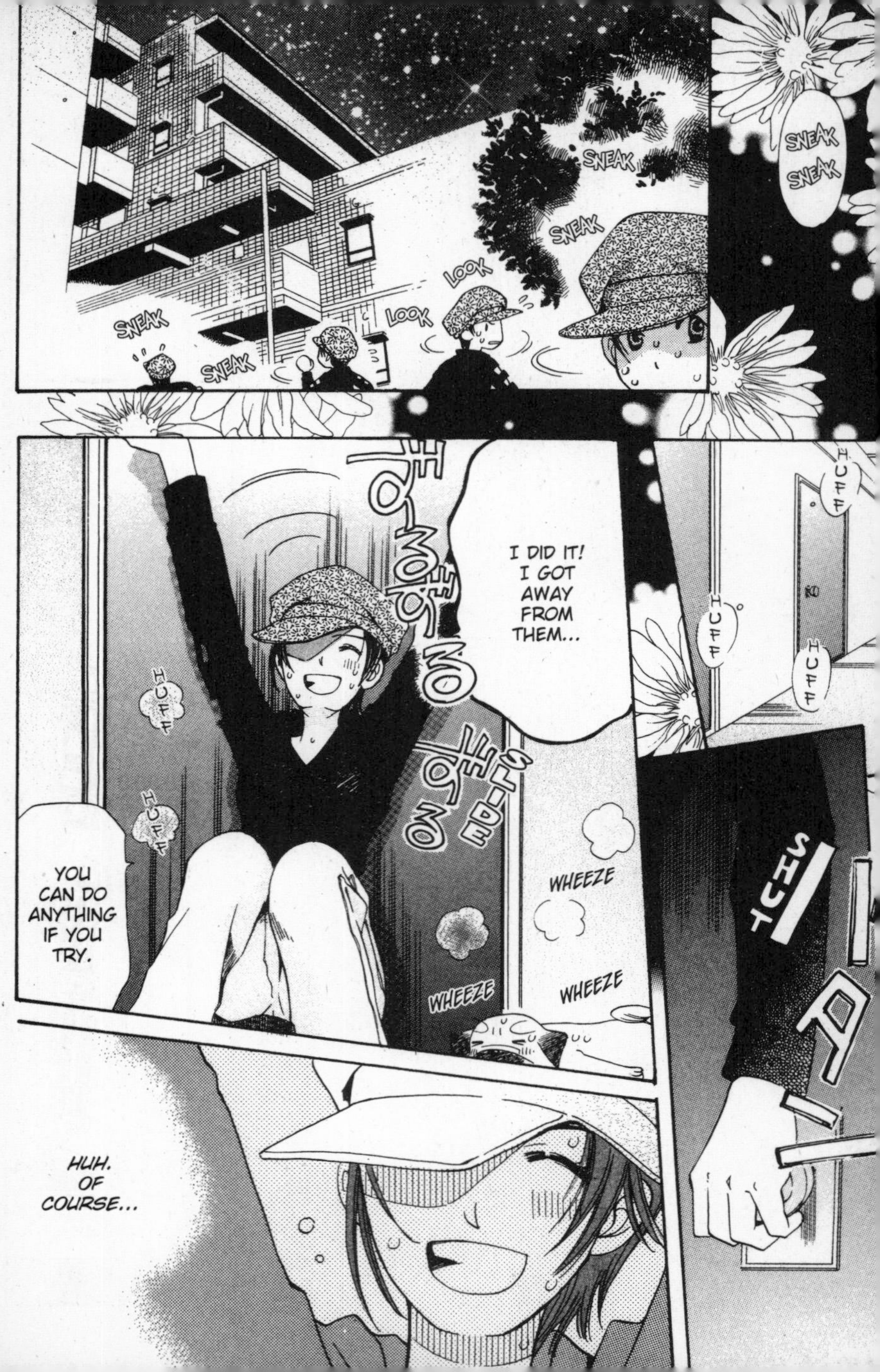
SNEAK
SNEAK
SNEAK
SNEAK
LOOK
LOOK
SNEAK
SNEAK
HUFF
HUFF
HUFF
SHUT
I DID IT! I GOT AWAY FROM THEM...
SLIDE
WHEEZE
WHEEZE
WHEEZE
HUFF
HUFF
YOU CAN DO ANYTHING IF YOU TRY.
HUH. OF COURSE...

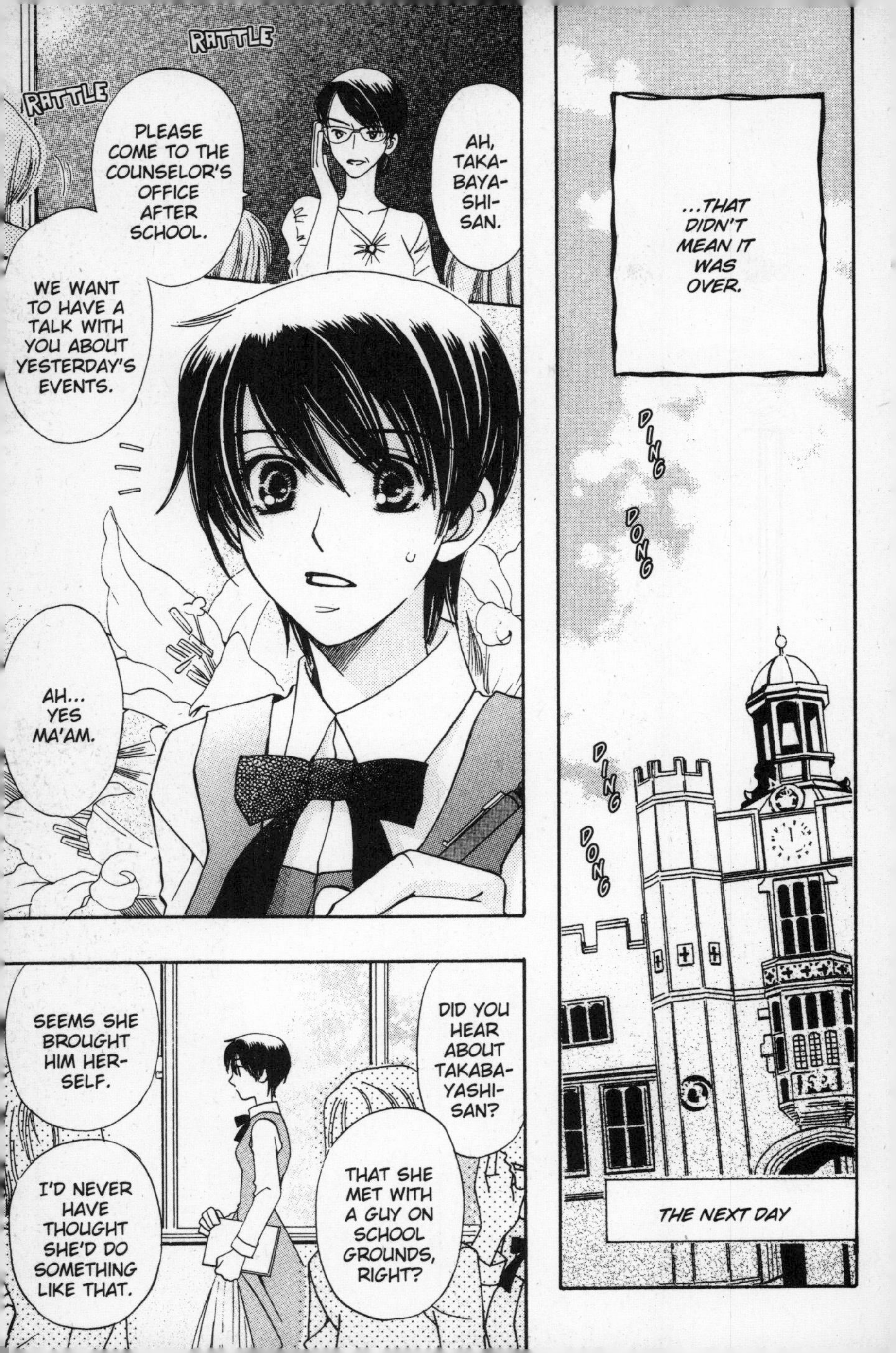
...THAT DIDN'T MEAN IT WAS OVER.
DING
DONG
DING
DONG
THE NEXT DAY
RATTLE
RATTLE
AH, TAKABAYASHI-SAN.
PLEASE COME TO THE COUNSELOR'S OFFICE AFTER SCHOOL.
WE WANT TO HAVE A TALK WITH YOU ABOUT YESTERDAY'S EVENTS.
AH... YES MA'AM.
DID YOU HEAR ABOUT TAKABAYASHI-SAN?
THAT SHE MET WITH A GUY ON SCHOOL GROUNDS, RIGHT?
SEEMS SHE BROUGHT HIM HERSELF.
I'D NEVER HAVE THOUGHT SHE'D DO SOMETHING LIKE THAT.

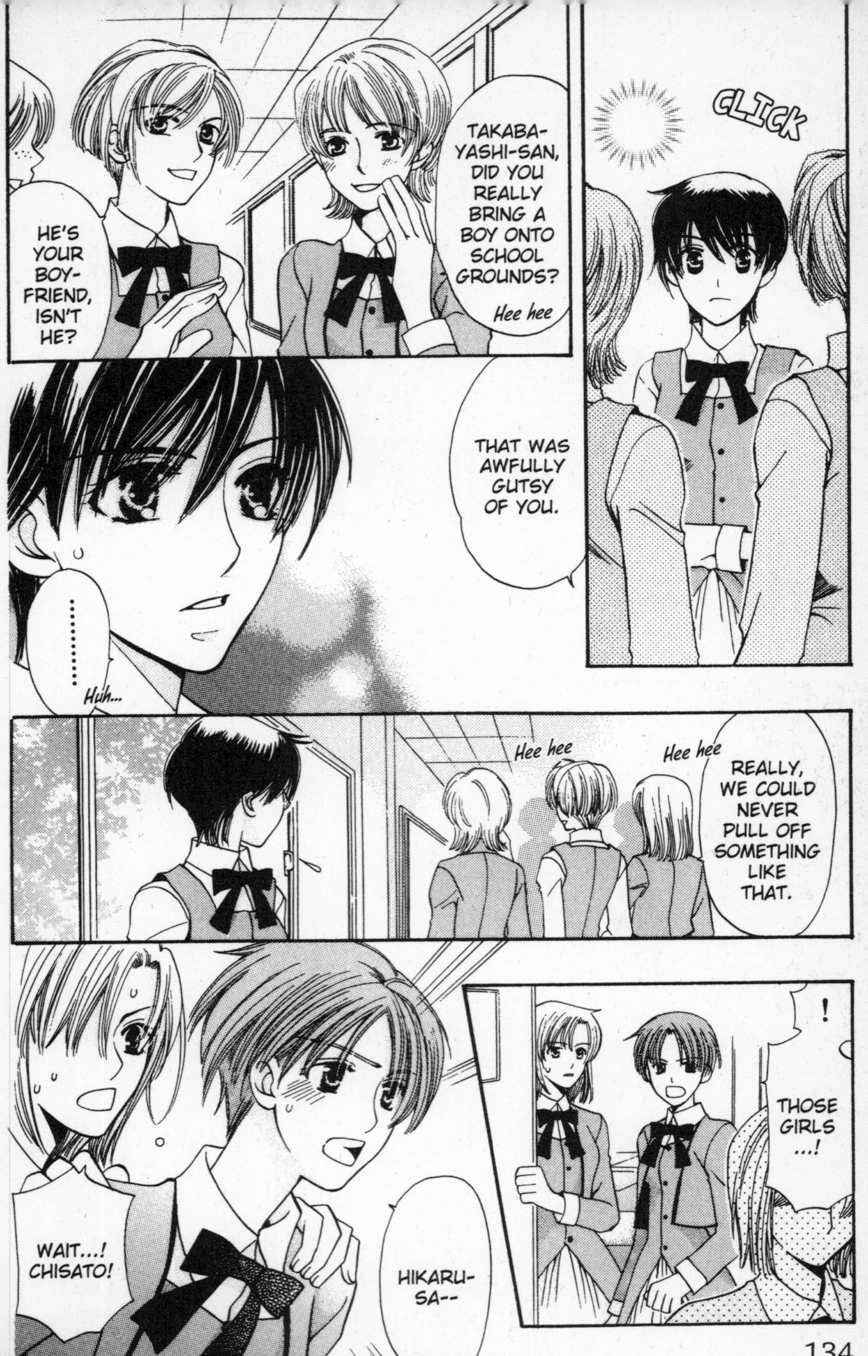
CLICK
TAKABA-YASHI-SAN, DID YOU REALLY BRING A BOY ONTO SCHOOL GROUNDS?
Hee hee
HE'S YOUR BOY-FRIEND, ISN'T HE?
THAT WAS AWFULLY GUTSY OF YOU.
....
Huh...
REALLY, WE COULD NEVER PULL OFF SOMETHING LIKE THAT.
Hee hee
Hee hee
!
THOSE GIRLS ...!
HIKARU-SA--
WAIT...! CHISATO!

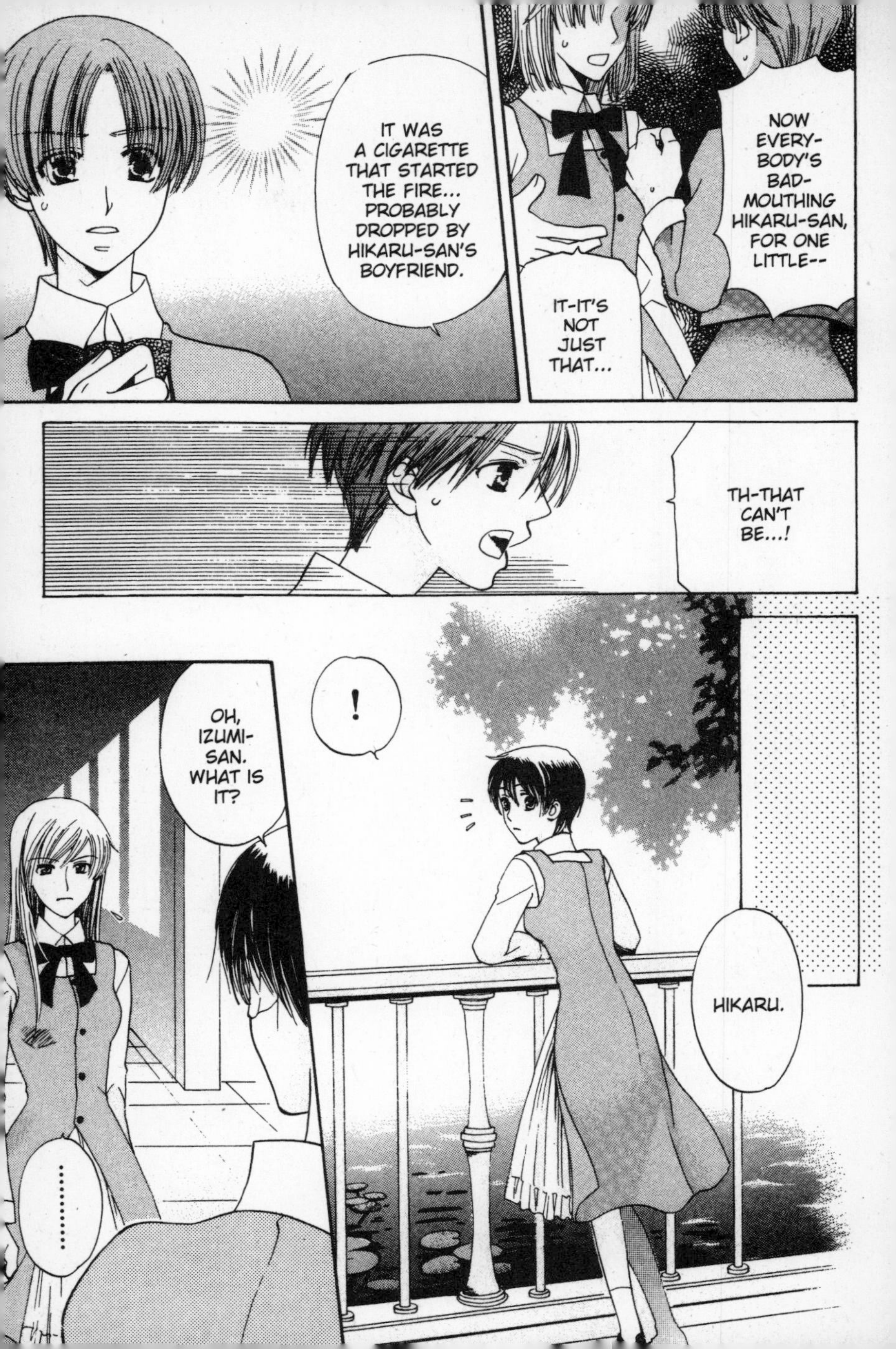
NOW EVERY-BODY'S BAD-MOUTHING HIKARU-SAN, FOR ONE LITTLE--
IT-IT'S NOT JUST THAT...
IT WAS A CIGARETTE THAT STARTED THE FIRE... PROBABLY DROPPED BY HIKARU-SAN'S BOYFRIEND.
TH-THAT CAN'T BE...!
HIKARU.
!
OH, IZUMI-SAN. WHAT IS IT?
......

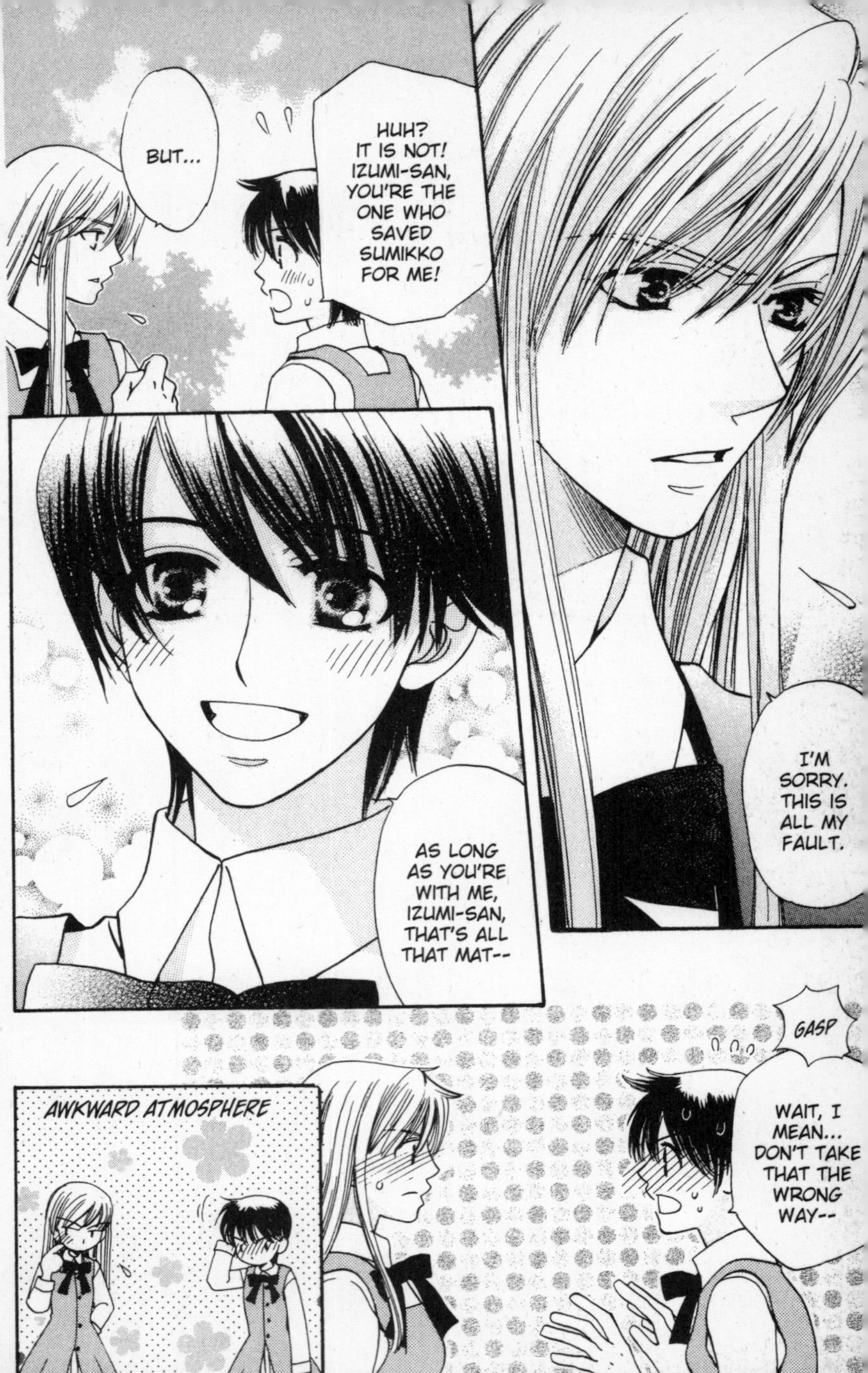
I'M SORRY. THIS IS ALL MY FAULT.
BUT...
HUH? IT IS NOT! IZUMI-SAN, YOU'RE THE ONE WHO SAVED SUMIKKO FOR ME!
AS LONG AS YOU'RE WITH ME, IZUMI-SAN, THAT'S ALL THAT MAT--
GASP
WAIT, I MEAN... DON'T TAKE THAT THE WRONG WAY--
AWKWARD ATMOSPHERE

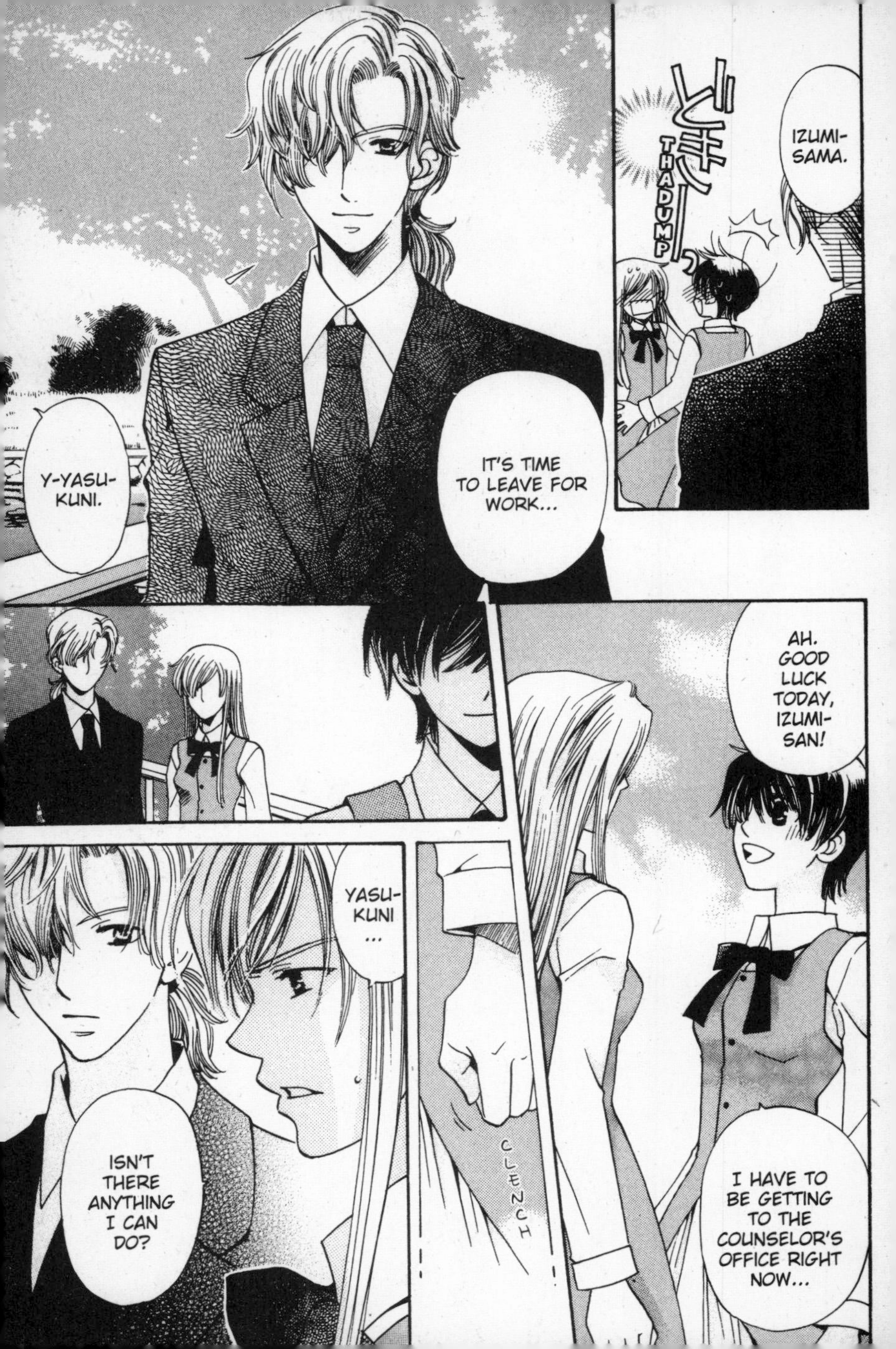
IZUMI-SAMA.
THADUMP
IT'S TIME TO LEAVE FOR WORK...
Y-YASU-KUNI.
AH. GOOD LUCK TODAY, IZUMI-SAN!
I HAVE TO BE GETTING TO THE COUNSELOR'S OFFICE RIGHT NOW...
CLENCH
YASU-KUNI ...
ISN'T THERE ANYTHING I CAN DO?

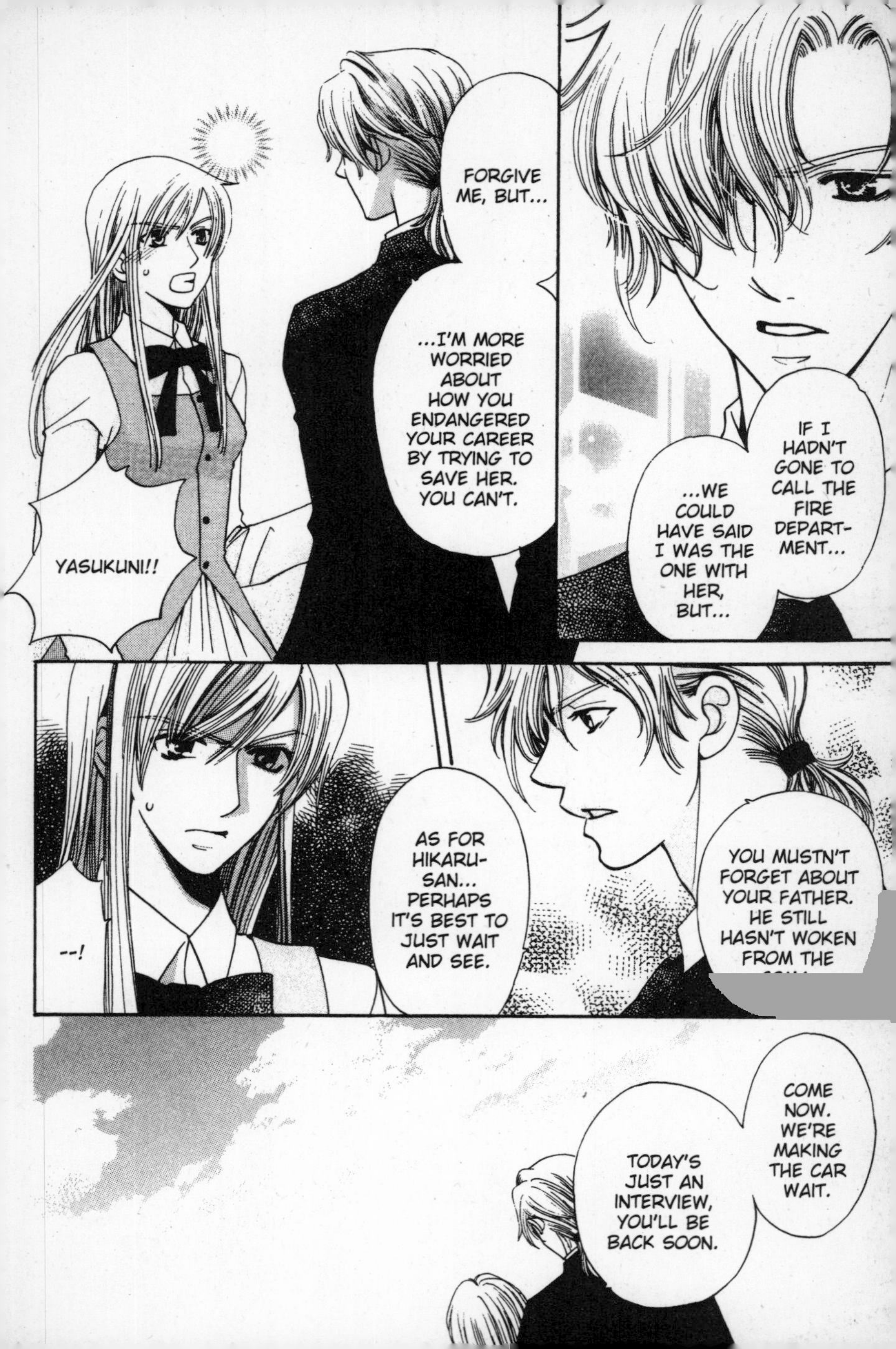
IF I HADN'T GONE TO CALL THE FIRE DEPART-MENT...
...WE COULD HAVE SAID I WAS THE ONE WITH HER, BUT...
FORGIVE ME, BUT...
...I'M MORE WORRIED ABOUT HOW YOU ENDANGERED YOUR CAREER BY TRYING TO SAVE HER. YOU CAN'T.
YASUKUNI!!
YOU MUSTN'T FORGET ABOUT YOUR FATHER. HE STILL HASN'T WOKEN FROM THE
AS FOR HIKARU-SAN... PERHAPS IT'S BEST TO JUST WAIT AND SEE.
--!
COME NOW. WE'RE MAKING THE CAR WAIT.
TODAY'S JUST AN INTERVIEW, YOU'LL BE BACK SOON.

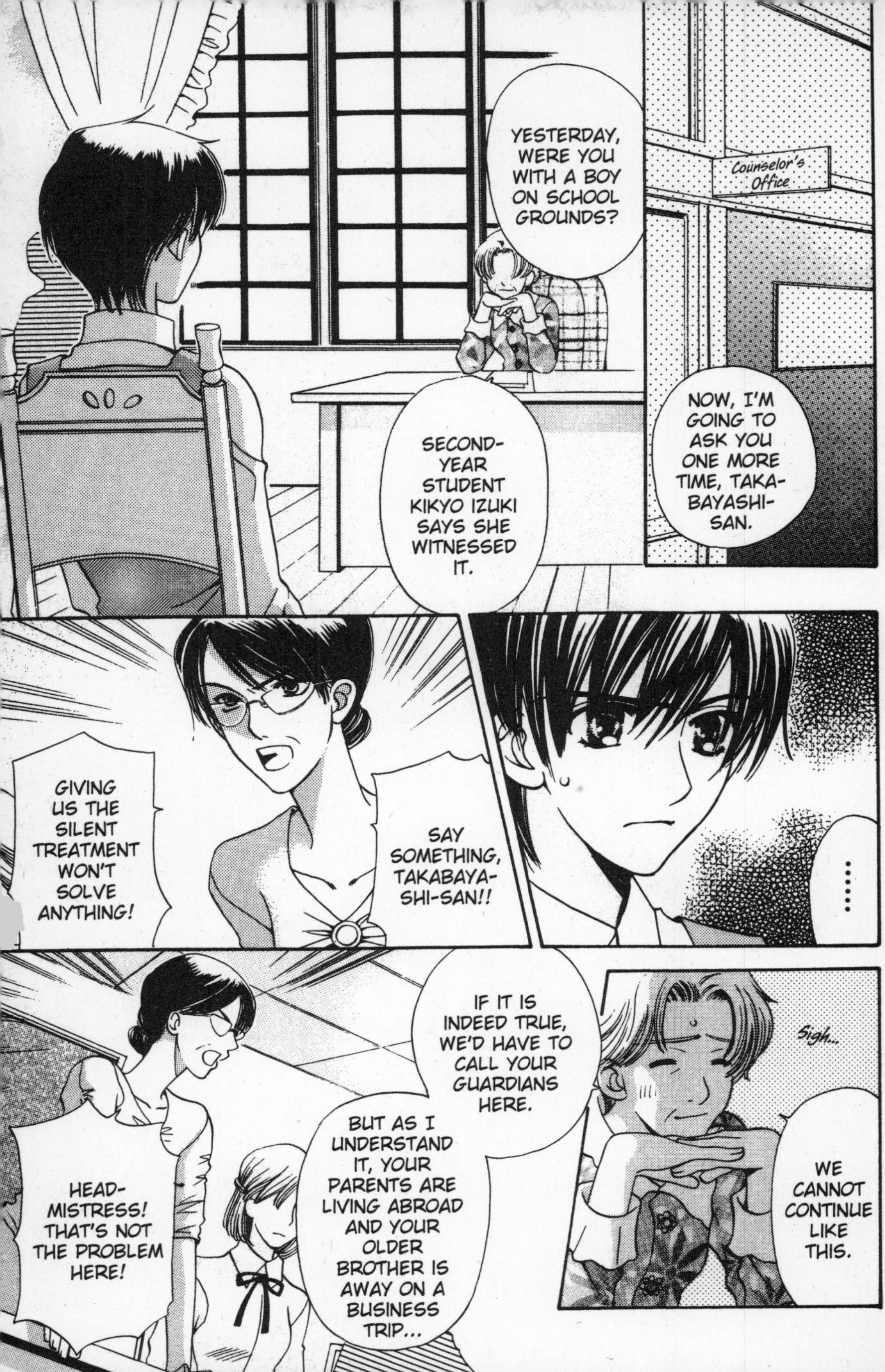
Counselor's Office
NOW, I'M GOING TO ASK YOU ONE MORE TIME, TAKA-BAYASHI-SAN.
YESTERDAY, WERE YOU WITH A BOY ON SCHOOL GROUNDS?
SECOND-YEAR STUDENT KIKYO IZUKI SAYS SHE WITNESSED IT.
......
SAY SOMETHING, TAKABAYA-SHI-SAN!!
GIVING US THE SILENT TREATMENT WON'T SOLVE ANYTHING!
Sigh...
WE CANNOT CONTINUE LIKE THIS.
IF IT IS INDEED TRUE, WE'D HAVE TO CALL YOUR GUARDIANS HERE.
BUT AS I UNDERSTAND IT, YOUR PARENTS ARE LIVING ABROAD AND YOUR OLDER BROTHER IS AWAY ON A BUSINESS TRIP...
HEAD-MISTRESS! THAT'S NOT THE PROBLEM HERE!

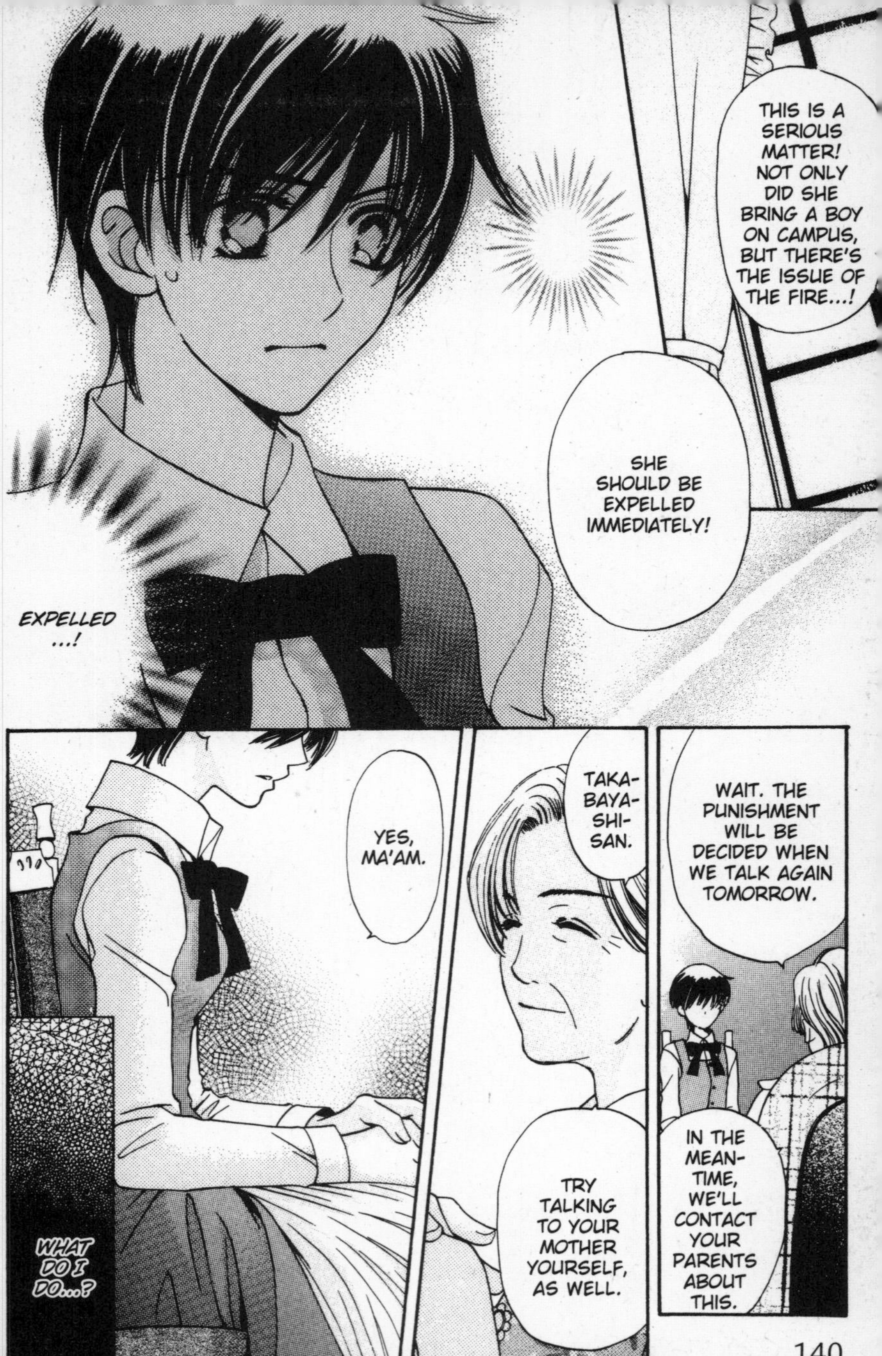
THIS IS A SERIOUS MATTER! NOT ONLY DID SHE BRING A BOY ON CAMPUS, BUT THERE'S THE ISSUE OF THE FIRE...!
SHE SHOULD BE EXPELLED IMMEDIATELY!
EXPELLED ...!
WAIT. THE PUNISHMENT WILL BE DECIDED WHEN WE TALK AGAIN TOMORROW.
IN THE MEAN-TIME, WE'LL CONTACT YOUR PARENTS ABOUT THIS.
TAKA-BAYA-SHI-SAN.
TRY TALKING TO YOUR MOTHER YOURSELF, AS WELL.
YES, MA'AM.
WHAT DO I DO...?

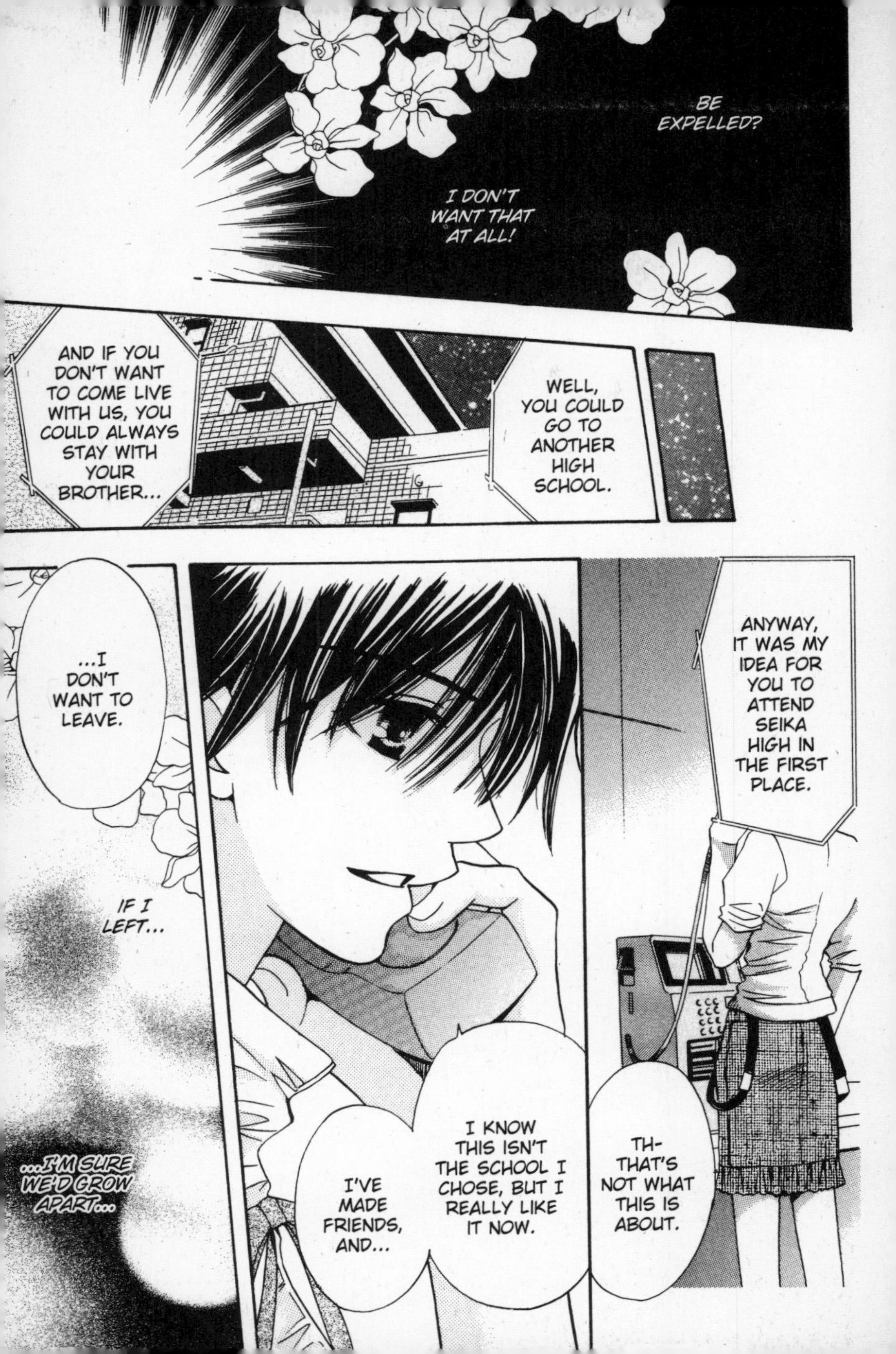
BE EXPELLED?
I DON'T WANT THAT AT ALL!
WELL, YOU COULD GO TO ANOTHER HIGH SCHOOL.
AND IF YOU DON'T WANT TO COME LIVE WITH US, YOU COULD ALWAYS STAY WITH YOUR BROTHER...
ANYWAY, IT WAS MY IDEA FOR YOU TO ATTEND SEIKA HIGH IN THE FIRST PLACE.
TH- THAT'S NOT WHAT THIS IS ABOUT.
I KNOW THIS ISN'T THE SCHOOL I CHOSE, BUT I REALLY LIKE IT NOW.
I'VE MADE FRIENDS, AND...
...I DON'T WANT TO LEAVE.
IF I LEFT...
...I'M SURE WE'D GROW APART...

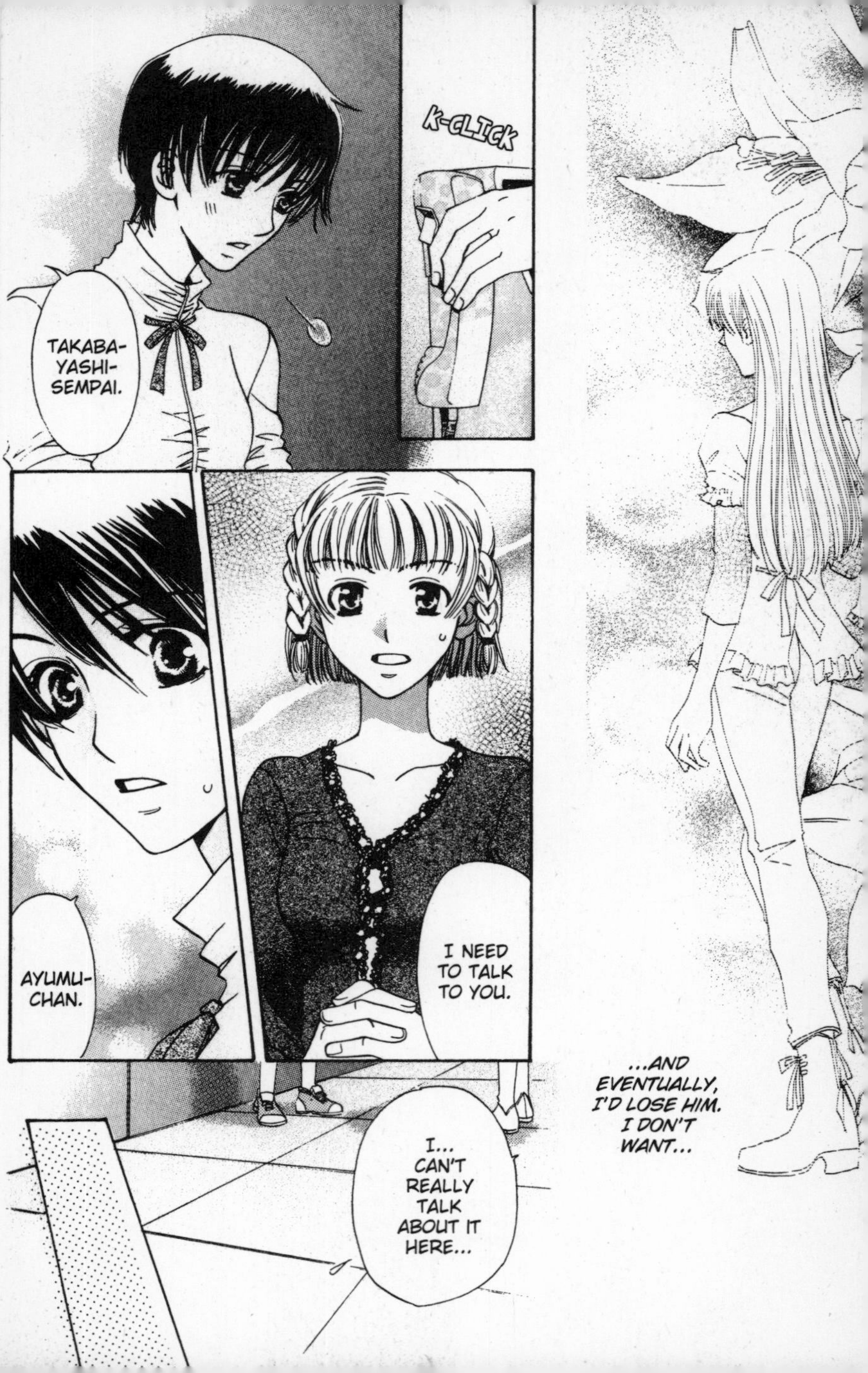
...AND EVENTUALLY, I'D LOSE HIM. I DON'T WANT...
K-CLICK
TAKABAYASHI-SEMPAI.
I NEED TO TALK TO YOU.
AYUMU-CHAN.
I... CAN'T REALLY TALK ABOUT IT HERE...

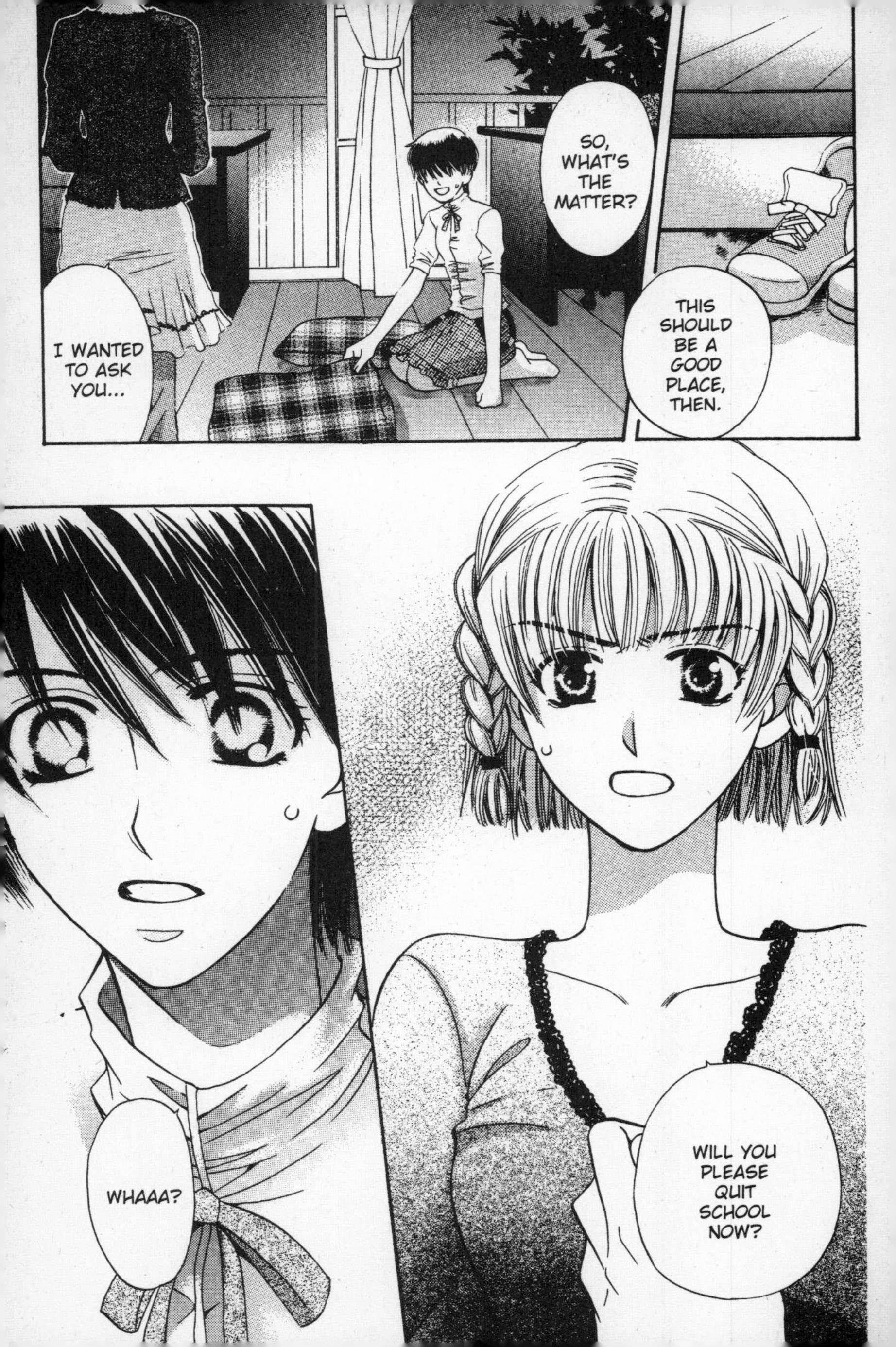
THIS SHOULD BE A GOOD PLACE, THEN.
SO, WHAT'S THE MATTER?
I WANTED TO ASK YOU...
WILL YOU PLEASE QUIT SCHOOL NOW?
WHAAA?

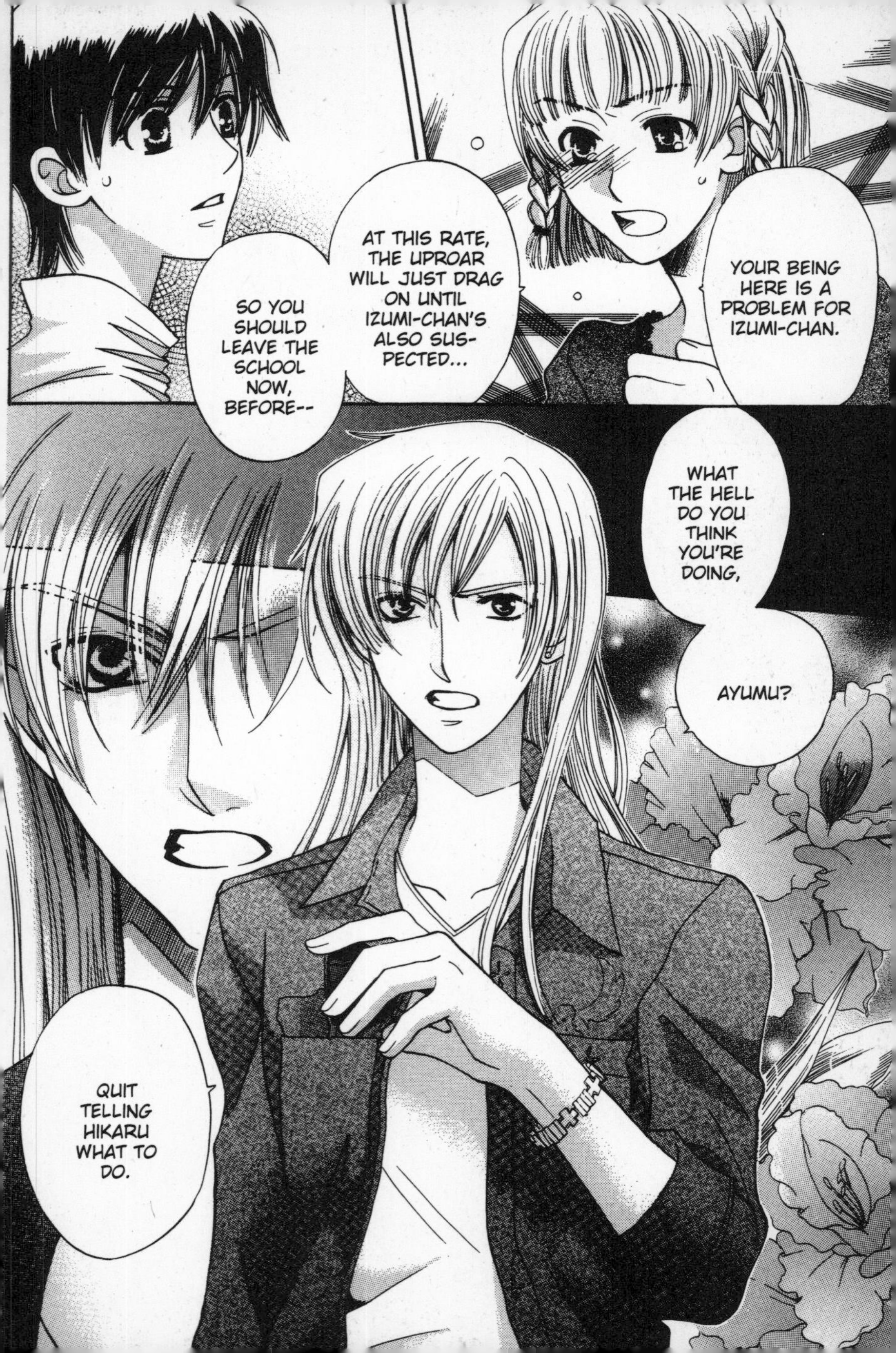
YOUR BEING HERE IS A PROBLEM FOR IZUMI-CHAN.
AT THIS RATE, THE UPROAR WILL JUST DRAG ON UNTIL IZUMI-CHAN'S ALSO SUS-PECTED...
SO YOU SHOULD LEAVE THE SCHOOL NOW, BEFORE--
WHAT THE HELL DO YOU THINK YOU'RE DOING,
AYUMU?
QUIT TELLING HIKARU WHAT TO DO.

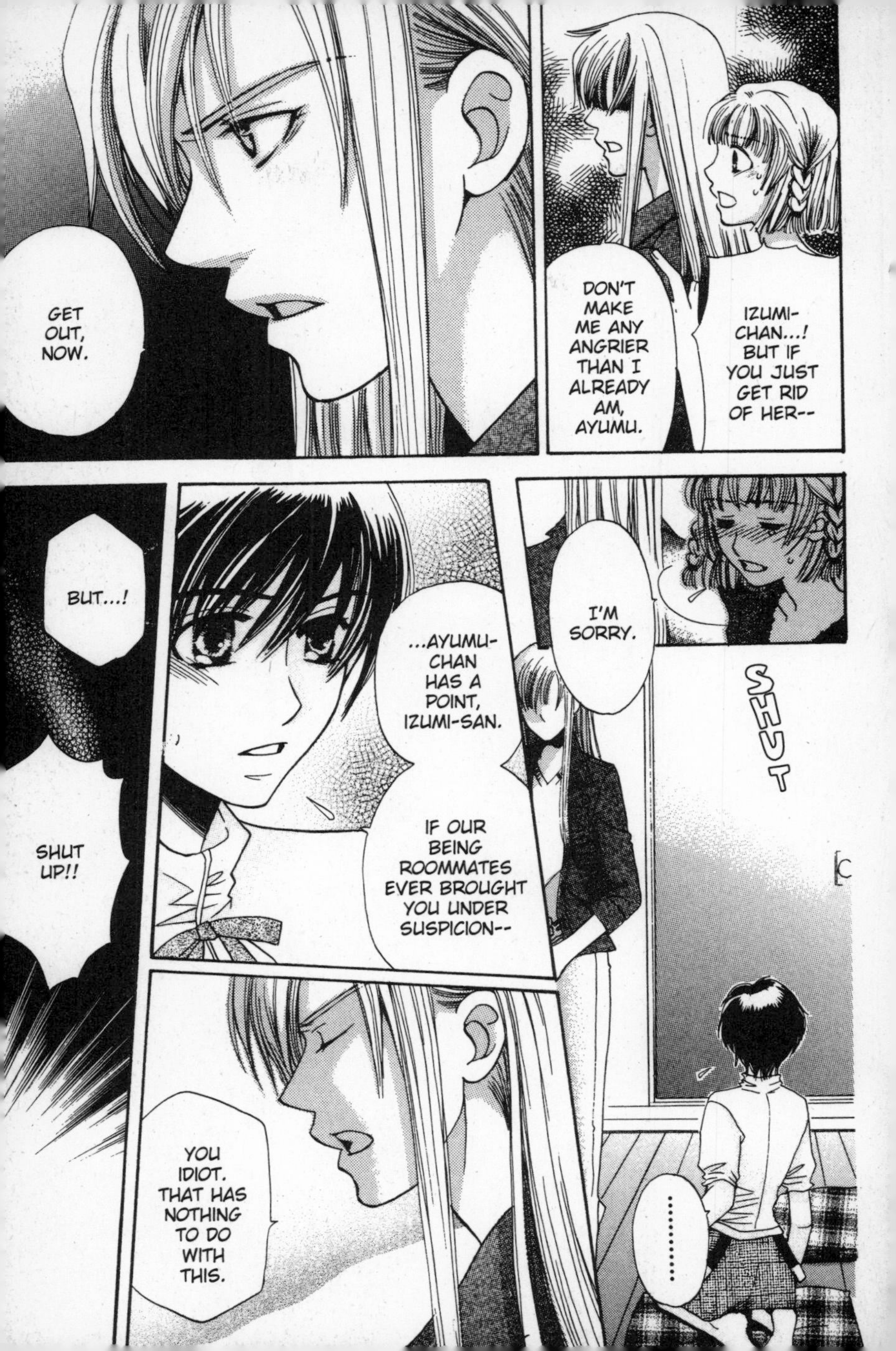
IZUMI-CHAN...! BUT IF YOU JUST GET RID OF HER--
DON'T MAKE ME ANY ANGRIER THAN I ALREADY AM, AYUMU.
GET OUT, NOW.
I'M SORRY.
SHUT
......
...AYUMU-CHAN HAS A POINT, IZUMI-SAN.
IF OUR BEING ROOMMATES EVER BROUGHT YOU UNDER SUSPICION--
BUT...!
SHUT UP!!
YOU IDIOT. THAT HAS NOTHING TO DO WITH THIS.

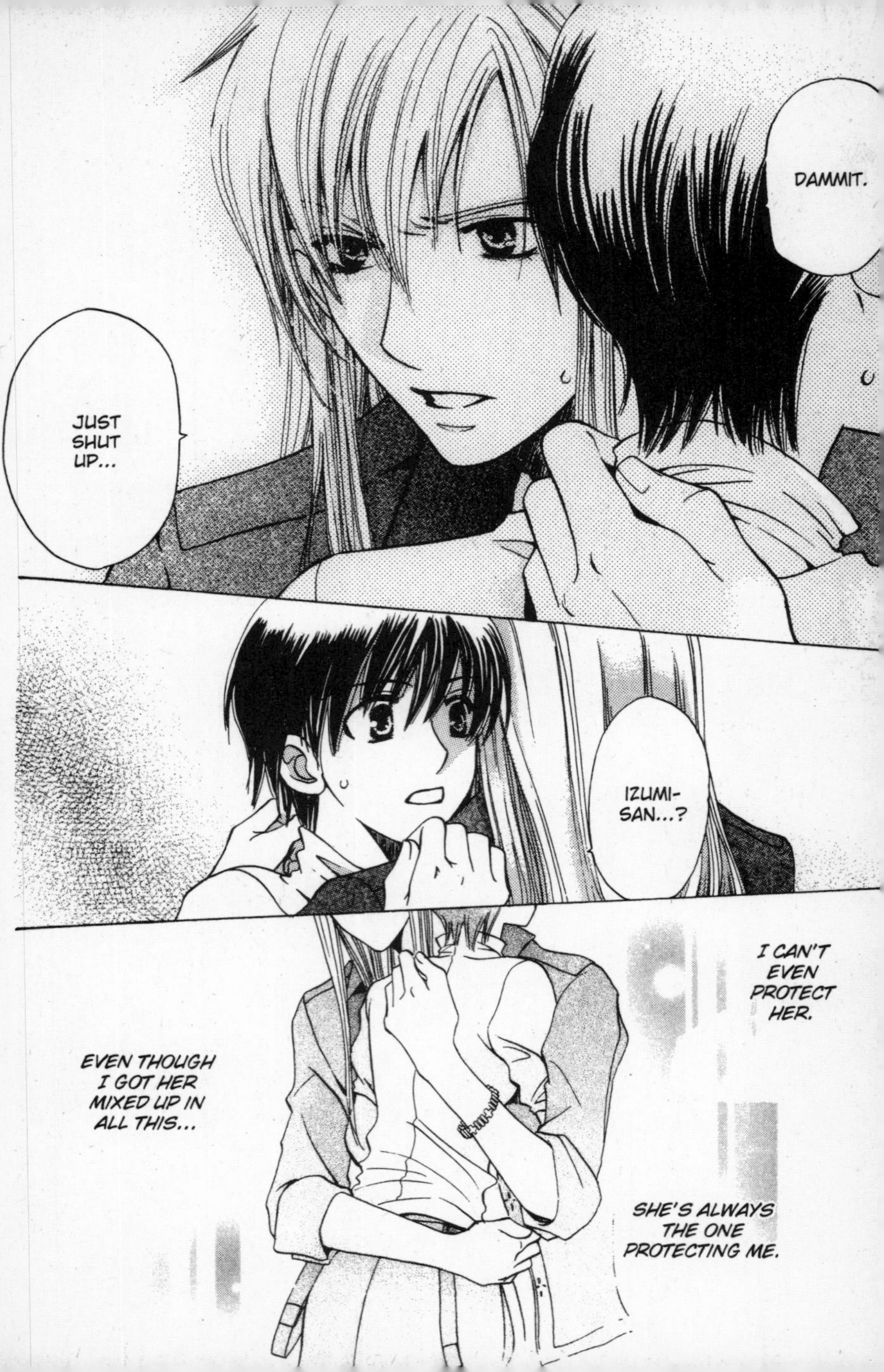
DAMMIT.
JUST SHUT UP...
IZUMI-SAN...?
I CAN'T EVEN PROTECT HER.
EVEN THOUGH I GOT HER MIXED UP IN ALL THIS...
SHE'S ALWAYS THE ONE PROTECTING ME.

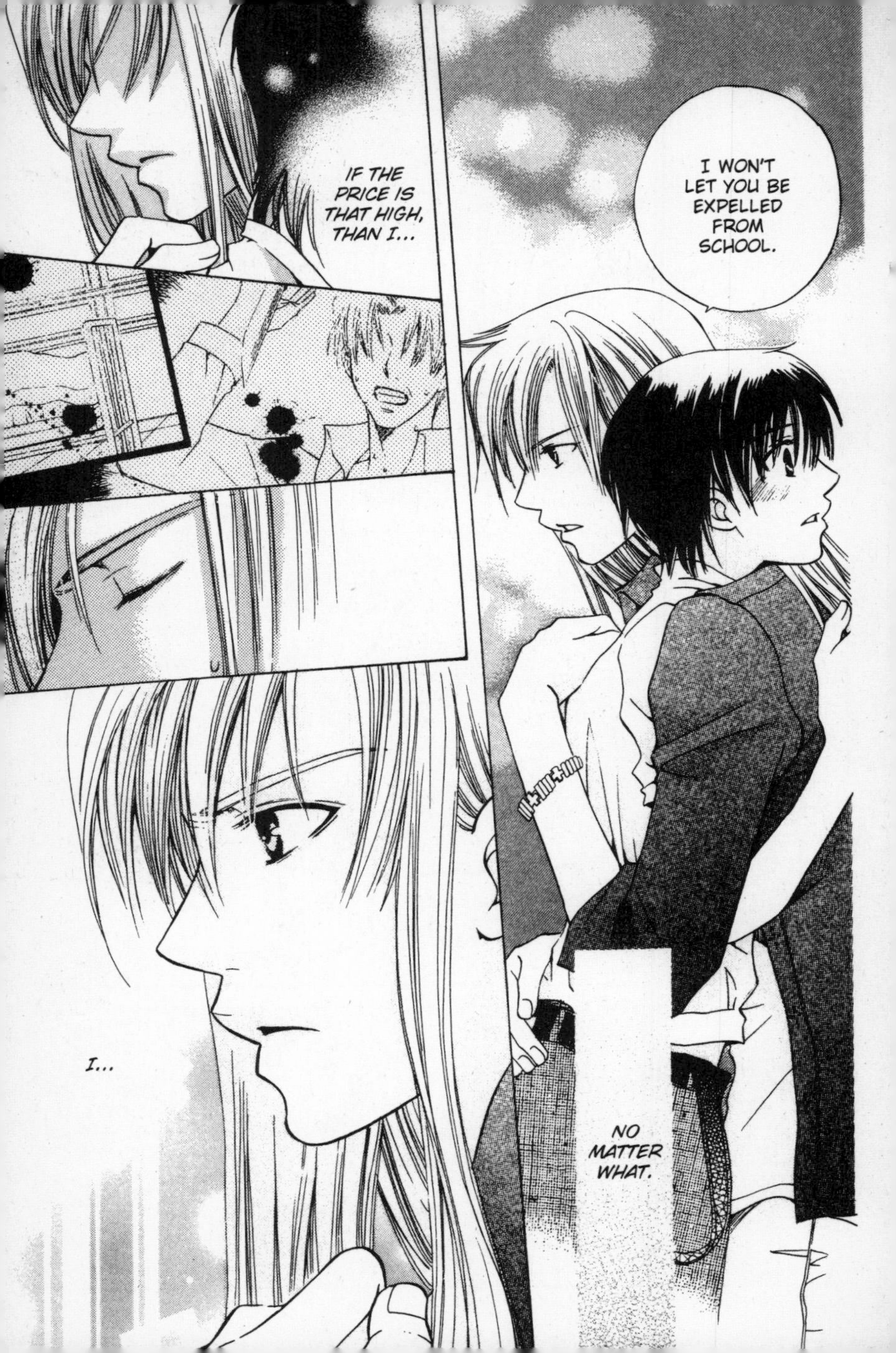
I WON'T LET YOU BE EXPELLED FROM SCHOOL.
NO MATTER WHAT.
IF THE PRICE IS THAT HIGH, THAN I...
I...

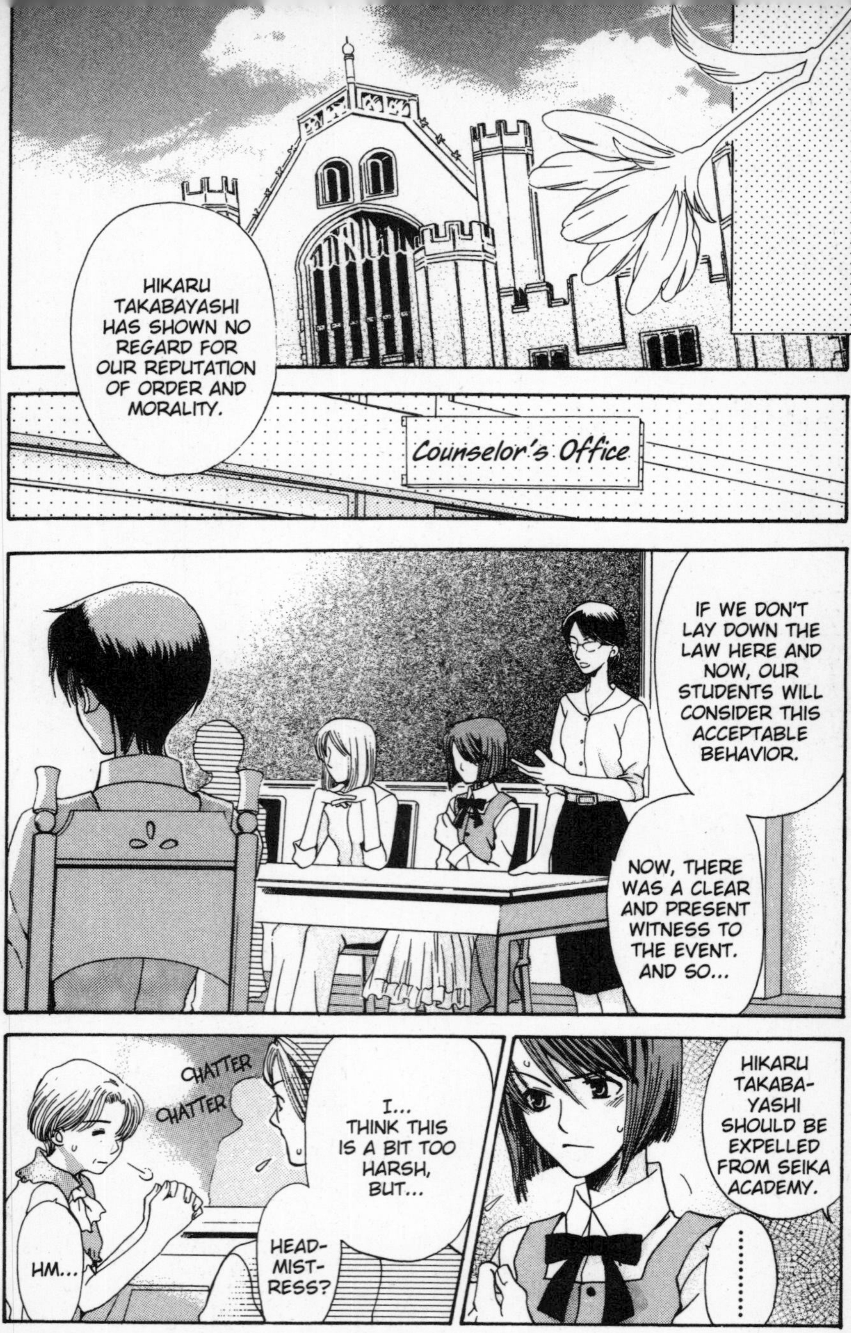
HIKARU TAKABAYASHI HAS SHOWN NO REGARD FOR OUR REPUTATION OF ORDER AND MORALITY.
Counselor's Office
IF WE DON'T LAY DOWN THE LAW HERE AND NOW, OUR STUDENTS WILL CONSIDER THIS ACCEPTABLE BEHAVIOR.
NOW, THERE WAS A CLEAR AND PRESENT WITNESS TO THE EVENT. AND SO...
HIKARU TAKABA-YASHI SHOULD BE EXPELLED FROM SEIKA ACADEMY.
......
I... THINK THIS IS A BIT TOO HARSH, BUT...
HEAD-MIST-RESS?
CHATTER
CHATTER
HM...

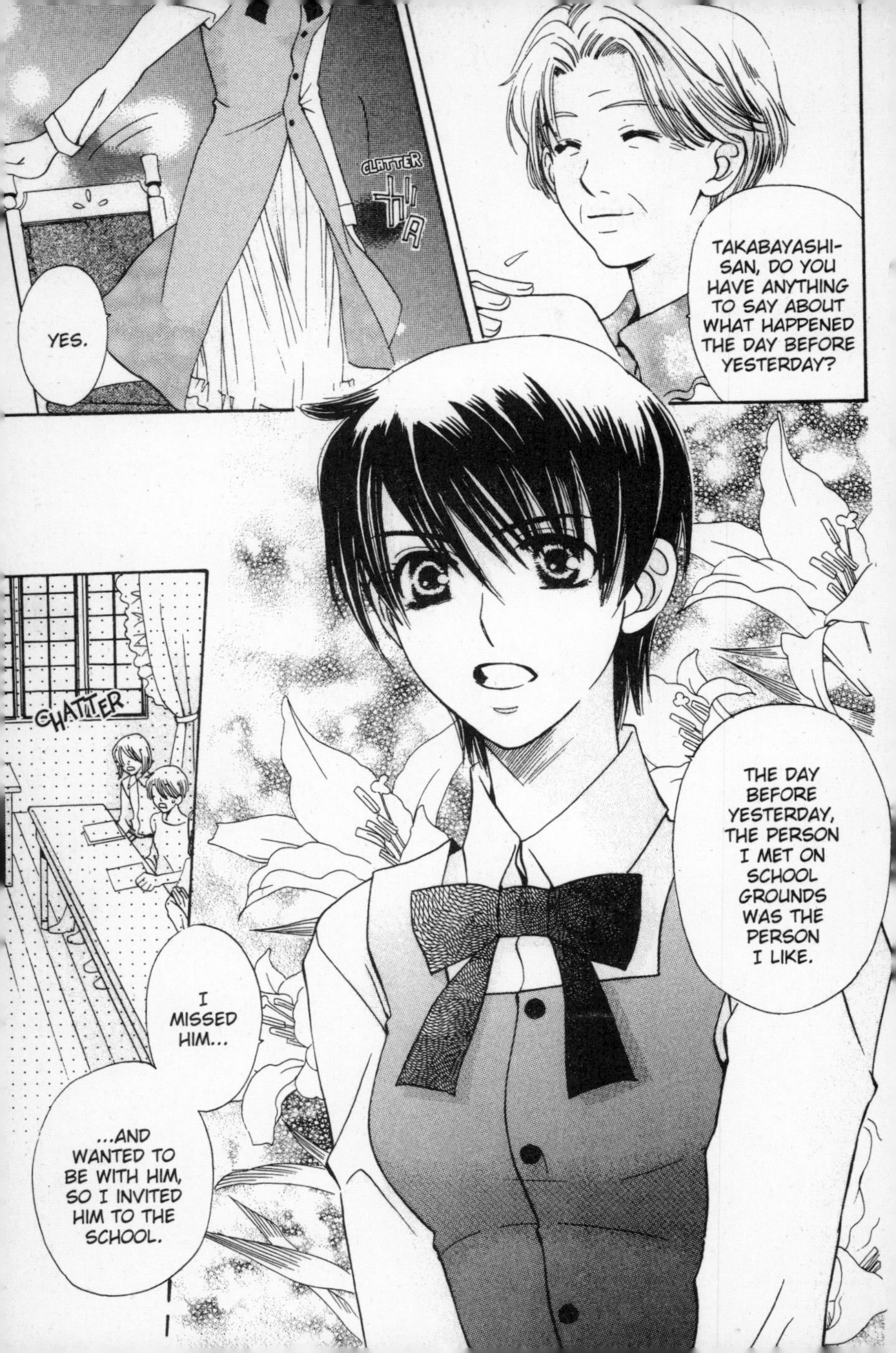
TAKABAYASHI-SAN, DO YOU HAVE ANYTHING TO SAY ABOUT WHAT HAPPENED THE DAY BEFORE YESTERDAY?
CLATTER
YES.
THE DAY BEFORE YESTERDAY, THE PERSON I MET ON SCHOOL GROUNDS WAS THE PERSON I LIKE.
I MISSED HIM...
...AND WANTED TO BE WITH HIM, SO I INVITED HIM TO THE SCHOOL.
CHATTER

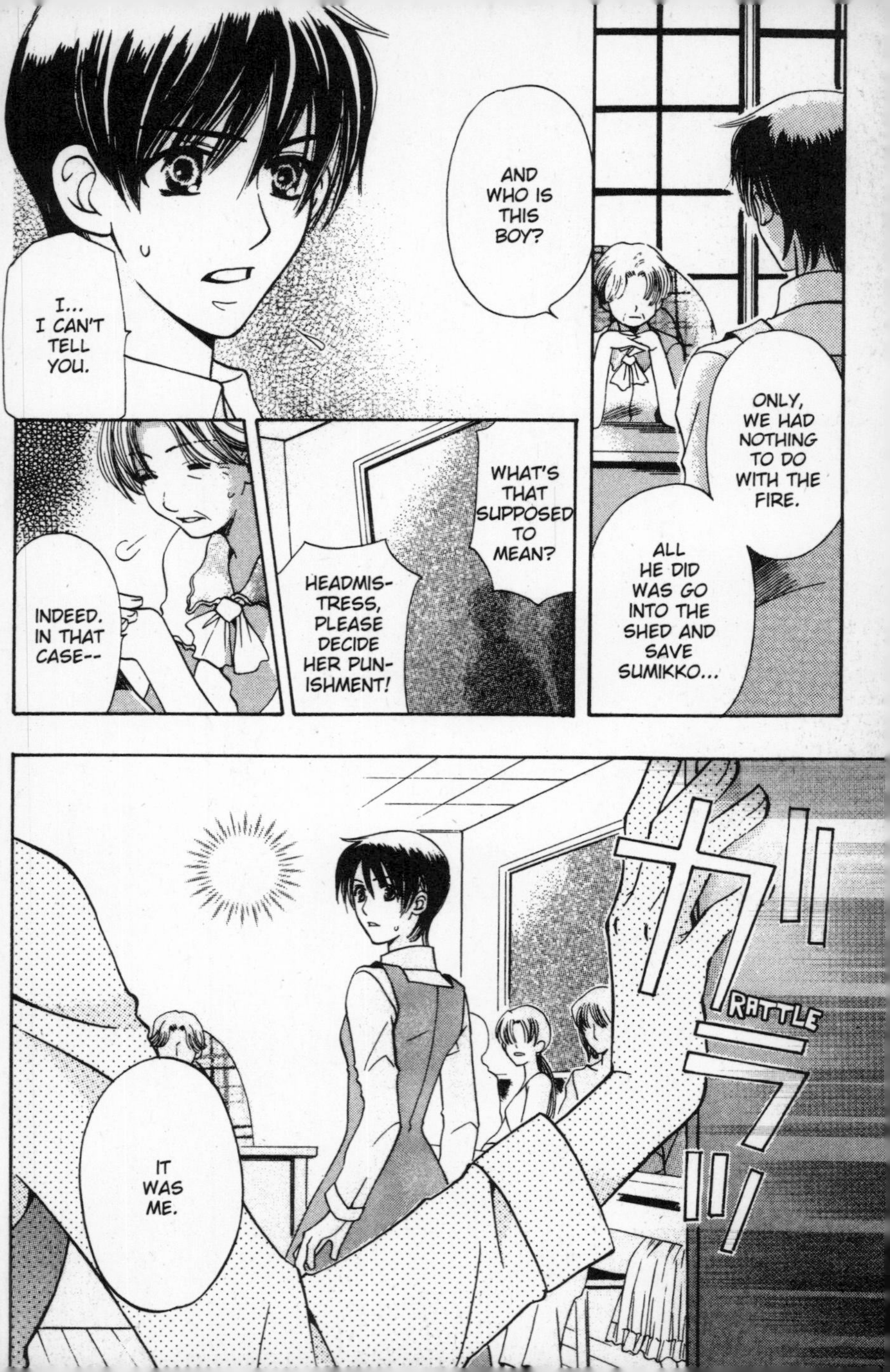
AND WHO IS THIS BOY?
I... I CAN'T TELL YOU.
ONLY, WE HAD NOTHING TO DO WITH THE FIRE.
ALL HE DID WAS GO INTO THE SHED AND SAVE SUMIKKO...
WHAT'S THAT SUPPOSED TO MEAN?
HEADMISTRESS, PLEASE DECIDE HER PUNISHMENT!
INDEED. IN THAT CASE--
RATTLE
IT WAS ME.

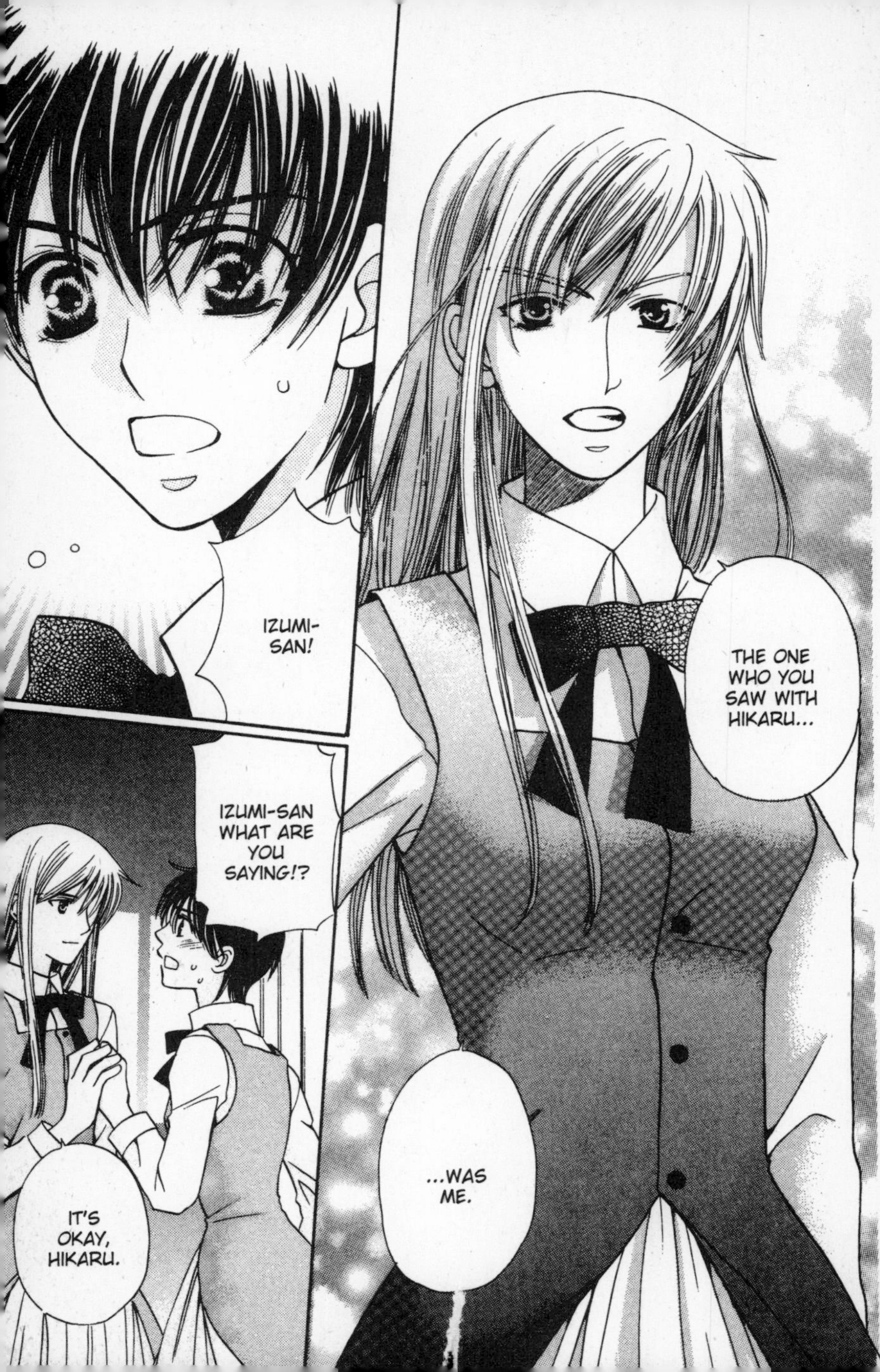
THE ONE WHO YOU SAW WITH HIKARU...
...WAS ME.
IZUMI-SAN!
IZUMI-SAN WHAT ARE YOU SAYING!?
IT'S OKAY, HIKARU.

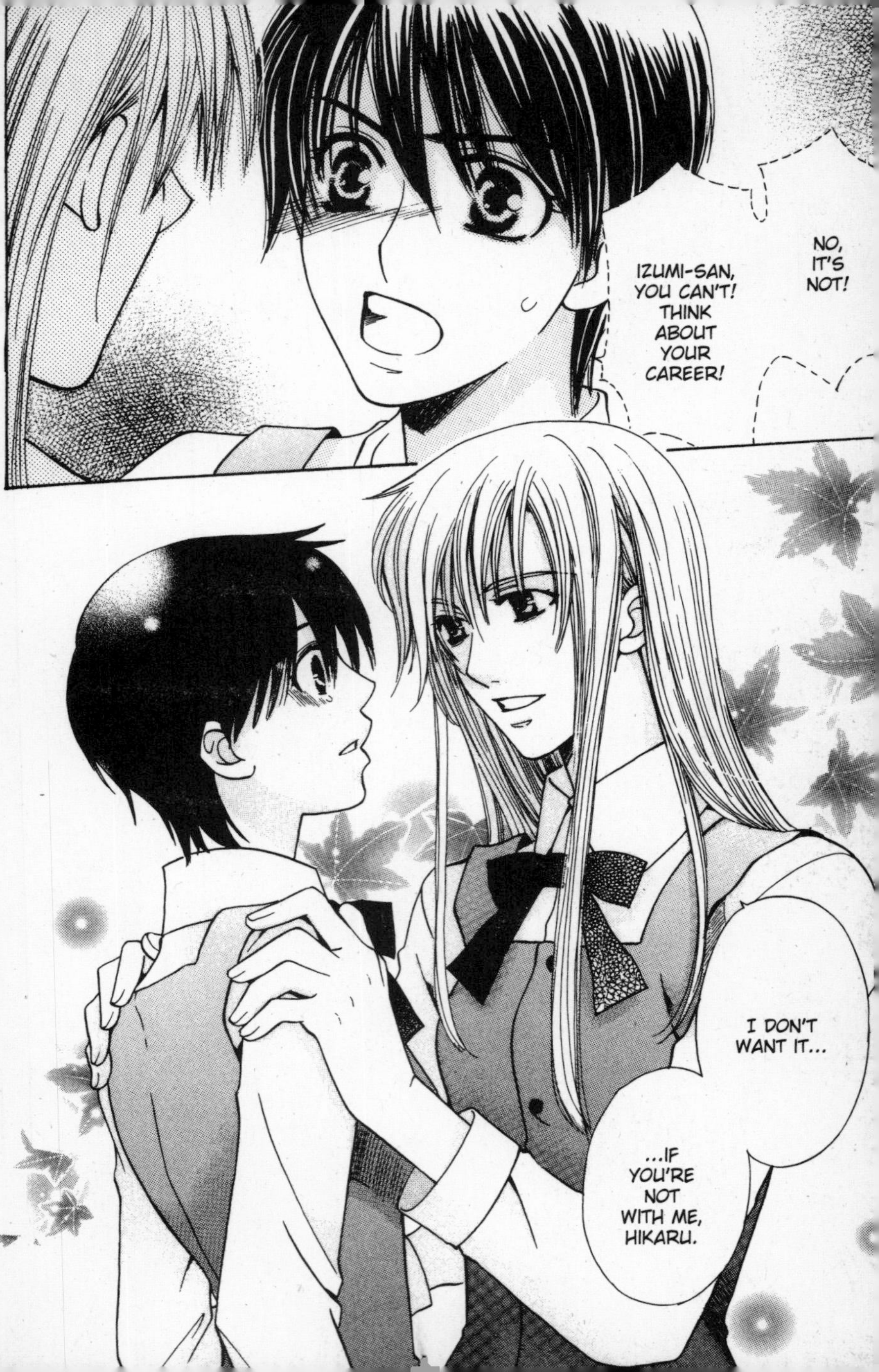

NO, IT'S NOT!
IZUMI-SAN, YOU CAN'T! THINK ABOUT YOUR CAREER!
I DON'T WANT IT...
...IF YOU'RE NOT WITH ME, HIKARU.

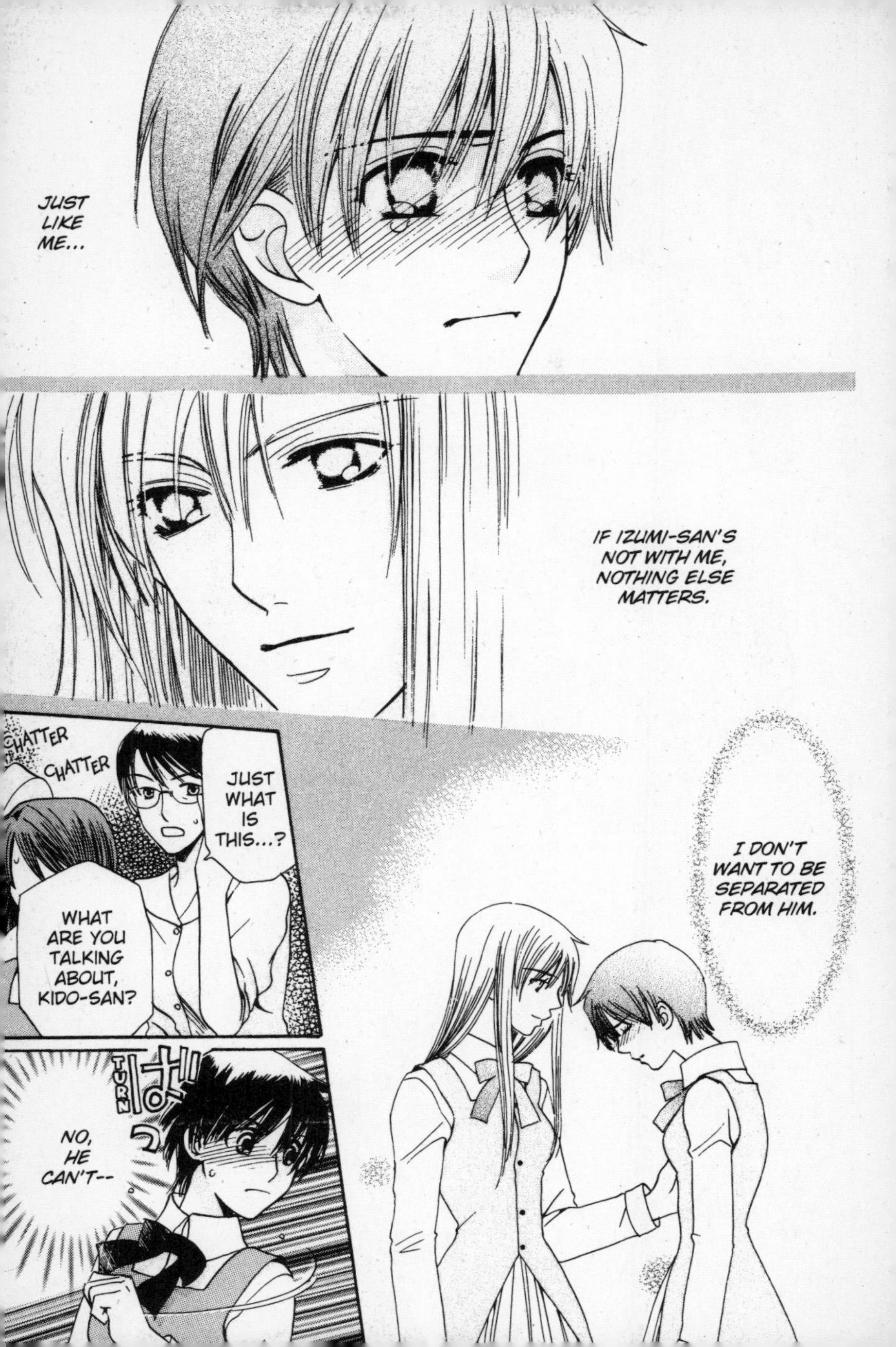
JUST LIKE ME...
IF IZUMI-SAN'S NOT WITH ME, NOTHING ELSE MATTERS.
I DON'T WANT TO BE SEPARATED FROM HIM.
JUST WHAT IS THIS...?
CHATTER
CHATTER
WHAT ARE YOU TALKING ABOUT, KIDO-SAN?
TURN
NO, HE CAN'T--

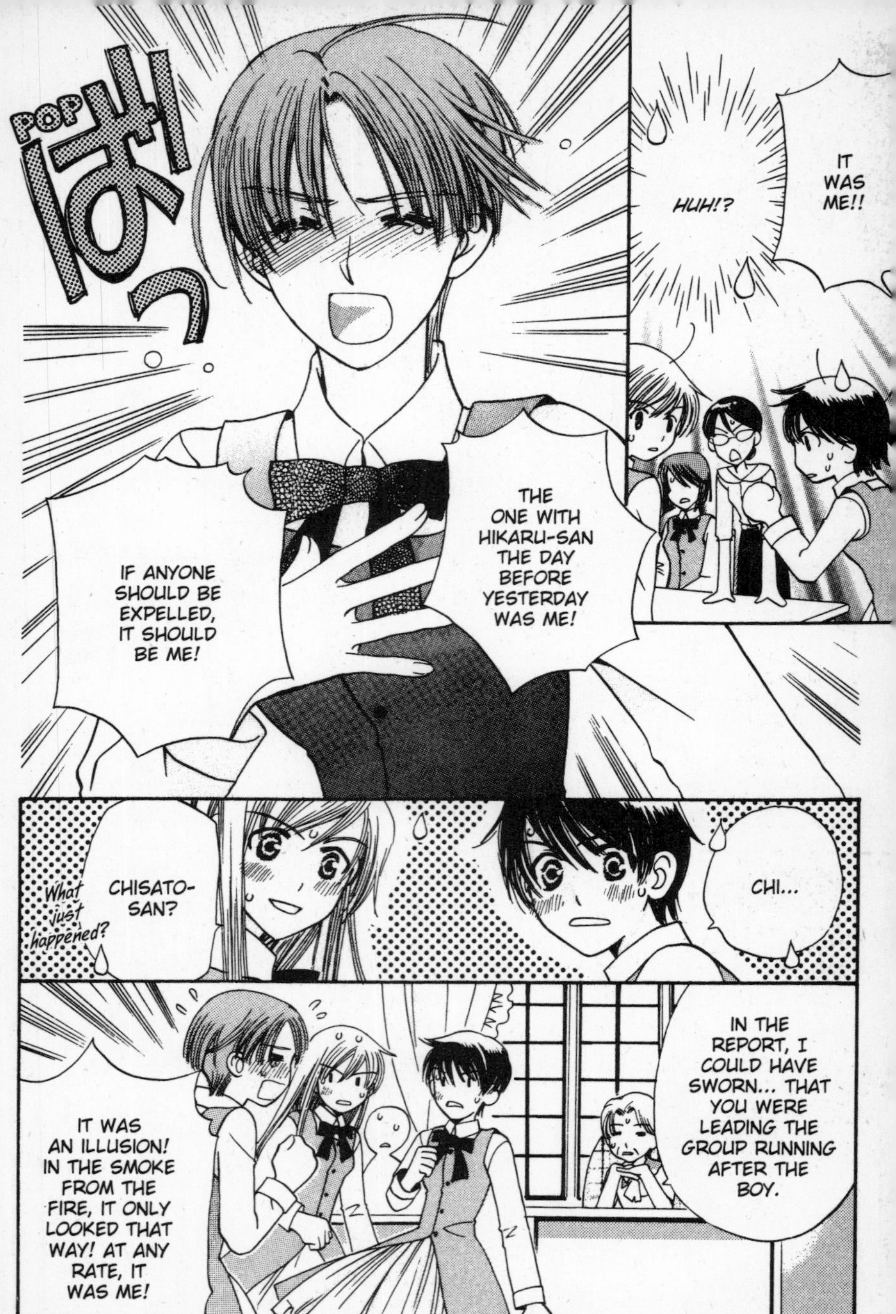
IT WAS ME!!
HUH!?
POP
ぱっ
THE ONE WITH HIKARU-SAN THE DAY BEFORE YESTERDAY WAS ME!
IF ANYONE SHOULD BE EXPELLED, IT SHOULD BE ME!
CHI...
CHISATO-SAN?
What just happened?
IN THE REPORT, I COULD HAVE SWORN... THAT YOU WERE LEADING THE GROUP RUNNING AFTER THE BOY.
IT WAS AN ILLUSION! IN THE SMOKE FROM THE FIRE, IT ONLY LOOKED THAT WAY! AT ANY RATE, IT WAS ME!

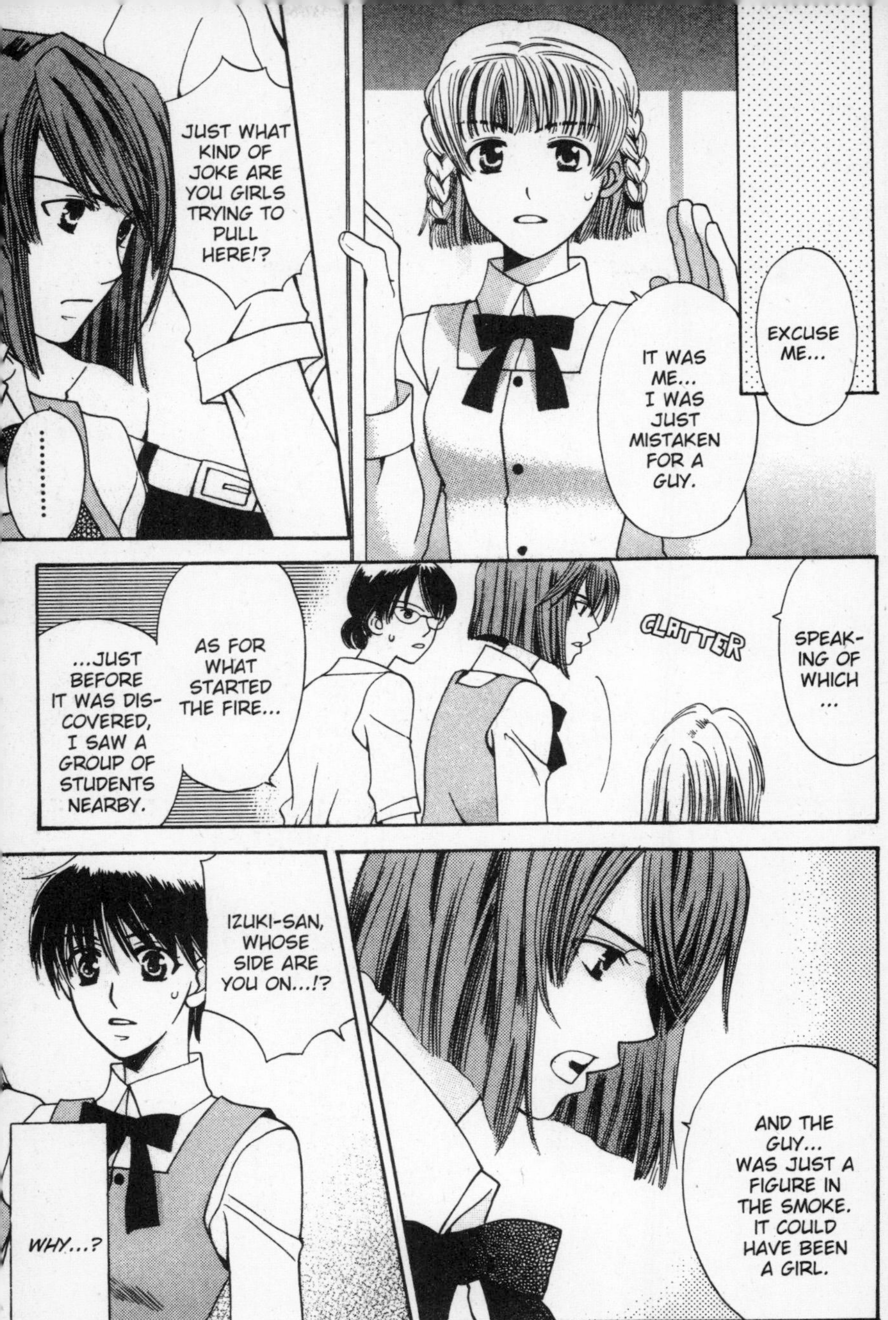
EXCUSE ME...
IT WAS ME... I WAS JUST MISTAKEN FOR A GUY.
JUST WHAT KIND OF JOKE ARE YOU GIRLS TRYING TO PULL HERE!?
......
SPEAK-ING OF WHICH...
CLATTER
AS FOR WHAT STARTED THE FIRE...
...JUST BEFORE IT WAS DIS-COVERED, I SAW A GROUP OF STUDENTS NEARBY.
AND THE GUY... WAS JUST A FIGURE IN THE SMOKE. IT COULD HAVE BEEN A GIRL.
IZUKI-SAN, WHOSE SIDE ARE YOU ON...!?
WHY...?

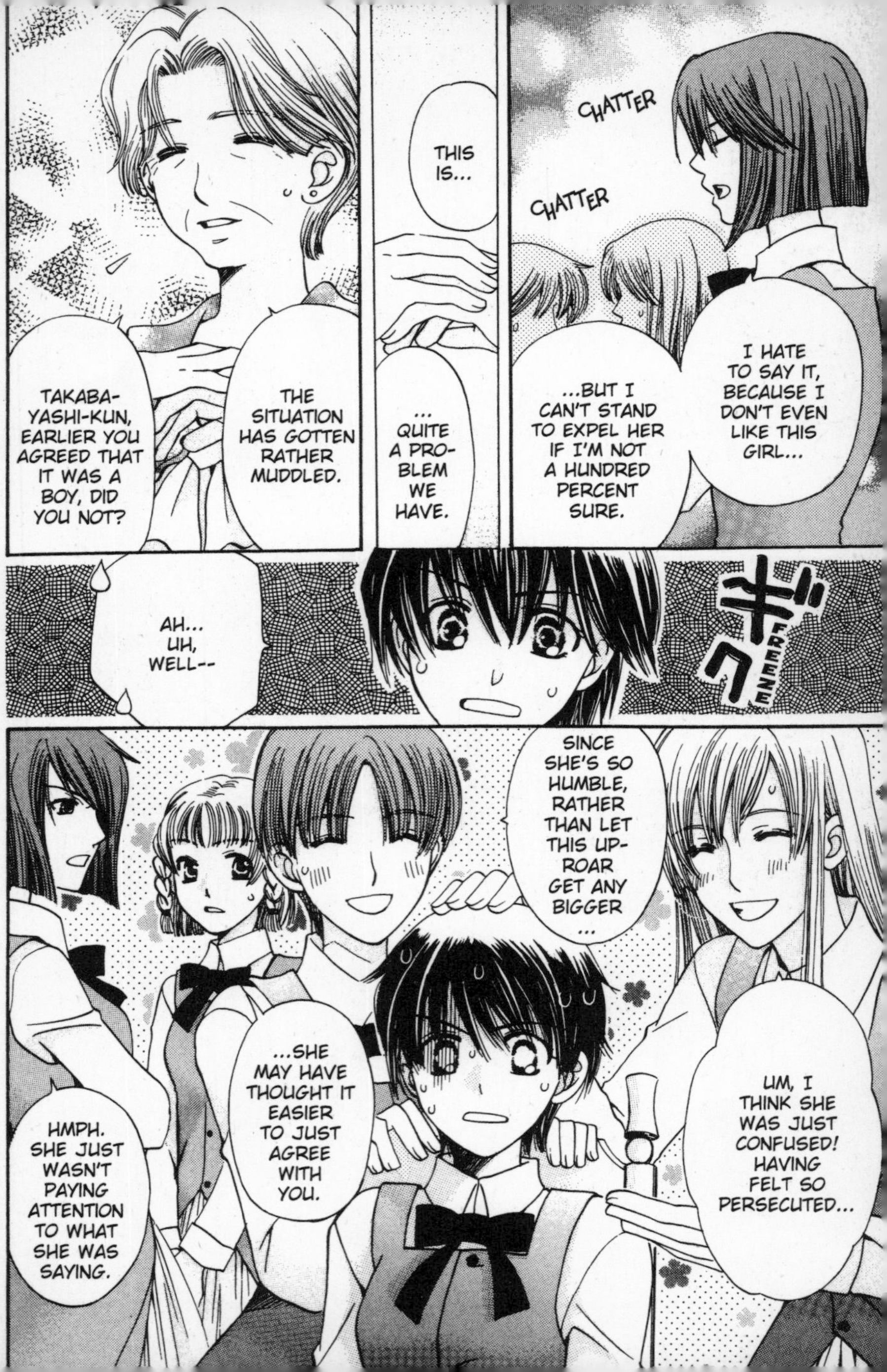
CHATTER
CHATTER
I HATE TO SAY IT, BECAUSE I DON'T EVEN LIKE THIS GIRL...
...BUT I CAN'T STAND TO EXPEL HER IF I'M NOT A HUNDRED PERCENT SURE.
THIS IS...
...QUITE A PRO-BLEM WE HAVE.
THE SITUATION HAS GOTTEN RATHER MUDDLED.
TAKABA-YASHI-KUN, EARLIER YOU AGREED THAT IT WAS A BOY, DID YOU NOT?
ギク
FREEZE
AH... UH, WELL--
SINCE SHE'S SO HUMBLE, RATHER THAN LET THIS UP-ROAR GET ANY BIGGER...
UM, I THINK SHE WAS JUST CONFUSED! HAVING FELT SO PERSECUTED...
...SHE MAY HAVE THOUGHT IT EASIER TO JUST AGREE WITH YOU.
HMPH. SHE JUST WASN'T PAYING ATTENTION TO WHAT SHE WAS SAYING.

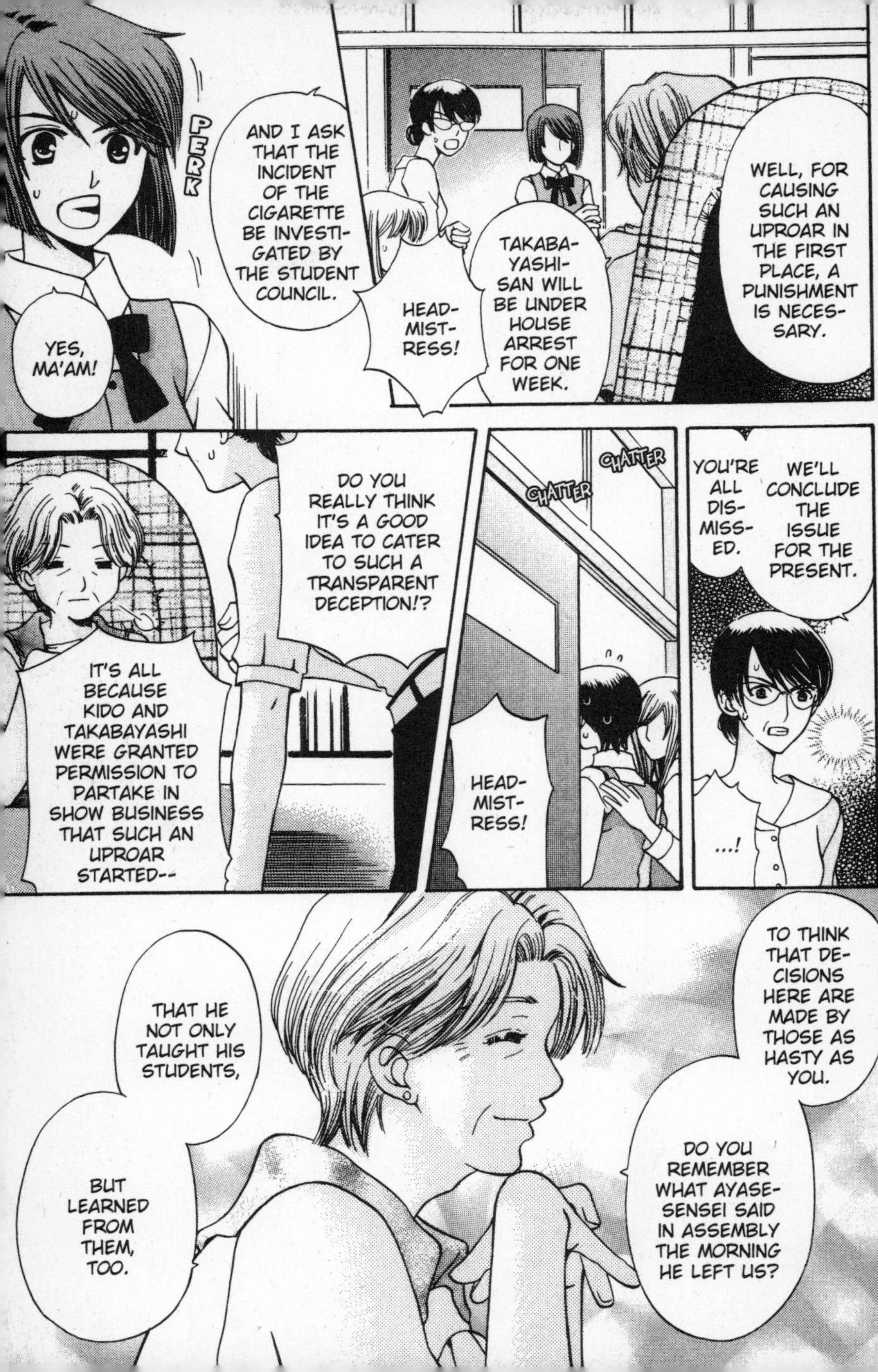
WELL, FOR CAUSING SUCH AN UPROAR IN THE FIRST PLACE, A PUNISHMENT IS NECESSARY.
TAKABAYASHI-SAN WILL BE UNDER HOUSE ARREST FOR ONE WEEK.
HEADMISTRESS!
AND I ASK THAT THE INCIDENT OF THE CIGARETTE BE INVESTIGATED BY THE STUDENT COUNCIL.
PERK
YES, MA'AM!
WE'LL CONCLUDE THE ISSUE FOR THE PRESENT.
YOU'RE ALL DISMISSED.
...!
CHATTER
CHATTER
HEADMISTRESS!
DO YOU REALLY THINK IT'S A GOOD IDEA TO CATER TO SUCH A TRANSPARENT DECEPTION!?
IT'S ALL BECAUSE KIDO AND TAKABAYASHI WERE GRANTED PERMISSION TO PARTAKE IN SHOW BUSINESS THAT SUCH AN UPROAR STARTED--
TO THINK THAT DECISIONS HERE ARE MADE BY THOSE AS HASTY AS YOU.
DO YOU REMEMBER WHAT AYASE-SENSEI SAID IN ASSEMBLY THE MORNING HE LEFT US?
THAT HE NOT ONLY TAUGHT HIS STUDENTS,
BUT LEARNED FROM THEM, TOO.

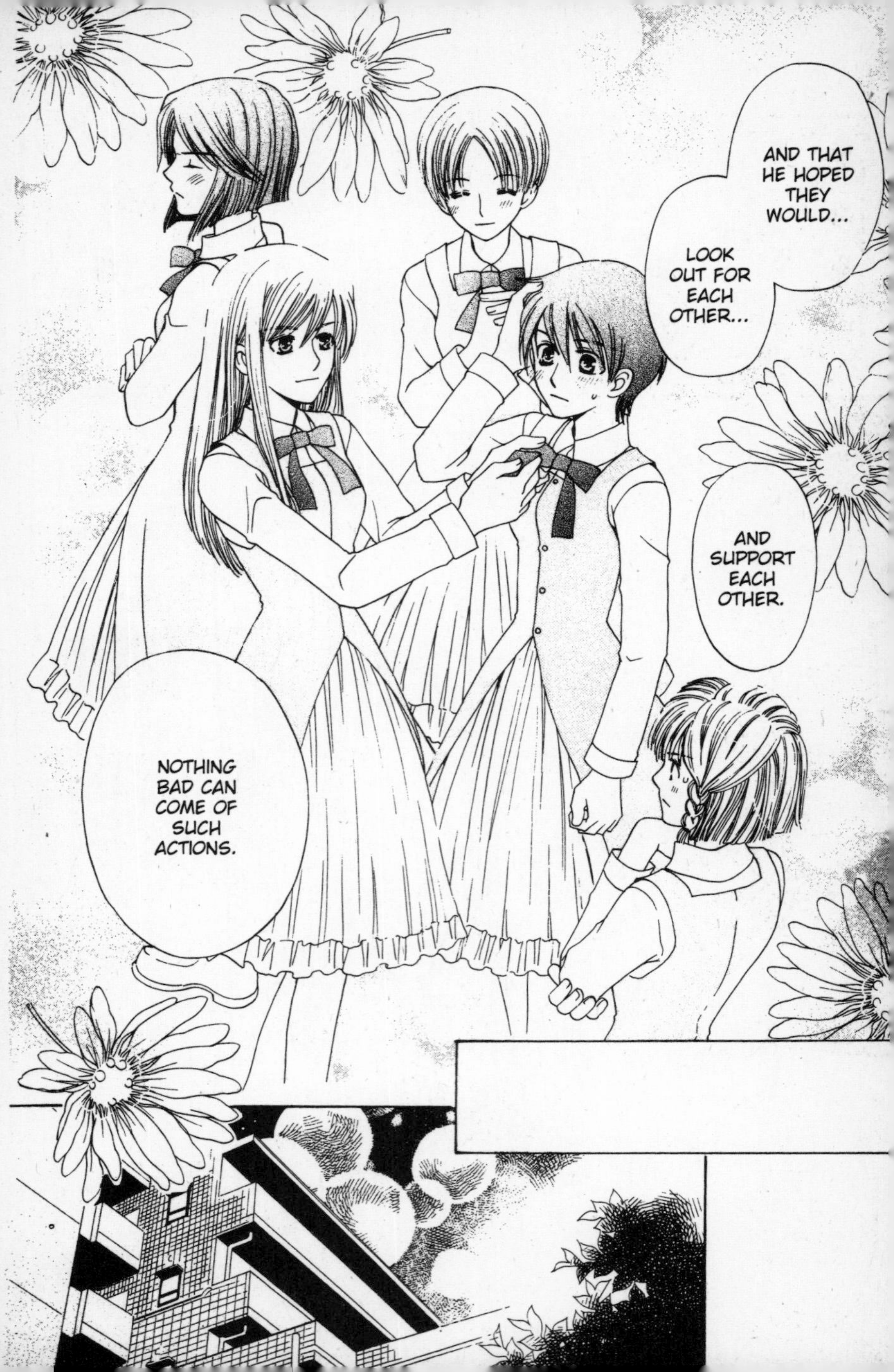
AND THAT HE HOPED THEY WOULD...
LOOK OUT FOR EACH OTHER...
AND SUPPORT EACH OTHER.
NOTHING BAD CAN COME OF SUCH ACTIONS.

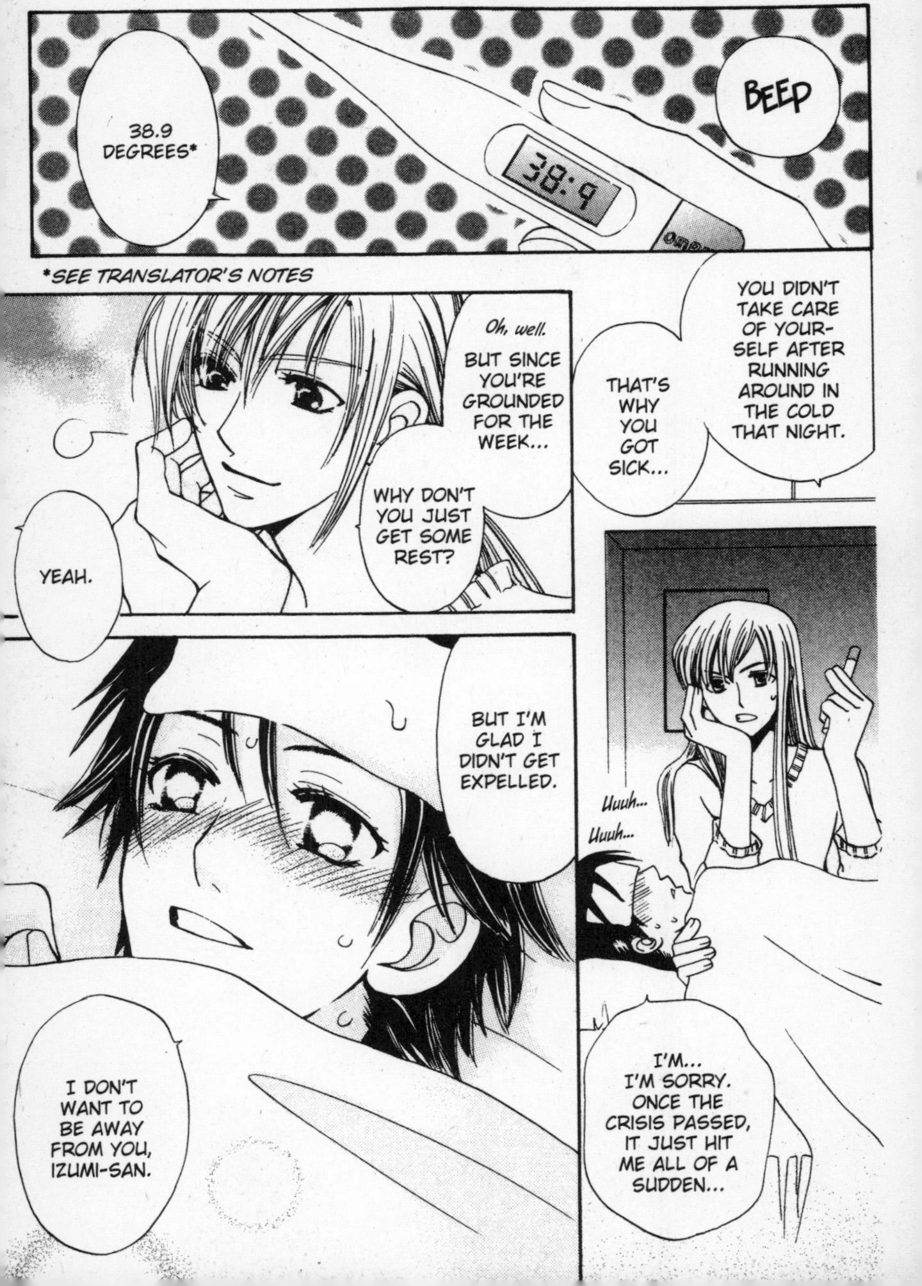
BEEP
38.9 DEGREES*
YOU DIDN'T TAKE CARE OF YOURSELF AFTER RUNNING AROUND IN THE COLD THAT NIGHT.
THAT'S WHY YOU GOT SICK...
Uuuh... Uuuh...
I'M... I'M SORRY. ONCE THE CRISIS PASSED, IT JUST HIT ME ALL OF A SUDDEN...
Oh, well.
BUT SINCE YOU'RE GROUNDED FOR THE WEEK...
WHY DON'T YOU JUST GET SOME REST?
YEAH.
BUT I'M GLAD I DIDN'T GET EXPELLED.
I DON'T WANT TO BE AWAY FROM YOU, IZUMI-SAN.

*SEE TRANSLATOR'S NOTES

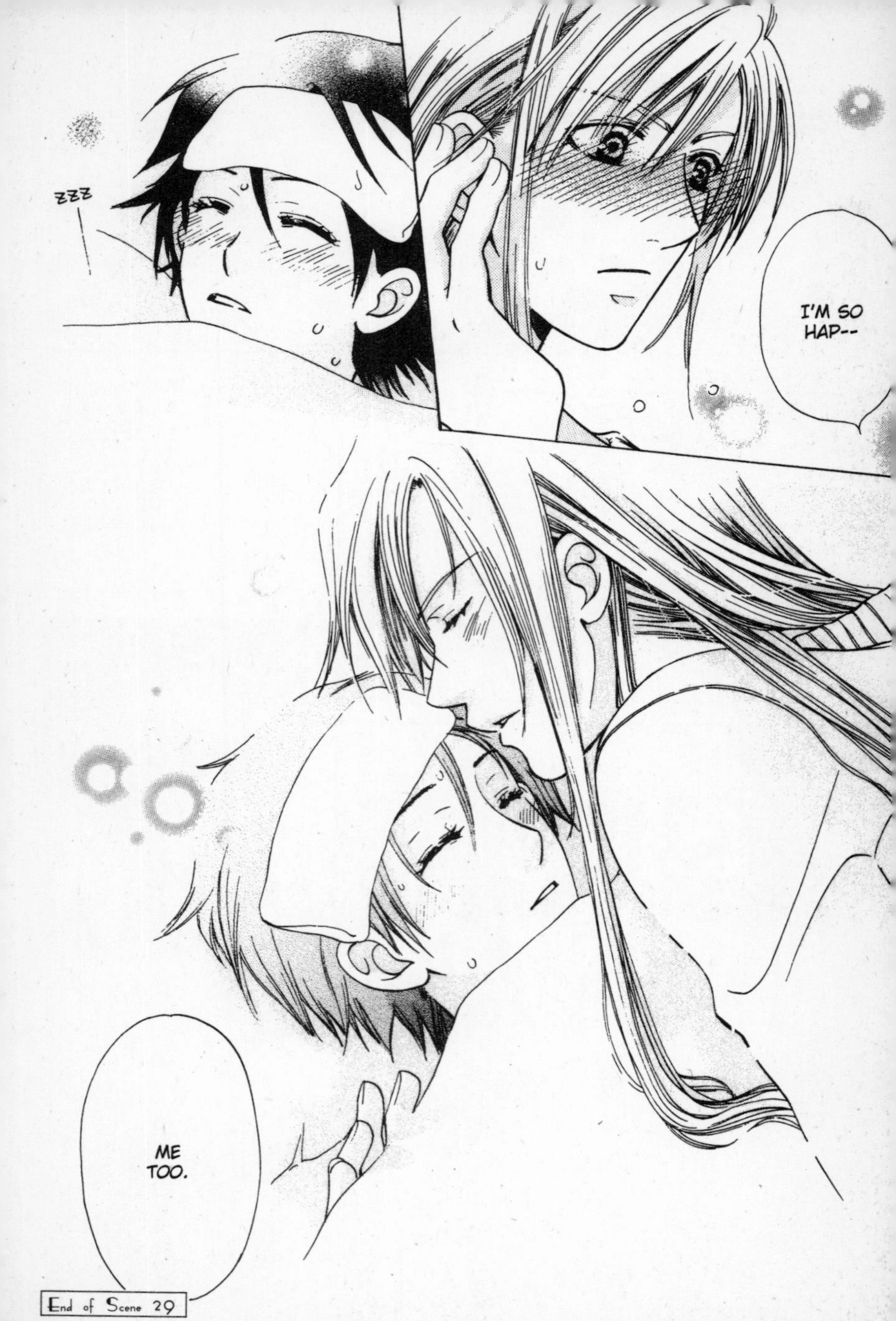
I'M SO HAP--
ZZZ
ME TOO.

End of Scene 29

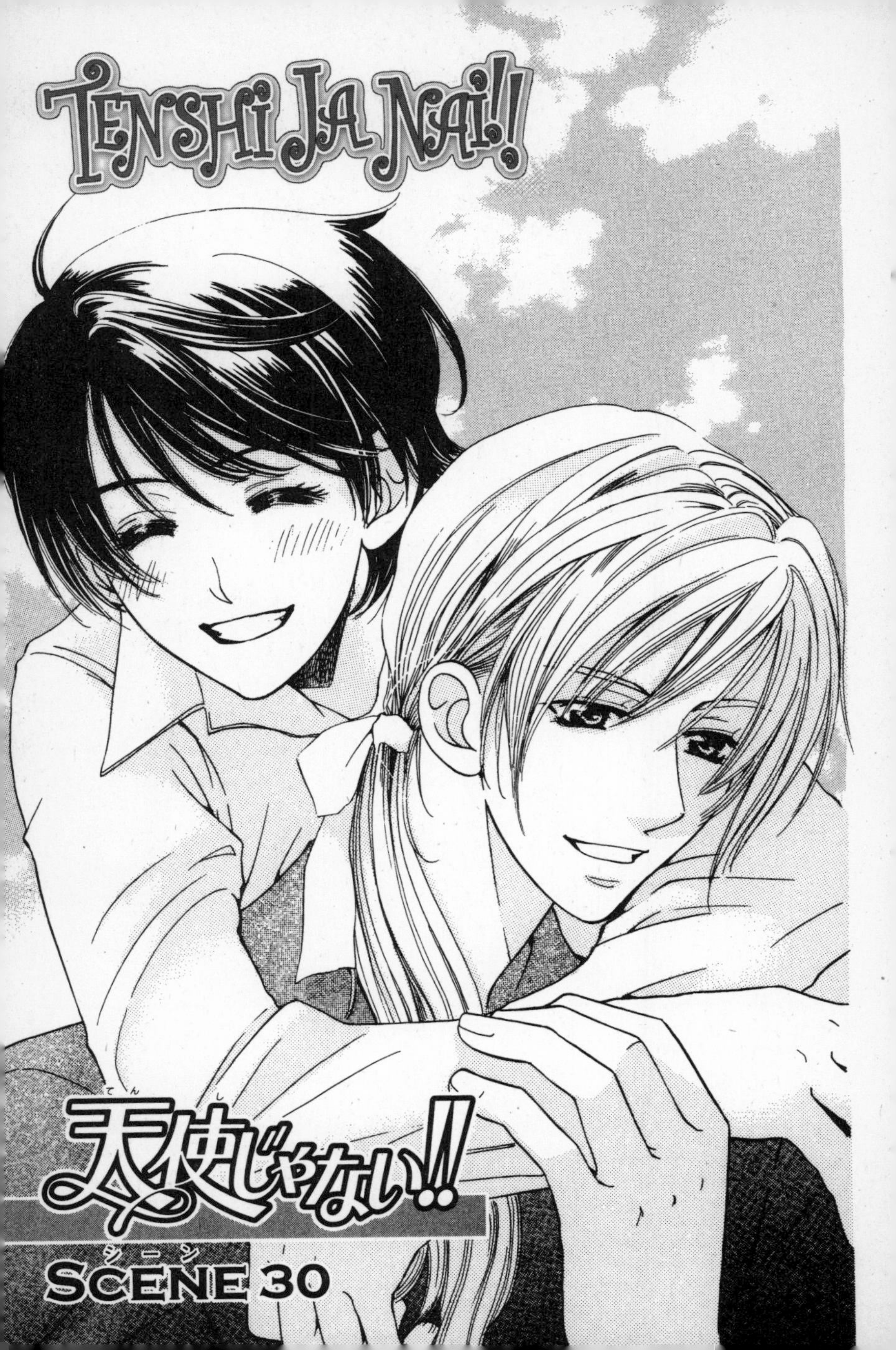

TENSHI JA NAI!!
天使(てんし)じゃない!!
SCENE(シーン) 30

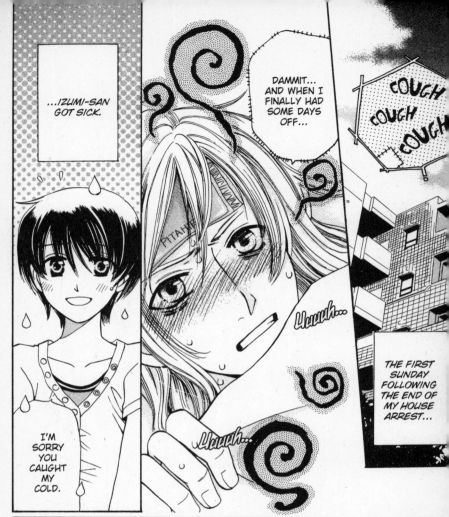

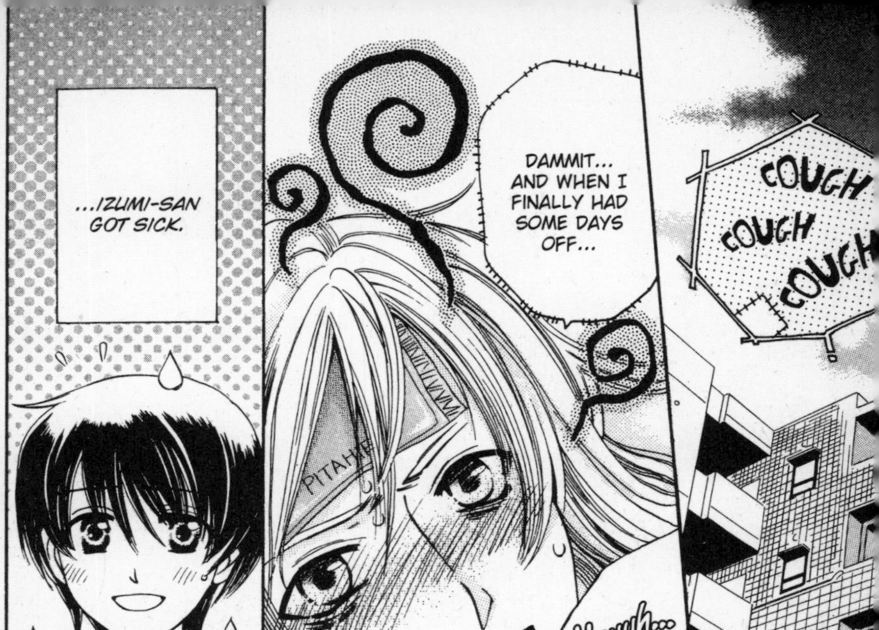
COUGH
COUGH
COUGH
THE FIRST SUNDAY FOLLOWING THE END OF MY HOUSE ARREST...
DAMMIT... AND WHEN I FINALLY HAD SOME DAYS OFF...
Uuuuh...
Uuuuh...
...IZUMI-SAN GOT SICK.
I'M SORRY YOU CAUGHT MY COLD.

Covers to Western books are so beautiful...

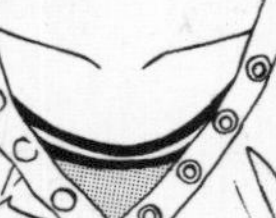
LOVE

They're all multicolored and get me all cheery about taking the big step and reading it!

My Current Addictions #2

What I'm working hardest at now is trying to get into reading Western literature. I'm starting with picture books on the internet. Sometimes I get happy when I can understand the English conversations that air on educational programs and the like. But I'm still only at the level of a kindergartener. (laugh) I suppose my greatest achievement so far has been losing my sense of fear when facing it.

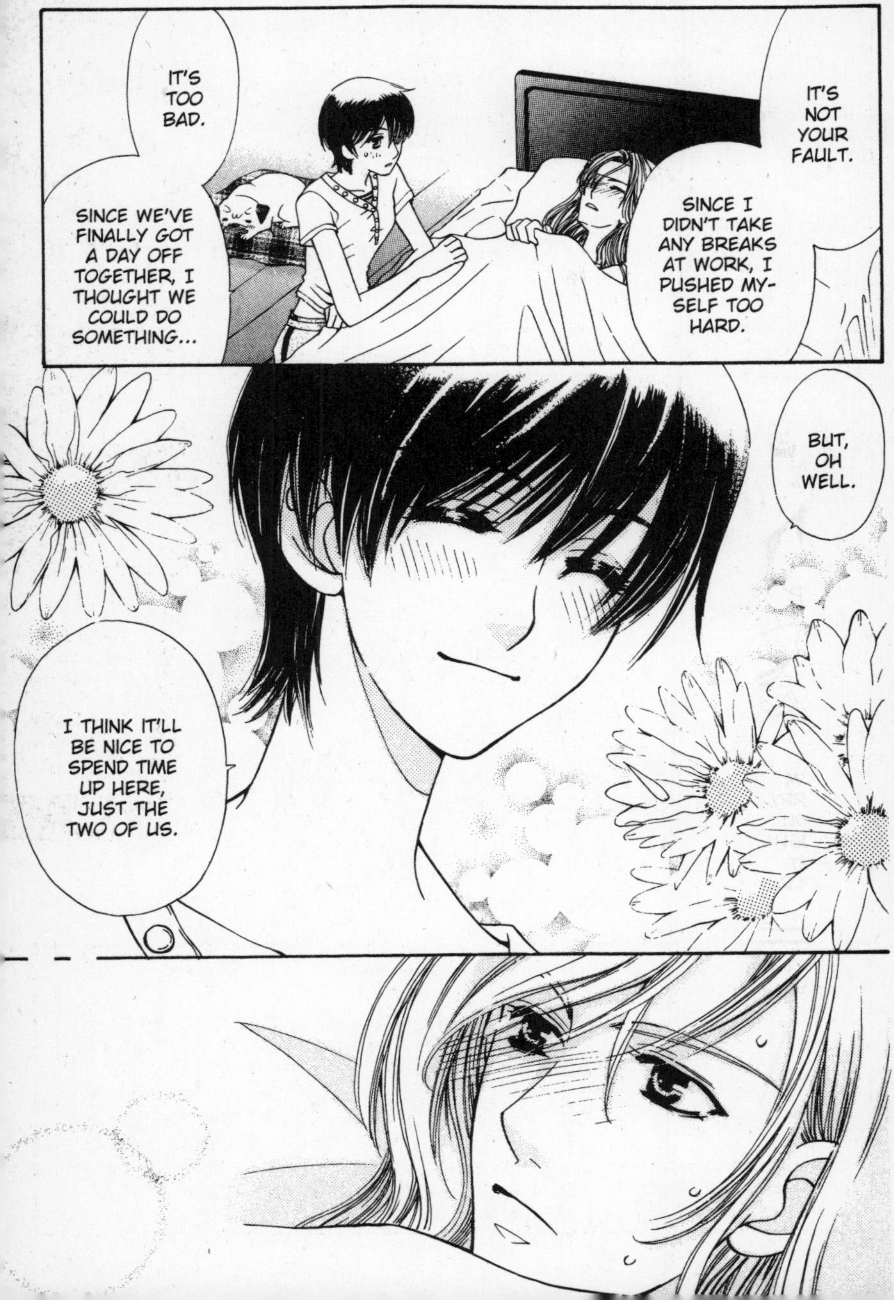
IT'S NOT YOUR FAULT.
SINCE I DIDN'T TAKE ANY BREAKS AT WORK, I PUSHED MY-SELF TOO HARD.
IT'S TOO BAD.
SINCE WE'VE FINALLY GOT A DAY OFF TOGETHER, I THOUGHT WE COULD DO SOMETHING...
BUT, OH WELL.
I THINK IT'LL BE NICE TO SPEND TIME UP HERE, JUST THE TWO OF US.

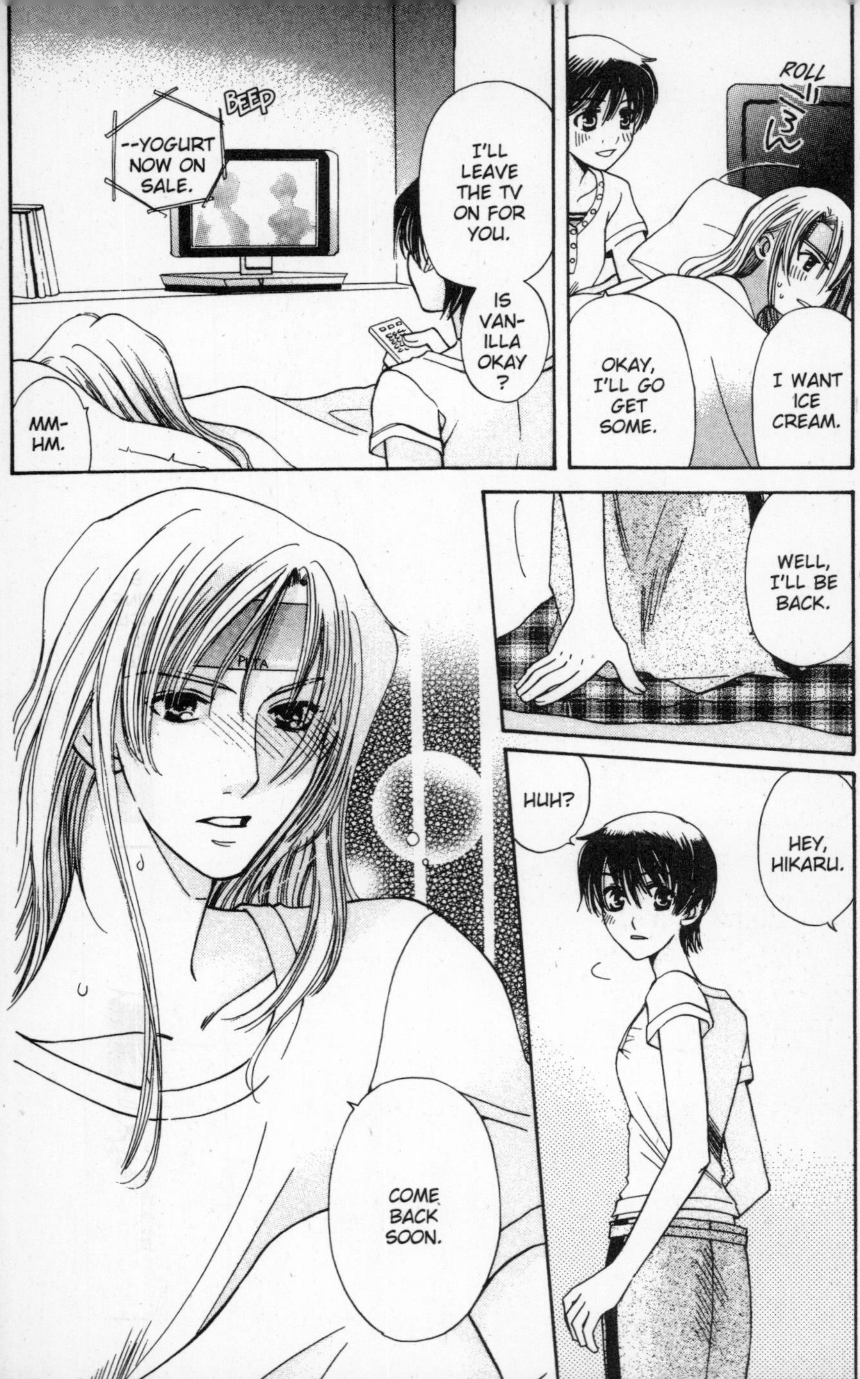
ROLL
I WANT ICE CREAM.
OKAY, I'LL GO GET SOME.
I'LL LEAVE THE TV ON FOR YOU.
IS VANILLA OKAY?
BEEP
--YOGURT NOW ON SALE.
MM-HM.
WELL, I'LL BE BACK.
HEY, HIKARU.
HUH?
COME BACK SOON.

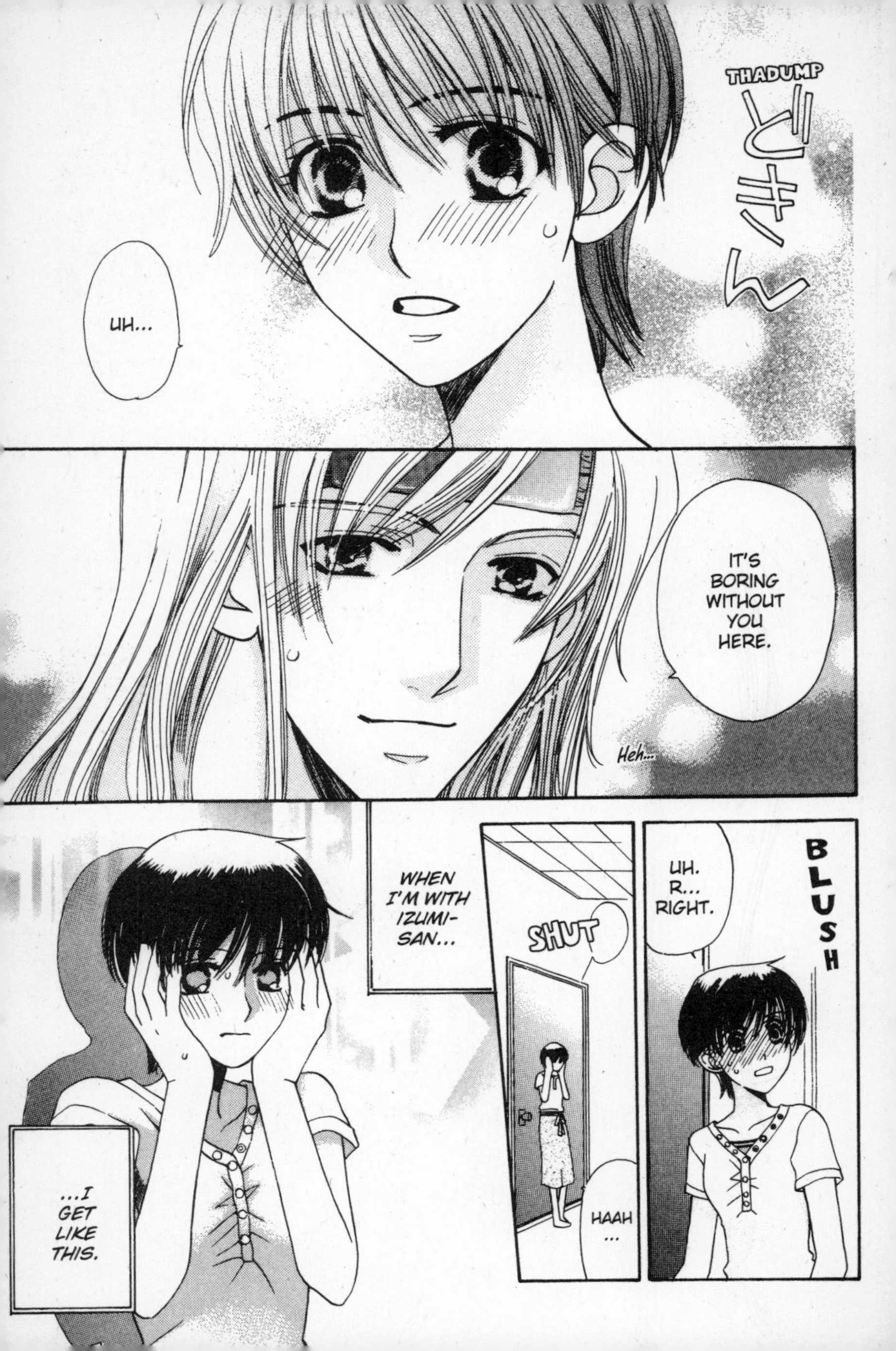
THADUMP
どきん
UH...
IT'S BORING WITHOUT YOU HERE.
Heh...
BLUSH
UH. R... RIGHT.
SHUT
HAAH ...
WHEN I'M WITH IZUMI-SAN...
...I GET LIKE THIS.

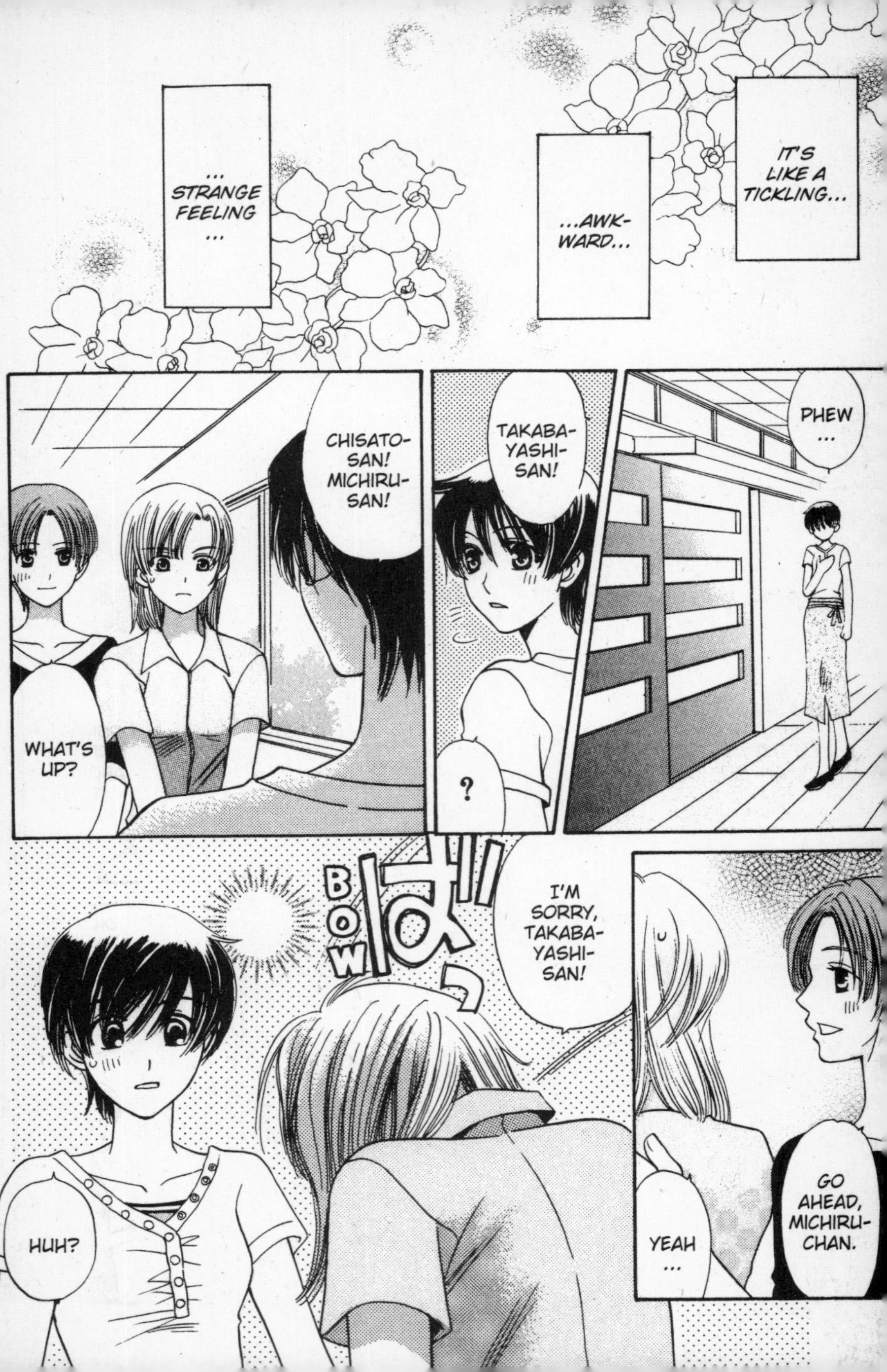
IT'S LIKE A TICKLING...
...AWK-WARD...
...STRANGE FEELING...
PHEW...
TAKABA-YASHI-SAN!
?
CHISATO-SAN! MICHIRU-SAN!
WHAT'S UP?
GO AHEAD, MICHIRU-CHAN.
YEAH...
I'M SORRY, TAKABA-YASHI-SAN!
ばっ
BOW
HUH?

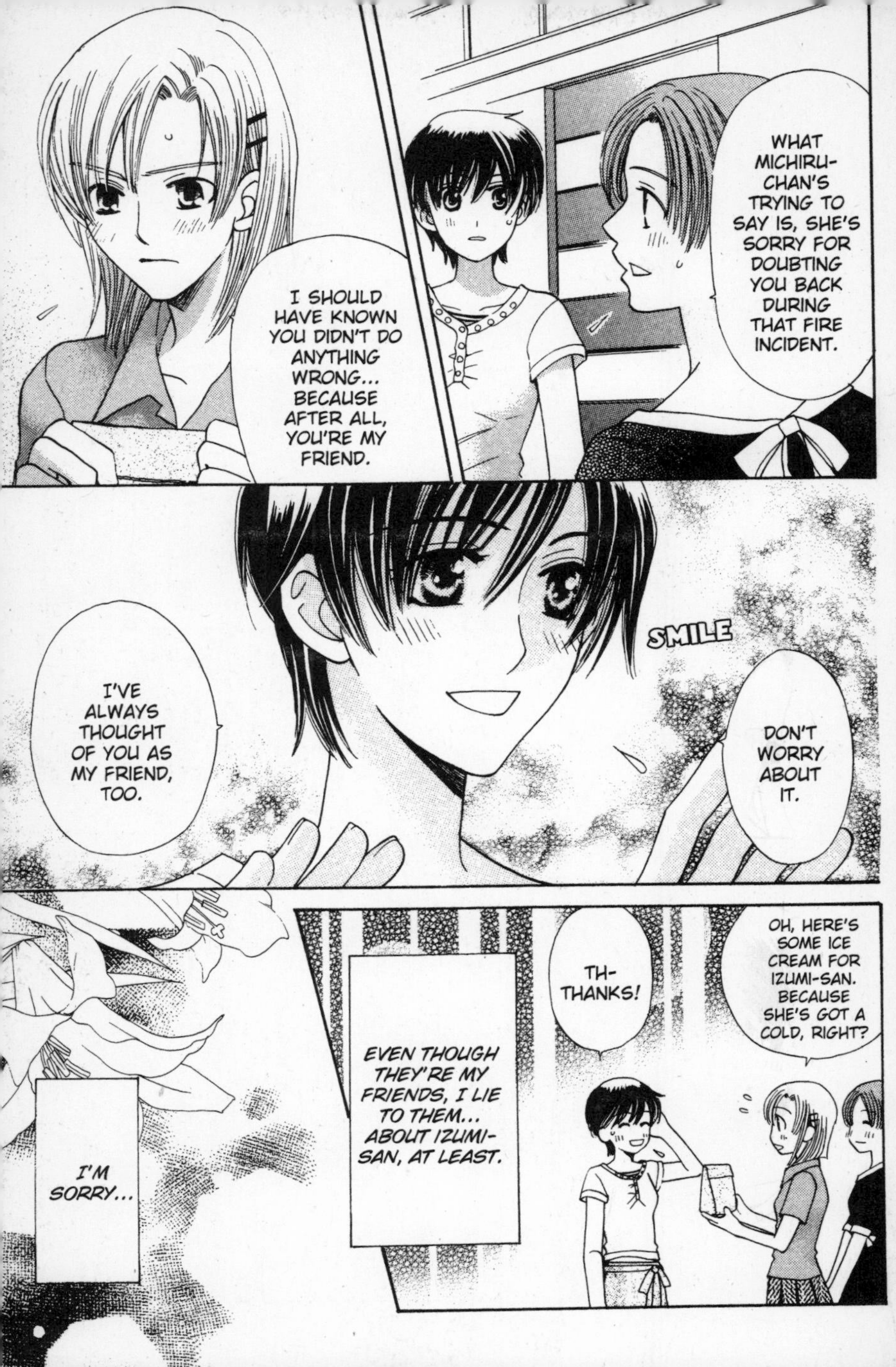
WHAT MICHIRU-CHAN'S TRYING TO SAY IS, SHE'S SORRY FOR DOUBTING YOU BACK DURING THAT FIRE INCIDENT.
I SHOULD HAVE KNOWN YOU DIDN'T DO ANYTHING WRONG... BECAUSE AFTER ALL, YOU'RE MY FRIEND.
SMILE
DON'T WORRY ABOUT IT.
I'VE ALWAYS THOUGHT OF YOU AS MY FRIEND, TOO.
OH, HERE'S SOME ICE CREAM FOR IZUMI-SAN. BECAUSE SHE'S GOT A COLD, RIGHT?
TH-THANKS!
EVEN THOUGH THEY'RE MY FRIENDS, I LIE TO THEM... ABOUT IZUMI-SAN, AT LEAST.
I'M SORRY...

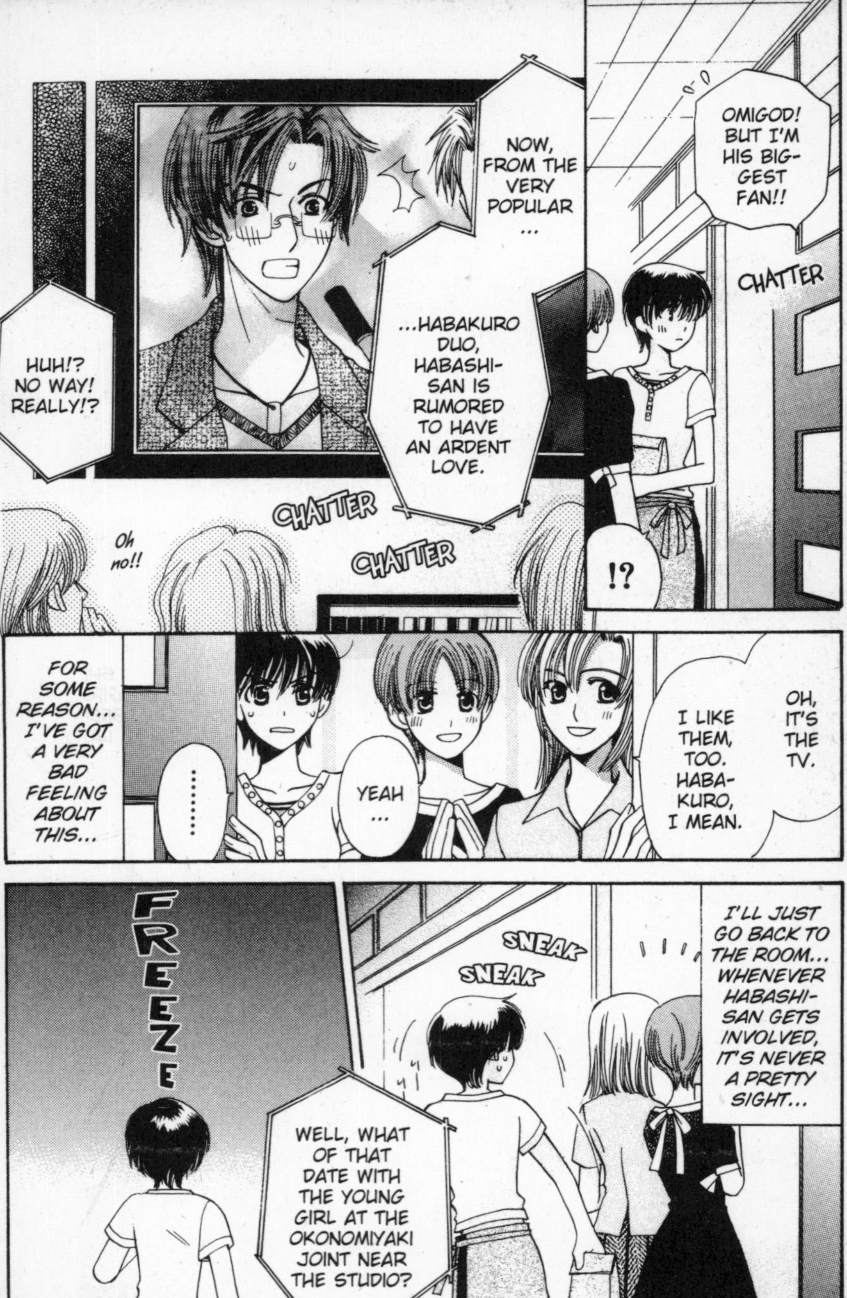
OMIGOD! BUT I'M HIS BIG-GEST FAN!!
CHATTER
!?
NOW, FROM THE VERY POPULAR ...
...HABAKURO DUO, HABASHI-SAN IS RUMORED TO HAVE AN ARDENT LOVE.
HUH!? NO WAY! REALLY!?
CHATTER
CHATTER
Oh no!!
OH, IT'S THE TV.
I LIKE THEM, TOO. HABA-KURO, I MEAN.
YEAH ...
......
FOR SOME REASON... I'VE GOT A VERY BAD FEELING ABOUT THIS...
I'LL JUST GO BACK TO THE ROOM... WHENEVER HABASHI-SAN GETS INVOLVED, IT'S NEVER A PRETTY SIGHT...
SNEAK
SNEAK
WELL, WHAT OF THAT DATE WITH THE YOUNG GIRL AT THE OKONOMIYAKI JOINT NEAR THE STUDIO?
FREEZE

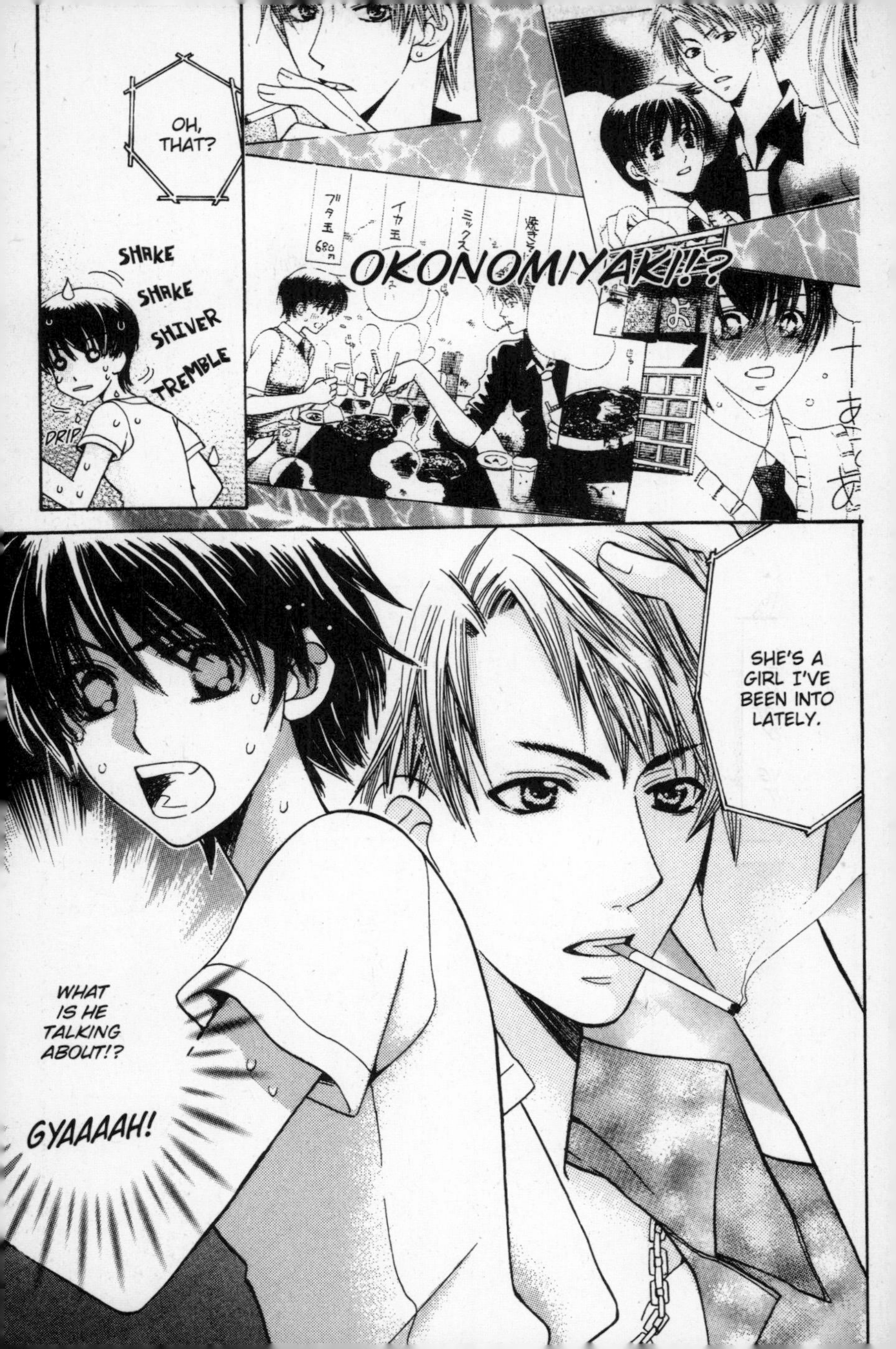

ミックス
イカ玉
ブタ玉
680円
OKONOMIYAKI!!?
OH, THAT?
SHAKE
SHAKE
SHIVER
TREMBLE
DRIP
SHE'S A GIRL I'VE BEEN INTO LATELY.
WHAT IS HE TALKING ABOUT!?
GYAAAAH!

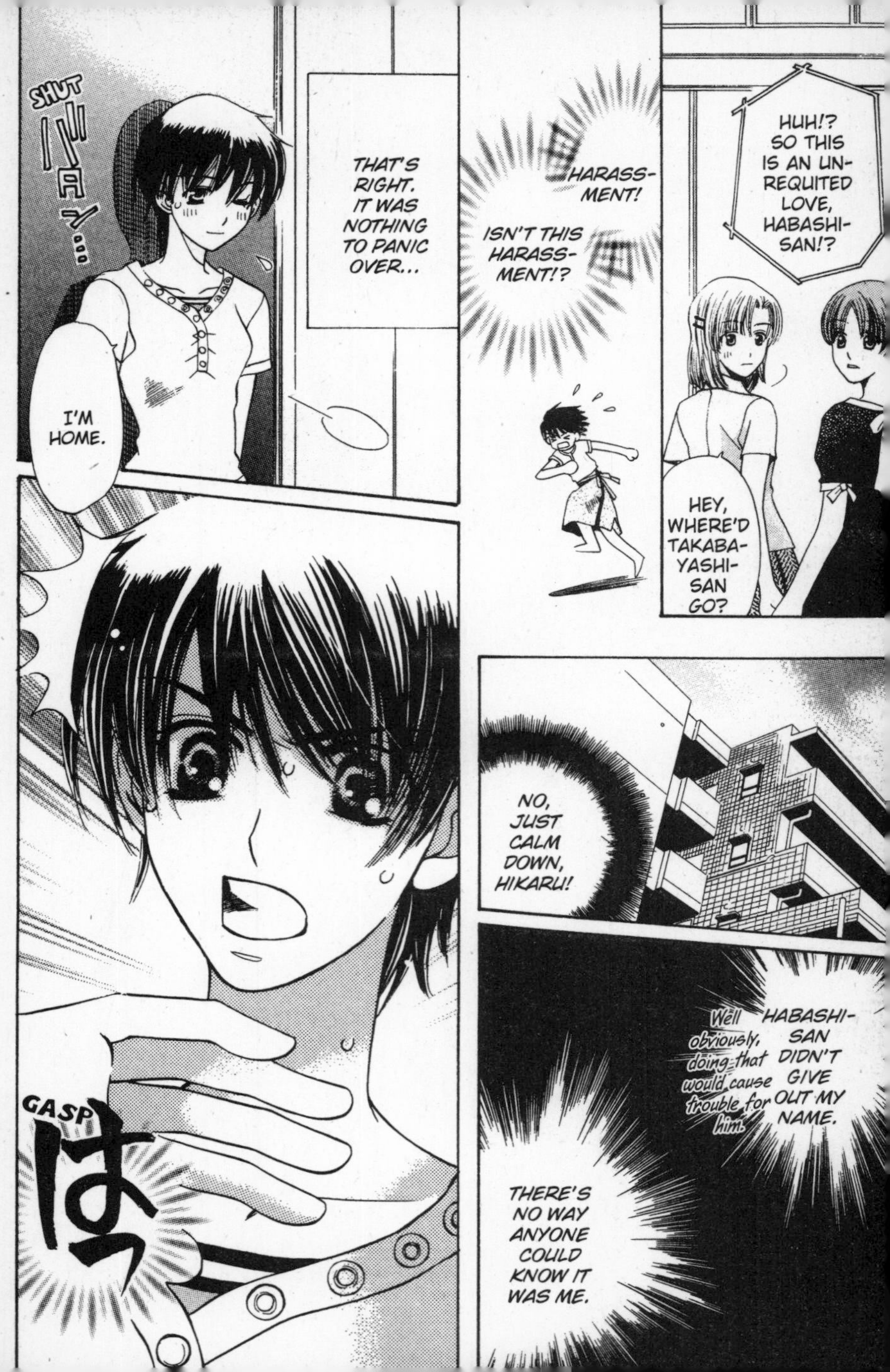
HUH!? SO THIS IS AN UN-REQUITED LOVE, HABASHI-SAN!?
HEY, WHERE'D TAKABA-YASHI-SAN GO?
HARASS-MENT!
ISN'T THIS HARASS-MENT!?
THAT'S RIGHT. IT WAS NOTHING TO PANIC OVER...
SHUT
バタン…
I'M HOME.
NO, JUST CALM DOWN, HIKARU!
HABASHI-SAN DIDN'T GIVE OUT MY NAME.
Well obviously, doing that would cause trouble for him.
THERE'S NO WAY ANYONE COULD KNOW IT WAS ME.
GASP
はっ

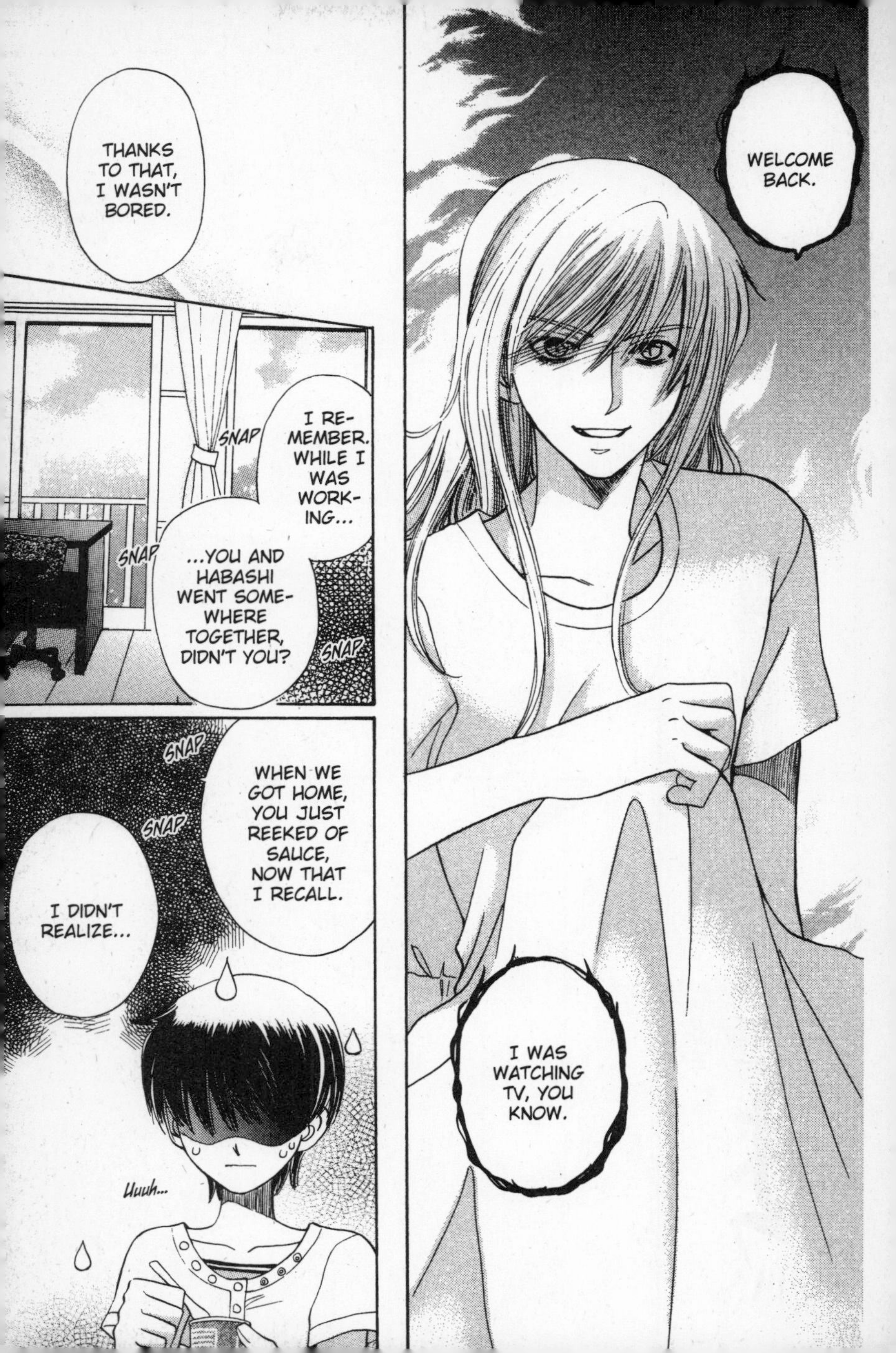
WELCOME BACK.
I WAS WATCHING TV, YOU KNOW.
THANKS TO THAT, I WASN'T BORED.
SNAP
I RE-MEMBER. WHILE I WAS WORK-ING...
SNAP
...YOU AND HABASHI WENT SOME-WHERE TOGETHER, DIDN'T YOU?
SNAP
SNAP
SNAP
WHEN WE GOT HOME, YOU JUST REEKED OF SAUCE, NOW THAT I RECALL.
I DIDN'T REALIZE...
Uuuh...

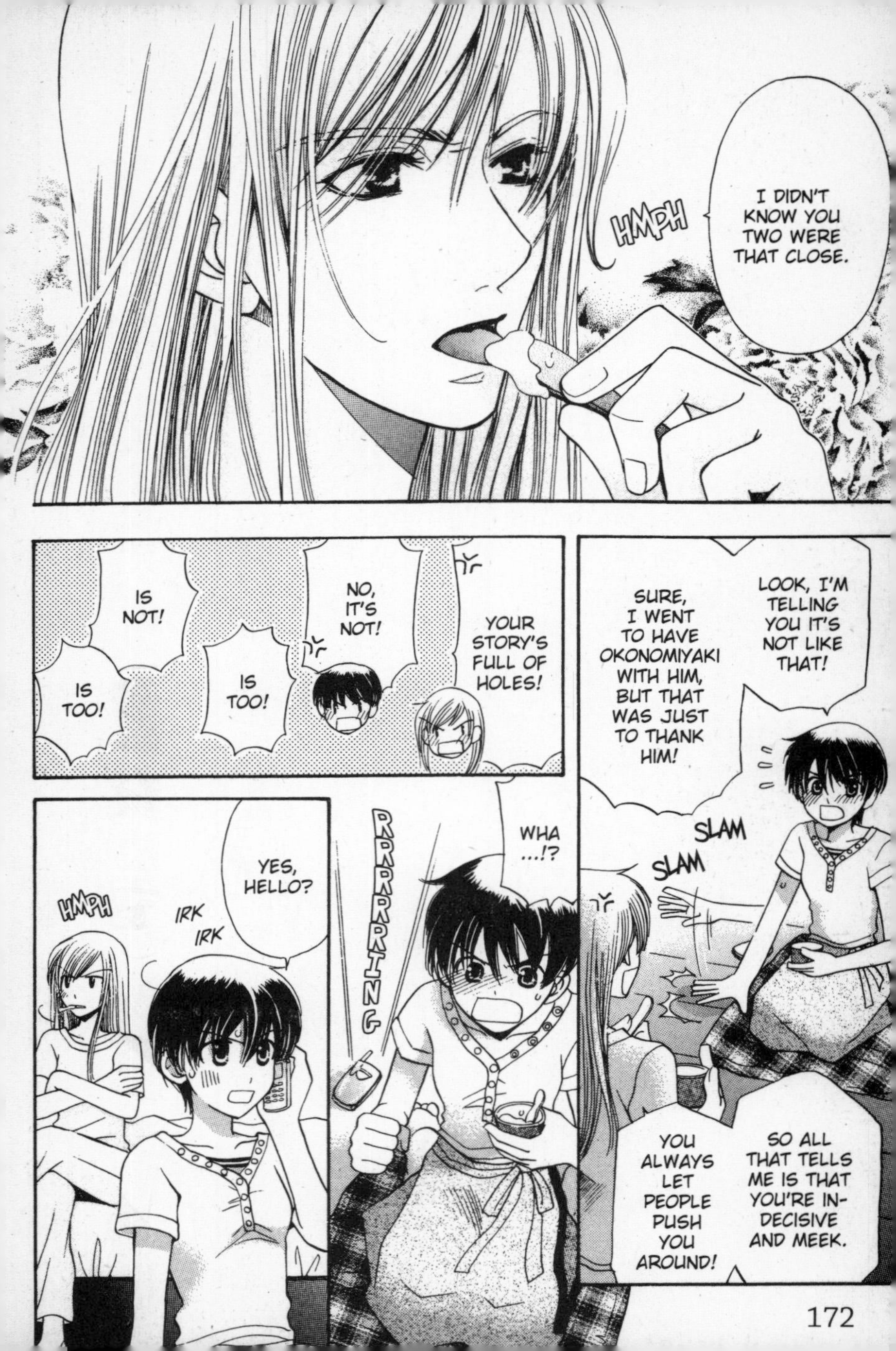
I DIDN'T KNOW YOU TWO WERE THAT CLOSE.
HMPH
LOOK, I'M TELLING YOU IT'S NOT LIKE THAT!
SURE, I WENT TO HAVE OKONOMIYAKI WITH HIM, BUT THAT WAS JUST TO THANK HIM!
SLAM
SLAM
SO ALL THAT TELLS ME IS THAT YOU'RE IN-DECISIVE AND MEEK.
YOU ALWAYS LET PEOPLE PUSH YOU AROUND!
YOUR STORY'S FULL OF HOLES!
NO, IT'S NOT!
IS TOO!
IS NOT!
IS TOO!
WHA ...!?
RRRRRRING
YES, HELLO?
IRK IRK
HMPH

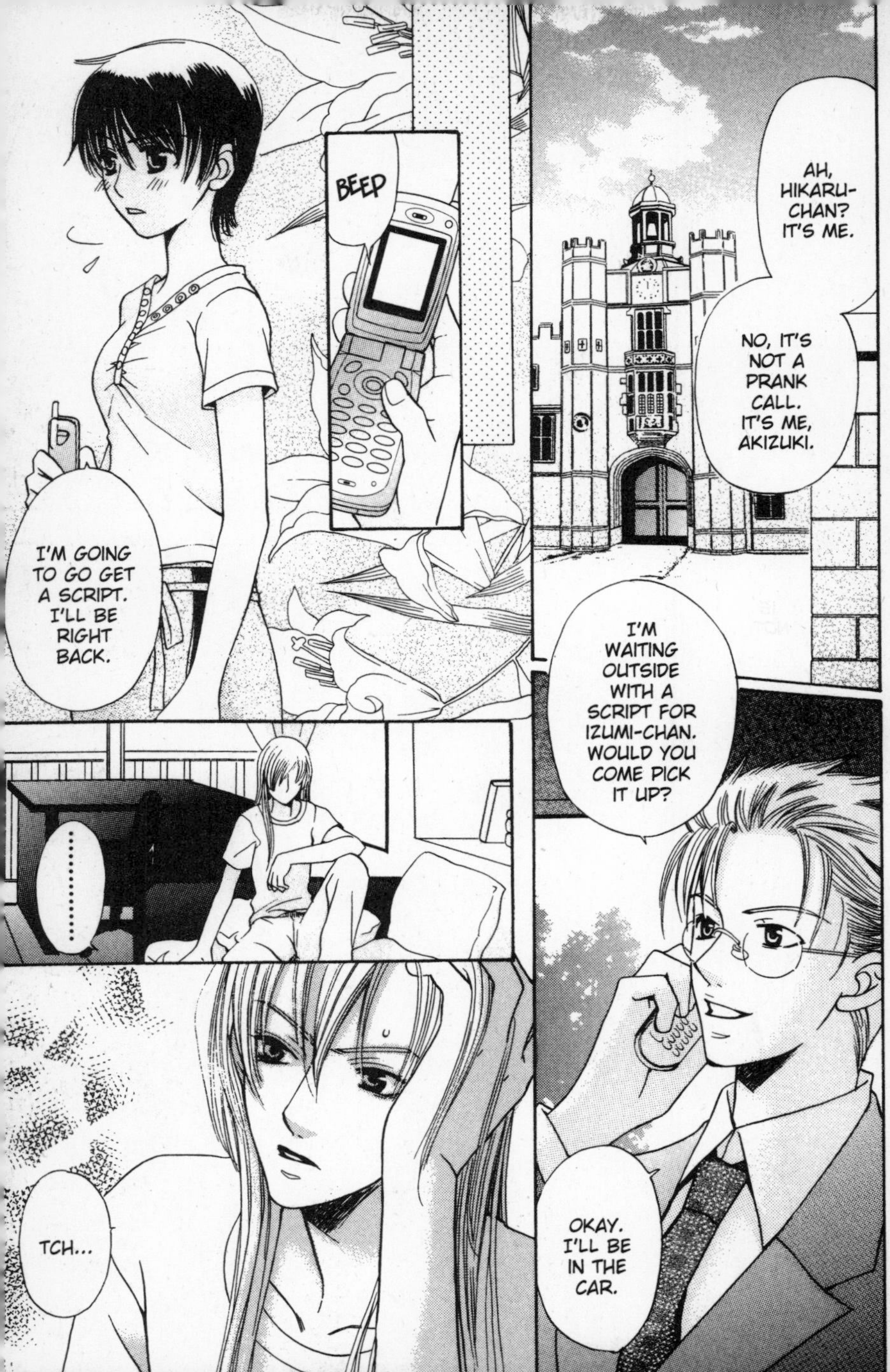
AH, HIKARU-CHAN? IT'S ME.
NO, IT'S NOT A PRANK CALL. IT'S ME, AKIZUKI.
I'M WAITING OUTSIDE WITH A SCRIPT FOR IZUMI-CHAN. WOULD YOU COME PICK IT UP?
OKAY. I'LL BE IN THE CAR.
BEEP
I'M GOING TO GO GET A SCRIPT. I'LL BE RIGHT BACK.
....
TCH...

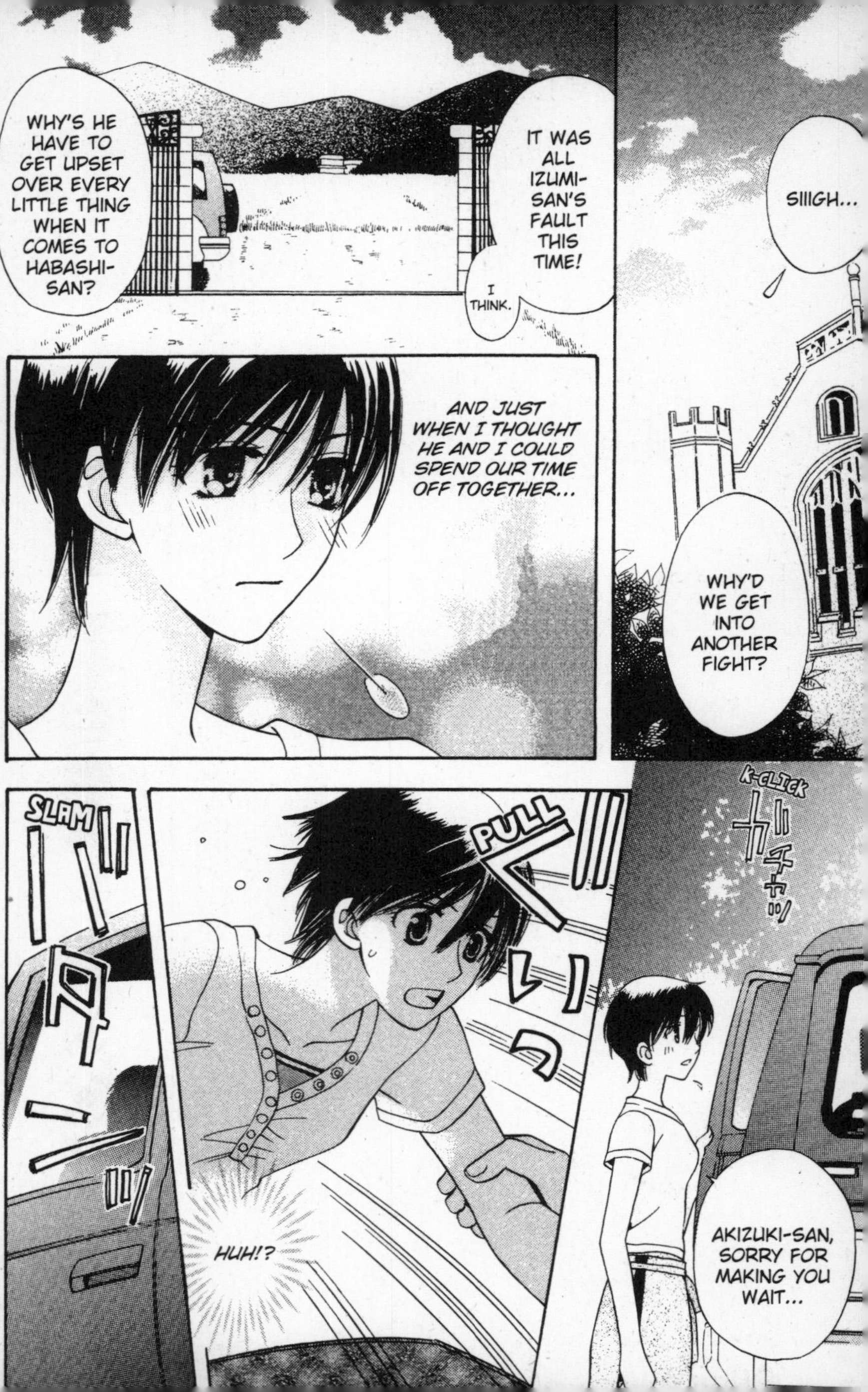
SIIGH...
WHY'D WE GET INTO ANOTHER FIGHT?
IT WAS ALL IZUMI-SAN'S FAULT THIS TIME!
I THINK.
WHY'S HE HAVE TO GET UPSET OVER EVERY LITTLE THING WHEN IT COMES TO HABASHI-SAN?
AND JUST WHEN I THOUGHT HE AND I COULD SPEND OUR TIME OFF TOGETHER...
K-CLICK
AKIZUKI-SAN, SORRY FOR MAKING YOU WAIT...
PULL
HUH!?
SLAM

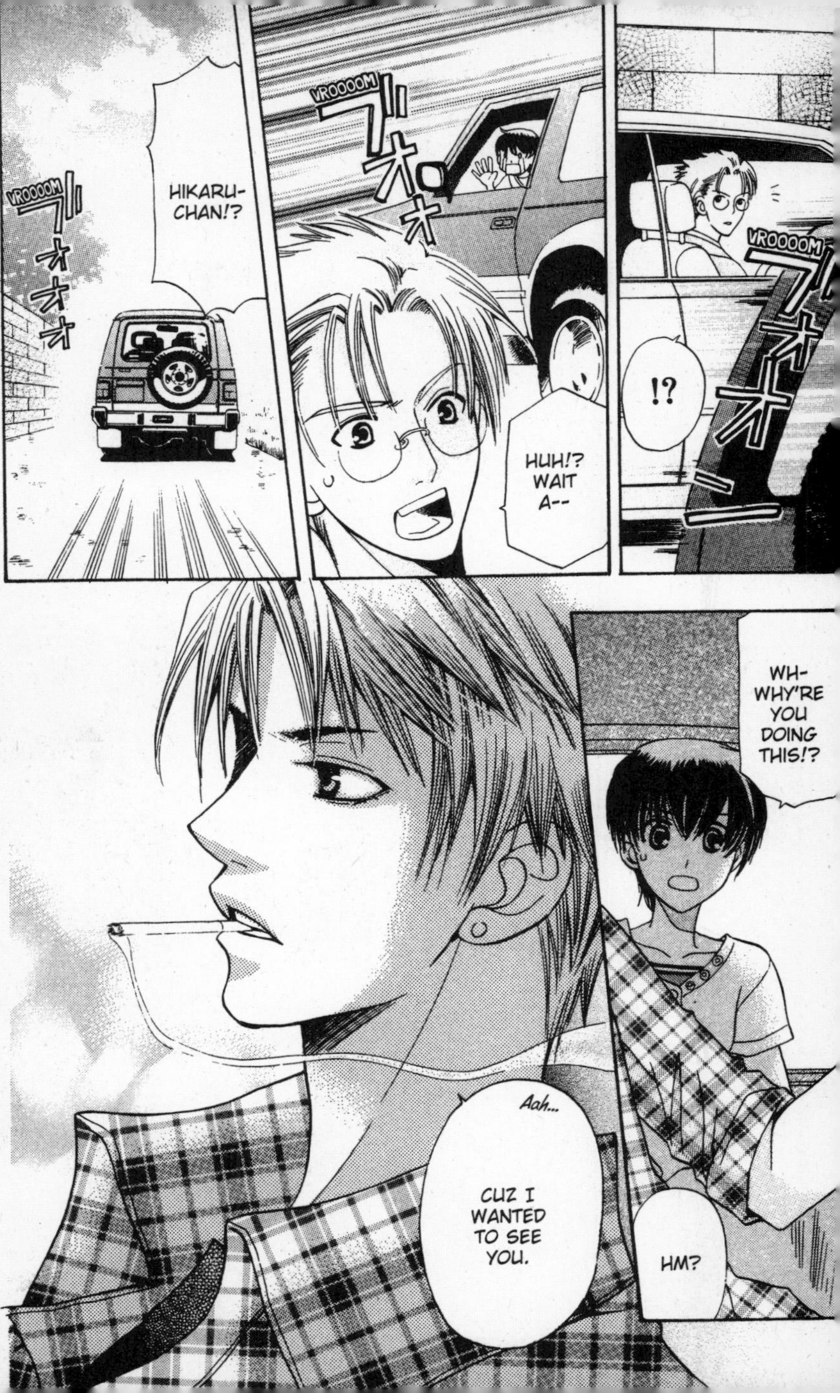
VROOOOM
!?
VROOOOM
HUH!? WAIT A--
HIKARU-CHAN!?
VROOOOM
WH-WHY'RE YOU DOING THIS!?
HM?
Aah...
CUZ I WANTED TO SEE YOU.

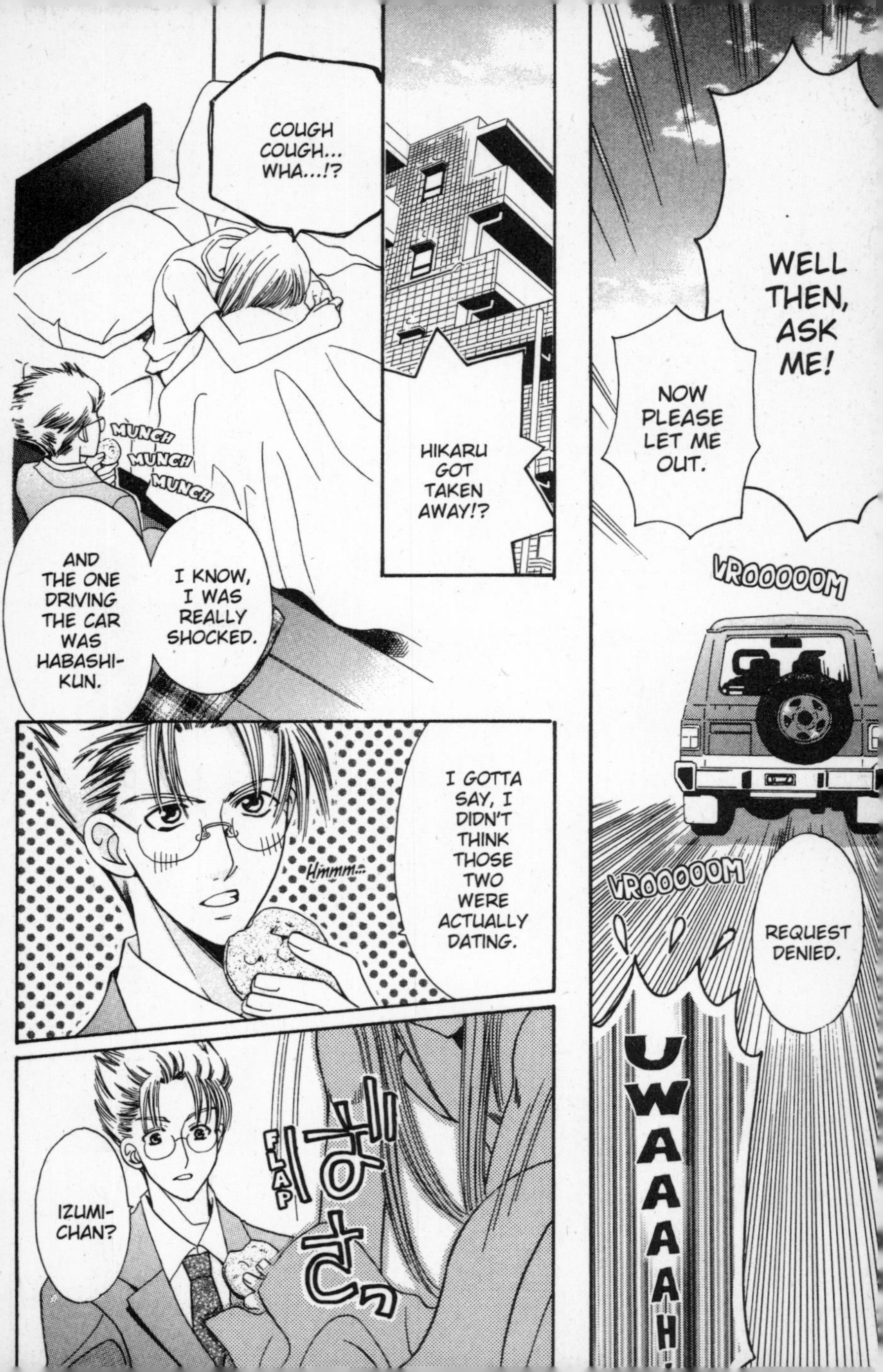
WELL THEN, ASK ME!
NOW PLEASE LET ME OUT.
VROOOOOM
VROOOOOM
REQUEST DENIED.
UWAAAAAH!
HIKARU GOT TAKEN AWAY!?
COUGH COUGH... WHA...!?
MUNCH MUNCH MUNCH
I KNOW, I WAS REALLY SHOCKED.
AND THE ONE DRIVING THE CAR WAS HABASHI-KUN.
I GOTTA SAY, I DIDN'T THINK THOSE TWO WERE ACTUALLY DATING.
Hmmm...
ばさっ
FLAP
IZUMI-CHAN?

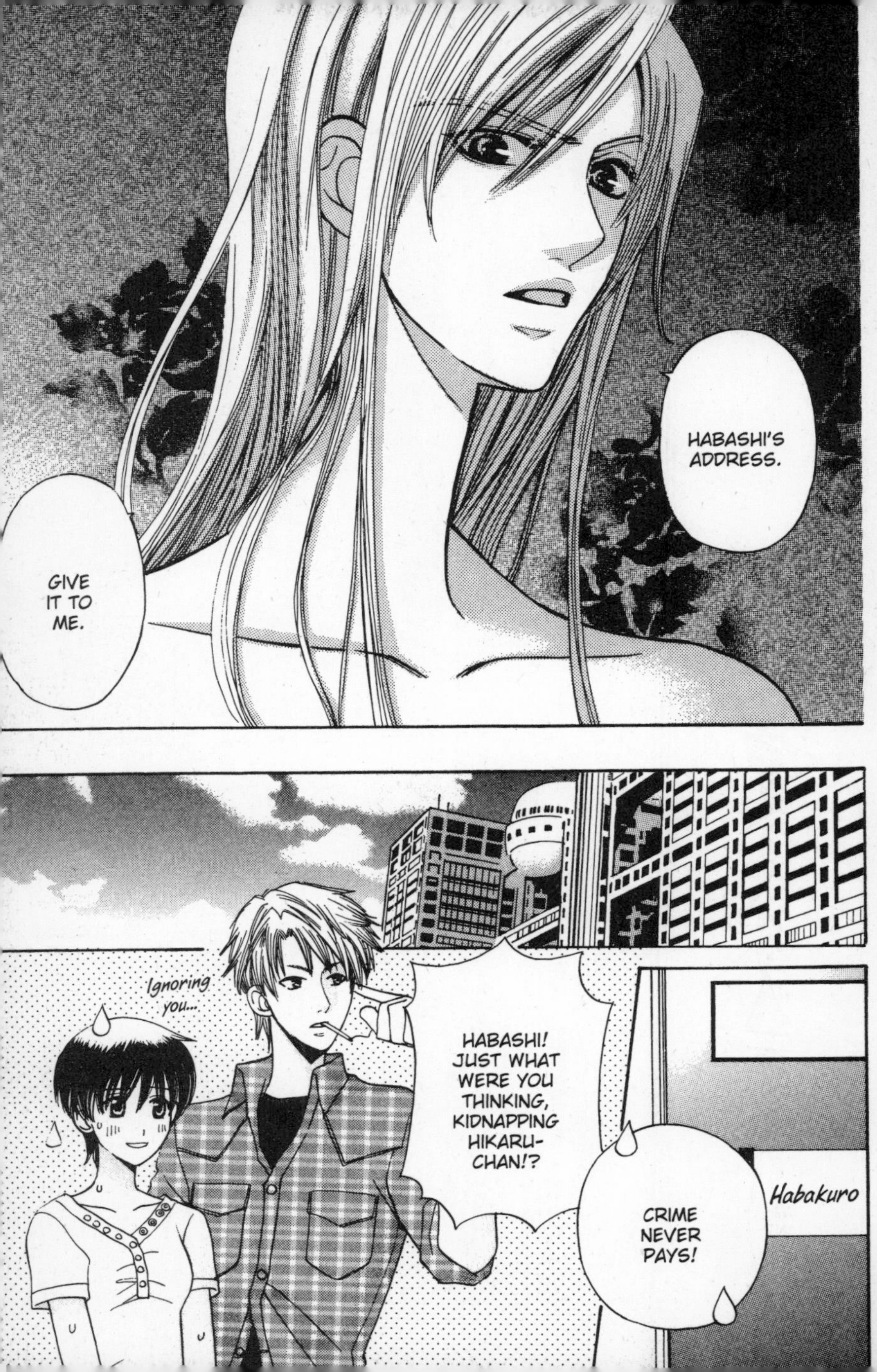
HABASHI'S ADDRESS.
GIVE IT TO ME.
Habakuro
HABASHI! JUST WHAT WERE YOU THINKING, KIDNAPPING HIKARU-CHAN!?
CRIME NEVER PAYS!
Ignoring you...

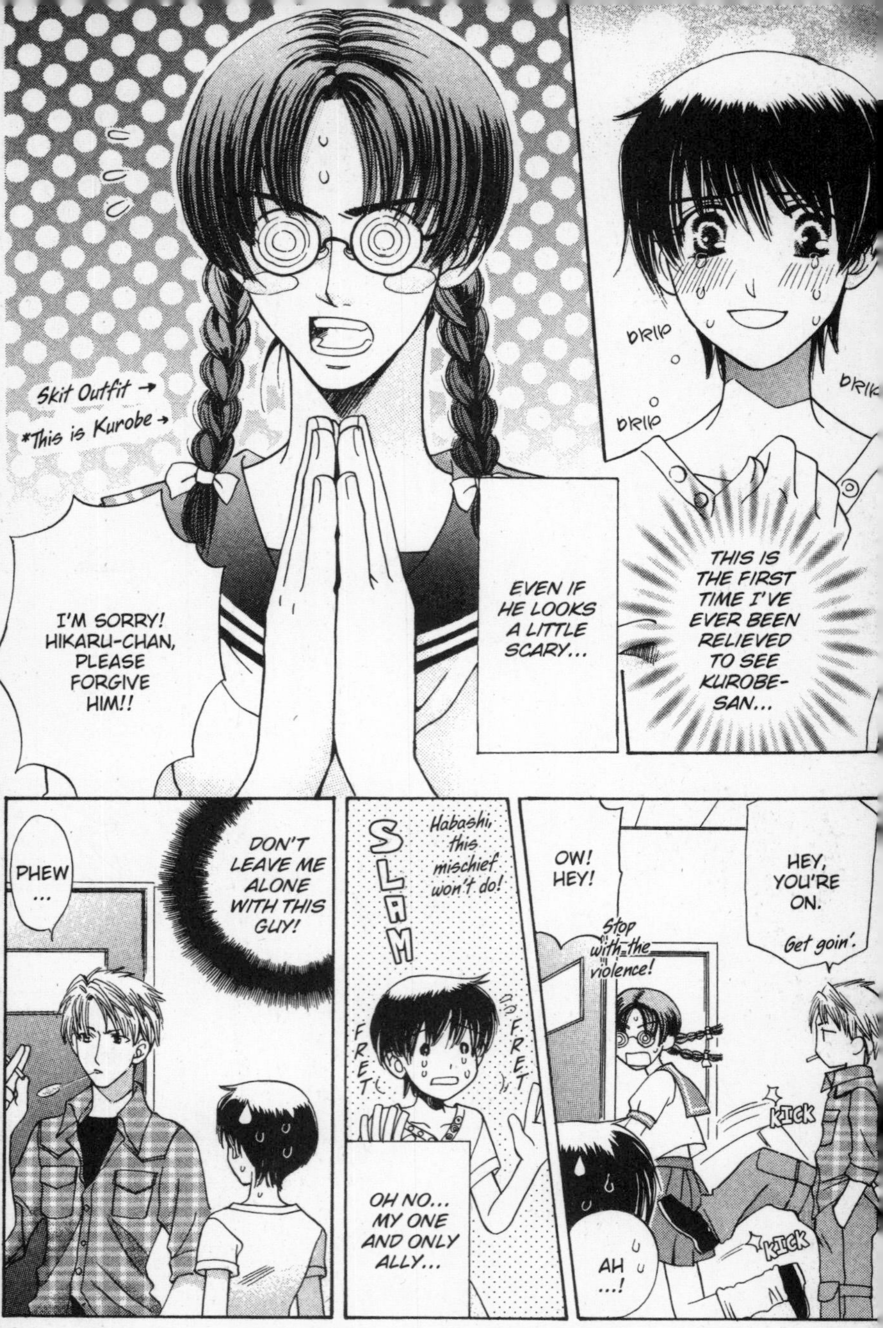
DRIP
DRIP
DRIP
THIS IS THE FIRST TIME I'VE EVER BEEN RELIEVED TO SEE KUROBE-SAN...
EVEN IF HE LOOKS A LITTLE SCARY...
I'M SORRY! HIKARU-CHAN, PLEASE FORGIVE HIM!!
Skit Outfit →
*This is Kurobe →
HEY, YOU'RE ON.
Get goin'.
OW! HEY!
Stop with the violence!
KICK
KICK
AH ...!
Habashi, this mischief won't do!
SLAM
FRET
FRET
OH NO... MY ONE AND ONLY ALLY...
DON'T LEAVE ME ALONE WITH THIS GUY!
PHEW ...

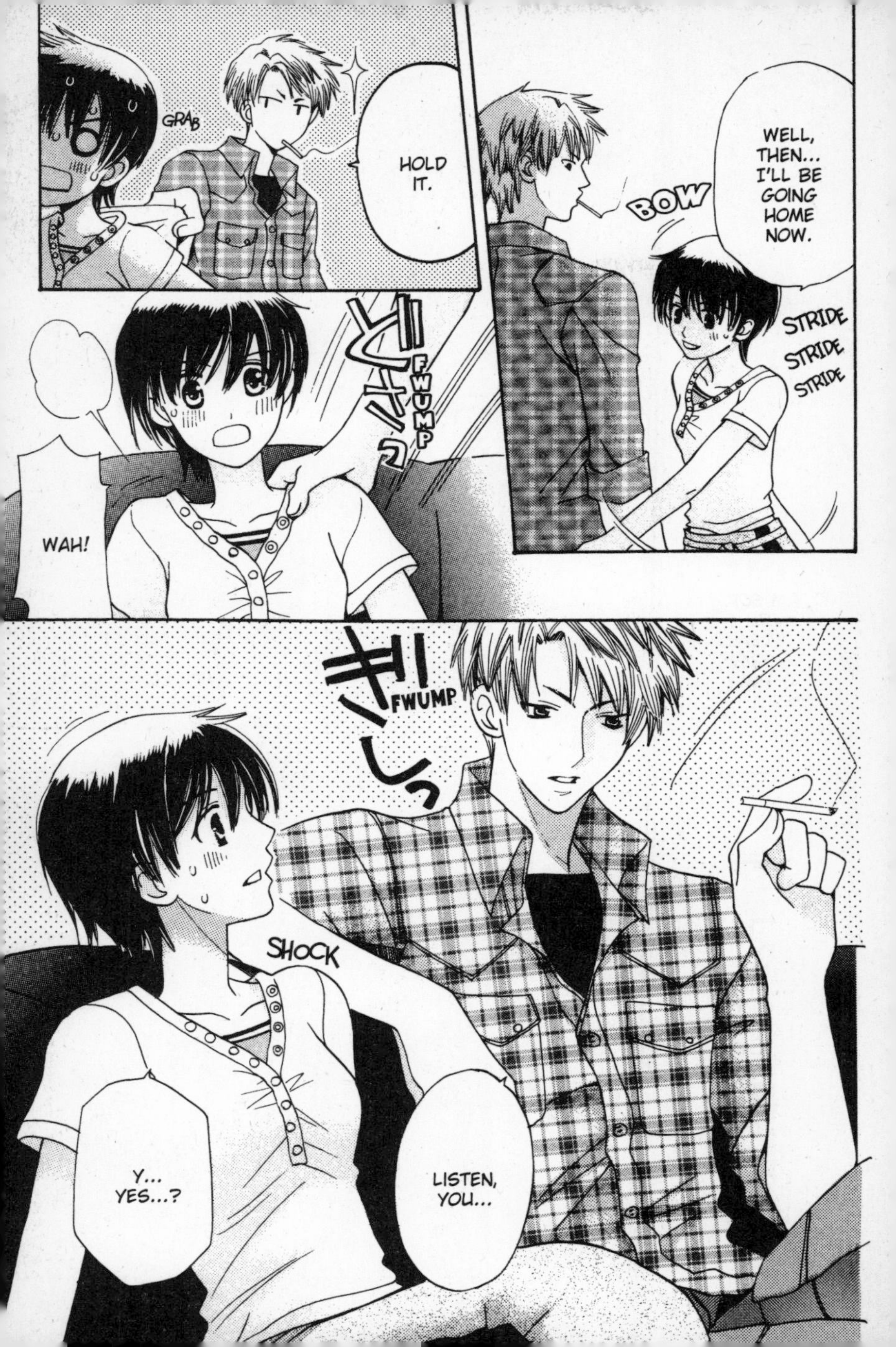

WELL, THEN... I'LL BE GOING HOME NOW.
BOW
STRIDE
STRIDE
STRIDE
HOLD IT.
GRAB
どさっ
FWUMP
WAH!
ぎしっ
FWUMP
SHOCK
LISTEN, YOU...
Y... YES...?

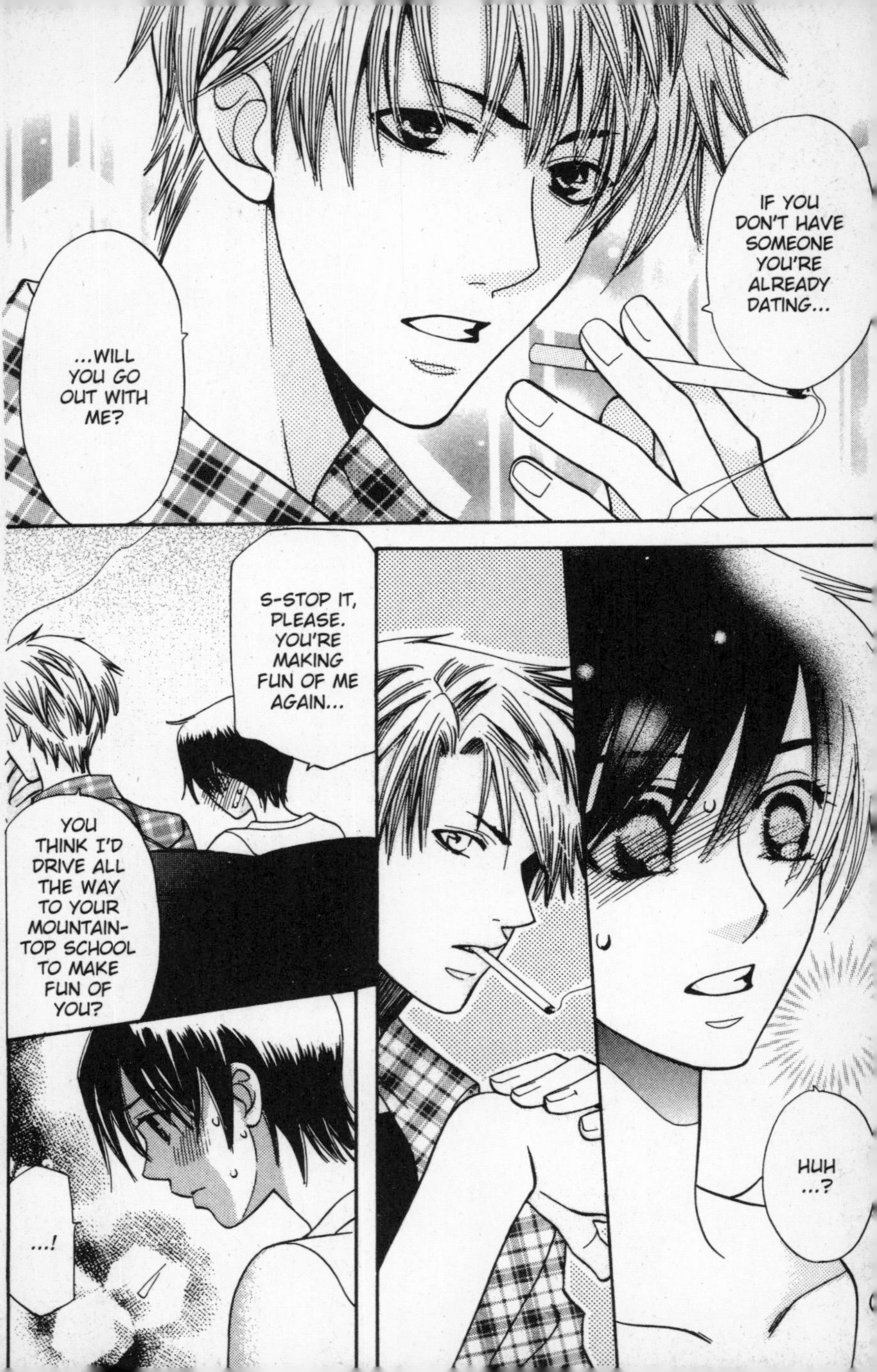
IF YOU DON'T HAVE SOMEONE YOU'RE ALREADY DATING...
...WILL YOU GO OUT WITH ME?
HUH ...?
S-STOP IT, PLEASE. YOU'RE MAKING FUN OF ME AGAIN...
YOU THINK I'D DRIVE ALL THE WAY TO YOUR MOUNTAIN-TOP SCHOOL TO MAKE FUN OF YOU?
...!

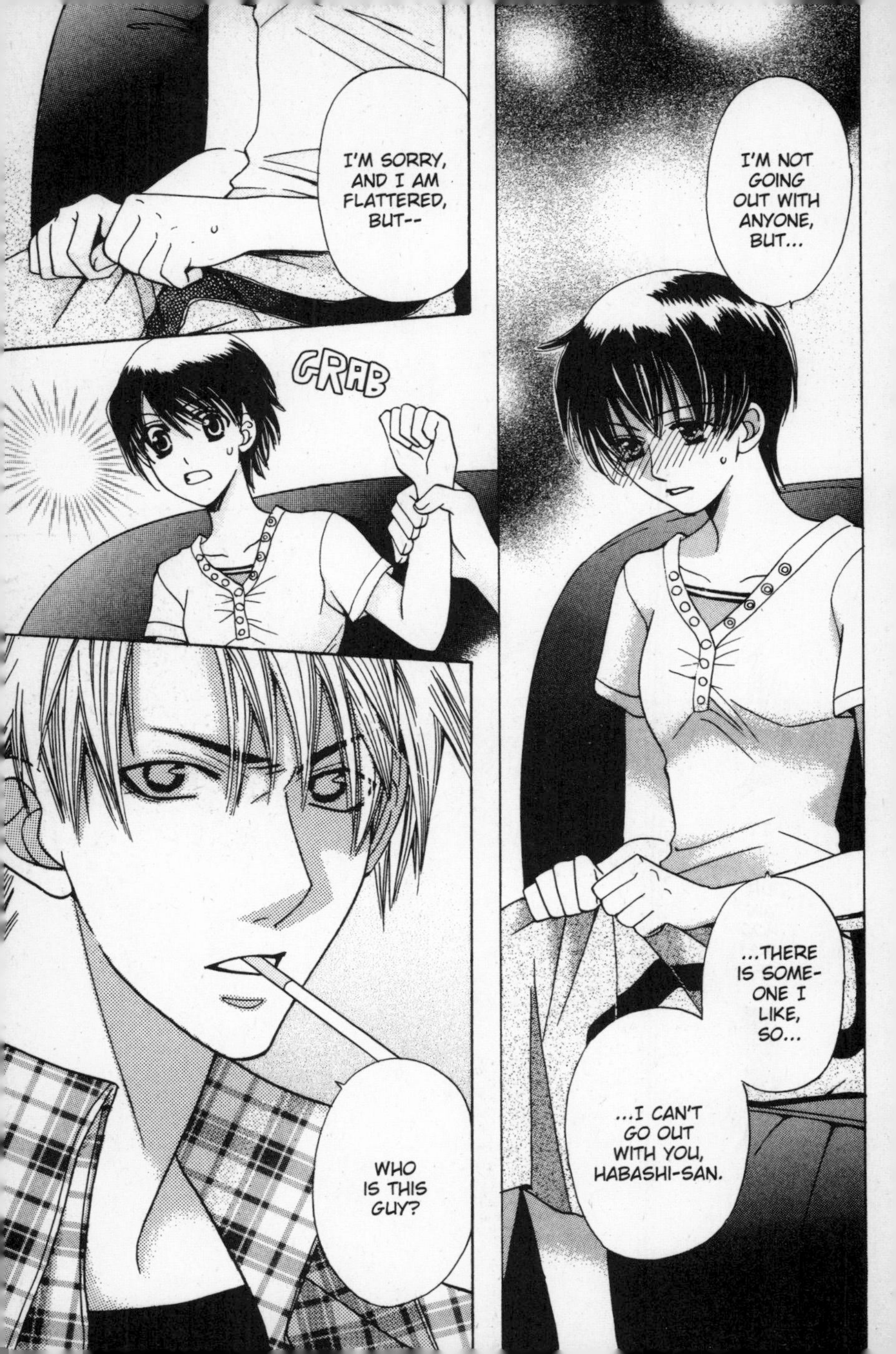
I'M NOT GOING OUT WITH ANYONE, BUT...
...THERE IS SOME-ONE I LIKE, SO...
...I CAN'T GO OUT WITH YOU, HABASHI-SAN.
I'M SORRY, AND I AM FLATTERED, BUT--
GRAB
WHO IS THIS GUY?

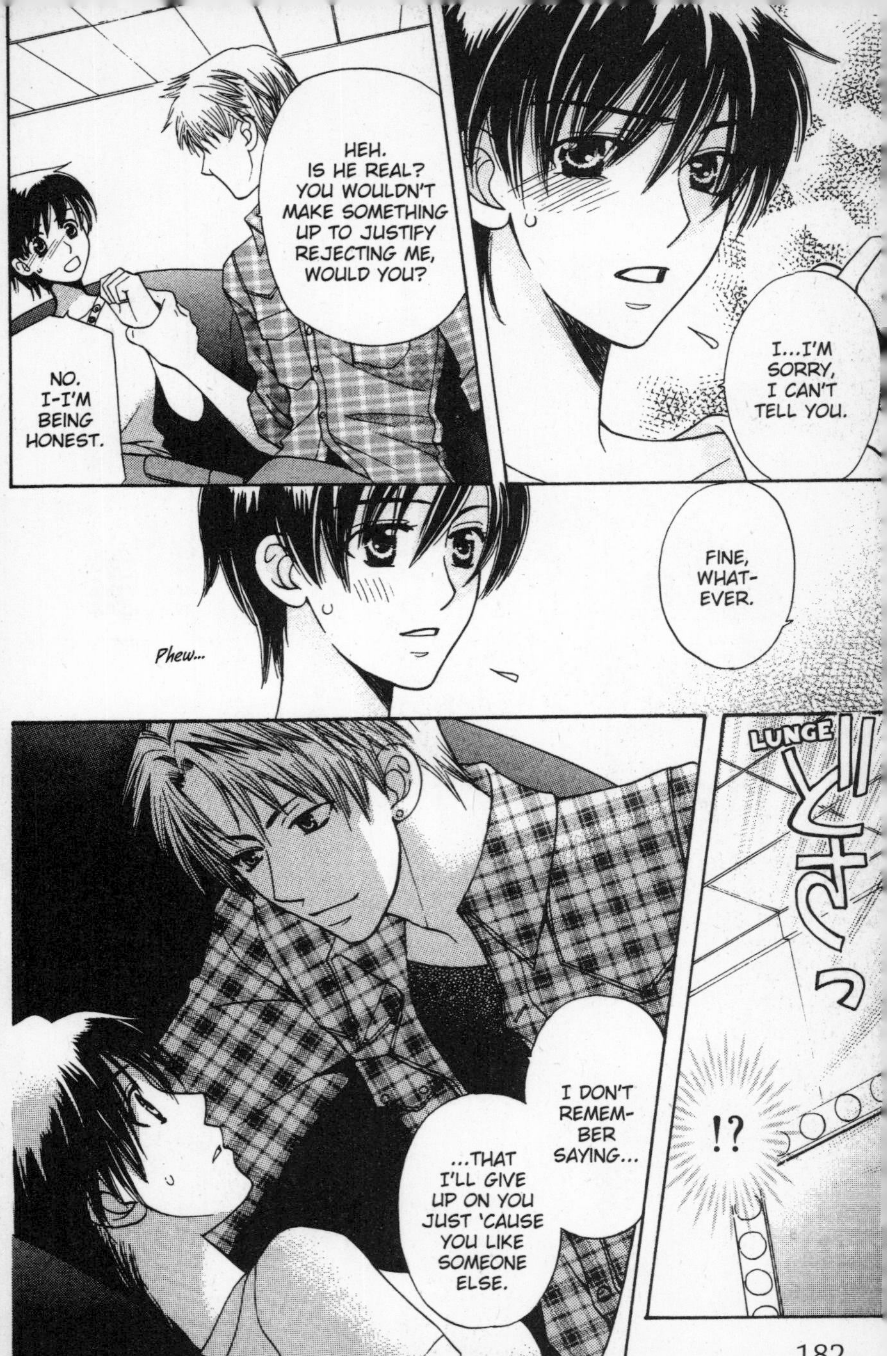
I...I'M SORRY, I CAN'T TELL YOU.
HEH. IS HE REAL? YOU WOULDN'T MAKE SOMETHING UP TO JUSTIFY REJECTING ME, WOULD YOU?
NO. I-I'M BEING HONEST.
FINE, WHATEVER.
Phew...
LUNGE
!?
I DON'T REMEMBER SAYING...
...THAT I'LL GIVE UP ON YOU JUST 'CAUSE YOU LIKE SOMEONE ELSE.

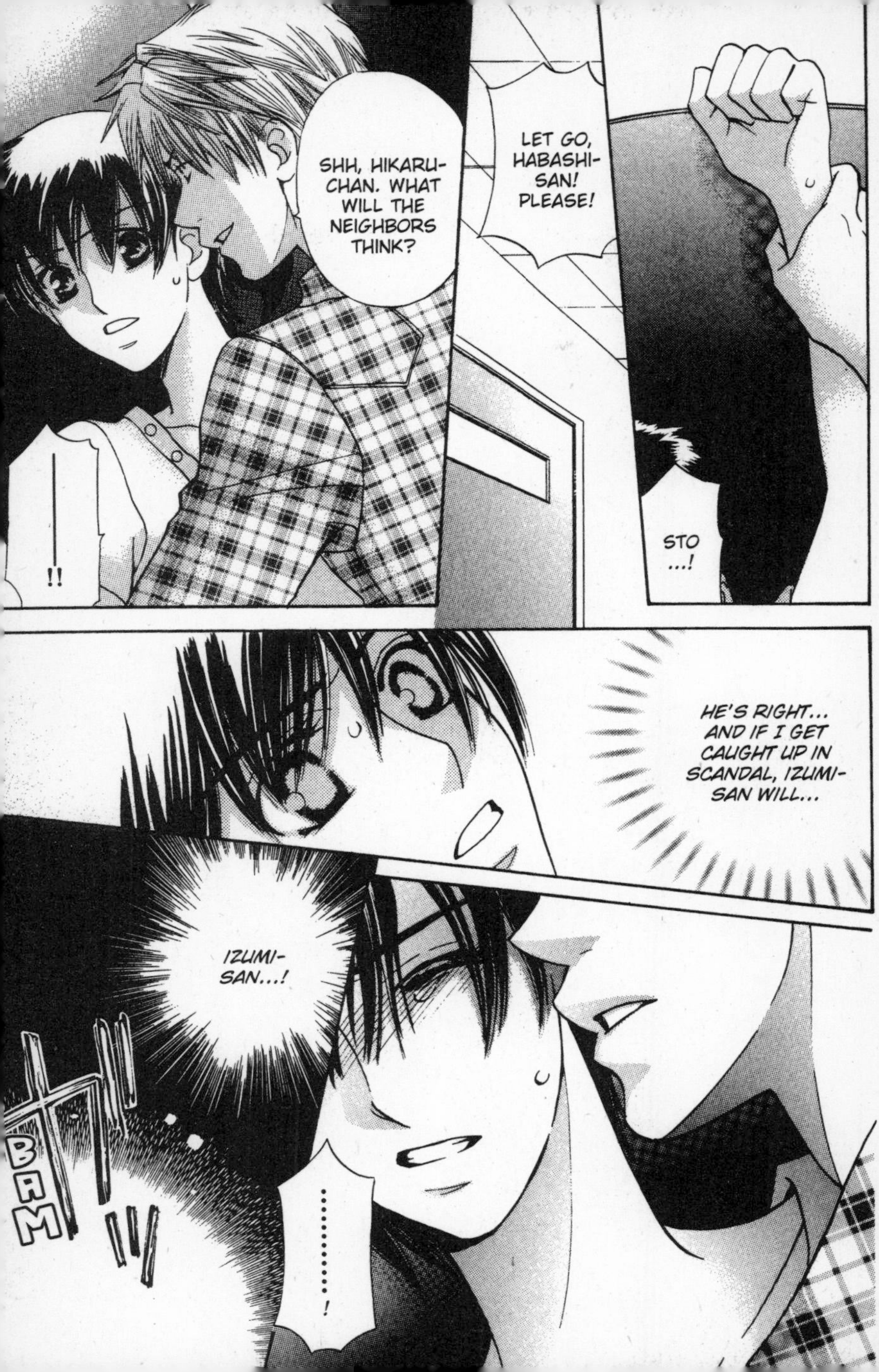
STO ...!
LET GO, HABASHI-SAN! PLEASE!
SHH, HIKARU-CHAN. WHAT WILL THE NEIGHBORS THINK?
!!
HE'S RIGHT... AND IF I GET CAUGHT UP IN SCANDAL, IZUMI-SAN WILL...
IZUMI-SAN...!
......!
BAM

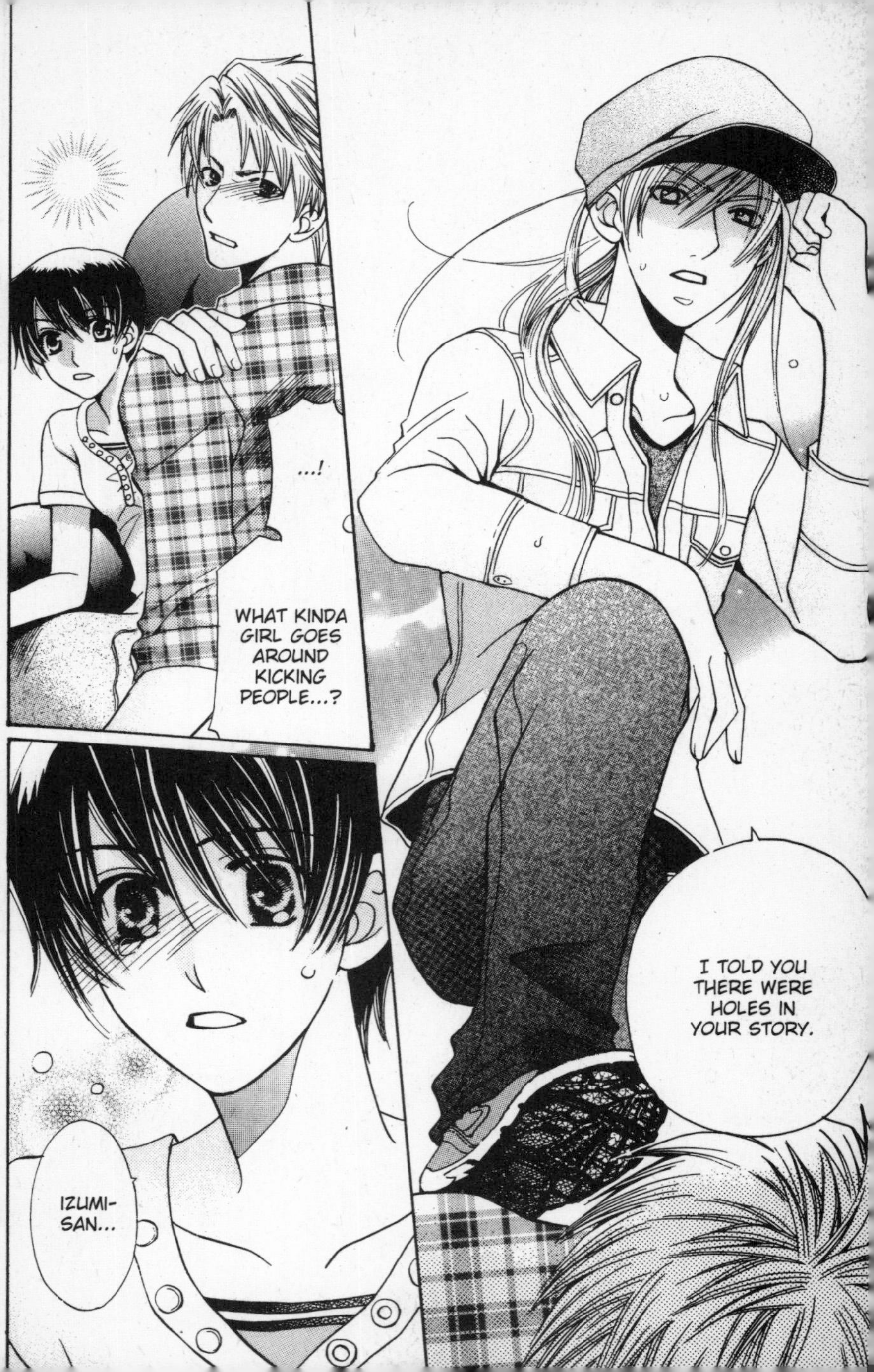
I TOLD YOU THERE WERE HOLES IN YOUR STORY.
...!
WHAT KINDA GIRL GOES AROUND KICKING PEOPLE...?
IZUMI-SAN...

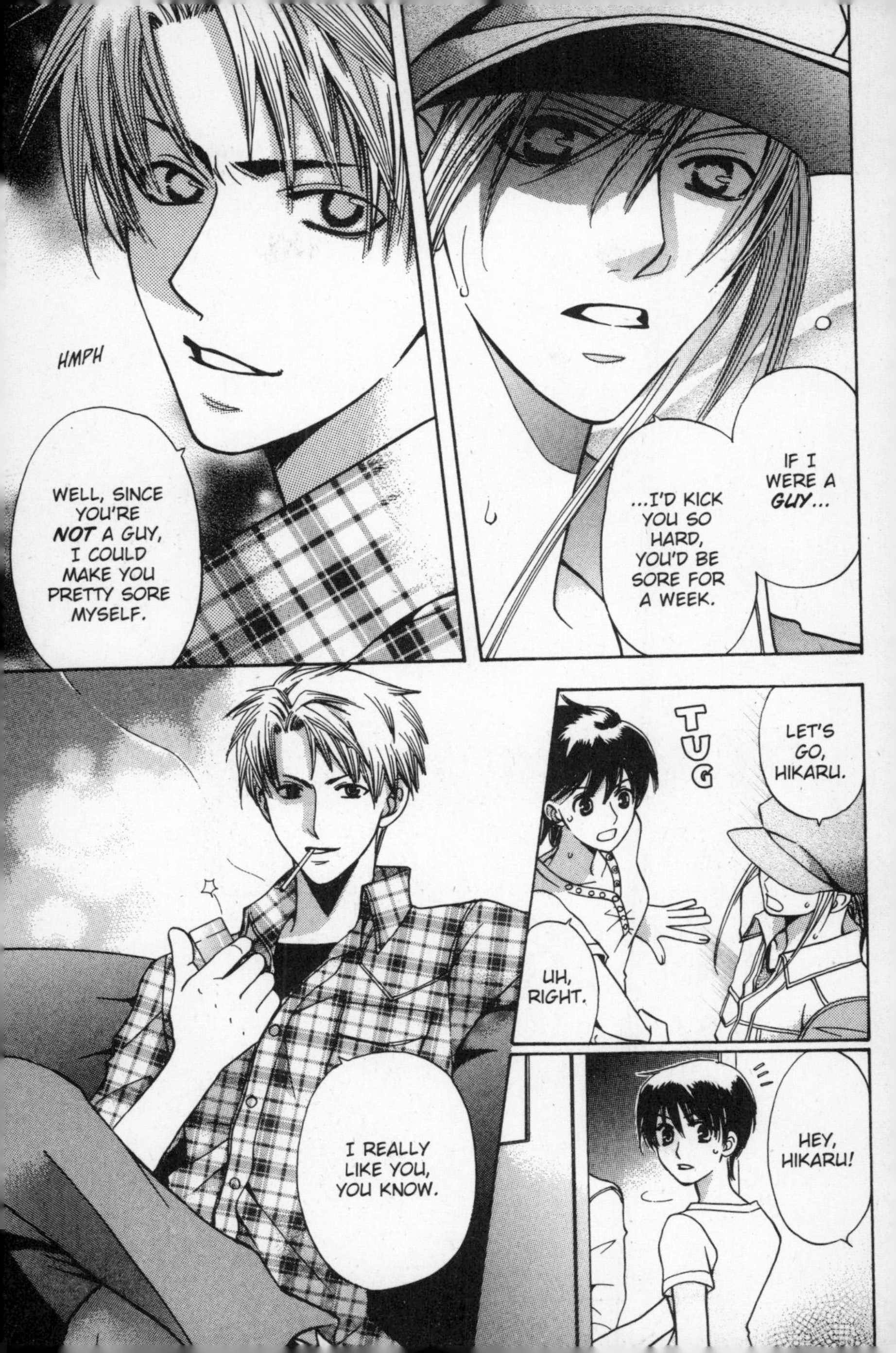
IF I WERE A GUY...
...I'D KICK YOU SO HARD, YOU'D BE SORE FOR A WEEK.
HMPH
WELL, SINCE YOU'RE NOT A GUY, I COULD MAKE YOU PRETTY SORE MYSELF.
LET'S GO, HIKARU.
TUG
UH, RIGHT.
HEY, HIKARU!
I REALLY LIKE YOU, YOU KNOW.

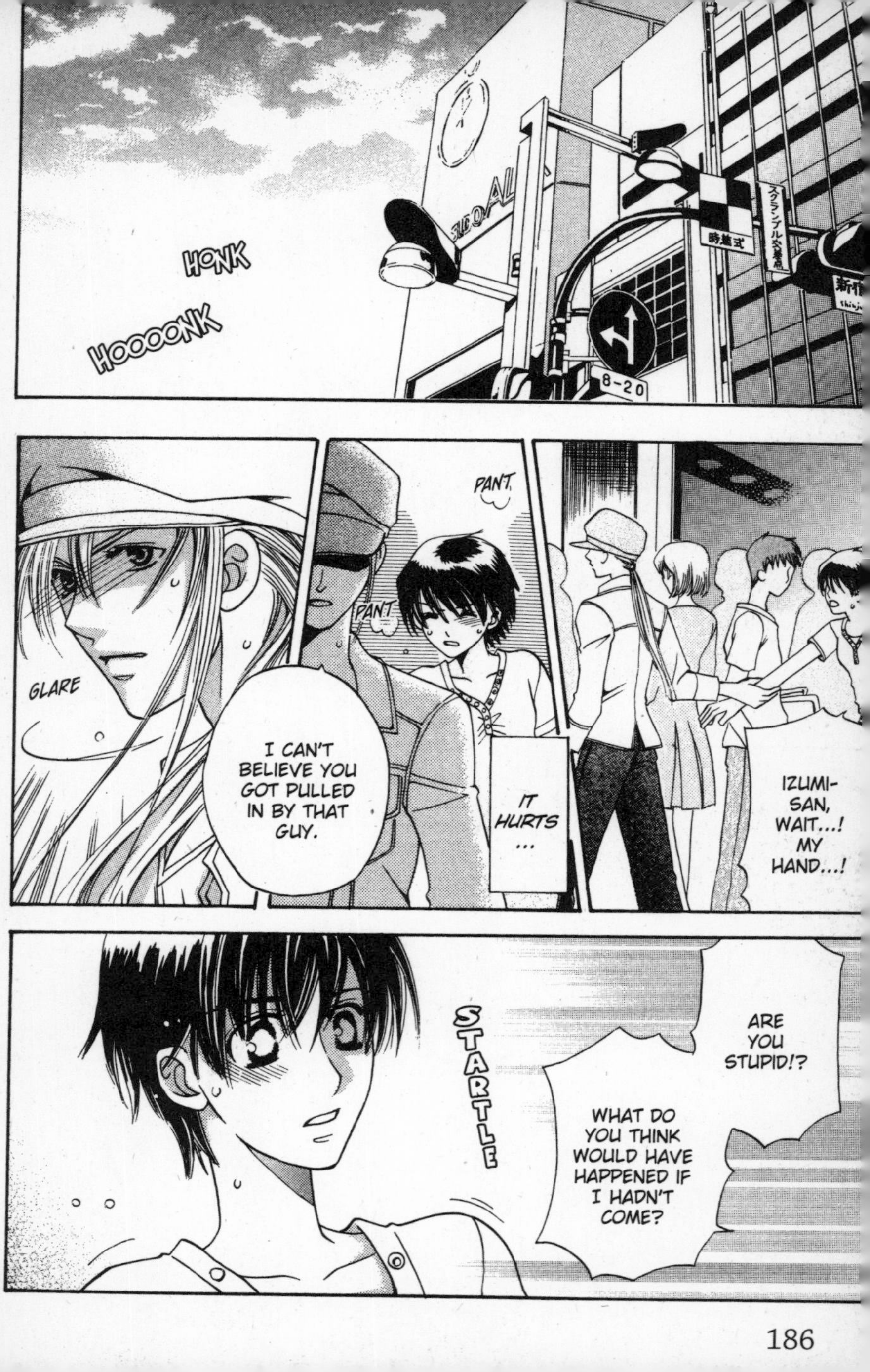

HONK
HOOOONK
時差式
8-20
IZUMI-SAN, WAIT...! MY HAND...!
PANT
PANT
IT HURTS...
I CAN'T BELIEVE YOU GOT PULLED IN BY THAT GUY.
GLARE
ARE YOU STUPID!?
WHAT DO YOU THINK WOULD HAVE HAPPENED IF I HADN'T COME?
STARTLE

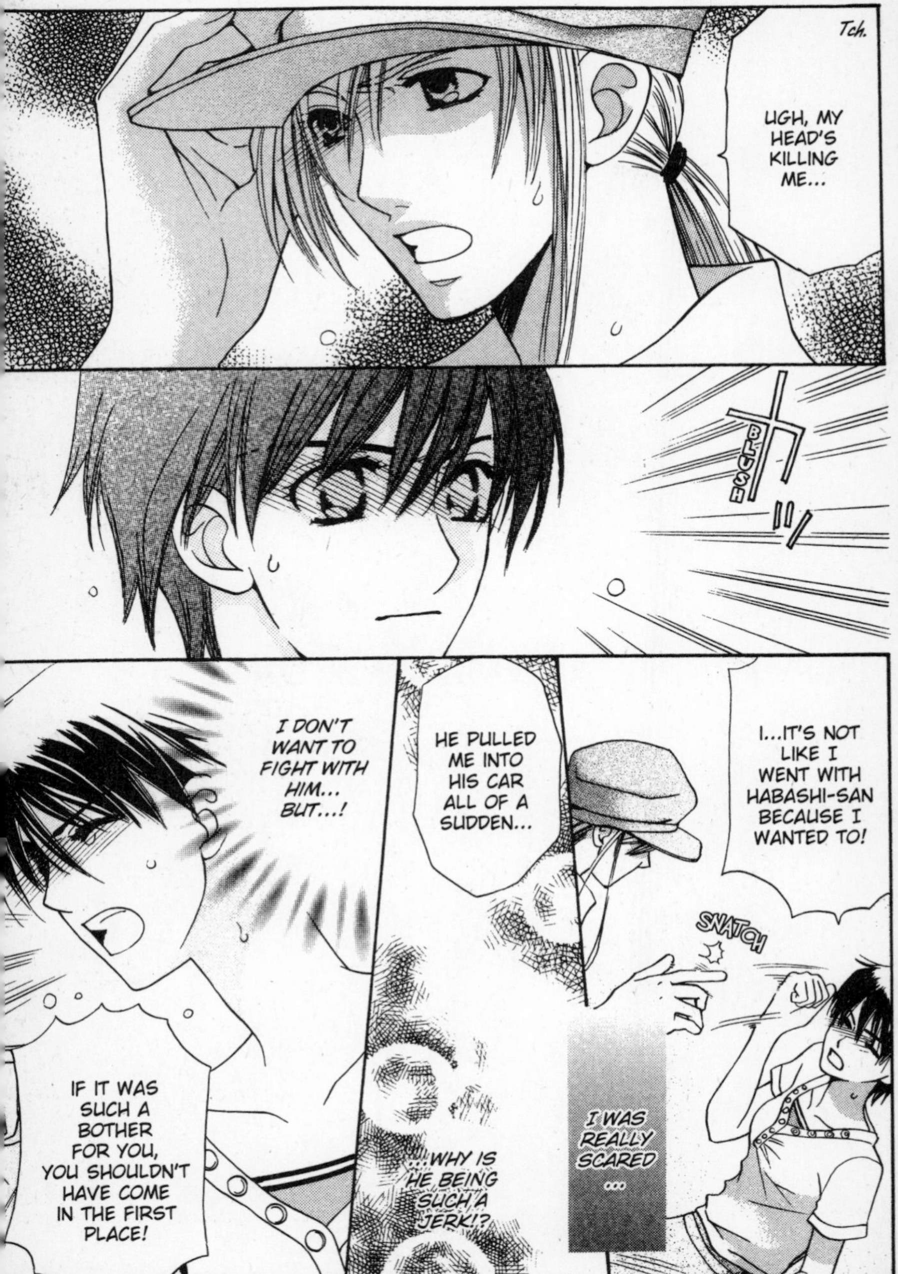
Tch.
UGH, MY HEAD'S KILLING ME...
BLUSH
I...IT'S NOT LIKE I WENT WITH HABASHI-SAN BECAUSE I WANTED TO!
SNATCH
I WAS REALLY SCARED...
HE PULLED ME INTO HIS CAR ALL OF A SUDDEN...
...WHY IS HE BEING SUCH A JERK!?
I DON'T WANT TO FIGHT WITH HIM... BUT...!
IF IT WAS SUCH A BOTHER FOR YOU, YOU SHOULDN'T HAVE COME IN THE FIRST PLACE!

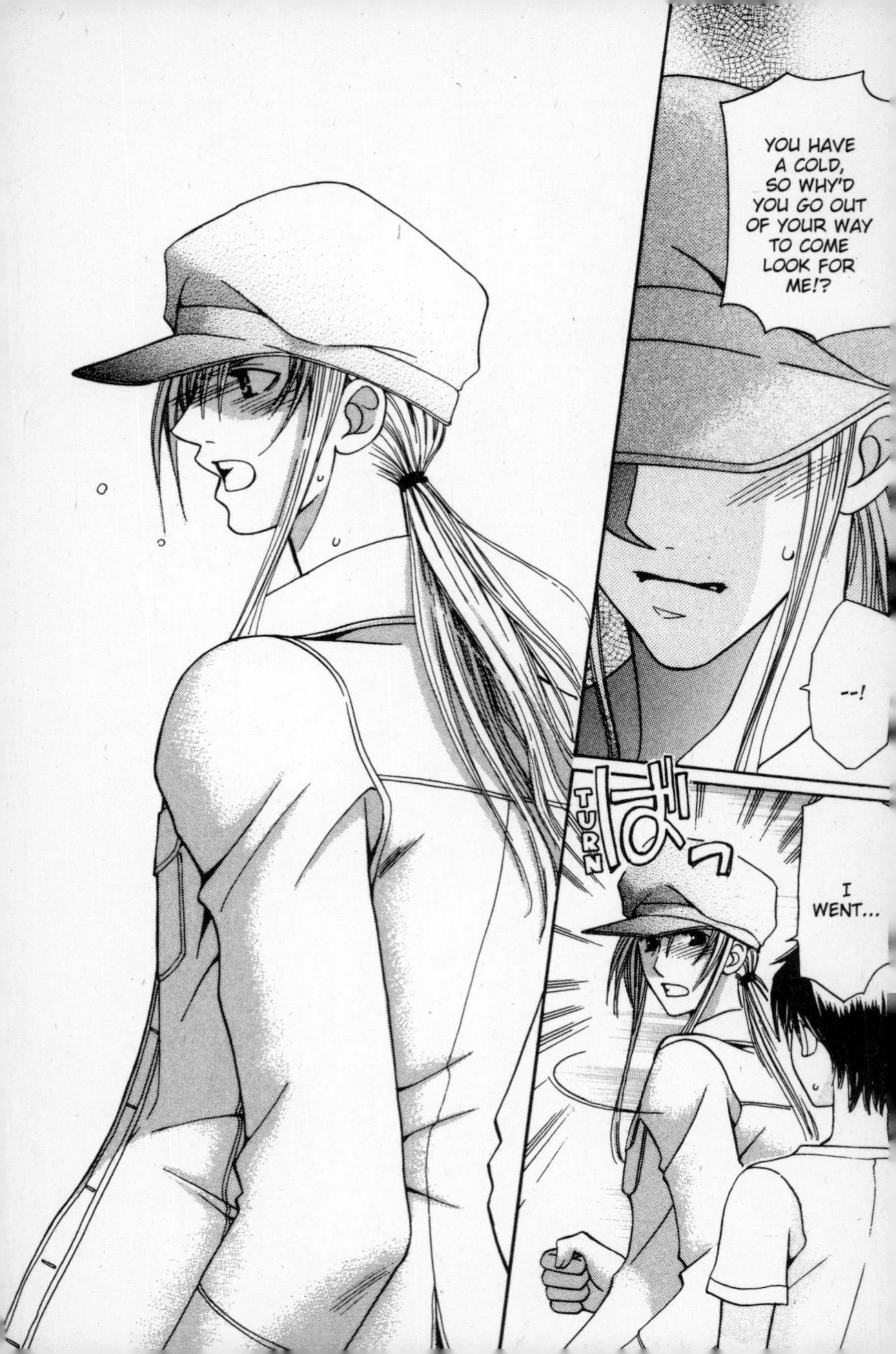
YOU HAVE A COLD, SO WHY'D YOU GO OUT OF YOUR WAY TO COME LOOK FOR ME!?
--!
I WENT...
TURN
ばっ

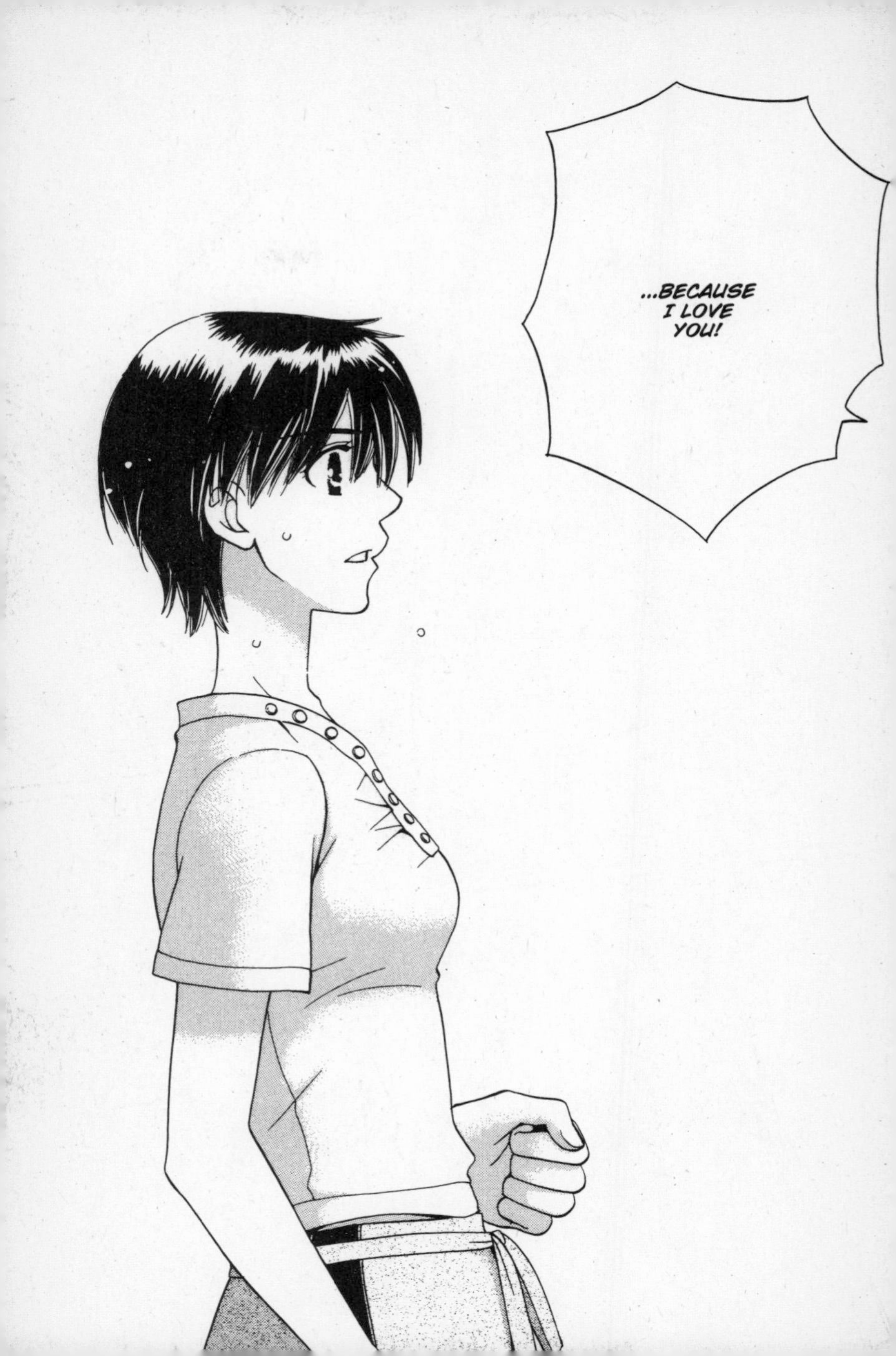
...BECAUSE
I LOVE
YOU!

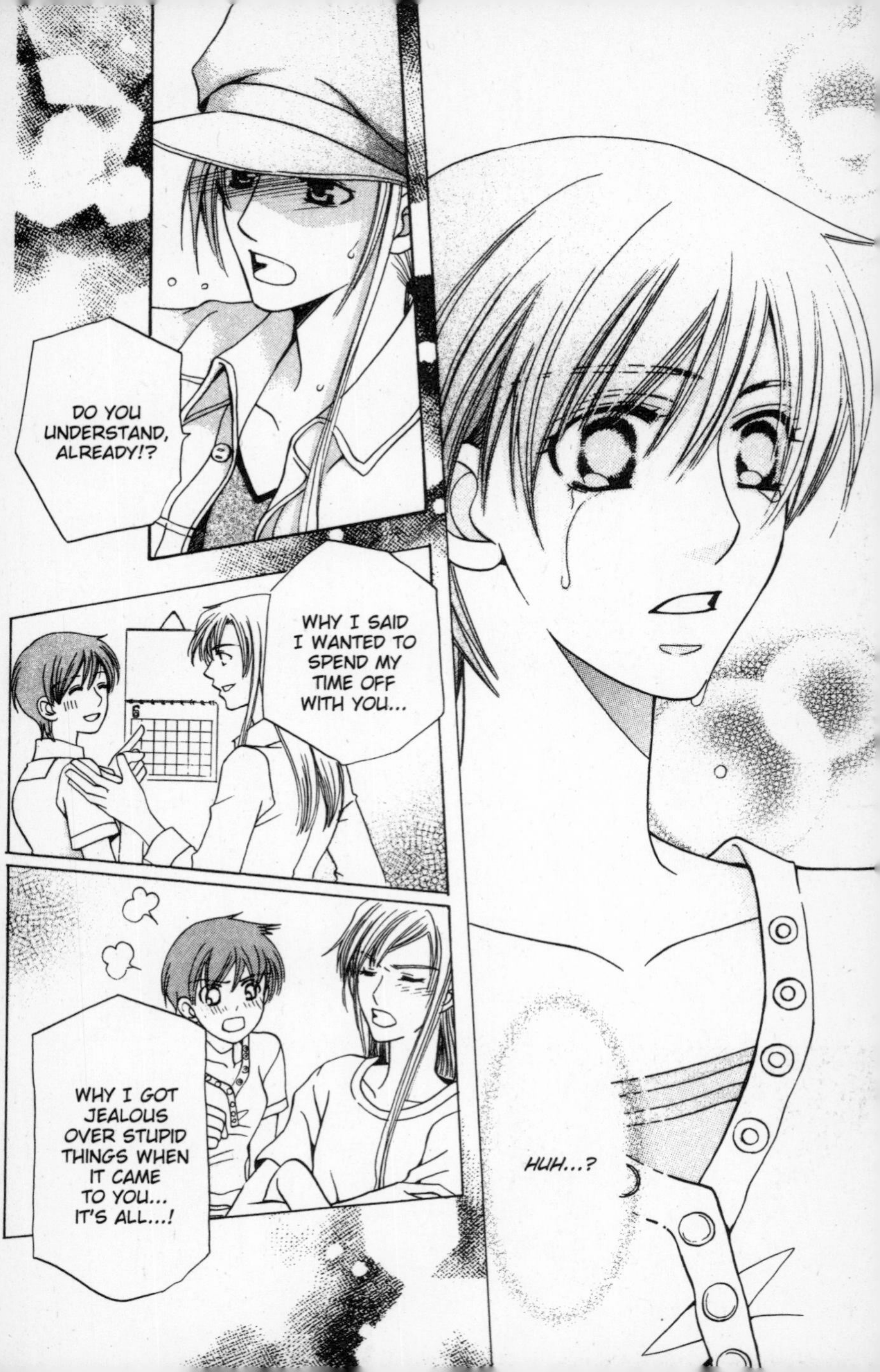
HUH...?
DO YOU UNDERSTAND, ALREADY!?
WHY I SAID I WANTED TO SPEND MY TIME OFF WITH YOU...
WHY I GOT JEALOUS OVER STUPID THINGS WHEN IT CAME TO YOU... IT'S ALL...!

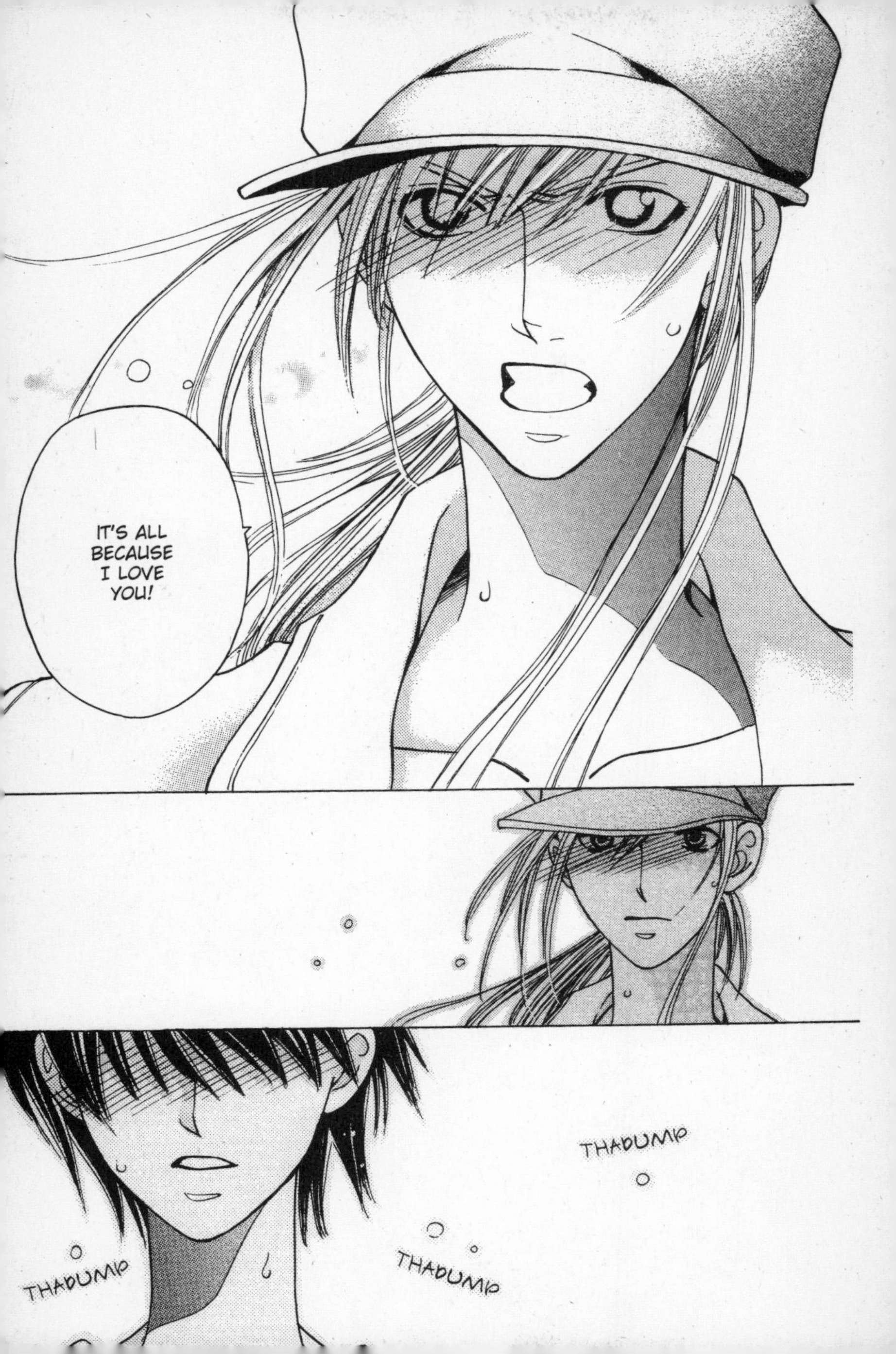
IT'S ALL BECAUSE I LOVE YOU!
THADUMP
THADUMP
THADUMP

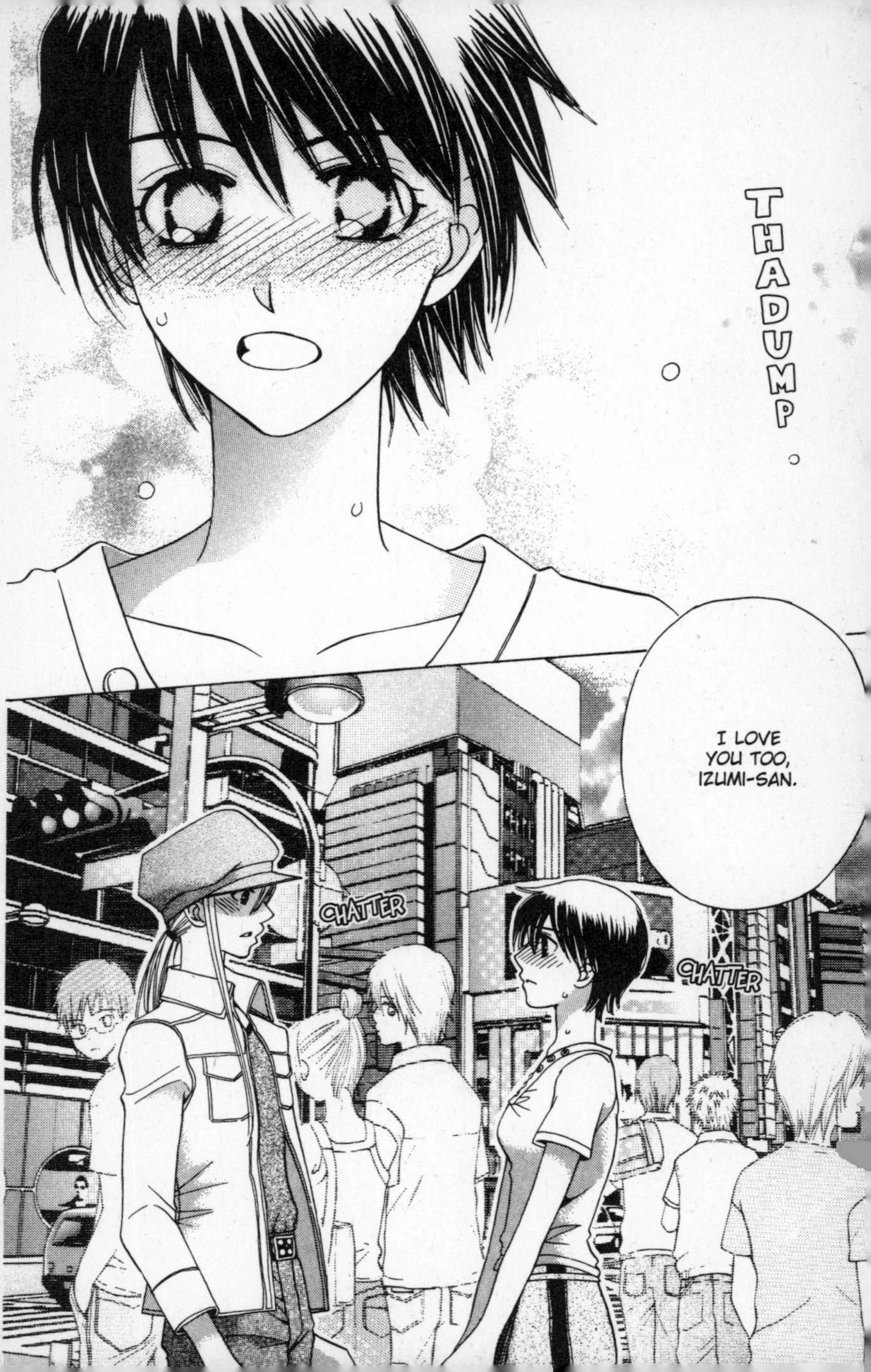
THADUMP
I LOVE YOU TOO, IZUMI-SAN.
CHATTER
CHATTER

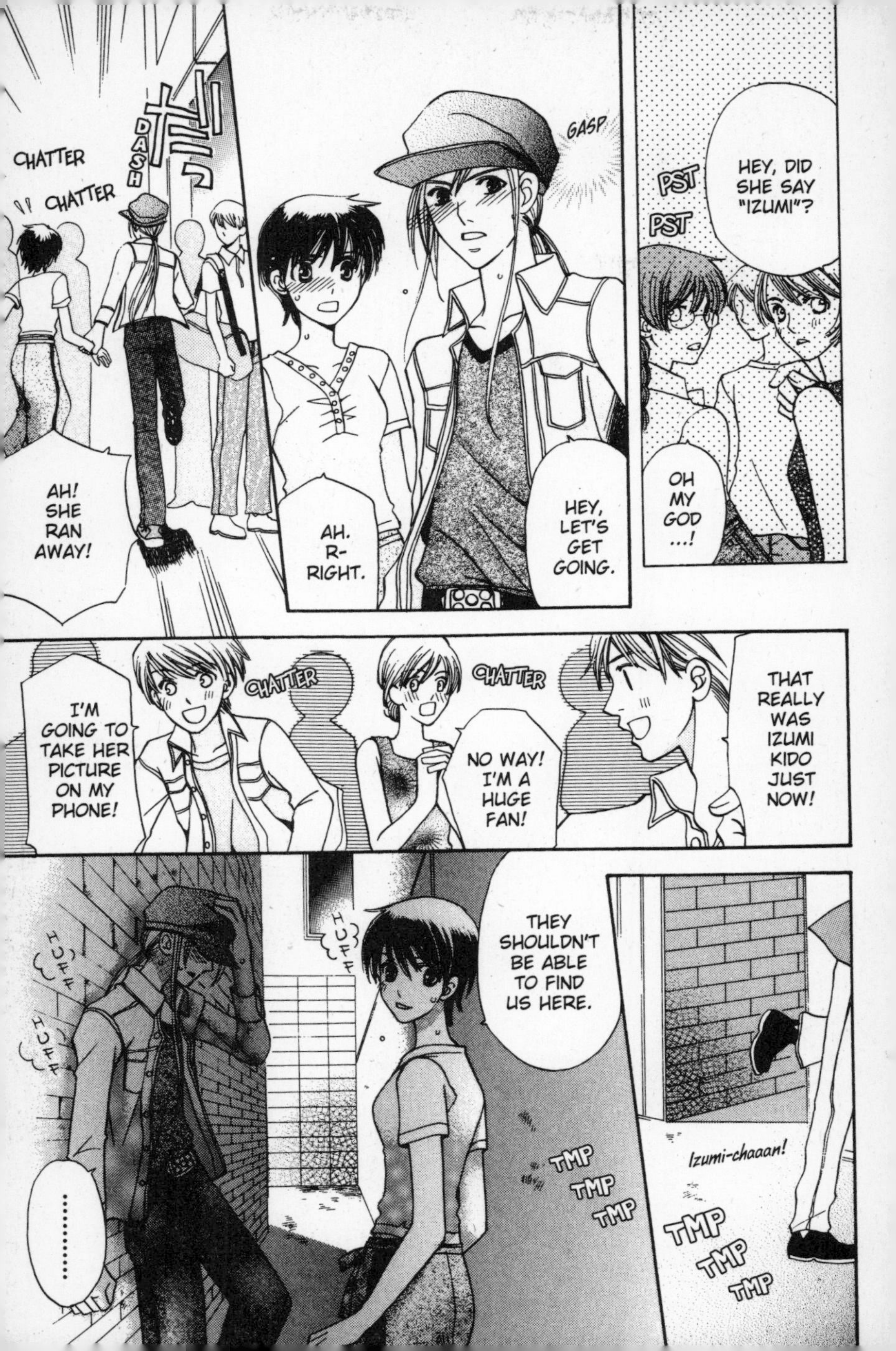
PST
PST
HEY, DID SHE SAY "IZUMI"?
OH MY GOD ...!
GASP
HEY, LET'S GET GOING.
AH. R-RIGHT.
CHATTER
CHATTER
DASH
AH! SHE RAN AWAY!
THAT REALLY WAS IZUMI KIDO JUST NOW!
CHATTER
NO WAY! I'M A HUGE FAN!
CHATTER
I'M GOING TO TAKE HER PICTURE ON MY PHONE!
Izumi-chaaan!
TMP TMP TMP
THEY SHOULDN'T BE ABLE TO FIND US HERE.
TMP TMP TMP
HUFF HUFF
HUFF HUFF
....

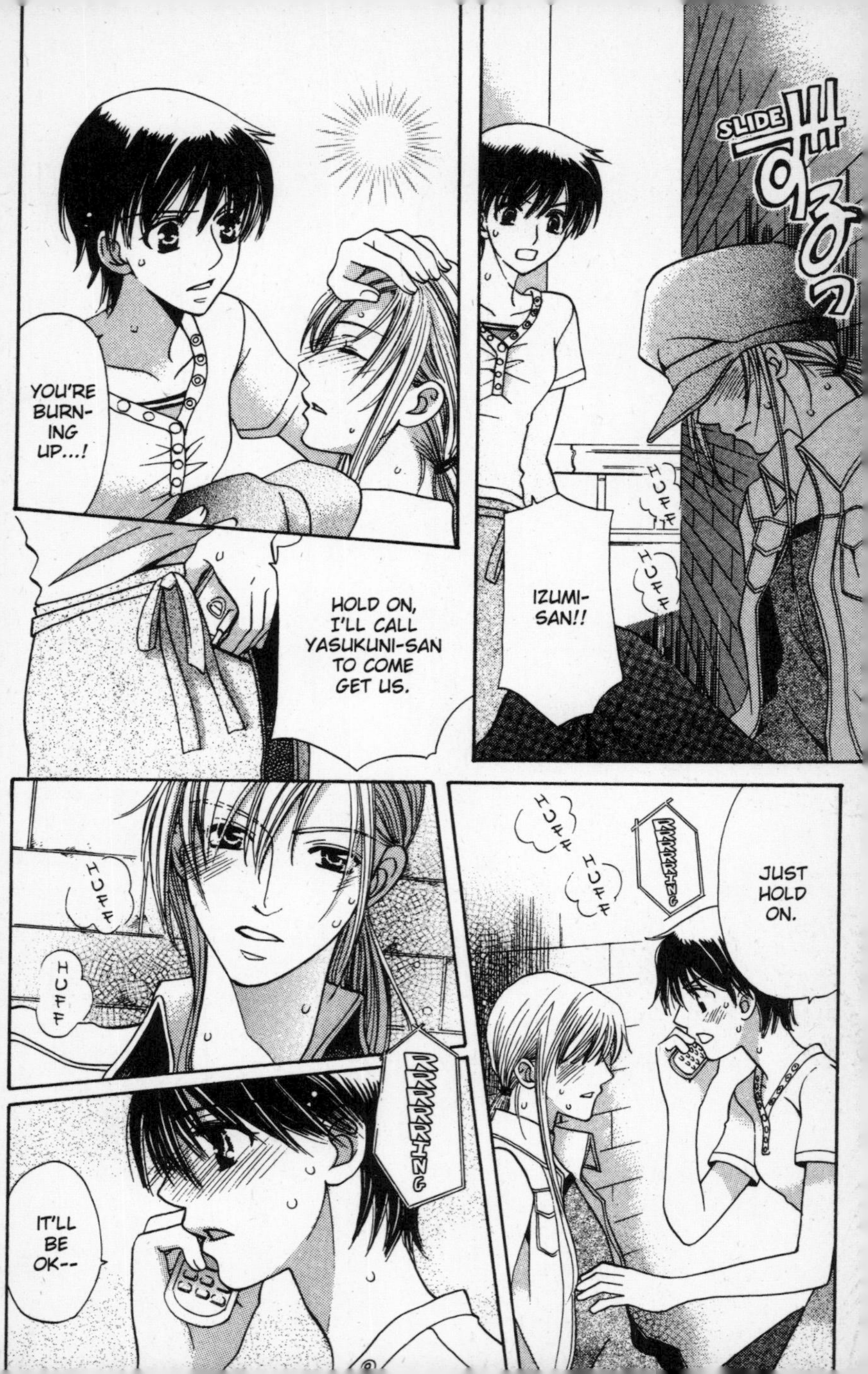
SLIDE
HUFF
HUFF
IZUMI-SAN!!
YOU'RE BURNING UP...!
HOLD ON, I'LL CALL YASUKUNI-SAN TO COME GET US.
HUFF HUFF
RRRRING
JUST HOLD ON.
HUFF
HUFF
RRRRING
IT'LL BE OK--

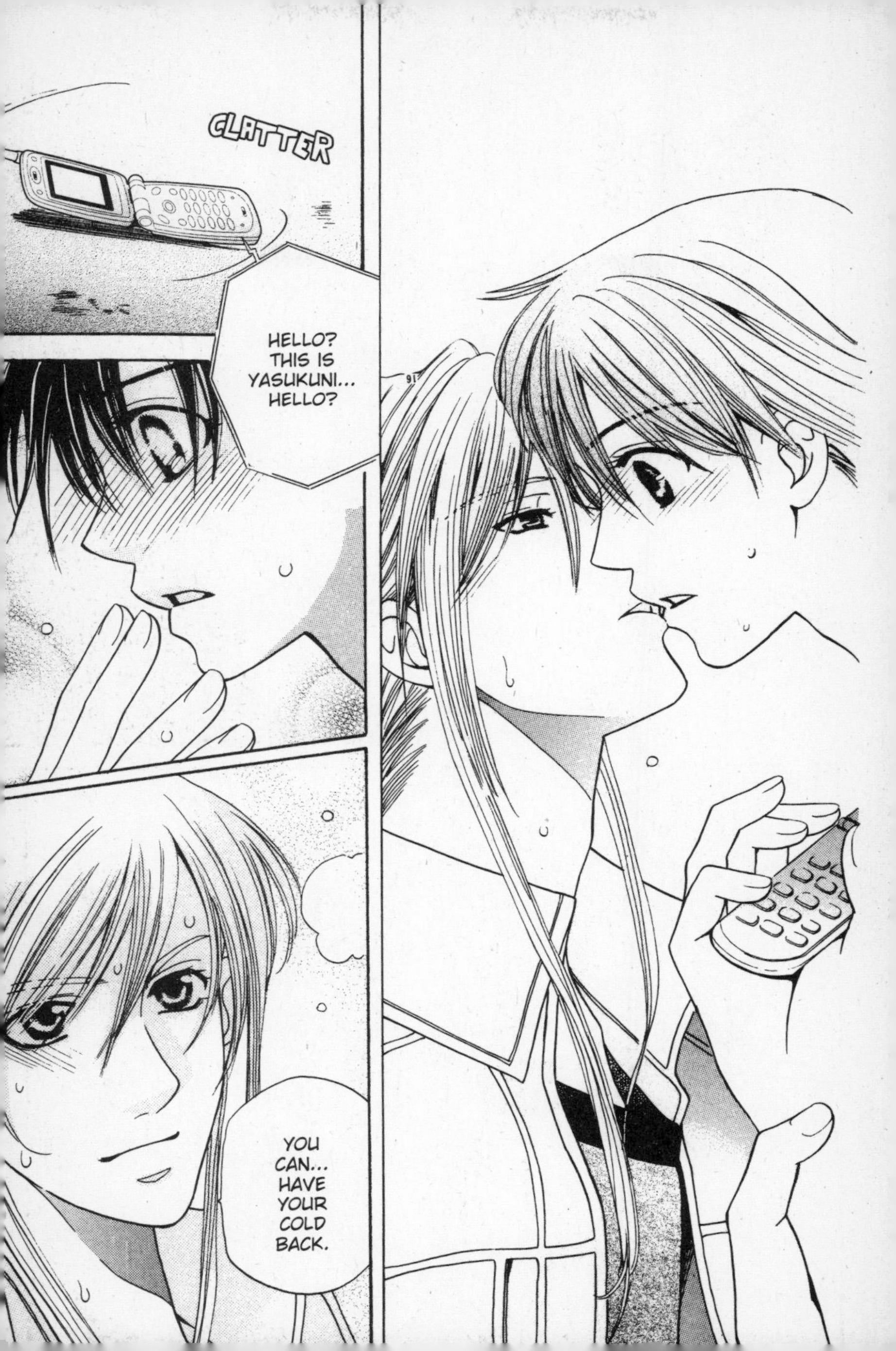
CLATTER
HELLO? THIS IS YASUKUNI... HELLO?
YOU CAN... HAVE YOUR COLD BACK.

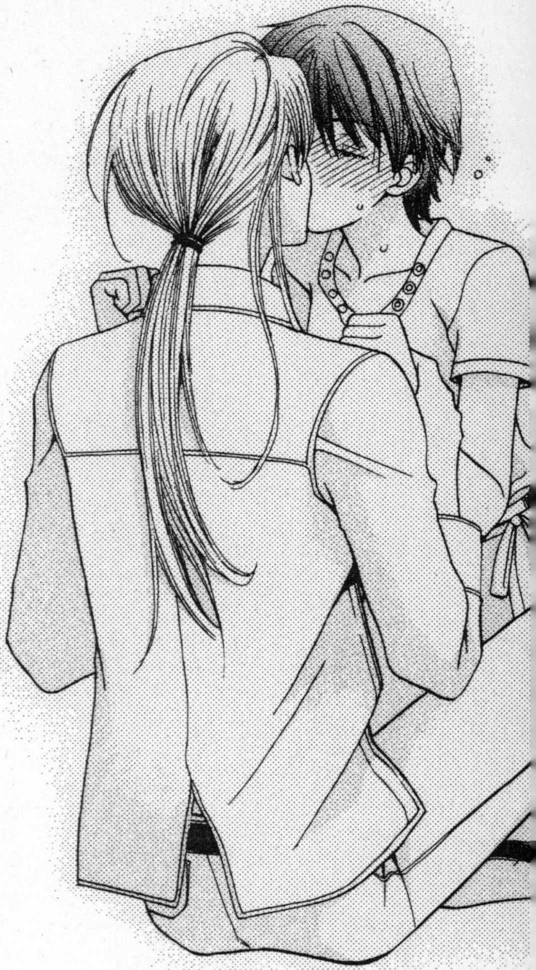

ON THAT DAY, IZUMI-SAN AND I...

...REALIZED OUR LOVE, AND SHARED OUR FIRST KISS.

End of Scene 30

Afterword & Special Thanks!

To all of you who read "Tenshi Ja Nai!!" volume 6, thank you very much! And to all of you who send letters and leave messages on my website, you are always an inspiration for me! To my assistants, you've helped me out a lot: Hariguchi-san, Hatayama-san, and my manager, Suguwara-san!

I owe you so much for this round, too! My deepest gratitude!

I can't wait to hear from you!

Go! Media Entertainment
5737 Kanan Rd. #591
Agoura Hills, CA 91301
Homepage URL is:
http://www5b.biglobe.ne.jpg/~taka_s/index.html

"TENSHI JA NAI!!" VOLUME 6 / END

Translator's Notes

Pg. 36 – *aojiru*
A healthy Japanese drink made of tree kale that's very nutritious, but tastes like grass.

Pg. 64 – *zenzai*
Originating in Okinawa, this drink is made from red beans, and is surprisingly refreshing and tasty. (But not to Izumi...)

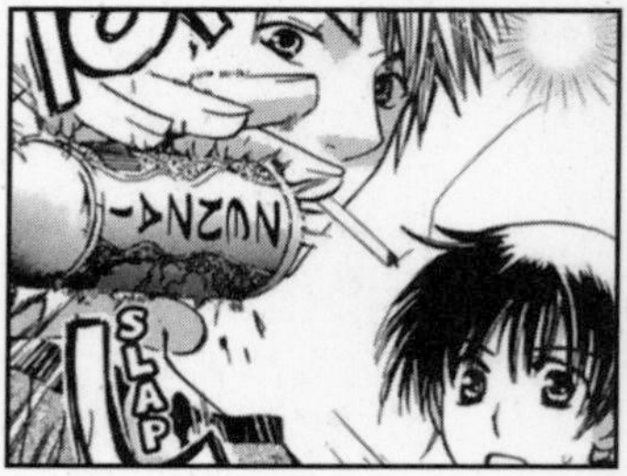
SLAP

Pg. 75 – *uchiwa*
A Japanese fan often used during festive occasions in the summer. They're disposable and make great advertising surfaces.

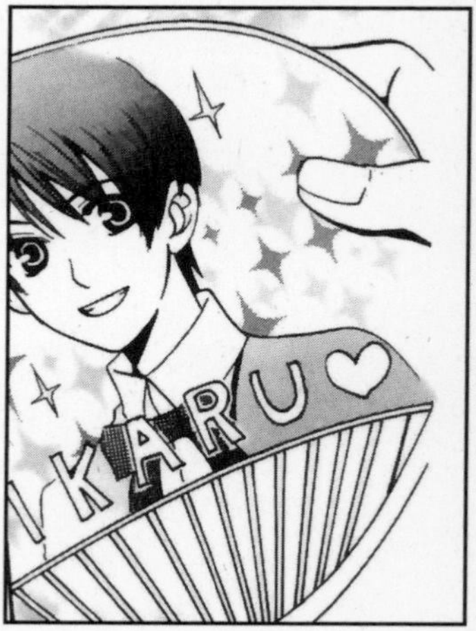
KARU

Pg. 84 – first-Magnitude Star
The brightest stars in the sky.

Pg. 85 – eighth Magnitude Star
The dimmest, most hard-to-notice stars in the sky.

Pg. 97 – *okonomiyaki*; *ikadama* and *butadama*
Okonomitaki means "as you like it grilled". It's a Japanese pan-fried batter cake you grill yourself, with vegetables or seafood and meats like ikadama (squid) and butadama (pork).

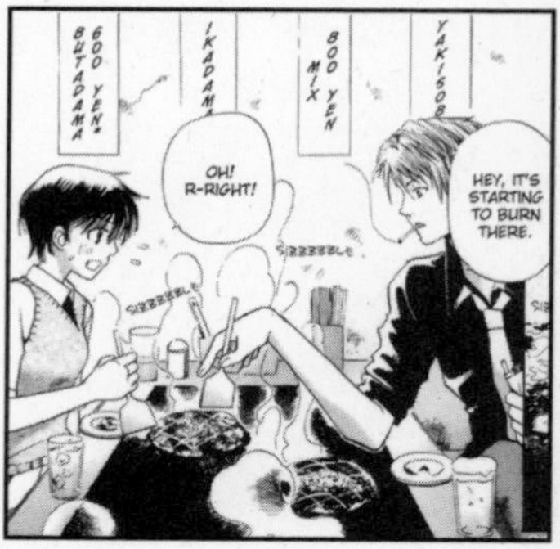
HEY, IT'S STARTING TO BURN THERE.
OH! R-RIGHT!
MIX 800 YEN
IKADAMA
BUTADAMA 600 YEN

Pg. 159 – 38.9 degrees
This is Celsius. That's 103.6 degrees Fahrenheit which is a pretty serious fever.

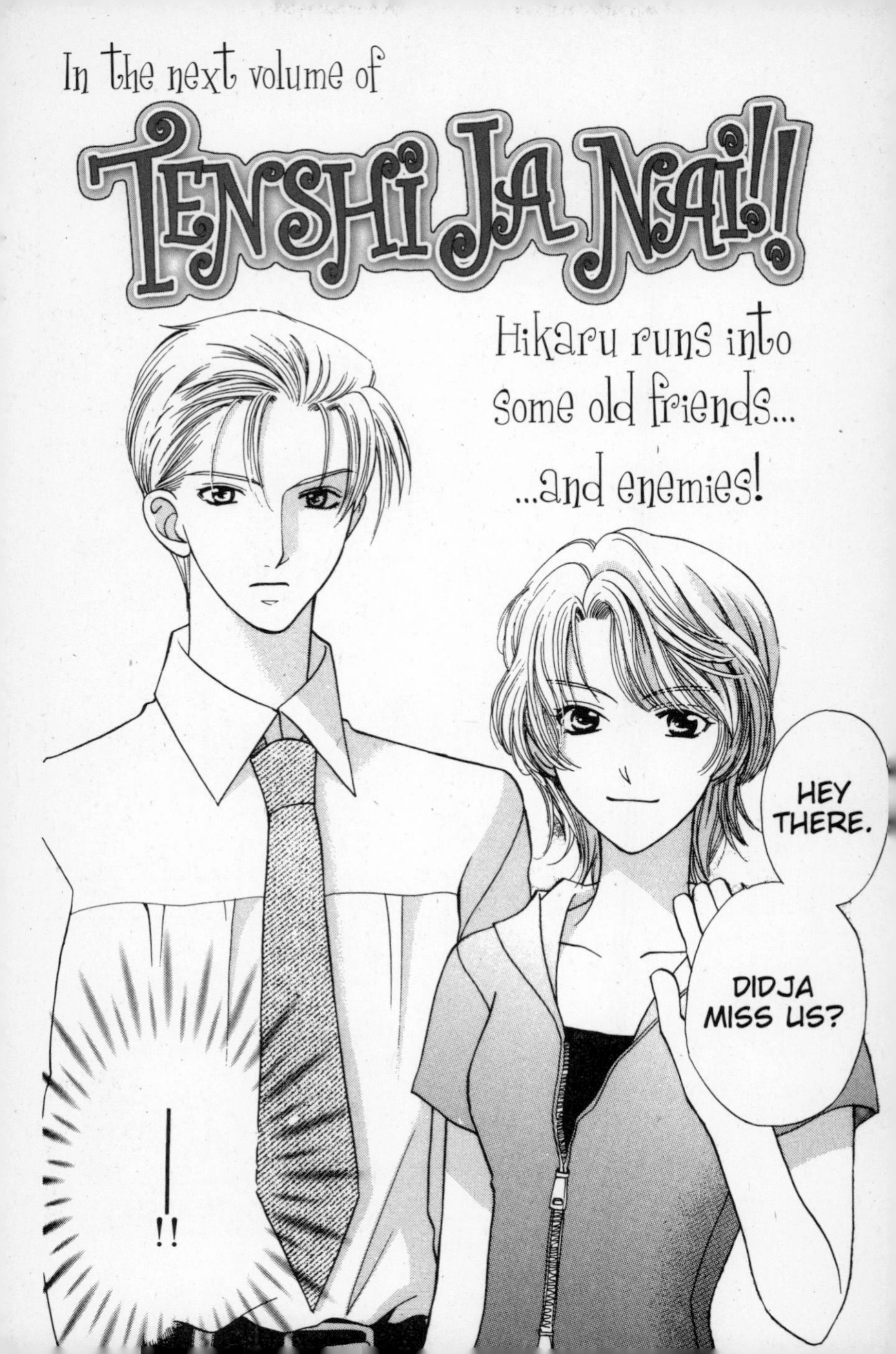
In the next volume of
TENSHI JA NAI!!
Hikaru runs into some old friends...
...and enemies!
HEY THERE.
DIDJA MISS US?
—!!

FAN ART

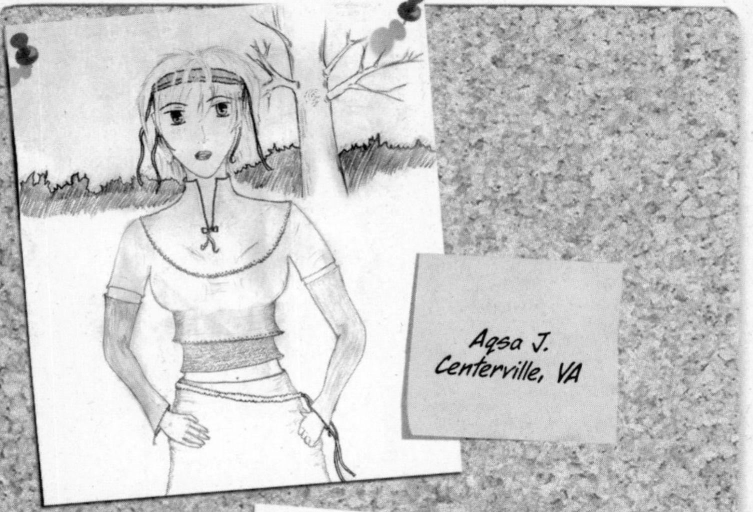

Aqsa J.
Centerville, VA

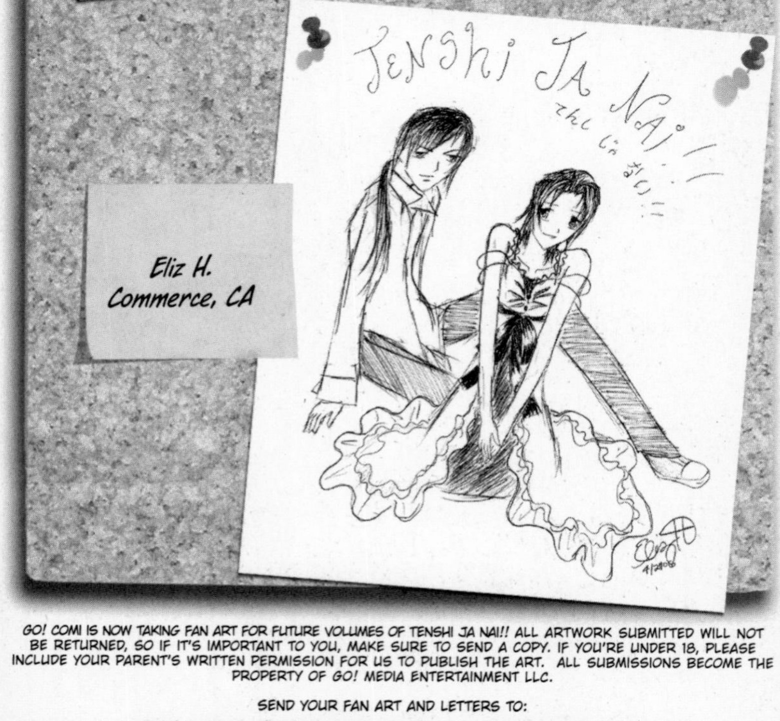
TENSHi JA NAi!!

Eliz H.
Commerce, CA

GO! COMI IS NOW TAKING FAN ART FOR FUTURE VOLUMES OF TENSHI JA NAI!! ALL ARTWORK SUBMITTED WILL NOT BE RETURNED, SO IF IT'S IMPORTANT TO YOU, MAKE SURE TO SEND A COPY. IF YOU'RE UNDER 18, PLEASE INCLUDE YOUR PARENT'S WRITTEN PERMISSION FOR US TO PUBLISH THE ART. ALL SUBMISSIONS BECOME THE PROPERTY OF GO! MEDIA ENTERTAINMENT LLC.

SEND YOUR FAN ART AND LETTERS TO:

GO! MEDIA ENTERTAINMENT ATTN: TENSHI JA NAI!!
5737 KANAN RD. #591 • AGOURA HILLS, CA 91301

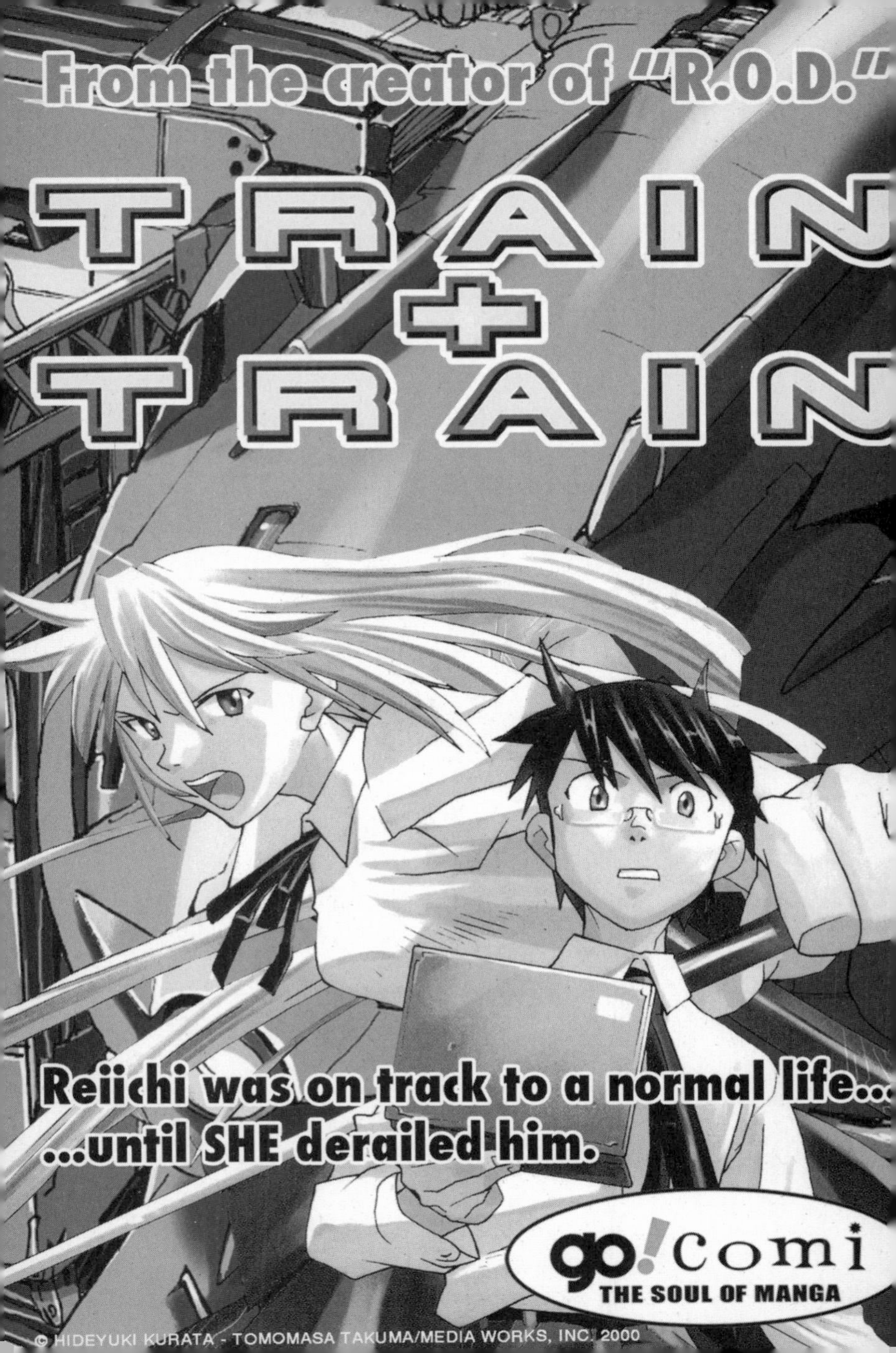
From the creator of "R.O.D."
TRAIN + TRAIN
Reiichi was on track to a normal life...
...until SHE derailed him.
go! comi
THE SOUL OF MANGA
© HIDEYUKI KURATA - TOMOMASA TAKUMA/MEDIA WORKS, INC. 2000

BLACK SUN SILVER MOON

SAVING THE WORLD...
ONE ZOMBIE AT A TIME.

go!comi
THE SOUL OF MANGA

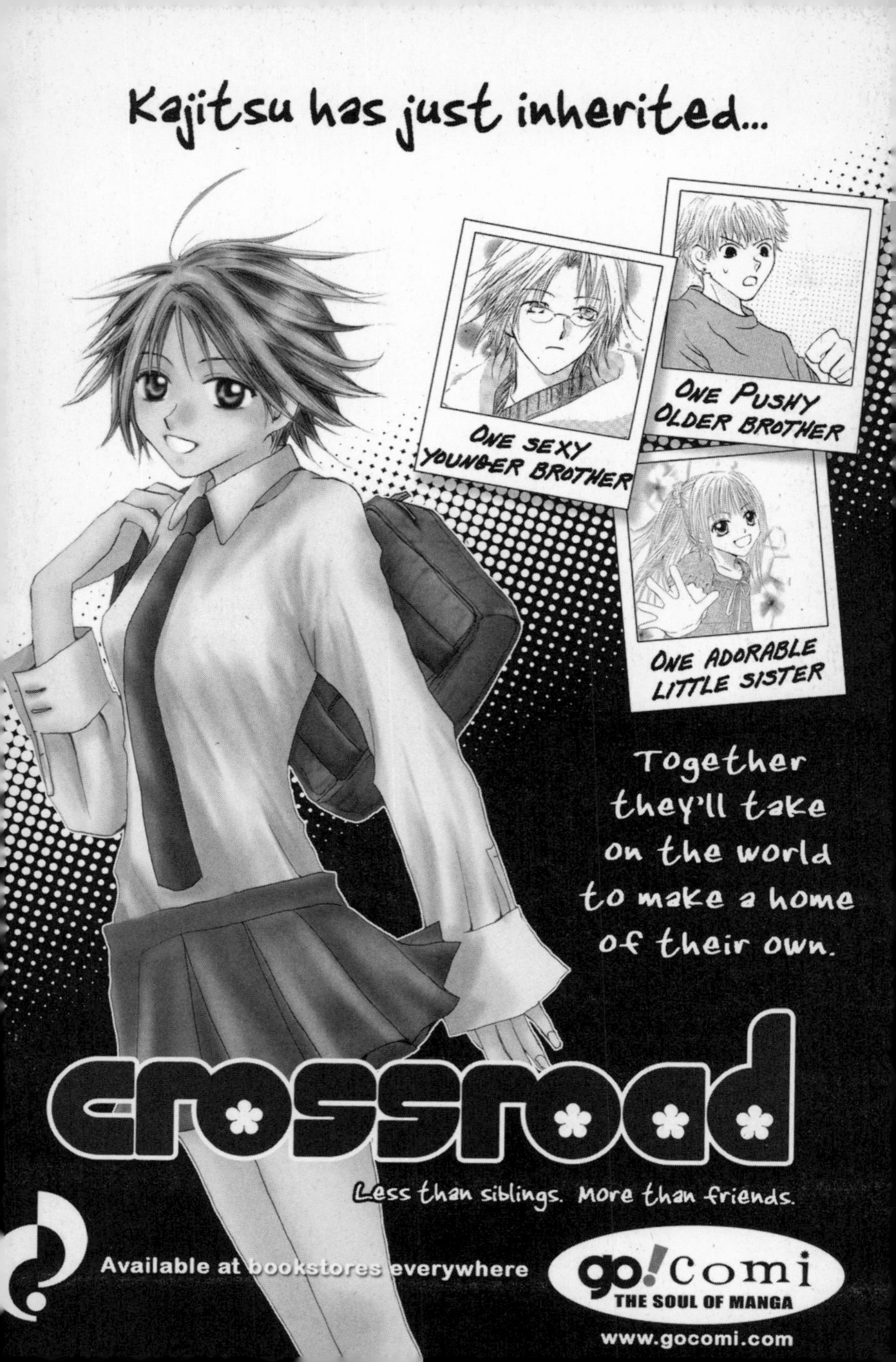
Kajitsu has just inherited...
ONE SEXY YOUNGER BROTHER
ONE PUSHY OLDER BROTHER
ONE ADORABLE LITTLE SISTER
Together they'll take on the world to make a home of their own.
crossroad
Less than siblings. More than friends.
Available at bookstores everywhere
go!comi
THE SOUL OF MANGA
www.gocomi.com

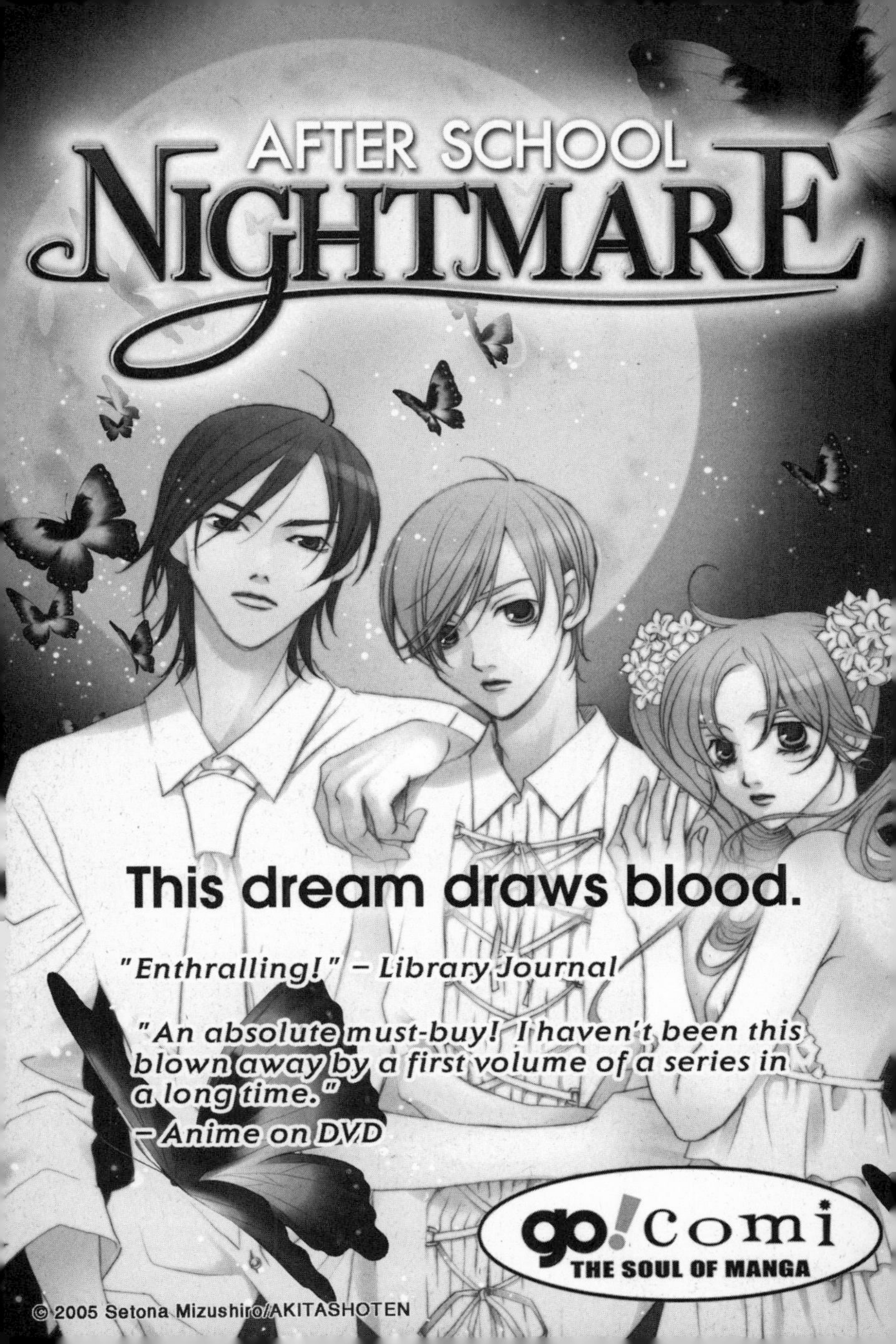
AFTER SCHOOL
NIGHTMARE
This dream draws blood.
"Enthralling!" – Library Journal
"An absolute must-buy! I haven't been this blown away by a first volume of a series in a long time."
– Anime on DVD
go!comi
THE SOUL OF MANGA
© 2005 Setona Mizushiro/AKITASHOTEN

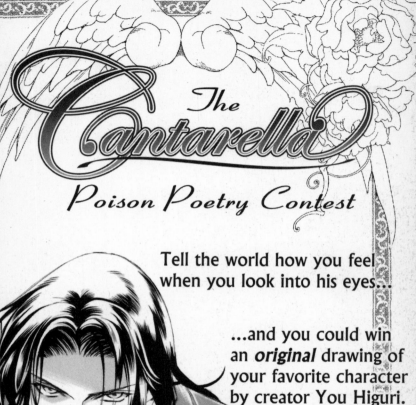

Author's Note

Thank you for picking up "Tenshi Ja Nai!!" volume 6! She's got that "deer in the headlights" look, but I'm sure my pet cat here is really happy (ha).

Visit Shigematsu-sensi online at
http://www5b.biglobe.ne.jp/~taka_s/